Wesley, Aquinas, and Christian Perfection

Wesley, Aquinas, and Christian Perfection

An Ecumenical Dialogue

Edgardo A. Colón-Emeric

BAYLOR UNIVERSITY PRESS

Cover Design by Andrew Brozyna, AJB Design.
Cover Image: "Camp meeting of the Methodists in N. America" / J. Milbert del.; M. Dubourg sculp. c. 1819, Courtesy of the Library of Congress Prints and Photographs Division, LC-USZC4-772.

Library of Congress Cataloging-in-Publication Data

Colón-Emeric, Edgardo Antonio, 1968-
Wesley, Aquinas, and Christian perfection : an ecumenical dialogue / Edgardo A. Colón-Emeric.
p. cm.
Includes bibliographical references (p.) and index.
ISBN 978-1-60258-211-8 (hardback : alk. paper)
1. Wesley, John, 1703-1791. 2. Perfection--Religious aspects--Methodist Church--Comparative studies. 3. Methodist Church--Relations--Catholic Church. 4. Thomas, Aquinas, Saint, 1225?-1274. Summa theologica. 5. Perfection--Religious aspects--Catholic Church--Comparative studies. 6. Catholic Church--Relations--Methodist Church. I. Title.
BT766.C63 2009
234'.8--dc22
2009020939

Printed in the United States of America on acid-free paper with a minimum of 30% pcw recycled content.

Contents

Introduction

Methodists and Catholics in Dialogue

Methodists and Catholics have been engaged in joint bilateral dialogues for over forty years.[1] From the beginning of these conversations, the participants were pleased to discover an eminent degree of spiritual kinship. The universal call to holiness announced by *Lumen Gentium*[2] echoed Wesley's insistence that all Christians, not just the clergy, are to "go on to perfection" (Heb 6:1). In the words of one of the earliest Methodist-Catholic reports: "Catholics and Methodists have always had one very important thing in common, though they have not fully realized it . . . the conviction of John Wesley that each man has a duty to seek holiness and 'Christian perfection.'"[3] Forty years of dialogue have confirmed the centrality of perfection in Methodist and Catholic ecclesiologies and affirmed the significance of sanctity for ecumenicity. "For Methodists and Catholics, the call to holiness and the call to be the Church belong together."[4]

In spite of strong joint statements on holiness, the doctrine of Christian perfection or "perfect love," as Wesley preferred to call it, has not been the subject of sustained ecumenical scrutiny.[5] Individual theologians have examined the doctrine of Christian perfection in an ecumenical context. These studies have frequently looked eastward for engaging in conversation.[6] Today, the working thesis among many Methodist theologians is that Catholicism teaches a static notion of perfection whereas Orthodoxy teaches a dynamic one, and that Wesley's is more like the latter than the former.[7] The originator of this thesis, or at the very least the one most credited with this theological approach, is Albert Outler. In an introduction to an anthology of Wesley sermons Outler states,

> [Wesley] was particularly interested in "Macarius the Egyptian" and Ephraem Syrus. What fascinated him in these men was their description of "perfection" (τελείωσις) as the goal (σκόπος) of the Christian in this life. Their concept of perfection as a process rather than a state gave Wesley a spiritual vision quite different from the static perfectionism envisaged in Roman spiritual theology of the period and the equally static quietism of those Protestants and Catholics whom he deplored as "the mystic writers." The "Christian Gnostic" of Clement of Alexandria became Wesley's model of the ideal Christian. Thus it was that the ancient and Eastern tradition of holiness as *disciplined* love became fused in Wesley's mind with his own Anglican tradition of holiness as *aspiring* love, and thereafter was developed in what he regarded to the end as his own most distinctive doctrinal contribution.[8]

Taking their cue from this statement by Albert Outler, recent evaluations of Wesley's doctrine of salvation have looked for affinities between Wesley's doctrine of Christian perfection and the patristic doctrine of *theosis*. A number of studies have been written that pair Wesley with Eastern Fathers like John Chrysostom.[9]

Valuable as these comparisons are for ecumenical rapprochement with the Orthodox, there are limitations to this approach, particularly when it is grounded in reconstructions of the historical sources of John Wesley's theology. Recent scholarship has seriously challenged the genetic dependence of Wesley's doctrine of perfection on Eastern Orthodox sources.[10] For instance, the avowal of a connection between Wesley's teaching of perfection and Macarius' understanding of *theosis* fails to give sufficient weight to the fact that Wesley appreciated what the Syrian monk had to say on the doctrine of sin, but was far less happy with his doctrine of divinization. In fact, in preparing the edition of Macarius' sermons for inclusion in the Christian Library, Wesley replaced all references to the term *theosis* with "sanctification," a change that arguably underlies not just a difference of vocabulary but of actual theological understandings.[11] Did Wesley appreciate and learn from the teachings of the Greek Fathers? Absolutely, but Wesley did not read Origen or Clement of Alexandria as Eastern Orthodox theologians but as Christian theologians belonging to the whole church; whenever he spoke of Orthodoxy at all, which was rare, it was in a largely negative light.[12]

In questioning the Orthodox provenance of Wesley's doctrine of perfection, I am not denying the possibility or fruitfulness of a Methodist-Orthodox dialogue on this or any other doctrine. If anything, such encounters between Wesley and the Eastern Fathers should be pursued more deeply and extensively. What I am questioning is the categorical validity of opposing an Eastern τελείωσις to a Western *perfectus*. It may be that the Latin Church of Wesley's day understood perfection in a manner altogether alien to Orthodoxy and Methodism, a static "perfected perfection" over and against a dynamic "perfecting perfection."[13] Yet, this contrast must surely not only be asserted but also substantiated. To put it into the form of a question: is the holiness to which *Lumen Gentium* calls all Christians a static, unattainable perfection? The answer to this question could greatly quench or quicken the ecumenical spirit of the joint Methodist-Catholic dialogues, but since judgments on the overall character of complex traditions like Catholicism are difficult to arrive at, it seems wiser to test Outler's thesis on an individual Catholic theologian rather than on the Catholic tradition as a whole.

This digression into Methodist soundings of patristic theology is nothing but a roundabout way of saying that the ecumenical encounter of Methodists and Catholics on the doctrine of Christian perfection is long overdue. A dialogue on this doctrine is facilitated by the fact that, as already observed, there is a certain measure of ecumenical agreement on this doctrine. Christian perfection constitutes a kind of common ground spiritually uniting Methodists and Catholics; what has yet to be determined is the depth and breadth of this ground. However, a dialogue on the doctrine of perfection is not simply important for the sake of the comprehensiveness of ecumenical efforts (that no doctrine is left behind, so to speak), but rather for the sake of the fruitfulness of these endeavors. There are at least two reasons why a dialogue on this doctrine is ecumenically significant.

First, although this doctrine does not have the same kind of theological *gravitas* as the doctrine of the Trinity or Christology, it is not peripheral to either tradition. Indeed, the doctrine of perfection serves as a kind of nexus for many other doctrines: sin, grace, atonement, and eschatology, to name a few. In other words, an exploration of this doctrine must treat many areas of theology, and can perhaps serve, given its already inchoate ecumenical acceptance, as the entry point to more disputed questions like the role of merit in salvation.

Second, there is growing recognition of the ecumenical significance of sanctity itself.[14] If unity is a gift of the Spirit, this unity is not only embodied by structures of unity (a United Methodist General Conference, the bishop of Rome), but also by people united to God and neighbor by perfect love, like saints. Hence, growth in the life of the Spirit is essential for the manifestation of greater visible unity. It is my conviction and hope that a better understanding of perfection can help clarify the goal which all Christians are called to attain and by doing so aid its actual attainment.

In light of the continuing need for ecumenical rapprochement between Catholics and Methodists, I propose to study the doctrine of perfection as taught by John Wesley and Thomas Aquinas. Three questions will guide our inquiry. First, what is perfection? Second, how is perfection attained? And finally, how would a generous reception of the doctrine of perfection contribute to the search for Christian unity?[15]

Wesley and Aquinas in Dialogue

Having explained the need for examining the doctrine of perfection in an ecumenical context, I must now explain the choice of Wesley and Aquinas as the central participants in this conversation. On the one hand, the choice is obvious. Whatever the fortunes of their popularity as theologians (both have experienced ups and downs through the centuries), both Aquinas and Wesley remain central to their respective ecclesial traditions: the former remains the unsurpassable *doctor communis* of the Catholic Church, the latter the irreplaceable founder of Methodism. The obviousness of their selection is compounded when one considers that, as is widely acknowledged, the doctrine of perfection is central to both their theologies. As we will see, the perfection of the human provides Aquinas with the organizing principle for the structure of the *Summa Theologiae* and Wesley with his missiological imperative. Thus, to study Wesley and Aquinas through this doctrine is to go to the heart of their respective theologies.

On the other hand, Wesley and Aquinas make something of an odd couple: the scholastic theologian and the evangelical revivalist. Each person is naturally or providentially suited to lead a certain kind of life, and these two men led very dissimilar lives. Aquinas was a monk who spent his life in contemplation. It was out of the fullness of this contemplation that his theological writings flowed.[16] Wesley's life was different; he could have remained at Oxford and lived his days reading and writing, but such was not his mission. Wesley was a man of action. Yes, he read and wrote profusely, but his main legacy to the church was to be found not in his books but in the movement he started. Almost all of Wesley's writings are either in defense or promotion of the people called Methodist, and for this reason his works bear an inevitably occasional and even polemical character. In any case, the point being made with these thumbnail sketches of Aquinas and Wesley is that a comparison of these two theologians on the basis of the style of their writings or their psychological makeup is doomed to fail, as will a strictly historical comparison. Obviously, Aquinas never read Wesley, and there is little evidence that Wesley knew much about Aquinas besides his name and that he was one of the "schoolmen."[17]

How can these two figures be meaningfully compared? Is not any comparison likely to get stuck in generalities or founder on their incommensurability? Perhaps, but the reader will have to judge to what extent this study succumbs to or escapes from this danger. Nevertheless, I am convinced that the attempt to bring Wesley and Aquinas together is not a futile one. I draw my inspiration from the theologian Otto H. Pesch[18] and the philosopher Jacques Maritain.[19] They too paired Aquinas with very unlikely figures—Luther in the former, John of the Cross in the latter—basing their pairings not on historical dependency, nor on personal affinities, nor even on similarity of theological styles, but on the commonality of their theological object. What I propose to show is that when Thomas Aquinas and John Wesley speak of perfection they are talking about the same reality albeit in different theological modes: Aquinas as *scientia*; Wesley as "practical divinity."[20] To put it in the language of Pesch, Aquinas' doctrine of perfection is sapiential, whereas Wesley's would best be called existential.[21] Or in the language of Maritain, Aquinas considers perfection as a speculatively practical science, whereas Wesley considers this doctrine as a practically practical science.[22] I am not suggesting that Wesley's theology fits neatly into Pesch's and Maritain's terms. Rather, these terms can help Wesley in describing his theological endeavors as practical divinity to find its place with respect to Aquinas' understanding of *sacra doctrina* as *scientia*. I am also suggesting that awareness of categories like those used by Pesch and Maritain can help dismiss facile oppositions or agreements between Wesley and Aquinas. In ecumenical dialogue, "much is already achieved when one clearly admits that different words often refer to the same content and, more important, that behind the same words there can be different concepts and even whole systems of categories."[23]

The foregoing terms for a comparison between Wesley and Aquinas belong to the speculative or sapiential realm. As such, these terms are abstract and their practical or experiential significance is not easily grasped. Hence, I offer a guiding image for this comparative study: the Methodist house and the Thomist cathedral.

On one occasion, Wesley describes his understanding of the essentials of the Methodist doctrine by means of the metaphor of a house. The image captures both the sense of movement, a Wesleyan way of theology, and the sense of discrete structural elements, specific doctrines. In Wesley's own words,

> Our main doctrines, which include all the rest, are three—that of repentance, of faith, and of holiness. The first of these we account, as it were, the porch of religion; the next, the door; the third, religion itself.[24]

The Methodist house of doctrine is no medieval cathedral. Methodist doctrine is simpler and plainer; its proportions are not as majestic and soaring as those of the great medieval *Summae*. Its scale is more human, I would almost say more biblical except that I would not want to be misheard as putting down the cathedral; indeed, at the heart of this study lies the conviction that the Thomist cathedral and the Methodist house need and complement each other.

Ecumenical Reception of Aquinas and Wesley

In this ecumenical encounter between Wesley and Aquinas we must be cognizant of the ongoing conversations between and about these two figures. There is a long history of a Catholic reception of Aquinas, a shorter one of a Methodist reception of Wesley, and a very brief history of a Methodist reception of Aquinas and a Catholic reception of Wesley. To trace the first of these three would divert our attention from the task at hand, and other authors have ably surveyed these.[25] Scholarly interest in Wesley and Aquinas has not been limited to their coreligionists nor to ecumenical joint commissions; indeed, the work of individual scholars on their ecclesial neighbors' chief theologian has both preceded and still continues the conversations of the official Methodist-Catholic bilateral dialogues.

Long before Vatican II, significant Roman Catholic theologians and historians embraced John Wesley as their separated brother. The pride of place falls here to Maximin Piette's *John Wesley in the Evolution of Protestantism*.[26] Father Piette's book, originally published in French in 1925, became a classic text among both Catholics *and* Methodists. The study traces in detail and with remarkable charity the twisted and tortuous path connecting Luther and the German Reformation to the Wesleyan revival. While some of his conclusions have been challenged, his comparison of Wesley to the religious founders of Catholic orders has never ceased to fire the imagination of ecumenicists. As Piette avers,

> John Wesley has been compared to St. Benedict as regards his liturgical sense and piety; to St. Dominic for his apostolic zeal; to St. Francis of Assisi for his love of Christ and detachment from the world; to St. Ignatius of Loyola for his genius as an organizer; to his contemporary, St. Alphonsus di Liguori, for those terrifying appeals to the judgment of God as the beginning of conversion.[27]

Piette's impulse to cast Wesley in the garb of a Catholic religious founder rather than those of a Protestant Reformer continues to be followed. In what is essentially a theological portraiture of John Wesley, the Catholic layperson John Todd not only compares Wesley with St. John of the Cross, but actually acknowledges that he prays through Wesley![28] Roman Catholic interest in Wesley, though naturally first attracted to the witness of his life, has more recently taken up an examination of his doctrine. Take, for example, Daniel Joseph Luby's study of Wesley's understanding of the perceptibility of grace[29] and Thomas Rigl's exploration of Wesley's soteriology.[30]

For what are no doubt complex reasons, Methodists have not shown much interest in the person and work of Thomas Aquinas.[31] Admittedly, this attitude of "benign" neglect has changed; a growing interest in virtue ethics as a remedy for the failures of situation ethics has turned some Methodist heads to Thomas Aquinas' account of the virtues in the *Summa Theologiae*. A noteworthy example is D. Stephen Long, whose book *John Wesley's Moral Theology: The Quest for God and Goodness* makes a strong case for understanding Wesley as the heir of medieval moral theology, rather than as the precursor of modern ethics.[32]

Toward a Dialogue on Perfection

Ecumenical engagement of Wesley and Aquinas is not new. However, it is still the case that more often than not, Catholic evaluations of Wesley and Methodist ones of Aquinas are based not on a close reading of primary sources but on dated, apologetic, secondary sources. So despite the forty years of rapprochement between Methodists and Catholics, with few notable exceptions (e.g., Stephen Long), it is still the case that the theologies of Wesley and Aquinas have not been studied together in a substantive way.

Over the next chapters we will engage Wesley and Aquinas on the doctrine of perfection. I begin with Wesley so as to disrupt any semblance of historical dependence of the one on the other. The first two expository chapters will deal with Wesley's doctrine of Christian perfection. Perfection for Wesley is the goal of all humans under the condition of grace. For this reason, his doctrine of perfection must not be treated in isolation from its trinitarian and soteriological framework. The Methodist house's plan is deceptively simple: a porch, a door, and the house itself. But each of these elements is supported by other doctrines. Christian perfection must be understood within the context of the *imago Trinitatis* and the *via salutis*.

Chapter 2 will focus on the theological and anthropological aspects of the doctrine. First, we look at what Christian perfection does not mean according to Wesley—divine, angelic, or Adamic perfection. Then, we look at what perfection does mean for him—freedom from sin, perfect love of God and neighbor, and holy tempers. Chapter 3 will consider the soteriological aspects of the doctrine as we examine how perfection is attained and for what. As we will see, the way to perfection is built on grace upon grace. Holiness is not obtained by human effort; it is a gift of God. The grace that sanctifies usually comes through certain established channels—means of grace that empower the exercise of the holy tempers. By grace, perfection is attainable in this life, and this perfection is a recognizable sign of God's presence for the church and the world.

After considering the simplicity of the Methodist house of holiness, chapters 4 and 5 introduce us into the sublime heights and sometimes dizzying depths of the Thomist doctrine of perfection. The shape of these chapters follows, not by accident, the shape of the *Summa Theologiae* itself. Aquinas' teaching of perfection is built on two pillars, the perfection of the form (*Prima Pars*) and the perfection of operation (*Secunda Pars*); these pillars are themselves grounded in the perfection of Christ (*Tertia Pars*). For Aquinas, sanctification is "Christification"; Christ is the measure of the perfect Christian. For this reason any discussion of the perfection that is the goal of the Christian life must be grounded in Christology. As with Wesley, the first expository chapter of Aquinas' doctrine of perfection will focus on what perfection (of the image) means; the second will focus on how perfection (union with Christ) is attained.

In chapters 5 and 6, Wesley and Aquinas will be brought into dialogue. I will juxtapose the Methodist house and the Thomist cathedral in order to consider their similarities, differences, and fundamental complementarity. In chapter 5, I will stake out the boundaries of the ecumenically recognized common ground between Wesley and Aquinas on perfection by considering how they each interpret the Sermon on the Mount. By bringing Wesley and Aquinas together in this way, I intend to make it clear that the commonality of their doctrine is grounded in the scriptural witness. In chapter 6, we will consider different aspects of the doctrine of perfection, including contested ones such as the place of purgatory on the way to salvation, the role of merit in final justification, and predestination. My hope is that by the end of this chapter the reader will be persuaded of two things.

First, I will argue that Aquinas offers Methodists the speculative theological principles that Wesley considered to fall outside "practical divinity" and hence never developed. Perhaps it is fortuitous and even fitting that Wesley has been compared to Catholic religious founders in general and to Ignatius of Loyola in particular, but never to Aquinas. After all, if when choosing the paradigmatic theologian for the Jesuits, Ignatius pointed to Aquinas instead of himself, might not we look to the *doctor communis* to serve a similar role for Methodists?

Second, I will argue that Wesley offers Catholics another practitioner of perfection next to St. John of the Cross, who applies the speculatively practical theology of Thomas Aquinas in a practically practical way, a way leading not up Mount Carmel to a life of contemplation but down the plain to a life of action.

In the final chapter, I will move the dialogue on perfection beyond the confines of a strictly doctrinal encounter, from "sitting ecumenism" in the direction of what I call a "kneeling ecumenism." Perhaps the most important contribution that a generous reception of the teaching of Aquinas and Wesley on perfection has to offer for the church universal is the affirmation of the ecumenical and ecclesial significance of sanctity. The saints are icons of ecclesial unity; they are not just Christian exemplars; they are themselves the actualization of the reconciling work of the church. The saint sees and embodies the whole; the holy ones are catholic par excellence: universal yet particular. Hence, the ecumenical movement might be well served in complementing joint declarations with joint hagiographies. By living in the doctrine of perfection as taught by Wesley and Aquinas we learn something of the grammar and genre of theological biographies.

Together Wesley and Aquinas may provide us with criteria for spiritual discernment superior to those employed by George Gallup's self-test for sanctity that determined that 13 percent of Americans are saints.[33] The problem with such a figure, besides the method employed for its computation, is not that it is too high but that it is too low. All Christians are called to holiness and for this reason, as Wesley realized, all of us are called to lead a disciplined life in the *spirit* of the counsels: holiness and poverty belong together. As Wesley (Charles this time) writes,

"Ye shall be perfect" here below,
He spake it, and it must be so;
But first he said, "Be poor;
Hunger, and thirst, repent, and grieve
In humble, meek obedience live,
And labour and endure."

Thus, thus may I the prize pursue,
And all th'appointed paths pass through
To perfect poverty,
Thus let me, Lord, thyself attain,
And give thee up thine own again,
Forever lost in thee.[34]

Chapter One

Wesley on Christian Perfection

The doctrine of Christian perfection is not simply one among others for Wesley. As we saw in the introduction, the Methodist house is built of various structural elements (the porch of repentance, the door of justification), but the house itself is constituted by holiness. The doctrine of perfection occupies a center stage in Wesley's theology because perfection is the goal of the Christian life. The whole purpose of the way of salvation is to turn a sinner into a saint fit to enjoy communion with the Triune God. Every Christian lives in expectation of and struggle toward this end, and Wesley, as a practical theologian, is intent on describing the way to this end and in leading us to attain it.

In this chapter I propose to examine Wesley's teaching on Christian perfection. The primary sources will be Wesley's sermons (with the exception of Wesley's "Sermons on the Sermon of the Mount," which I will treat independently in another chapter) and his "Plain Account of Christian Perfection." I will also draw on other writings and hymns as necessary to round out the exposition. I am not the first Methodist theologian to study Wesley's doctrine of perfection. My own interpretation derives from critical and grateful engagement with Lindström, Maddox, and Collins,[1] among others. Maddox and Collins define the current state of the questions through their voluminous and valuable writings on this subject; we have already encountered them in the introduction to this book and will do so again throughout. However, Lindström's work *Wesley and Sanctification* is still the classic study of the question of perfection in Wesley, and as such bears words of special recognition.

In *Wesley and Sanctification*, Lindström provides his readers with a theological analysis of the role of sanctification in Wesley's theology. Lindström begins by observing the happy rise of interest in the "theoretical element" in Wesley. No longer is Wesley's historical significance measured by such practical contributions as the Methodist revival, but more and more his thinking, while always practical in bent, is being examined for its theological content. These efforts have led to a reappraisal of Wesley; no longer does he come clothed in the garb of an eighteenth-century evangelist but in those of a theologian of experience, the forerunner of Schleiermacher and William James, or even a proto-Barthian. Amidst this variety of incompatible assessments of Wesley and his place in the church, Lindström identifies two main trends of Wesleyan interpretation: the Reformed gives pride of place to Wesley's teaching of justifaction by faith; the Arminian privileges Wesley's emphasis on sanctification.

Against this background of partisan readings of Wesley, readings which have tended to isolate aspects of Wesley's soteriology, Lindström elucidates the connection between justification and sanctification, sin and atonement, in order to help us understand the significance of John Wesley's teaching of Christian perfection in his overall theology. This approach results in a very readable and detailed exposition of John Wesley's doctrine of salvation. What Lindström does not offer is a theological assessment of this doctrine; he seeks to understand Wesley, not defend, critique, or correct him. By contrast, my own study of this doctrine arises chiefly from a theological rather than a historical perspective. For that very reason, I will not always address nor settle important questions of context, chronology, and sources disputed by students of Wesley's thought. Instead, I will engage in a theological evaluation of Wesley's work and at times (very few to be sure) offer gentle corrections of Wesley's teaching of perfection.

As I begin it is important to state the obvious: Wesley's thoughts on Christian perfection developed throughout his ministry. Scholars typically identify three discrete phases of Wesley's theology.[2] The "early Wesley" (1733–1738) is characterized by an emphasis on the necessity of attaining holiness in order to be acceptable to God. After the experience of Aldersgate, the "middle Wesley" (1738–1765) came to emphasize the primacy of grace in justification by faith.[3] Finally, chastened by perfectionist controversies in the societies, the "late Wesley" (1765–1791) integrated the primacy of grace with the necessity of human response in a mature synthesis that overcame the dialectical tensions of his middle period. This "late Wesley" will be the basis for the present exposition, and the reader should know that even when I appeal to texts from the early and middle periods of Wesley's theological life, I will be reading them from the vantage point of his most mature reflections.[4]

What Christian Perfection Is Not

The exploration of the Methodist house of holiness begins by distinguishing it from its counterfeits. The way of remotion was one that Wesley often adopted when speaking of the doctrine of perfection. By starting out saying what Christian perfection is not, Wesley refuted many of the objections of his detractors as directed at something Wesley did not teach.

Christian Perfection Is Not Divine Perfection

In the Sermon on the Mount, Jesus exhorts his disciples to be perfect as the heavenly Father is perfect (cf. Matt 5:48). We will have the opportunity to study Wesley's interpretation of the Sermon on the Mount later, but I recall this text now in order to remind us that there is in Scripture a deep correlation between the perfection of God and the perfection of the Christian. For this reason, our inquiry into Christian perfection begins by considering key aspects of Wesley's understanding of divine perfection.

First, God is all perfect. In assessing a fellow Christian's spiritual state, the first question Wesley asks is: "Dost thou believe his being, and his perfections?"[5] God's perfections express the nature of the divine being, and if there is to be any catholicity of spirit among people they must at least agree that God exists and they must have sufficient knowledge of his divine attributes so as to distinguish God from an idol.

Wesley consistently distinguishes between "the natural and moral attributes of God."[6] To the former he ascribes such attributes as omnipresence and eternity; and to the latter, God's holiness and love. The distinction between natural and moral does not mean that there is division in the divine being. The divine perfections interpenetrate and condition each other, as Wesley states: "All his attributes are inseparably joined: They cannot be divided, no, not for a moment."[7] Indeed, for Wesley, the chief error in the doctrine of predestination as taught by his Calvinist foes lies precisely in that one of God's natural attributes, divine sovereignty, is isolated and raised above all others.[8]

The doctrine of the divine attributes in Wesley has a strong soteriological focus. For him, "every major attribute of God had implications for understanding what humans are to be and to do."[9] This soteriological and doxological emphasis extends to both the moral and the natural attributes. As Maddox says,

> Wesley became increasingly convinced of the formative (and *de*formative) influence of our understanding of these attributes toward the end of his ministry, publishing several sermons on them.[10]

Significantly, Wesley does not neglect consideration of God's natural attributes. Indeed, he writes a sermon dedicated to showing the practical inferences of the ubiquity of God,[11] but it is clearly the moral attributes in general, love in particular, that are the focus of his theological reflection. For Wesley, the reason for this "caritative" concentration is not merely methodological—the exigencies of practical over speculative theology—but scriptural. As Wesley states, "It is not written, 'God is justice,' or 'God is truth': (Although he is just and true in all his ways:) But it is written, 'God is love.'"[12] Love is the nature of God, his chief perfection, "the very brightness of his glory,"[13] his "darling attribute,"[14] and "best name."[15]

Second, God's perfection is the source of all perfection. Many perfections are commonly attributed to God: "His eternity, immensity, wisdom, power; his justice, mercy, and truth."[16] But these do not exhaust God's nature. For Wesley, these attributes are only some of the properties of God's essence that he has been pleased to reveal so that we might attain happiness.

> The boundless perfections of his nature are an eternal ground of delight to every creature capable of apprehending them. And the numberless exertions of all those perfections on our behalf lay the strongest claim to our gratitude.[17]

For Wesley, as for Augustine, we are made for God, and the contemplation of the divine attributes inflames our hearts with a desire to seek him and rest in him.[18] In other words, pious knowledge of God's perfections perfects the person.

Third, many of God's attributes are incommunicable. God does not share his name,[19] his honor,[20] or his "form"[21] with any creature. The justice that God executes by vengeance belongs to him alone.[22] Omnipresence is "an attribute which cannot be allowed to any but the Almighty Spirit."[23] Eternity before time began to be (*aeternitas a parte ante*) can only be attributed to God. But regarding everlasting life, life without end (*aeternitas a parte post*), Wesley confidently affirms: "This is not an incommunicable attribute of the great Creator; but he has been pleased to make innumerable multitudes of his creatures partakers of it."[24] Simply put, some of God's perfections—mercy, justice, truth—are communicable. For this reason, true religion "is a participation of the divine nature, the life of God in the soul of man."[25] And the more we practice these "imitable perfections,"[26] the more we are filled with the life of God.[27]

At this point some readers might well ask: has Christian perfection become univocal with divine perfection? Consider the following verse from a hymn approved for singing in Methodist societies.

Come, Father, Son, and Holy Ghost,
And seal me thine abode!
Let all I am in thee be lost,
Let all be lost in God![28]

The stanza is part of a larger hymn written for believers who are longing for a rest that lies beyond the peace of justification. This second rest where "pure enjoyment reigns" can be attained "now" by a simple faith. As Christians come to genuine belief that God could work such a mighty act of salvation, they enter into a Sabbath rest of perfect love. They become so full of God that they lose themselves in his immensity. The expression, though poetic and not to be interpreted literally, still raises a question: has Wesley overstepped the Creator-creature distinction? The short answer is no.

For Wesley, as for most of the Christian tradition, the relation between divine perfection and human perfection is analogical; Christian perfection is both like and unlike divine perfection.[29] There is a similarity—God's perfection is communicable and imitable here below—within a greater dissimilarity—we do not become God *simpliciter* here or above. Human perfection, of which Christian perfection is a subset, is always a relative perfection and is dependent upon God's. As Wesley strongly insists, "Absolute perfection belongs not to man, nor angels, but to God alone."[30]

Christian Perfection Is Not Angelic Perfection

There is nothing in Wesley like a fully developed angelology, though the subject of angels is one that comes up in his sermons on several occasions. Angels play an important role in Wesley's understanding of God's providence; they are after all ministering spirits whom God has appointed as our guardians and guides. Angels also play an important role in Wesley's epistemology. The angelic state marks the upper limit of human knowledge. By meditating on their nature we learn how low humans have fallen and how high God will lift us up in Christ. As such it is incumbent upon us to examine Wesley's teaching on angels if we are to understand his doctrine of Christian perfection.

Angels are pure spirits; they are "not clogged with flesh and blood."[31] Like humans, angels have bodies. Unlike humans, these bodies are not made of matter but "of a finer substance."[32] However we understand the metaphysical implications of this statement (and perhaps Wesley's fumbling for the right words is an example of the conceptual clarity and coherence to be gained by adopting a more rigorous scholastic metaphysic with its distinction between form and matter), the basic point is incontrovertible: angels are both like and unlike humans. And it is precisely this analogous relation of humans to angels that makes angelology an important component of Wesley's anthropology, his epistemology in particular.

Angels, at least the good ones, have not fallen from the state in which they were created; they have retained their original intellectual perfection. Granted, angelic understanding is not exhaustive—angels are not God—but their intellect is "perfect in its kind."[33] Angels "take in one view the whole extent of creation."[34] Their mode of knowledge is not discursive, moving slowly along a lengthy chain of reasoning, rather "they see at one glance whatever truth is presented to their understanding; and that with all the certainty and clearness we mortals see the most self-evident axiom."[35] Interpreters of Wesley have reasonably labeled this manner of immediate understanding as intuitionist. In any case, the incontestable and essential point is that the angelic mode of knowledge is different than the human one.

The extent of angelic understanding is greater than ours. On the one hand, angels know more than we do because they are angels. As angels, they have a greater knowledge of the nature and attributes of God. Moreover, they far better understand the workings of divine providence in creation. They even have knowledge of the thoughts of those humans over which they have received a particular charge. According to Scripture, only God "knows the hearts of all people" (Acts 1:24); the angels, as spirits, are able to read our thoughts as they occur with greater ease than the most seasoned psychologist can discern a person's state by looking at his or her face and bearing. Angels know more than we do because they are older. Since they sang together at the dawn of creation, they have had a long time to contemplate God and observe his works with a corresponding growth in wisdom. Wesley's description of the extent and manner of the angelic perfection may strike some as somewhat unguarded and rhetorically overcharged, but the point he makes is clear and important: angelic knowledge is free from any kind of error, if not from every kind of ignorance. Because angelic understanding is unerringly true, angelic affections are always rightly ordered; hence their actions are unceasingly oriented toward fulfilling the will of God.[36] The perfection of understanding and affections results in perfect actions and in return a greater perfection of understanding and affections. To put it another way, angelic knowledge grows in perfection, and Wesley speculates that this may be one of the reasons why God charges us to their care. God employs angels in his governance of creation, because "by exercising the goodness they have already they continually acquire more, and swiftly too."[37] A startling conclusion follows from this statement—the perfection of angels and the perfection of humans are somehow linked. The more an angel performs acts of benevolence toward humanity, the more that angel grows in virtue and happiness: in virtue because repeated acts of virtue strengthen the associated habit, and in happiness because "the greater goodwill they bear to men, the greater must be their joy when these men, in the fullness of time, are received into that glory appointed for them."[38] So in a way, the glorification of humans contributes to angelic beatitude. As Charles Wesley writes,

> Angels, rejoice in Jesus' grace,
> And view with man's more favour'd race,
> The blood that did for us atone
> Confer'd on you some gift unknown,
> Your joys thro' Jesus' pains abound,
> Ye triumph by his glorious wound.
>
> Or stablish'd and confirm'd by him
> Who did our lower world redeem,
> Secure ye keep your blest estate
> Firm on an everlasting seat,
> Or rais'd above yourselves, aspire,
> In bliss improv'd, in glory higher.
>
> But who of all your hosts can tell
> The mystic bliss unspeakable,
> The joy that issu'd from his side,
> And how the pure it purified,
> The grace supreme by Jesus given,
> When heaven itself was double heaven![39]

Talk of angelic improvement, like talk of angelic habits and bodies, will doubtless trouble Thomists. It is true that there are some important historic differences in the understanding of perfection that might underlie Wesley's reflections on the angels. For example, there is Gregory of Nyssa's vision of perfection as endless growth in contrast to the scholastic understanding of perfection as a fully realized act. It is clear that Wesley thinks that there can be growth in perfection in heaven on account of the incarnation of the Word and the ministry of the church. What is not so clear is whether there will be growth into eternity or whether such growth will achieve its mature consummation at the final judgment and resurrection. In my opinion, certain passages in the late Wesley suggest the latter.[40] In any case, Wesley's chief point in these and other passages is that angels grow in joy as they work with God for the salvation of sinners.

On this point, at least, Thomists should agree, for Aquinas says as much, "the joy of angels can be increased with regard to the salvation of such as are saved through their ministrations."[41]

Christian perfection is not angelic perfection for two reasons: first, humans are not angels. The seraphim and cherubim are the "elder sons of God,"[42] the Lord's "first born children,"[43] the highest link of the chain of being, and no human, not even Adam before the fall, can lay claim to such titles. Second, humans have fallen from their original perfection. Even under the influence of grace, they do not possess perfect understanding; they lack a clear vision of what Wesley calls the angelic law: "a complete model of all truth, so far as was intelligible to a finite being, and of all good, so far as angelic minds were capable of embracing it."[44] Humans see only in part; we abide in corruptible bodies. The intellect not being perfect, the affections will not always be rightly guided and our words and deeds will not actually and constantly tend to fulfilling God's will. So if Christian perfection is equated with angelic perfection, in keeping with angelic law, then the only conclusion one can reach is that perfection is not to be found on earth or in heaven.[45]

Christian Perfection Is Not Adamic Perfection

Wesley's reflections on angels, though an important side note to his reflections on perfection, are largely marginal to his overall thought. However, his consideration of what has been called the original state, the nature and life of the first Adam before the fall, is a persistent theme in his theology. The doctrine of the image of God lies at the heart of Wesley's theological anthropology and soteriology. As Maddox asserts, "Wesley assumed a two-dimensional anthropology: humans exist in this world as embodied souls/spirits."[46] Humans are by nature a composite of spirit and matter. Even though the soul can live separated from the body in the state between death and resurrection, the final felicity of the human is a beatified soul in a glorified body. In short, the body matters.[47] Nevertheless, as important as the body is for Wesley, it is the soul as a spiritual reality that is capable of bearing the image of God who is Spirit.

According to the Bible, humanity was created in the image of God, which means, as Wesley immediately clarifies, in the image of the Holy Trinity. Humans are not brutes by nature as some philosophers of Wesley's and our time claim, but rather to be human is to be

> an incorruptible picture of the God of glory; a spirit that is of infinitely more value than the sun, moon, and stars put together; yea than the whole material creation.[48]

To be made in the image of God means that one is "an image of his own eternity,"[49] even "transcripts of the Trinity."[50] Borrowing language from Isaac Watts' *Ruin and Recovery of Mankind*,[51] Wesley considers the perfection of the image of God in three aspects: the natural image, the political image, and the moral image:

> "And God," the three-one God, "said, Let us make man in our image, after our likeness. So God created man in his own image, in the image of God created he him." Not barely in his *natural image*, a picture of his own immortality, a spiritual being endued with understanding, freedom of will, and various affections; nor merely in his *political image*, the governor of this lower world, having "dominion over the fishes of the sea, and over the fowl of the air, and over the cattle, and over all the earth"; but chiefly in his *moral image*, which according to the Apostle, is "righteousness and true holiness."[52]

Adam enjoyed the full splendor and perfection of the natural image of God. He enjoyed the perfection of self-motion appropriate to a spirit "lodged in an earthly tabernacle";[53] the strength of his body and the swiftness of its response to all commands was unparalleled by anything else in creation except the angels. In the state of innocence, human nature was, in a sense, impassible, "it had no alloy of sorrow or pain, whether of body or mind,"[54] and even immortal since at that time the body "had no seeds of corruption within itself and adopted none from without."[55] The perfection of the natural image of God in the human in the paradisiacal state needs to be considered with respect to the three constitutive faculties of this image: understanding, the will, and liberty. Let us examine each of these in turn.

Adam's understanding was "perfect in its kind."[56] His intellect did not err in distinguishing truth from falsehood or in drawing the right inferences from given premises. "He was equally a stranger to error and doubt; either he saw not at all, or he saw plainly."[57] The greatness of his understanding is evident in the ease with which he named all the living creatures that passed before him, showing a profound grasp of their natures.[58] If human understanding was so perfect, how could Adam sin? Wesley does not say whether Adam saw or did not see the Beatific vision, but he does say that humans in their original state can be deceived. Hence, the understanding of Adam was perfect, but it lacked the certain security of heaven.

The perfection of his will follows the perfection of his understanding. Adam's affections and tempers unfailingly guided by the right reason led the will to tend only toward the good appropriate there and then.

Indeed in Adam's case it may be inaccurate to speak of affections and tempers per se, since he knew only one—love. In paradise, "man was what God is, Love."[59] Love filled his inmost being and was the principle of all his actions.

In paradise, Adam also enjoyed perfect liberty. Wesley's understanding of this aspect of the natural image is somewhat puzzling. On the one hand, he says that Adam's understanding guided his liberty: "he chose or refused according to its direction."[60] On the other hand, Wesley describes this liberty as "an entire indifference, either to keep or change his first estate: it was left to himself what he would do; his own choice was to determine him in all things."[61] The former account presents liberty as a faculty that is directed by reason and ultimately by truth; the latter presents liberty as a power of the soul that is *indifferent* before truth or falsehood, good or evil. Wesley's inclusion in his theological anthropology of the nominalist notion of a liberty of indifference is problematic. Consider the following passage from his sermon "What Is Man?"

> I have not only what is termed a "liberty of contradiction," a power to do or not to do, but what is termed a "liberty of contrariety," a power to act one way or the contrary. To deny this would be to deny the constant experience of all human kind. . . . And although I have not an absolute power over my own mind, because of the corruption of my nature, yet through the grace of God assisting me I have a power to choose and do good as well as evil.[62]

Does it make sense to say that I need God's grace to do evil? At this point, I find myself in fundamental agreement with Stephen Long's assessment of Wesley's eclectic approach to the various philosophical currents of his day.

> Wesley was not a profound philosopher, but he was a faithful church theologian. He received these sources within the context of the church's tradition and that gave him a richer context than he would have had if he only received them in an architectonic system with a well-established epistemology because he still had a world oriented by the church's practices.[63]

Even if we excuse Wesley for using philosophical terms loosely and confusing the orders of nature and grace, the question remains whether it is appropriate to speak of a liberty of contrariety in the original state. There is a sense in which, as Wesley explains, "the liberty of man necessarily required that he should have some trial; else he would have had no choice whether he would stand or no, that is, no liberty at all."[64] However, does human freedom necessarily require that humans have a trial to choose between means to an end or between ends themselves? Indeed, is not this distinction between means and ends crucial to understanding the original sin itself? After all, in believing the words of the serpent, Eve was not choosing between ends (good versus evil) but between means to the end (the fruit of the tree versus obedience). In any case, Wesley would surely want to say that perfect liberty is found not in a state of indifference before God and the devil but beyond such indifference in actually choosing God over the devil.[65]

The crown of all perfections of the natural image and the whole purpose of their institution is to render the human capable of God, capable of attaining the likeness of God, or as Wesley calls it, capable of attaining God's moral image. Adam's moral perfection consisted in the fact that he knew, loved, obeyed, and enjoyed the author of his being. It is this capacity for God that makes humans rank highest in the chain of being in the visible creation. What distinguishes humans from animals is not that one is rational whereas the other is not, but that "man is capable of God; the inferior creatures are not."[66] This capacity for God is not a static endowment; rather, it is a vocation that if fulfilled truly makes us temporal transcripts of the eternal Trinity, but if forsaken leads to eternal death.

Adam was not only capable of God; he actually experienced God's indwelling in a profound way. Hence, Adam's moral image was perfect. He was free from all blemish of sin; he was holy. The law was written directly on the heart.[67] So for Adam, the law was not chiefly an external command, a positive law. The only positive law Adam received, according to Wesley, was the command to refrain from eating from the tree at the center of the garden. This law was not what is sometimes called the "ceremonial law," nor was it the Mosaic law. The law that was written on his heart was the moral law. In essence, this law is the same as the angelic law, only it is in proportion to human nature: the law of love.

The doctrine of the law is central to John Wesley's understanding of the moral image. The moral law, as Collins avers, "highlights the similarities between the nature of God and the nature of humanity as originally created."[68] The law that was written on human and angelic nature participates in the law of God. Indeed, this law is coeternal with God. As Wesley says,

> This law is an incorruptible picture of the high and holy One that inhabiteth eternity. It is he whom in his essence no man hath seen or can see, made visible to men and angels. It is the face of God unveiled; God manifested to his creatures as they are able to bear it; manifested to give and not to destroy life; that they may see God and live. It is the heart of God disclosed to man.[69]

Wesley explains the nature of this law in language that is unmistakably christological.

> The law of God (speaking after the manner of men) is a copy of the eternal mind, a transcript of the divine nature; yea, it is the fairest offspring of the everlasting Father, the brightest efflux of his essential wisdom, the visible beauty of the Most High. It is the delight and wonder of cherubim and seraphim and all the company of heaven, and the glory and joy of every wise believer, every well instructed child of God upon earth.[70]

Wesley cautions his readers that he is only "speaking after the manner of men," but his use of christological terminology is deliberate. The Law and Christ are not exactly identical, nonetheless they are *strongly* related, so much so that Methodist scholars have not unreasonably described Wesley's Christology in terms of "Christ as Torah incarnate."[71]

Not only was the law of love written on Adam's heart, Adam actually loved God with his whole heart, soul, mind, and strength. And because Adam loved God perfectly, he was perfectly holy. And because he was perfectly holy, he was perfectly happy. As Wesley rhapsodizes,

> [T]hen indeed to live was to enjoy, when every faculty was in its perfection, amidst abundance of objects which infinite wisdom had purposely suited to it, when man's understanding was satisfied with truth, as his will was with good; when he was at full liberty to enjoy either the Creator or the creation; to indulge in rivers of pleasure, ever new, ever pure from any mixture of pain.[72]

In short, in paradise Adam enjoyed a profound vision of God, which resulted in the moral perfection of his nature and also in the perfection of the political aspect of God's image stamped on his soul. One could say that if the natural image reflects Wesley's understanding of what it means to be made "in God's image," and the moral image his understanding of what it means to be made "after God's likeness," the political image expresses what it means to have dominion: "Man was God's vicegerent upon earth, the prince and governor of this lower world; and all the blessings of God flowed through him to the inferior creatures. Man was the channel of conveyance between his Creator and the whole brute creation."[73] In the beginning, dominion was not given to Adam as a charter for the exploitation of creation but for the sake of its benediction.

In the original state, Wesley insists, animals too had a principle of self-motion; they too were endued with understanding, will, and liberty; they even had some kind of moral goodness and happiness because "as a loving obedience to God was the perfection of men, so a loving obedience of men was the perfection of brutes."[74] Though it is true that what distinguishes animals from humans is that "man is capable of God; the inferior creatures are not,"[75] it is also true that the perfection of the human and the perfection of the animal realm were linked in Adam through the perfection of the political image.

In the state of Adamic perfection, the human as *capax Dei* served as a means of blessing for the animal world. Humans were a kind of sacrament for creation that allowed the cosmos to fulfill its *telos* of serving and loving the creator through the human. In a similar fashion, the animal realm as *capax hominis* served as a means *to* grace insofar as by lovingly discharging his high commission as God's vice-regent Adam perfected the perfection of his original image.

Before concluding these reflections on Wesley's doctrine of the image, I should point out that the political aspect of this doctrine is one of the most underdeveloped loci of Wesley's theology. Nevertheless, at present, it is possible to identify two strands of reflection on this Wesleyan teaching. On the one hand, Maddox explores the implications of this doctrine for the development of Wesleyan ecological ethics.[76] After all, if Wesley is right and animals become *capax Dei* in the age to come,[77] should not such a consideration soften our hearts today "towards the meaner creatures"?[78] On the other hand, Theodore Weber explores the potential of this doctrine for the development of Wesleyan political ethics.[79] After all, if humans are made in the political image of God, then political responsibility in the organization of the state is a task for all humans, and to exclude people from the political process is to deny them their full humanity.[80]

Both Maddox and Weber present important ways of creatively appropriating Wesley's doctrine of God's image for Christian life today. A thorough engagement with their rich proposals exceeds the scope of my investigation. However, there are two questions I need to ask because they directly impinge on the doctrine of perfection.

First, what understanding of nature allows us to speak of dogs as *capax Dei* in the life to come? Wesley seems to consider the capacity for God to be a gift of grace rather than a given in nature. As we will see in the next section, this supposition is what allows Wesley to say that after the fall the capacity for God is gone, but that by the gift of prevenient grace humans are made *capax Dei* again. It is this understanding of the capacity for God as a graced endowment which does not come in the way of nature that allows Wesley to speculate that animals can be made *capax Dei*. True, with God all things are possible, and if it suited his purpose God could make a dog become an angel, but in such a case it would cease being a dog. Moreover, it seems to me that a dog singing the *sanctus* would be a less doggy dog than a dog chasing a squirrel and therefore a less perfect dog.[81]

Second, if we understand perfection of the image of God in the human to require the perfection of the political realm, is it possible for humans to be made perfect in love in this life? Weber asks but does not answer this question.[82] If we answer no—if, in this life, we dismiss the attainment of perfection as a utopian dream because "systemic sin," so called, cleaves to all our deeds—then I believe we have parted company with Wesley's doctrine of the *imago Dei*. As we will see in the final chapters of this book, such an understanding of the perfection of the political image, rather than being wholistic and Wesleyan, is actually reductionist and Niebuhrian.

In this life, Christian perfection cannot mean Adamic perfection. It cannot mean the full restoration of the natural image because in this life no one can be so perfect as to be delivered from all ignorance. In the present state, Christians are ignorant not just of the deep things of God (how God can be three in one, the time of the *parousia*, etc.), but even of the most common natural phenomena: the physics of wind currents, the chain of causality. Because Christians do not know all but only that which is necessary for salvation, they are not free from error. They can make errors of judgment when it comes to evaluating actions or people. They can even be mistaken in their interpretation of Holy Scripture (except in things essential to salvation). Furthermore, Christians are not free from all defects that come from living in a fallen world. Slowness of mind, faulty memory, and ineloquent speech may be found among the perfect. None can expect complete deliverance from these defects until they walk by sight in the presence of God in the life to come. Moreover, Christians must expect to be tempted and even to make mistakes; what they will not do is to willfully and knowingly sin against God or neighbor.

In this life, Christian perfection cannot mean the full restoration of the moral image to its paradisiacal state. The keeping of the Adamic law was the basis for "the covenant of *works*, made with Adam while in paradise."[83] God required of Adam perfect obedience to this law, and Adam's moral perfection consisted precisely in this. He did indeed obey this law, keep this covenant, and was capable of keeping it fully without interruption or hesitation. Work was no sweat, and prayer came so easily that he could do it in his sleep. Adam could do this in the state of innocence because he was "upright and perfect"[84] in his understanding, affections, and tempers. However, such perfection is not possible in this life. Even with the law of love written on our hearts by grace, the holiest of persons will be distracted from their worship of God by a bad bout of indigestion.

In this life, Christian perfection cannot mean the full restoration of the political image. One can speak of God's grace as encouraging humans to be more responsible in their care of animals. Yet, even under the condition of grace, dogs do not always obey their Christian masters; pious parents beget rebellious children, and saints sometimes support politically faulty causes. Of course, there are people like St. Francis whose relations to animals give us a glimpse of what the perfection of the political image, at least as far stewardship of creation, can look like. However, the full perfection of the political image can only be attained in the heavenly polis, where there are no resident aliens but only full citizens. One of our chief tasks as Christians, and here I am in complete agreement with Weber, is "to anticipate that heaven below" by "going on to perfection" and striving for "the imaging of God in our shared, interactive, public existence."[85]

What Christian Perfection Means

So far, we have been considering what Christian perfection is not. We began our study of the Methodist house of holiness by the way of remotion so as to clear away some of the misconceptions and objections arising from the application of the term "perfection" to Christian life. Striving for and attaining Christian perfection does not mean one becomes the fourth person of the Holy Trinity, nor does it mean that one becomes like the angels in heaven, nor that paradise has been regained. To be made perfect, to be saved to the uttermost, means to be holy as God is holy. Chiefly, Christian perfection means the renewal of the moral image.

Christian Perfection Means Freedom from Sin

The doctrine of Christian perfection has both a negative and a positive aspect. Wesley once said: "Know your disease! Know your cure!"[86] Sin and salvation need to be thought of together. It is characteristic of Wesley's theology that he never considers the effects of the fall in isolation from God's economy of salvation: original sin with prevenient grace, actual sins with justifying grace, inbred sin with sanctifying grace. Entire sanctification entails both freedom *from* sin and freedom *for* love. Let us first consider the negative aspect of Wesley's doctrine of perfection (the sickness of sin) to which the positive aspect of the doctrine (perfect love) is the remedy.

The Fall and Original Sin

Tragically, our first parents sinned, and the consequences of this original sin have been grave for all humanity. After the fall, God's favor and the primitive perfection of Adam were lost. The divine image which humans once bore as their crown has been totally corrupted but, most importantly, not destroyed. As Maddox helpfully states, "depravity is not the obliteration of human faculties, but their debilitation when devoid of God's empowering presence."[87]

As a result of the fall, the natural image has been sorely wounded. The body is now a weak thing that is prone to sickness and subject to death. The light of human understanding has been dimmed leading to many errors of discernment and judgment. As a result of this corruption of the intellect, the affections and tempers have become disordered resulting in an evil will and a loss of liberty.

The fall was not without consequence for the political image. The gift and vocation of what it means to be human has also been affected. By cutting themselves off from God, humans became incapable of serving as channels of God's blessings for the world; creation was submitted to futility.[88] "As man is deprived of *his* perfection, his loving obedience to God, so brutes are deprived of *their* perfection, their loving obedience to man."[89]

However, the chief consequence of the fall was the total corruption of the moral image.[90] Now, the human does not and cannot love God, and therefore the human is not and cannot be happy. As Wesley explains:

> No man loves God by nature, no more than he does a stone, or the earth he treads upon. What we love, we delight in: but no man has naturally any delight in God.[91]

The fall has poisoned and twisted Adam's capacity to love. The *imago diaboli* has been etched over the *imago Dei*.[92] Instead of being children of God, we now have the devil as our father. Like the devil, humans are full of unbelief, pride, and self-will. Unlike the devil, who only loves himself, humans love the world.

To summarize, humanity has fallen from its paradisiacal state of righteousness into a state of total depravity. To be children of wrath is now the "natural" state of humankind; it is "natural" not because it is original but because it is universal. All humans without distinction are born into this world with an inclination to evil; all thoughts, tempers, and actions are out of harmony with the divine will. A distorted threefold desire has become inbred into human nature.[93]

First, there is the desire of the flesh. Since the fall, there is present in humans a disordered tendency to delight in the creaturely. Sensual pleasures have the power to captivate our intellectual powers and shape the volitional dispositions of both peasant and epicure. Even though some people, whether by natural constitution or moral education, resist the immediate gratification offered by the desire of the flesh, no one is completely immune to it. As Wesley observes, "man, with all his good breeding and other accomplishments, has no preeminence over the goat."[94]

Second, there is the desire of the eyes. Since the fall, there is present in humans a diseased fascination that delights not so much in what is beautiful as in what is new. Daily experience confirms that humans are attracted to what is unusual and familiarity breeds contempt. Like drinking seawater, the more one tries to quench this thirst for novelty, the more burning it becomes. Wesley draws particular attention to the ways in which this sick search for happiness in novelty infects the way we relate to the world around us. For instance, we devise more "creative" forms of apparel and amusement in order to gratify our imagination. More seriously, the desire of the eyes spoils even our noblest human endeavors. Delirious with the desire of the eyes, philosophers can forsake their love of truth for the latest theory and end up being curious instead of wise.

Third, there is the pride of life. Since the fall, there is in humans a sickened desire for praise. In the high-born, this is often called a thirst for glory; and in the low, a concern for good reputation. In either case, it is a distorted desire that looks for approbation and honor from our neighbors instead of from God. Is there anyone who does not want to hear praise over dispraise? Indeed, is it not a mark of sound judgment to seek the approbation of others? The danger with the desire to be deemed worthy is that under the condition of our illness it easily begets pride.

Freedom from Sin

Now that we have considered the illness, we can consider the cure. Christian perfection means freedom from the *triplex concupiscentia* that has afflicted all humans since Adam and Eve: freedom from inbred sin, the desire of the flesh, the desire of the eyes, and freedom from the pride of life.[95] To be made perfect means to be freed from evil tempers, evil thoughts, and even from wanderings in prayer.[96]

Christian perfection does not mean freedom from all defects. Wesley acknowledges a whole class of "failings" that are not sin because they are involuntary. For instance, in Christian charity one judges a person more highly than one ought. Or because of an inadequate knowledge of Scripture, one violates a divine law without intending to. The origin of these "infirmities" is not a corrupt will but the postlapsarian constitution of a corruptible body and weakened intellect. On account of this involuntary character, these infirmities are not properly called sins. As Wesley avers:

> Though these are deviations from the holy and acceptable and perfect will of God, yet they are not properly sins, nor do they bring any guilt on

> the conscience of "them which are in Christ Jesus." They separate not between God and them, neither intercept the light of his countenance, as being no ways inconsistent with their general character of "walking not after the flesh, but after the Spirit."[97]

For Wesley, "Sin, properly speaking, is neither more nor less than 'a voluntary transgression of a known law of God.'"[98] This definition of sin can sound excessively narrow, but it is not. Wesley's understanding of "sin, properly speaking" covers both outward and inward sins, as well as sins of omission. Looking ahead for a moment, I will later claim that this distinction between "sin, properly speaking" and "failings" closely parallels the distinction that Aquinas draws between mortal and venial sins. In other words, whoever has trouble with Wesley on this point will also have trouble with Aquinas. However, the reader will need to wait until the next-to-last chapter of this book for the substantiation of this claim.

Christian perfection means freedom from "sin, properly speaking" but it does not mean freedom from temptation, and for this reason Christian perfection does not mean freedom from falling. As Wesley observes, "There is no such height or strength of holiness as it is impossible to fall from."[99] In other words, once attained, Christian perfection can be lost. According to Wesley, it is not uncommon for those entirely sanctified to lapse from this state before being established in it. In any case, the fall from perfection does not happen all at once. In fact, the sad testimonies of backsliders shed light on the well-trod-upon path leading from the house of holiness to the wilderness of sin. According to Wesley the pilgrim's recess is as follows:

> First, into negative, inward sin, not "stirring up the gift of God which was in him," not "watching unto prayer," not "pressing on to the mark of the prize of his high calling": Then, into positive inward sin, inclining to wickedness with his heart, giving way to some evil desire or temper: Next, he lost his faith, his sight of a pardoning God, and consequently his love of God; and, being then weak and like another man, he was capable of committing even outward sin.[100]

Even the youngest "babe in Christ" has sufficient grace so as to *not* follow this pattern from grace into outward sin. Yet, the freedom of these children of God is a conflicted one. The *triplex concupiscentia* still tugs at their hearts. The desire of the flesh, the desire of the eyes, and the pride of life are still there, but they are seldom gratified. Sinful tempers are still present but they are held in check more often than not. Sins remain, "though not *reign*, in him that is born of God."[101]

By contrast, in the perfect Christian, the "inbred leprosy"[102] has been cleansed and the "fatal disease"[103] has been cured.[104] In a real sense, such a person is no longer *simul justus et peccator* but holy.[105] However, while in this life, the possibility of sin (though not its necessity or inevitability) remains even for the sanctified. Even when saved from sin to the uttermost, the Christian remains absolutely dependent on the merits and intercession of Jesus Christ. No one ever outgrows Jesus, not in this life nor in the life to come. From repentance to glorification, at every stage along the way of salvation, the Christian lives from and in communion with Christ.

> [O]ur perfection is not like that of a tree, which flourishes by the sap derived from its own root, but, as was said before, like that of a branch which, united to the vine, bears fruit; but, severed from it, is dried up and withered.[106]

Christian Perfection Means Perfect Love

So far our study of the doctrine of Christian perfection has followed the way of remotion. We have defined Christian perfection by distinguishing it from what it is not (divine, angelic, Adamic) and by describing what it is incompatible with, namely sin, "properly speaking." It is now time to turn to the positive content of this doctrine as we enter the house itself: holiness.

Throughout his writings, Wesley offers his followers a rich collage of scriptural images of Christian perfection.[107] Christian perfection means having the same mind "which was also in Christ Jesus" (Phil 2:5) so that our whole intellect, affections, and tempers are rightly ordered toward God and humanity. The perfect person is the one who has opened herself to that "glorious constellation of graces"[108] which Paul refers to as the "fruit of the Spirit" (Gal 5:22-23). To be perfect entails "putting on the new man, which is created after God in righteousness and true holiness" (Eph 4:24). In short, perfection signals the renewal of the moral image of God in the human. The perfection that we aspire to reach is comprehensive and universal, inward and outward; it is characterized by holiness of heart "and in all manner of conversation" (1 Pet 1:15); it is constituted by the offering of the whole person (body and soul) as "living sacrifice unto God" (Rom 12:1) so that we might "be preserved blameless unto the coming of our Lord Jesus Christ" (1 Thes 5:23).

The range of biblical images of perfection utilized by Wesley is extensive, and yet these images are but so many depictions of the same underlying reality: "This is the sum of Christian perfection: it is all comprised in that one word, love."[109] Humans need not live up to the demands of

Adamic perfection, nor be like the angels in order to be fit for glory. In Wesley's words,

> Faith working or animated by love is all that God now requires of man. He has substituted not sincerity, but love, in the room of angelic perfection.[110]

To be perfect here below is to be made perfect in love. The identification of Christian perfection with perfect love is a persistent and consistent theme in Wesley's theology. Perfection in love is a fitting end for humans in the condition of grace, for such perfection entails participation in the very nature of the God who is love.[111]

For Wesley, love is the highest thing that can be predicated of God. It is God's chief attribute and ought to be ranked above omniscience, omnipotence, or eternity. "Love is the very image of God: it is the brightness of his glory."[112] Because God is love, love is the only religion worthy of God. Love is "the medicine of life, the never failing remedy for all the evils of a disordered world, for all the miseries and vices of men."[113] Wesley does not overlook the divinely immanent dimensions of God's love, but he focuses his attention on the divine economy: God's love *ad extra*. "Love is the end, the sole end, of every dispensation of God, from the beginning of the world to the consummation of all things."[114]

Lest Wesley's language of love be dismissed as amorphous and his doctrine of God be misunderstood as teaching that God does not judge, it is important to affirm that Wesley strongly links God's love with his holiness. God's love is a holy love. As Collins states,

> For Wesley, then, God is not love in an indulgent way, nor is God holy in an abstract sense; rather, holiness is that divine attribute which informs *every one* of the divine perfections, but especially love.[115]

God's holy love is shown *ad extra* in his creation of a good universe where everything was "perfect in its kind."[116] From the highest angels in the golden chain of being to the basic constitutive elements of inert matter every part was in harmony with the rest and oriented toward the glory of God. God not only created all that is but watched over it with providential care. None are neglected by God; not the sparrow, not the orphan. "Remember," Wesley states, "that God *ita praesidet singulis sicut universis, et universis sicut singulis*."[117] Yet, God's love toward his creatures is not egalitarian; there is distinction and differentiation in his care of creation, "a threefold circle of divine providence."[118] The "outermost circle" encompasses all of humanity, on whom God lavishes without distinction the blessings of creation: rain, bountiful harvests, and the like. The "interior circle" encloses all the baptized, all who invoke the name of Christ. God offers these the Scriptures and the means of grace. The "innermost circle" includes only the "real Christians," the "invisible church," those who worship God in spirit and truth. These are truly the apples of God's eye, and it is these that Jesus intends when he says, "even the hairs of your head are numbered" (Luke 12:7). Because God's love is holy, it draws distinctions. Full communion with the God who is holy love requires that "God would first, by this inspiration of his Spirit, have wrought in our hearts that holy love without which none can enter into glory."[119]

Chiefly, the flame of God's love *ad extra* burns most brightly not in his care of creation but in the sacrifice on the cross: "God's love was revealed among us in this way: God sent his only Son into the world so that we might live through him" (1 John 4:9). It is in the divine economy of salvation that the depths of God's love, as well as the Triune origin of God's love, are made known with exceeding intensity and clarity.

> Unless then *many* had been made sinners by the disobedience of one, by the obedience of one many would not have been "made righteous." So there would have been no room for that amazing display of the Son of God's love to mankind. There would have been no occasion for his "being obedient unto death, even the death of the cross." It could not then have been said, to the astonishment of all the hosts of heaven, "God so loved the world," yea, the ungodly world which had no thought or desire of returning to him, "that he gave his Son" out of his bosom, his only-begotten Son, "to the end that whosoever believeth on him should not perish, but have everlasting life."[120]

For Wesley, as for much of the Christian tradition, the fall of Adam is indeed a *felix culpa* because it leads to the incarnation of the Word. "Unless all the partakers of human nature had received that deadly wound in Adam it would not have been needful for the Son of God to take our nature upon him."[121] Hence, the fall allows the human to attain greater heights of holiness, happiness, and perfection (these three being synonyms in Wesley's theological lexicon) than would have been possible had Adam not fallen.[122] So, perfection in love is not a consolation prize for a lost Adamic perfection, but a perfecting of that perfection.

At its heart, Christian perfection consists in the perfection of our love for God. But our love of God is only possible in response to God's love for us. "We love because he first loved us" (1 John 4:19). This Johannine saying, so central to Wesley's soteriology, expresses Wesley's conviction that the divine economy of salvation is a kind of circle of love.

> It immediately and necessarily implies the continual inspiration of God's Holy Spirit: God's breathing into the soul, and the soul's breathing back what it first receives from God; a continual action of God upon the soul, and re-action of the soul upon God; an unceasing presence of God, the loving, pardoning God, manifested to the heart, and perceived by faith; and an unceasing return of love, praise, and prayer, offering up all the thoughts of our hearts, all the words of our tongues, all the works of our hands, all our body, soul, and spirit, to be an holy sacrifice, acceptable unto God in Christ Jesus.[123]

As we love God our hearts are filled with the very life of God, and only as our hearts are filled with the life of God can we love. In love there is a mutual indwelling of us in God and God in us, and where there is love, "there are virtue and happiness, going hand in hand. There is humbleness of mind, gentleness, long-suffering, the whole image of God."[124] Love of God is the one thing needful, the only fitting response of the creature to the Creator, "the proper worship of a reasonable creature."[125] Love is the way to happiness for "by love man is not only made like God, but in some sense one with him."[126] Love is the source of our life (we were made out of love) and the goal of our life (we were made for love).[127]

As is apparent from these statements, Wesley's understanding of the role of love in perfection is both causal and teleological. On the one hand, God's love is the source of our love.

> Just as sanctification is now regarded as a consequence of saving faith in atonement, so love to God and our neighbor, which is the essence of sanctification, is linked up with faith in atonement and assurance of forgiveness. Love is seen as the direct fruit of the justifying faith.[128]

On the other hand, God's love is the goal of our love.

> God's love in atonement and justification aims at the establishment of the law of love in the human heart . . . The object of salvation is the restoration in man of the love of God. This is effected by faith. But faith is only the means, the end is love.[129]

To be made perfect in love means to be ruled by love so that everything we do in this life is motivated by and for the sake of love. Love of God is the end; faith in God is the means. According to Wesley, the love that is the source and goal of our strivings can be considered in two ways: love of complacency and love of gratitude. These two kinds of love correspond to the teleological and causal structure of God's love. In the first of these, love of complacency or delight, one loves God for who God is, for his perfection, his wisdom, his goodness, and his infinity. This delight in God is in a sense possible for all reasonable creatures that see the invisible things of God in the things that God has made (cf. Rom 1:20). The second kind of love, love of gratitude or benevolence, is properly found only in the Christian. Only one who believes that Jesus died for the sins of the world knows this kind of love (cf. 1 John 4:19). These two kinds of love are distinct, but they are not meant to be separate. As Wesley avers,

> When these fountains have once united their streams, they flow with redoubled violence, and bear the Christian strongly forward to please and obey the All-merciful, and to be made one with the all perfect.[130]

In other words, the perfect love of God includes both gratitude and delight, a love of God for what he has done for me and for who he is in himself. Moreover, the conjunction of gratitude and delight is perfective of love. Gratitude for our redemption strengthens delight because it is on the cross that I apprehend most clearly who God is. Delight strengthens gratitude because the more that I reflect on God's nature *in se* the more that I marvel that he is *pro me*.

Christian perfection consists in obeying that command which calls us to love the Lord our God with our whole heart, soul, mind, and strength. All of Christ's commands in both the Old and New Testaments are about love. The various and sundry prohibitions in the Bible are nothing else "but so many cautions against what estranges us from the love of God."[131] The hard "Thou shall nots" of the law serve as warnings: "we must not love anything more than God . . . we must entertain no love which is contrary to the love of him."[132] The positive commands in Scripture either direct us to those means of grace whereby our love of God is inflamed or to those virtues whereby this love is exercised. In either case, as Lindström states, "the idea of Christian love is closely bound up with the idea of Law."[133] The process of sanctification consists chiefly in the interiorization of the revealed law, so that it ceases to be only an exterior command but becomes written on the heart.

It is important to underscore this point, for at times Wesley's interpreters set logos and ethos at odds with each other.[134] For Wesley, love has a basis in God's eternal reason. Love of God presupposes knowledge of God, and knowledge of God requires the exercise of the intellect. We will consider the relation of knowing and loving more closely when we study Aquinas' doctrine of perfection. Suffice it to say for now, that reason cannot by itself move us to love God; however, our love of God is "always consistent with reason."[135] Hence, according to Wesley, love of God is not some amorphous feeling of dependence but a holy habit that is ordered by and toward the fulfillment of the divine law. Wesley draws attention to the fulfillment of this law not only because it is the "greatest commandment" but also because the command to love God has its roots in the nature of human existence. What makes this ordering of love humanly possible is God's imparting of the holy tempers, but more of that in a moment.

The perfection of the love of God might seem to leave little room for other loves.[136] However, Wesley accepts Jesus' synthesis of Deuteronomy 6:5 and Leviticus 19:18 as normative for Christian life. Love of God and love of neighbor are, in a sense, one commandment. Many Wesley hymns express this synthesis. For instance,

> Turn the full stream of nature's tide;
> Let all our actions tend
> To thee, their source; thy love the guide,
> Thy glory be the end.
>
> Earth then a scale to heaven shall be;
> Sense shall point out the road;
> The creatures all shall lead to thee,
> And all we taste be God.[137]

In other words, the creature is loved for the sake of the creator. We desire the things of this world insofar as they lead us to what is most desirable—the vision of God. This understanding of the love of neighbor, based on the Augustinian distinction between *frui-uti*, is easily misunderstood as expressing a longing for an individualistic beatitude of *solus cum solo*. And yet, for Wesley, tender affections toward family members and delight in the virtues of the saints are neither prohibited by Scripture nor discouraged but positively commanded. However, it is important to note that the perfect love of neighbor is not one that is motivated by natural kinship but by the gift of the Holy Spirit.

> Whosoever feels the love of God and man shed abroad in heart feels an ardent and uninterrupted thirst after the happiness of all his fellow-creatures.[138]

The perfect love of neighbor is motivated by God's sake. We love because he first loved us and we love others as he loves us. Love is ordered according to its objects. Just as God's relation to creation can be described in terms of concentric circles of providence where God shows greater care for things closer to the center than for those on the periphery, there are circles of love in our relation to the neighbor.[139] In the outermost circle, we are to regard all humankind (even our enemies) with universal benevolence and esteem. Wesley lays particular emphasis on the love of enemies as a mark of perfection. When the whole mind that was found in Christ Jesus comes to rule among us,

> [W]e shall love every man so as to be ready "to lay down our life for his sake"; so as, by this love, to be freed from anger, and pride, and from every unkind affection.[140]

In the inner circle, we are to love all Christians (regardless of their denomination) as children of God and joint heirs of the kingdom. In the innermost circle, we are to love with greatest fervor the saints, those real Christians who are, by grace, closer to us than our closest kin. For Wesley, the distinction between these circles of love is a distinction in degree not in kind, but it is a real distinction.

Contrary to critics of Augustine and Wesley, the doctrine of perfect love does not treat the creature as a mere stepping-stone on the way to God. Dissimilarly, our perfection and the perfection of our neighbors are greatly linked on earth and in heaven. On earth, we need neighbors to love and neighbors to love us if we are to grow in holiness. Hence, the need for society and the real basis for the most famous of Wesley's adages: "no holiness but social holiness."[141] In heaven, the spirits of the righteous grow in happiness and holiness not only as they contemplate God but also as they become acquainted with their benefactors among humans and angels. Because although it is in Jesus Christ that are hidden all the treasures of wisdom and knowledge (Col 2:3), "it is certain human spirits swiftly increase in knowledge, in holiness, and in happiness, conversing with all the wise and holy souls that lived in all ages and nations from the beginning of the world."[142] But this increase in joy among the saints is not merely an intra-heavenly affair, as Wesley asks (rhetorically): "may we not probably suppose that the spirits of the just, though generally lodged in paradise, yet may sometimes, in conjunction with the holy angels, minister to the heirs of salvation?"[143] Indeed, "how much happiness will that add to the happiness of those spirits which are already discharged from the body, that they are permitted to minister to those whom they have left behind!"[144]

Why would God work this way? Is he not almighty and able by his immediate power to meet all the needs of his creatures on earth and in heaven? Nevertheless, God is pleased to work through subordinate means, which is in keeping with God's character and with his nature of love. As Wesley explains, "The grand reason why God is pleased to assist men by men, rather than immediately by himself, is undoubtedly to endear us to each other by these mutual good offices, in order to increase our happiness both in time and eternity."[145] Nor is this happiness of creatures in other creatures a temporary stage to be overcome in the *eschaton*. In the new creation, "there will be a deep, an intimate, an uninterrupted union with God; a constant communion with the Father and his Son Jesus Christ, through the Spirit; a continual enjoyment of the Three-One God, *and of all the creatures in him!*"[146] By way of anticipation, I should say that Aquinas' understanding of primary and secondary causality offers Wesley a way of conceptually elucidating these surprisingly traditional affirmations of faith in the communion of saints.

Christian perfection as we have just been discussing consists chiefly in the perfect love of God and neighbor. Is there room for self-love in the perfect? After all, the Lord's command to love our neighbor as ourselves presupposes some measure of self-love. Moreover, according to Wesley, "the love which is shed abroad in my heart by the Holy Ghost, destroys all self-love; so that I could lay down my life for my brethren."[147] Lindström states Wesley's solution well, "Unregulated self-love is an expression of sin and thus proper self-love acquires the character of regulated love."[148] What Lindström does not discuss in as much detail as warranted is how this regulated character is attained by the exercise of the holy tempers, and it is to their consideration that we now turn.[149]

The tempers play an integral role in Wesley's understanding of human psychology.[150] Wesley grew up in an environment where the reigning moral philosophy traced its origins back to Plato. For many Anglicans, including Wesley's mother, the greatest obstacle to moral action was the passions. The "dark horse" of the emotions and the white horse of the spirit need to be reigned in by the charioteer of reason. Only when reason is in charge are actions good. Maddox refers to this moral psychology as "habituated rational control."[151] Wesley's early pastoral practice adopted this model. The practices of scriptural reading and the Eucharist were not chiefly means of grace but of ordinances. Love was important in this account not as a moral motivation but as an ethical obligation.

Through his interactions with the English Moravians, Wesley encountered an Augustinian account of the will that throughly challenged the assumptions of his moral psychology of "habituated rational control." From an Augustinian perspective, humans are created to love God with a love of enjoyment (*frui*) and to love creatures with a love of use (*uti*). The first is the end or purpose of our existence; the latter is a means to that end. The human predicament is that because of the fall our loves have become disordered. We have swapped the objects of these two loves. We love God with the love of *uti*, and we love the creature with the love of *frui*. No human faculty or relation has been left unaffected by our disordered loves. Take the will, for instance. Augustine distinguishes two levels of the will: *theleitas* and *voluntas*. The former represents the level of the will that is closest to action. Reason has control over this level of operation. I can choose to type or not to type. I can type one word or another. The latter represents the level of the will that reflects my loves and the fundamental orientation of my life. It is at this deep level that the will is disordered. Reason cannot reorder this level of the will. I cannot reason my way into doing something out of love. Only an infusion of God's own love can restore our loves to their proper order.

The adoption of this Augustinian psychology prompted a radical shift in Wesley's theology and practice. To mention just one example, whereas his earlier piety had sought for certainty of his love for God, he now sought evidence of God's love for him. This shift in piety signals a move away from the Platonic psychology of his household that said that humans are moved to act by reason. Instead, he adopted the empiricist psychology of his alma mater, which claimed that humans are moved to act by being "experientially affected."[152]

Wesley could not altogether accept this "affective" moral psychology. It seemed to compromise human freedom and reduce moral action to a Pavlovian response to external stimuli. One way in which Wesley avoided this unhappy consequence was by ranking liberty as an integral component of the image of God, different from the will. By insisting on the liberty of indifference Wesley sought to safeguard human freedom. As we have already seen there are philosophical and theological problems with this move. The other way in which Wesley emphasized the significance of love for moral theology was by reflecting on the nature of the tempers. What is a temper? Let us listen to Maddox.

> Wesley used the term in specific reference to the human affections. While our affections are responsive, he was convinced that they need not be simply transitory, they can be focused and strengthened into enduring dispositions. Thus, in his terminology, the capacity for simple responsive love is an affection, while a developed enduring disposition to love (or to reject love!) is a temper.[153]

By centering his mature moral psychology on tempers Wesley comes very close to Aquinas' "virtue ethic."[154] The late Wesley regarded the holy tempers as seeds of God's sanctifying grace. These seeds are implanted in human nature for the purpose of grounding holy actions on holy affections. For this reason, Maddox refers to this moral psychology as "habituated holistic affections."[155]

The central role of holy tempers in the perfection of believers is the reason why Wesley can claim that "True religion is right tempers toward God and man."[156] Holy tempers keep Christian life on an even keel, as far removed from ironic indifference as from excessive affection, thus "preserving the mean in every circumstance of life."[157] Christians attain the fullness of perfection when love becomes the sole principle of all those tempers that are found in the mind of Christ.[158] When this happens the affections are not destroyed or rooted out but healed.[159]

Holy tempers are what regulate Christian love so that it does not become un-Christian zeal. Etymologically, zeal refers to heat and it is ascribed to particularly strong emotions such as anger, indignation, or jealousy. As such, zeal can and has been a very destructive passion throughout history. As Wesley avers "pride, covetousness, ambition, revenge, have in all parts of the world slain their thousands, but zeal its ten thousands."[160] It was zeal that provoked the Crusades. It was zeal that fueled the fires during the reign of "Bloody Mary." It was zeal that led to the massacre of the French Huguenots. But these instances of zeal are not worthy of the name Christian. True zeal, or Christian zeal, is a religious zeal that is united with charity. Simply put, Christian zeal is love, and not just any common degree of love, but that love which fills up the whole of human nature with the "flame of love."[161] In true zeal, holy tempers such as humility, meekness, and patience are present with such a burning intensity that all turbulent passions are purged away. Zeal has the good as its object; it is directed toward everything that is good in the sight of God but, "[zeal] is always *proportioned* to that good, to the degree of goodness that is in its object."[162]

Wesley understands this proportion of love to the good as a set of concentric circles or steps. The outermost circle and also the first step is the church; Christians are to love the church; obey it; work to extend its boundaries; pray for is members. Next, the ordinances of God: the Lord's Supper, prayer, searching the Scriptures, fasting; Christians are to be zealous toward these by observing them and recommending them to others. Next are the works of mercy. We should be more zealous toward these than toward the aforementioned works of piety because "God desires mercy and not sacrifice" (Hos 6:6). As Wesley avers: "Even reading, hearing, prayer, are to be omitted, or to be postponed, 'at charity's almighty call.'"[163] Further inward and upward are holy tempers; we are to be zealous in cultivating the whole train of holy habits that alone give eternal worth to our efforts. Some of these tempers can be described as "passive graces"[164] or "passive virtues";[165] such tempers presuppose suffering for their existence and operation.[166] Without suffering, for example, there would be no true meekness or resignation. Even if God were to sow the seeds of these tempers in our souls, there would be no occasion for their exercise and growth. Other tempers, like benevolence, pertain more to the active life of good works. In either case, active and passive, the holy tempers are both means of grace and means to greater grace. The stronger these holy habits become the holier we become, and the holier we become the happier we will be.

> To sum up what has been said under this head. As the more holy we are upon earth the more happy we must (seeing there is an inseparable connection between holiness and happiness); as the more good we do to others the more of present reward redounds in our own bosom; even as our sufferings for God lead us to "rejoice" in him "with joy unspeakable and full of glory."[167]

We will consider this connection between perfection, happiness, and holy tempers in a later chapter when we compare Aquinas' interpretation of the Sermon on the Mount to Wesley's.

Finally, at the center of it all is love. Church, sacraments, social service, and the life of the virtues are not enough; "all is nothing without love,"[168] for without love there is no stable ground or goal for the Christian life.

> The heaven of heavens is love. There is nothing higher in religion; there is in effect nothing else; if you look for anything but *more love*, you are looking wide of the mark, you are getting out of the royal way.[169]

It is for the sake of preserving the sublimity of love that Wesley warns those who claim to have attained perfection to beware of enthusiasm. An undue interest in visions, dreams, divine voices, and the like can lead one to despise the means of grace as too ordinary and common. A misunderstanding of the state of perfection as different in kind, not simply in degree, from the state of justification can provoke the "perfect" to look down on lesser-blessed believers as not real Christians at all. The main difference between the perfect and those going on to perfection is not that the former know more but that they love best. Christian perfection does not consist in the gift of prophecy or in the discernment of spirits. Love alone is the highest gift of God and the holiest of tempers.

Conclusion

In this chapter, we have examined the principal structural elements of the Methodist house of holiness. This inquiry has yielded two results that would be worth restating and some problems that need acknowledgment. First, Wesley makes it clear that Christian perfection is not to be confused with the absolute perfection of God, or with the perfection of angels, Adam, or heaven. Second, Christian perfection consists primarily in the renewal of the moral aspect of the divine image; entire sanctification marks the perfect coincidence of freedom and love (or as perfect as these can be in this life). This emphasis on the moral image is important so as to avoid an overly realized expectation of perfection. If, for instance, Christian perfection consisted in the renewal of the natural image, one would look for its exemplars among the most beautiful and intelligent specimens of humanity. However, since perfection pertains primarily to the heart's affections and tempers, its exemplars can be found among the physically handicapped and perhaps even among the mentally infirm. The emphasis on the renewal of the moral image need not exclude the restoration of other aspects of the image of God. Wesley did not say so, but one way to make theological sense of people like Saint Francis is to read the stories of his relations to animals as an earthly anticipation of the perfection of the political image that Wesley expected would be fully attained only in the new creation. The same could be said of other hagiographical accounts which relate wondrous manifestations of a saint's physical subtlety, corporeal incorruptibility, or spiritual understanding.

One problem with the doctrine of Christian perfection that still needs acknowledgment is Wesley's understanding of sin. Thomas Rigl correctly observes that Wesley's teaching stands or falls on the basis of its *verkürzten Sündenbegriff* of sin, "properly speaking."[170] Clearly, Wesley's doctrine of sin covers sins of omission. Moreover, only on the basis of Christ's merits is invincible ignorance not culpable. But, how perfect is the freedom of Christian perfection? It seems to me that Wesley's concept of sin becomes abbreviated when the corporate dimension of sin and salvation is lost and the assurance of personal holiness is purchased at the cost of Christian solidarity with sinners. Since the perfection of a Christian is, in a sense, yoked to that of the neighbor, we should expect that perfect love would cast out the distinction between what is mine and what is yours as much as possible—even when it comes to sins (cf. 1 Cor 12:26)!

Chapter Two

Wesley on the Way to Christian Perfection

As we saw in the last chapter, Christian perfection consists in freedom from sin and perfection in love. The freedom falls short of the perfect freedom of *non-posse peccare*. The love falls short of the perfect act of love possible for a beatified mind and glorified body. In other words, Christian perfection falls short of heavenly perfection. However, Christian perfection is truly perfection as it is attainable in this life, and differs from the perfection of heaven only in degree, not in kind.

Perfect love and freedom are the two pillars that hold up the Methodist house of the doctrine of perfection. We now turn our attention to a different set of considerations of this house. First, how is the house of holiness attained? Is entire sanctification a Pelagian achievement? Is it attained by faith alone? What is the role of the church in sanctification? Is there perfection outside the church? Second, why is this doctrine an important teaching? What is Christian perfection for? Does it need to be attained in this life? Third, how do we recognize Christian perfection? Is public recognition desirable or even necessary for this doctrine to fulfill its purpose? Fourth, for whom is this doctrine written? Are all called to perfection in this life or only a few?

The Way to Christian Perfection

Salvation, for Wesley, means more than "going to heaven." Salvation covers "the entire work of God, from the first dawning of grace in the soul till it is consummated in glory."[1] The way of salvation is built on grace upon grace. "Grace is the source, faith the condition, of salvation."[2] What is grace? At its heart, grace is the love of God, a love that is shown *for* us in Christ's atoning work and *in* us by the Spirit's sanctifying presence. Daniel Luby's words on Wesley's doctrine of grace are worth heeding:

> Grace for Wesley is the pardoning, transforming love of God, present to us in the indwelling person of the Holy Spirit. It is congenial with, but radically different from, our natural endowment, and is ordered to our participation in the divine life, to a relationship with God of intimacy and mutual love.[3]

There are two aspects of this quote that are worth highlighting. First, there is a close relation between Wesley's doctrine of grace and the doctrine of the Spirit.[4] Grace has a pneumatological shape in Wesley's theology. His alleged "optimism" of grace is really an affirmation of faith in the presence and power of the Holy Spirit.[5] Second, for Wesley, grace is both revelatory and transformative. Grace opens our eyes to see God and the world in a new way. God loves us, even while we are still sinners. He loves us so much that he sent his Son to die on the cross for us. As I accept his atoning work by faith, my sins are forgiven, and I know myself to be a child of God. Our affections are reordered by the light of faith; the perception of being loved by God moves us to become lovers of God and neighbor. The dependence of transformation on revelation underscores the significance of perception in Wesley's theology. Luby observes that

> Wesley sees Christian love as properly motivated only by a truly personal response to the love of God for us. In order for such a response to be genuinely ours it must be preceded by a conscious awareness of the love to which we are responding.[6]

Christian life is difficult and the gift of assurance, the conscious awareness that God loves me, belongs to the ordinary privileges of all children of God.[7] Wesley speaks of faith in three ways: as intellectual assent, as trust, and as spiritual sense. It is in this last way that humans perceive invisible realities like the indwelling presence of God or the testimony of the Spirit. Such spiritual perception is immediate in the sense that it is not the result of ratiocination or abstraction, but it is not *sine mediis*.[8] Indeed, Wesley often links his own experiences of assurance with his reception of the Eucharist. I will say more about this later when we consider how Wesley understands the means of grace.

Two interwoven leitmotifs dominate Wesley's doctrine of grace: free grace and universal grace. On the one hand, grace is "free in all," that is to say, it is freely given without any prior consideration of works or merits on the part of the receiver.[9] Whatever good we do, whatever right tempers we have, or noble things we propose are the effects of grace, not their cause. The sole meritorious cause of grace is Christ, and *in this sense* Christ can be considered the only means of grace.[10] On the other hand, grace is universal; it is "free for all."[11] It is not limited to a small select band predestined for glory, but rather it is available to all humankind. Like the profligate sower of Jesus' parable, God scatters his graces liberally on the human race so that "No man sins because he has not grace, but because he does not use the grace which he has."[12]

The emphasis on the freedom of grace "in all" and "for all" shines a spotlight on the controversy between Calvinists and Wesleyans on their doctrines of grace and in particular on the resistibility of grace. We will consider this topic in greater detail in the final sections of our study of Aquinas and Wesley when we consider their respective teachings on merit and predestination. For now, let me simply say that for Wesley grace is a gift that can be turned down; it is resistible. Admittedly, "the grace which brings faith, and thereby salvation in the soul, is irresistible *at that* moment."[13] Furthermore, it is true "that most believers do at some other times find God *irresistibly* acting upon their souls."[14] Nevertheless, Wesley insists "that the grace of God both before and after those moments, may be, and hath been, resisted; and [t]hat, in general, it does not act irresistibly, but we may comply therewith or may not."[15]

Grace is both God's favor and God's gift; it is God working for us and in us; it reconciles us with God and renews us after the image of Christ. As Wesley explains,

> As soon as ever the grace of God (in the former sense, his pardoning love) is manifested to our soul, the grace of God (in the latter sense, the power of his Spirit) takes place therein.[16]

These various senses of grace do not represent actually different kinds or "flavors" of grace. Rather, they describe different effects of grace, effects that are suited to meet the needs of the person at the state of the journey in which they find themselves. As Luby avers, "grace in all is one; but the situation of the individual changes the way we talk about that one grace, and it changes the specific way in which grace affects us."[17] Let us now consider some of these specific ways.

The way to perfection begins with the operation of God's prevenient grace. This grace restores to the human a measure of the freedom lost in the fall. As we saw in the last chapter, Adam's rebellion did not result in God's abandonment of humanity. On account of original sin, all humans are by nature dead in their sins, void of anything like free will, and incapable of seeking God, but there is no human that lives in this purely "natural" state. For Wesley, the phenomenon of "pure nature" without grace is an abstraction, a logical but not historical possibility because by the incarnation of the Word a measure of free will has been restored to the human. In Lindström's words,

> [Wesley] does not regard such discernment as something emanating from natural man's own resources, a consequence of the survival after the Fall of a certain residue of the *imago Dei*, but instead as deriving from prevenient grace.[18]

All humans have a conscience, and unless they persistently act against it, this conscience gives them a rough sense of the difference between good and evil. Thus, the phenomena of heathen religions and morality are not strictly speaking natural phenomena; rather they are the evidence that God has not completely abandoned his creatures, and continues to confer on all people without distinction a measure of grace. In other words, for Wesley, natural conscience is not a natural capacity but an effect of grace, or more specifically, prevenient grace.

In sum, the universal phenomenon of conscience is in truth supernatural in origin. But as as most people ignore this grace, the human condition even after Christ is characterized not by freedom of conscience but by a false peace. As Wesley states, "The 'natural man' neither fears nor loves God."[19] He neither struggles nor fights against whatever goes against conscience but sins willingly and happily. Such is the state of pagans and nominal Christians. They feel no condemnation for the sins they commit; they are essentially sleepwalkers. A vague awareness of the need for God does not suffice. The religious *cor inquietum* is not enough; humans need a genuine conviction of personal sinfulness.

The first overture of prevenient grace needs to be followed by the operation of "convincing grace." If the first grace is not shunned and stifled, God gives a second grace which awakens humans to their sinful predicament. Convincing grace has the effect of bringing humans "under the law." Those who are "under the law" are conscious of their pride, their idolatry, and above all, the *triplex concupiscentia* inbred into their souls—the desire of the flesh, the desire of the eyes, and the pride of life. But "under the law," the awakened sinner knows no rest from these disordered desires. As Wesley puts it, "the man under the law fights with sin, but cannot conquer."[20] What needs to be done in order to be found acceptable to God is clear, and yet as Paul explains in Romans 7:15, "I do not do what I want, but I do the very thing I hate." When such persons measure their lives by the demands of God's moral law, they find that they come up short. Under the law, the awakened conscience diagnoses itself as sinful, as ill to the very core; yet the law offers no cure for this sickness but only a prognosis—death.

The effects of convincing grace make it sound like an unwelcome guest. However, with the graced stirring of sorrow over sin, the way to perfection begins in earnest. Now the human begins to offer, if time allows, works for repentance, which, though not meritorious, are a fitting preparation for the gift of justification.

It might be helpful at this point to remember something we looked at in passing in the last chapter. According to Wesley, sin and grace must be considered together—the sickness with the cure. The soteriological orientation of Wesley's doctrine of sin is exemplified in his correlation of the twofold character of sin and salvation. Sin and salvation have, in Lindström's words, an objective-juridical aspect and a subjective-medical one.[21] Under its objective-juridical aspect, sin is guilt and its remedy is justification, the forgiveness of sin. The basis for this justification and acceptance by God lies in the atonement: Christ died for me. The death of Christ on the cross is not for Wesley a merely representational act in the name of humanity, an example of the way to salvation, but it is salvific itself. At Calvary, Christ did something: he paid the ransom for my sins, and merited my justification by his act of passive obedience; his suffering took the place of our suffering, but, and this is key for Wesley, his obedience to the law does not substitute for ours. By the grace of justification, I am forgiven for all *past* sins.[22] Under its subjective-therapeutic aspect, sin is sickness and salvation is healing: the restoration of health to the soul. If justification is what Christ does for me, a *relative* change, sanctification is what Christ does in me, a *real* change. Not only am I forgiven, I am born again and I begin to be made holy. By sanctifying grace, the moral image lost to sin begins to be restored, and the natural and political reordered. The restoration to spiritual health is central to Wesley's doctrine of grace. As Wesley explains, Christianity is a therapeutic faith.

> It is θεραπεία ψυχῆς. God's method of healing a soul which is thus diseased. Hereby the great Physician of souls applies medicine to heal this sickness; to restore human nature, totally corrupted in all its faculties.[23]

The work of grace has both juridical and therapeutic aspects, but these must not be played off each other as though they belong to separate economies of salvation. On the contrary, these two aspects exist in a teleological relation; the former is for the sake of the latter—we are forgiven in order to be healed; we are justified in order to be sanctified.

To return to our discussion of justifying grace, those who have been born again live "under grace"; they have been set free from the Adamic covenant of works and enjoy the liberty of the children of God. As we have already seen, Wesley is persuaded that even the youngest "babe in Christ" has sufficient grace so as to walk free from outward sin. However, the babe in Christ has not yet come to maturity. This person has faith, but it is weak and mixed with doubt. The person "under grace" is, as Luther adverted, *simul justus et peccator*. Indeed, all of the aforementioned stages along the way to perfection are often mixed, for seldom is a person in the "natural state" wholly unacquainted with pangs of conscience, or one "under the law" totally void of hope. God does not hide his countenance from the mass of humanity. "The wise and gracious God rarely suffers this; for he remembereth that we are but dust."[24] It is for this very reason, because the stages along the way to perfection are mixed states, that Wesley insists that the declaration of the law and the invitation to repentance are not things that pertain only to those "under the law" but also to those "under grace," albeit in a different way.

> The repentance consequent upon justification is widely different from that which is antecedent to it. This implies no guilt, no sense of condemnation, no consciousness of the wrath of God. It does not suppose any doubt of the favour of God, or any "fear that hath torment." It is properly a conviction wrought by the Holy Ghost of the "sin" which still "remains" in our heart, of the φρόνημα σαρκός, "the carnal mind," which "does still remain," as our Church speaks, "even in them that are regenerate"—although it does no longer reign, it has not now dominion over them.[25]

For Wesley, Christians are even more aware than unbelievers of the sin that continues to remain in their mortal bodies. Even after justification, or especially after justification, the Christian must lead a life of repentance and good works with the support of the means of grace that God has made available for sanctification. Those "under grace" fear God but not as those "under the law": their fear is filial, not servile; it is the bold reverence that a child owes a loving parent, not the cowering attitude of a slave before a cruel master. For these persons, the law of God does not thunder condemnation but offers good news because it presents opportunities for joyful obedience. Inbred sin, pride, the *triplex concupiscentia*, all these abide in those "under grace." The work of restoration is not finished; they have not been saved to the uttermost.

As wonderful and transformative as the effects of justifying grace are for the believer, they do not mark the end of the journey. At some point, whether soon after justification or years after, God will complete the work he started and entirely sanctify the Christian through "sanctifying grace."

The work of sanctification began at the same time as that of justification. By being born again the person begins to be renewed after the likeness of God. However, the work remains incomplete until the person attains Christian perfection, "the highest state of grace."[26]

It might be misleading to call Christian perfection a "state" since entire sanctification was not for Wesley a static achievement. Still, it is not inappropriate to refer to it as a "state" in that Wesley conceives entire sanctification as a new mode of divine operation and a higher degree of Christian existence. Unlike the justified, those who are entirely sanctified have the assurance not only of the forgiveness of sin but of the eradication of their tendency to sin. This fullness of assurance increases humility, because the person knows that perfection is a gift from God and not the result of their own striving.

Wesley in continuity with the great Christian tradition is convinced that salvation is all of grace: "the very first motion of good is from above, as well as the power that completes it."[27] God alone saves; God alone justifies; God alone sanctifies. If we do nothing with the grace that God has given us, if we treat his gift as our private possession and hoard it, then we lose it. The divine gift of salvation elicits and empowers human responsibility, and this is why Wesley approvingly adopts an Augustinian dictum, ("one of the noblest he ever uttered"):[28] *Qui fecit nos sine nobis, non salvabit nos sine nobis*.[29] If we "stir the spark of grace"[30] in us God will give us more grace; his favor for us will be clearer; his presence in us more intense; his gifts more fruitful. "Growth in grace" is grace upon grace.[31]

Growth in grace is gradual. Wesley affirms that God does not give all of his graces at once; children do not grow up in a day (even if they do go through growth spurts). The dying to sin and growing in grace that constitute the goal of Christian life can take years. Indeed, as Wesley himself admits, "many of those who have died in the faith, yea, the greater part of those we have known, were not perfected in love till a little before their death."[32] But, however long the way to perfection may be, the attainment of perfection itself occurs in an instant.

> A man may be dying for some time; yet he does not, properly speaking, die, till the instant the soul is separated from the body; and in that instant he lives the life of eternity. In like manner, he may be dying to sin for some time; yet he is not dead to sin, till sin is separated from his soul; and in that instant he lives the full life of love.[33]

Because this great work of salvation is instantaneous, perfection need not be deferred to the deathbed. Today could be the day that God completes the work he began when he called us to faith. Now could be the very moment when God pours into our hearts the perfect love that casts out all fears. Wesley impresses upon his listeners the urgency of perfection in the following manner:

> Do you believe we are sanctified by faith? Be true then to your principle; and look for this blessing just as you are, neither better nor worse; as a poor sinner that has still nothing to pay, nothing to plead, but "Christ died." And if you look for it as you are, then expect it now. Stay for nothing: Why should you? Christ is ready; and He is all you want. He is waiting for you: He is at the door![34]

The high state of grace can be attained today because the only requisite for sanctification is faith. If sanctification were by works, or by faith plus works, then one would expect that certain conditions would need to be met—repentance for the remnants of sin in the heart, fruits of this repentance (works of piety and works of charity)—but "these fruits are only necessary conditionally, if there be time and opportunity for them."[35] Faith is the only condition absolutely necessary for entire sanctification; one cannot be sanctified without it, and it alone suffices. By "sanctifying faith," Wesley means the evidence and conviction that, first of all, God has promised to make us holy; moreover, God is able to make us holy; finally, God is able and willing to make us holy—now.[36] For this reason, the Christian's preparation for sanctification is to "expect it by faith, expect it as you are, and expect it now! To deny one of them, is to deny them all; to allow one, is to allow them all."[37]

Wesley's strong assertion of the instantaneous aspect of perfection is motivated by pastoral and theological concerns. First and foremost, by insisting on the "now" Wesley intends to disturb his listeners from their antinomian slumber and goad them into surrendering all to God, now and always. As he admits,

> For suppose we were mistaken, suppose no such blessing ever was or can be attained, yet we lose nothing: Nay, that very expectation quickens us in using all the talents which God has given us; yea, in improving them all; so that when our Lord cometh, he will receive his own with increase.[38]

Second, by insisting on the "now," Wesley is equally concerned to defend the gratuitousness of grace against those who put works on the same level as faith and suggest that one can actually be deserving of sanctification. One can certainly raise legitimate questions about the theological coherence of the gradual versus instantaneous aspects of Wesley's doctrine of grace; we will consider these questions further after we study Aquinas' doctrine of perfection.

In sum, for Wesley, Christian perfection is instantaneous. However, Wesley introduces an important caveat at this point—that we must *seek and strive* for perfection. God is not irrational or arbitrary in the dispensing of his gifts. "God does not, will not, give that [perfect] faith, unless we seek it with all diligence, in the way which he hath ordained."[39] The way that leads to perfection consists of absolute obedience, zealous observance of the commandments, and self-denial. Those who expect to be made perfect in this life cannot follow the way of quietism and settle for an indolent, indifferent waiting on God. We witness our expectation of perfection by actively waiting within the means of grace.

Wesley's reflections on the means of grace arise in critical dialogue with English Moravians like Philip Molther. In Wesley's view, Molther's one-sided emphasis on *sola fide* and his fear of abusing the ordinances of God led to the embrace of antinomianism and the rejection of the means of grace altogether.[40] In his own thought and practice of the means of grace, Wesley steers clear of the quietism of the Moravians. Consider the following definition:

> By "means of grace" I understand outward signs, words, or actions ordained by God, and appointed for this end—to be the *ordinary* channels whereby he might convey to men preventing, justifying, or sanctifying grace.[41]

I wish to highlight a number of points in this definition. The means of grace are just that: they are "means" to an end, not the end itself. The words and matter from which these means are constituted are not grace in and of themselves, but outward signs. For this reason Wesley warns his listeners: "Before you use any means let it be impressed in your soul: There is no *power* in this. It is in itself a poor, dead, empty thing: separate from God, it is a dry leaf, a shadow."[42] This does not mean that the means of grace are empty signifiers; these ritual acts really serve as channels of God's grace. The image that comes to mind is that of an irrigation channel. In and of itself an irrigation channel is an empty ditch, but when the sluice gate is opened it becomes a life-bearing conduit for the crops. So it is with the means of grace; by themselves they are just words, or rituals, or elements, but in union with God these become the bearers of God's good gifts, which become efficacious for me when I receive them in faith.[43] The grace is real even if the manner is unknown.[44] In the words of a Wesley hymn on the Lord's Supper,

O the depth of Love Divine,
th' unfathomable Grace!
Who shall say how bread and wine
God into man conveys?
How the bread his flesh imparts,
fills his faithful peoples' hearts
with all the life of God![45]

God leads Christians along the path to perfection by way of certain instituted means of grace. God institutes these means so that the Christian way to holiness of heart and life is clearly marked and stocked. Prayer, fasting, and searching the Scriptures (reading, hearing, and meditating) are among the ordinary channels of God's grace, and chief among these is the Eucharist.

The Prayer, the Fast, the Word conveys,
When mixt with Faith, thy Life to me,
In all the Channels of thy Grace,
I still have fellowship with Thee,
But chiefly here is my soul fed
With fullness of Immortal Bread.[46]

In addition to the instituted means of grace there are prudential means of grace: class meetings, covenant renewal service, works of piety of all sorts (practicing the presence of God,[47] the art of holy dying), and works of mercy of all sorts (friendship with the poor, almsgiving). These means are prudential in that they are not obligatory; they are not divinely appointed by God but by wise and experienced Christians; these prudential helps are "grounded on reason and experience, in order to apply the general rules given in Scripture according to particular circumstances."[48]

What I hope is clear from this present consideration of the "how" Christian perfection is, is that it is only possible through grace. It is not a Pelagian or semi-Pelagian athletic achievement. The Christian waits on God to finish the work he began in justification, but this waiting occurs within the means of grace. Wesley makes it clear that God's grace is present in the sacraments, but he also insists that the performing of works of charity can be of greater significance to the strengthening of holy tempers than attending to works of piety. For instance, nothing strengthens the virtues of resignation to God's will and meekness as an active life of service to the poor, and for this reason nothing slows our growth in grace as growing in riches.

The means of grace are apportioned in an order that corresponds to the needs along the way to perfection. As Wesley observes, "There is a kind of order wherein God himself is generally pleased to use these means in bringing a sinner to salvation."[49] Typically, a person is convicted of sinfulness by a sermon, or by a providential encounter with a friend. Such a person acquires a desire to flee from the wrath to come and searches the Scriptures to learn how this can be done. Upon reading the Scriptures, he begins to meditate and ponder upon what he finds there and begins haltingly to talk or pray to God. He then seeks the comfort and companionship of those who know God. In other words, he goes to church. In the congregation he meets other awakened sinners approaching the Lord's Table; he does not consider himself worthy yet he imitates them; he walks forward and receives communion.

> And thus he continues in God's way—in hearing, reading, meditating, praying, and partaking of the Lord's Supper—till God, in the manner that pleases him, speaks to his heart, "Thy faith hath saved thee; go in peace."[50]

The way of salvation outlined above is the ordinary way in which God works and leads people unto salvation, but it is not the only way. God can work through extraordinary means or through none at all because "God is above all means."[51] The assurance of pardon might come to someone from receiving communion, as it often did for Wesley, or it might come from outside the instituted means of grace, as it did for the thief on the cross. For Wesley the differentiation of grace into preventing, justifying or sanctifying has nothing to do with the variety of means (as if some means were more efficacious in bearing certain graces), but with the variety of states or stages of the Christian pilgrimage. For this reason, Wesley encourages his followers to attend to *all* the ordinances of grace.

> The sure and general rule for all who groan for the salvation of God is this—whenever opportunity serves, use all the means which God has ordained. For who knows in which God will meet thee with the grace that bringeth salvation?[52]

Since Wesley does not limit the work of grace to the instituted means of grace, it is not too surprising that he ponders the possibility of grace without church. After all, if God is above all means is he not also above the church? Can grace not bypass the church's sacramental mediation? Is there salvation outside the church? Wesley wisely refuses to exclude definitively from salvation those outside the church.[53] The reason for his reserve has nothing to do with universalism or theological indifferentism. On the contrary, the beliefs and practices of Christianity have profound soteriological consequences for all peoples, not just for Christians. Rather, Wesley's refusal to indissolubly link salvation and church for both believers and non-believers comes from his conviction of the superiority of loving over knowing.

> I believe the merciful God regards the lives and tempers of men more than their ideas. I believe he respects the goodness of the heart rather than the clearness of the head; and that if the heart of a man be filled (by the grace of God, and the power of his Spirit) with the humble, gentle, patient love of God and man, God will not cast him into everlasting fire prepared for the devil and his angels because his ideas are not clear, or because his conceptions are confused. Without holiness, I own, no man shall see the Lord; but I dare not add, or clear ideas.[54]

This "credo" admirably expresses the extent of Wesley's catholic spirit. It is this generous orthodoxy (or perhaps we should say generous *orthokardia*[55]) that allows him to recognize signs of holiness in the most unusual of places—even in Popery! We shall return to this point in the final chapter of this study when we consider the way in which Wesley recognizes holiness beyond the bounds of his church. However, before moving on to explore the purpose of Christian perfection, I should clearly state that Wesley never considers grace apart from Christ's life and work. Although Wesley refuses to doom all non-Christians to eternal punishment, he wisely refrains from naming any names. His reticence on recognizing holiness outside the church stands in marked contrast with his remarkable openness to exemplars of perfection outside Anglicanism and Protestantism.

The Purpose of Christian Perfection

Throughout his many writings and works, Wesley's passion does not consist of offering the people called Methodist a coherent account of Christian perfection, though his account is, I think, quite successful in this regard. Instead, his real passion consists in leading his people to go on to perfection. Indeed, Wesley understands such a commitment to be integral to the divine commission of Methodism. As the "Large Minutes" record,

> Q. What may we reasonably believe to be God's design in raising up the Preachers called Methodists?
>
> A. Not to form any new sect; but to reform the nation, particularly the Church; and to spread scriptural holiness over the land.[56]

This is a rich quote, and many aspects of it are worthy of exploration. At present, I want to call attention to the way that Wesley links together the preaching of perfection and the reformation of church and nation.

Ultimately, the adequacy of Wesley's doctrine of perfection must not be judged by its internal coherence but by its external appeal. Perfection is a sign: a personal sign, an ecclesial sign, a missional sign. Let us consider each of these in order.

First and foremost, Christian perfection is a sign of personal fitness for heaven. The bond between the state of perfection and the state of glorification in Wesley's theology is strong. No one can enter fully into the presence of God without first having been freed from sin and perfected in love. Only a perfectly holy person could truly enjoy the life of heaven. The relational change that occurs in justification is not by itself sufficient to prepare us for glorification. As Wesley explains,

> The righteousness of Christ is, doubtless, necessary for any soul that enters into glory. But so is personal holiness, too, for every child of man. But it is highly needful to be observed that they are necessary in different respects. The former is necessary to entitle us to heaven; the latter, to qualify us for it. Without the righteousness of Christ we could have no claim to glory; without holiness we could have no fitness for it.[57]

But where does this transformation from embattled Christian to triumphant saint take place? When does one put on the wedding garment of holiness? Wesley admits that there is a difference of opinion on this matter:

> Some believe it is attained before death; some, in the article of death; some, in an after-state, in the Mystic or the Popish purgatory. But all writers, whom I have ever seen till now, (the Romish themselves not excepted,) agree, that we must be "fully cleansed from all sin" before we can enter into glory.[58]

Roman Catholic tradition canonizes those whom God's grace radically transformed while in this life, but it also recognizes that for most Christians their entire sanctification and preparation for the life of heaven does not take place on earth but in purgatory. Wesley could not accept such an explanation; there was no room in his *via salutis* for postmortem purgation. Wesley did allow for an intermediate state between heaven and earth, but this place was definitely not purgatory (a place of suffering) but paradise (a place of rest). As Wesley explains,

> In paradise the souls of good men rest from their labours, and are with Christ from death to the resurrection. This bears no resemblance at all to the Popish purgatory, wherein wicked men are supposed to be tormented in purging fire, till they are sufficiently purified to have a place in heaven. But we believe, (as did the ancient church,) that none suffer

> after death, but those who suffer eternally. We believe that we are to be here saved from sin, and enabled to love God with all our heart.[59]

Leaving aside the inadequacies of Wesley's reading of the Catholic teaching on purgatory, it is clear that for him we cannot defer holiness to the hereafter; sin must be dealt with in this life or not at all. In addition to rejecting the existence of an intermediate state of purgation as taught by Roman Catholics, Wesley also repudiated the Calvinist belief that entire sanctification was accomplished by an operation of divine power at the hour of death.[60] One cannot lead a mediocre, half-Christian life on earth and upon breathing one's last breath expect God to irresistibly and instantaneously render one as pure and holy as the greatest of saints. Such a scenario was not plausible for Wesley. It violated his understanding of the divine economy of salvation—*Qui fecit nos sine nobis, non salvabit nos sine nobis*.[61] For the imperfect Christian, death is not a shortcut to perfection but a dead end; Christian perfection must be attained in this life or not at all! "If we are not renewed in the spirit of our mind by the love of God shed abroad in our hearts by the Holy Ghost, given unto us, we cannot enter into life eternal."[62]

Clearly, there seems to be a problem with understanding the relation of Christian perfection and final salvation along the lines that I have just sketched. At his best, Wesley links Christian perfection and glorification in a practical manner. By insisting that holiness is the norm for the Christian life and should not be treated as an exception, and by refusing to treat the promise of a ripening in paradise as an excuse for indolence on earth, Wesley is offering sound practical advice for helping his people go on to perfection. At his worst, Wesley allows the link between perfection on earth and glorification in heaven to assume too much speculative weight so that in effect he ends up saying: "without perfection below no salvation above." As Sangster has observed, if perfection in this life, even if only the perfection of love, is necessary to be fit for heaven then most Christians are destined for hell.[63]

In his later years, Wesley became increasingly aware of this difficulty and attempted to nuance his teaching on this issue while continuing to affirm his key pastoral and theological concerns.[64] In his sermon "The More Excellent Way" Wesley distinguishes between two orders or levels of Christians. There is a common level of Christian life: "The one lived an innocent life, conforming in all things not sinful to the customs and fashions of the world, doing many good works, abstaining from gross evils, and attending the ordinances of God."[65] But there is a more excellent way, a higher level of Christian existence, a superior order of Christians that avoided evil, did good, and attended to all the ordinances of grace, but "this one thing they did, they spared no pains to arrive at the summit of Christian holiness."[66] This more excellent way is set before all the justified; the Holy Spirit invites and incites all newborn babes in Christ "to choose the narrowest path in the narrow way, to aspire after the heights and depths of holiness, after the entire image of God,"[67] in short to "go on to perfection" (Heb 6:1). If Christians decline the offer they lapse into the lower order. Wesley concedes that this lower path leads not to hell but to God; these Christians at the end of their lives will find mercy for their failings by the blood of Christ. But "they will not have so high a place in heaven as they would have had if they had chosen the better part. And will this be a small loss?"[68] Wesley is not saying that on account of this loss there will be sorrow in heaven, for after all, stars differ from one another in glory (cf. 1 Cor 15:41). However, Wesley asks: "will it be a little thing to have lower place than you might have had in the kingdom of your Father?"[69] In short, the degree of perfection that we attain on earth is not without consequence to our degree of glorification in heaven.[70]

It appears that Wesley's understanding of this subject shifted over the years, but as with his cautious admission of the possibility of non-Christian salvation, the possibility of nonperfect glorification is marginal to his theology. He expects and hopes for perfection in this life because he believes that this is what God promises. Wesley focuses his theological and hagiographical attention on the perfect rather than on the almost perfect because he is convinced that at the conclusion of the life of grace, saints are the norm and the "average Christian" is the exception. I agree, as does Aquinas, but more on that later. We will revisit the question of purgatory again when we bring Aquinas and Wesley into conversation.

In addition to being a sign of fitness for heaven, Christian perfection is a sign of God's presence and power for the church. The promise of entire sanctification was not merely a comfort for the person who received this blessing but also a sign for believers that the goal was indeed attainable. Wesley expected that those whose hearts had been entirely cleansed from every wrongful thought and temper would want to testify to what God has done. The love burning in their breast would not be held back by common sense which might counsel silence, given the likelihood of adverse reactions from other people. As Wesley observes,

> [God] does not raise such a monument of his power and love, to hide it from all mankind. Rather, he intends it as a general blessing to those who are simple of heart. He designs thereby, not barely the happiness of that individual person, but the animating and encouraging others to follow after the same blessing. His will is, "that many shall see it" and rejoice, "and put their trust in the Lord."[71]

Personal perfection requires ecclesial recognition, because its purpose is not just the joy of the individual but the strengthening of the community. Since all Christians are called to perfection and a certain kind of perfection is attainable by every Christian in this life, there must be exemplars, living proofs, as it were, of the truthfulness of the doctrine. In this sense, the perfect are signs given by God for the perfection of others.

Admittedly, in the early Methodist societies, the presence of the perfect was both a source of encouragement and of contention. The unequal distribution of charisms in the community easily engendered jealousy in those who had not attained perfection and pride in those who had. Aware of these dangers, Wesley warns those on the way to perfection against projecting one model of Christian perfection unto the perfect. The perfect are not all cut from the same cloth, so to speak. The perfect are found in all walks of life. For instance, some might possess a more timid temperament than others. Some are simple people; some are professionals (perhaps even professional theologians). Some are single; some are married. In this last case, Wesley insists that we are not to judge the perfection of the parents by the perfection of the children. Wesley also cautions the perfect against pride, enthusiasm, and antinomianism. They must never lose the opportunity to do good works, lest they fall into sins of omission. Chief and foremost, they are to beware of schism.

In one of the saddest chapters of early Methodist history, the self-proclaimed perfect identified themselves as the only real Christians and wrote off the rest as almost Christians. These misunderstandings were to some extent inevitable. Wesley too struggled with defining and describing the nature of the true Christian. In his 1741 sermon on Christian perfection, while describing in what sense Christians are perfect, Wesley stated that only those who had grown to the stature of the fullness of Christ were "properly Christians."[72] The implication was all too clear: if you were not entirely sanctified you were not a real Christian; you were outside the house of Christian holiness. That this interpretation was not based on a forced reading of the text is evident from the fact that after 1750 Wesley changed the phrase "proper Christians" to "perfect Christians," thereby making it clear that Christian and perfect are not coextensive terms. However the ambivalence remained, for in "A Plain Account of Christian Perfection" he describes the "perfect Christian" by quoting "without alteration" from his 1742 tract, "The Character of a Methodist."

> A Methodist is one who . . . "loves the Lord his God with all his heart, with all his soul, with all his mind, and with all his strength." . . . He is therefore happy in God, yea, always happy, as having in him "a well of water springing up unto everlasting life," and "overflowing his soul with

> peace and joy." "Perfect love" having now "cast out fear," he "rejoices evermore."[73]

The correlation appeared to be incontrovertible, at least to Wesley's foes; the Methodist is one who is perfect and does not sin in thought, word, or deed.[74] Interestingly, before quoting this text, Wesley inserts the Pauline qualifying statement: "Not as though I had already attained" (Phil 3:2). This scriptural interpolation is very significant. Wesley never claimed to have attained perfection but was haunted to the end of his life by fears of missing the mark. I will say more about Wesley's "dark night" in the next-to-last chapter of this study, so let us return to the semiotic significance of perfection.

Third, Christian perfection is a sign for the world. The gift of holiness is not something given primarily for the benefit of the individual or the few but for the sake of the community so that no one will settle for a halfhearted pattern of Christian discipleship but will aspire to conformity with Christ. The perfect do not constitute a self-enclosed holy club; they are leaven; they are signs for the church and lights for the world. How does the sanctification of the person point to the perfection of the world? Is a social utopia a correlative of personal perfection? Wesley was certainly concerned with the conditions of society. At times, his critique of many kinds of public diversions, fashions, and manners can sound petty and puritanical to modern ears.[75] At any rate, Wesley was not afraid of speaking out against the great social evils of his day. His increasingly insistent call for the abolition of slavery and persistent denunciation of poverty and its causes suggest a desire to change hearts and transform society. But a few words of caution are in order lest Wesley be dressed too quickly in a beret and fatigues.

Wesley's primary concern in addressing the issues of the day is motivated by a desire to eliminate social obstacles to personal holiness. It is in this context that we are to interpret his regulations for Sabbath observance. Since resting on the seventh day is a way of imitating God,[76] breaking it, for example, to see a horse race stunts our growth in grace. When it comes to reforming the nation, Wesley's main social proposal is not some kind of governmental initiative or political action program, but it is the people called Methodist.[77] The Methodists are to model a rightly ordered social life for England. This is why Wesley insisted that if the Methodists became rich[78] or if they separated from the Church of England,[79] they would betray their very raison d'être—to reform the nation, *and particularly the church.*

Given these caveats, how are we to think of the relationship between the perfect and the world? What kind of sign are they to the world? Do the perfect represent those who have conquered the world by abandoning it? Or do they represent the highest form of political activism?

Rather than answering these questions directly by appealing to Wesley, I want to approach them obliquely by looking briefly at Pope Benedict XVI's first encyclical, *Deus Caritas est*. By making this switch from historical theology to ecumenical theology, I am suggesting that some of the most Methodist of questions call for the most Catholic of answers.

Benedict XVI invites Catholics and all Christians to reflect on the nature and practice of love. Like Wesley, Benedict asserts that Christianity is not an abstract ideal but the response to the divine love made manifest in creation and throughout salvation history. He even quotes that most Wesleyan of passages in support, "We love because he first loved us" (1 John 4:19). The "we" in this affirmation is ecclesial; it is the church that is constituted as a community of love, and by its works of charity the church makes the Trinitarian love manifest. In other words, the church is loved into being and it is sustained by love. Since love lies at the very core of the church's existence, the practice of charity is the responsibility of all Christians and of the church as a whole. Works of mercy, to use the Methodist phrase, cannot be outsourced to secular institutions.

The church's service of love does have an institutional aspect that mirrors that of its secular counterparts. For the sake of its mission, the church configures its charitable activities in an organized, orderly fashion. And yet, where the church's unique contribution lies is not chiefly at the programmatic level but at the personal. The church does not simply provide structures for charitable activities, but it provides persons who have both professional competence and a "formation of the heart" so that they will carry out their activities with a wisdom that transcends the bounds of human prudence and philanthropy. In short, what the church primarily offers the world is not an idea, a structure, or a program, but saints. The saints "stand out as lasting models of social charity for people of good will."[80]

The message of *Deus Caritas* is clear on this point and sheds light on what Wesley means by social holiness. Sanctity has social significance. For this reason, a church without saints forgets how to serve.[81] Faced with the enormity of the problems of this present age, a church without saints easily falls prey to presumption (the right ideology or technology can fix everything) or despair (all love's labors are lost). A church without saints easily forgets that "time devoted to God in prayer not only does not detract from effective and loving service to neighbor but is in fact the inexhaustible source of that service."[82] A church without saints easily overlooks the fact that "Those who draw near to God do not withdraw from men, but rather become truly close to them."[83] We will return to these considerations on the ecclesial and social significance of sanctity in the final chapter of this work.

The Recognition of Christian Perfection

As we have just seen, Christian perfection is a sign for the person, the church, and the world. Given the semiotic significance of perfection in Wesley's theology, it should come as no surprise to learn that Wesley struggled over the question of recognition of holiness. How do we recognize the perfect? At times, Wesley allows the discernment of holiness to be initiated by an act of self-examination followed by communal confirmation. The perfect testify and the community ratifies (or does not). As the holiness controversies of mid-nineteenth-century Methodism show, when the discernment of perfection is based on an act of self-recognition, what the community receives is not a witness of perfection but a witness of presumption, wishful thinking, and self-deception. Charles Wesley was more keenly aware of the incongruity of such a witness of sanctification than his brother John. According to Charles the truly perfect are like the man who finds the treasure hidden in the field.

> He did not proclaim to all that passed by,
> How happy I am, How sanctified am I,
> But finding a measure of heavenly power
> Conceal'd the rich treasure and labour'd for more.[84]

The pretenders to perfection act differently:

> The modern Pharisee is bold
> In boasting to surpass the old;
> Triumphant in himself, he stands,
> Conspicuous with extended hands,
> With hideous screams and outcries loud
> Proclaims his goodness to the crowd,
> Glories in his own perfect grace,
> And blasphemies presents for praise!
> "Again I thank thee, and again,
> That I am not as other men,
> But holy as Thyself and pure,
> And must, O God, like Thee endure;
> Thyself I now to witness call,
> That I am good and cannot fall,
> Thee to exalt, repeat the word,
> And thus I glory in the Lord!"[85]

John Wesley was not always as naïve as his younger brother sometimes thought. John acknowledged the importance of right recognition and gave his followers a list of criteria for discerning true claims from false claims. The criteria went as follows: First, the community must witness a change in the behavior of the perfect person. There must be a clear difference between the once and the now. Second, the perfect must be able to offer an account of the exact time and fashion in which the change occurred. Third, the community must continue to witness signs that the change is an abiding one. The words and deeds of the perfected must remain above reproach and truly holy.

Wesley fills out these guidelines by appealing to Clement of Alexandria's description of the true gnostic in book 7 of the *Stromata*. Clement of Alexandria distinguishes the true gnostic (the Christian) from the false by distinguishing the knowledge (*gnosis*) that comes from faith from the wisdom (*sophia*) acquired through learning.[86] Only an "acquaintance with divine things" through faith perfects humans as humans by rendering them conformable to God in Christ. Wesley finds himself in strong agreement with the understanding of perfection expressed in the *Stromata*, particularly with its emphasis on love of God, though he considers Clement's language too Platonic.

In defending himself from charges of sectarianism, Wesley describes the character of a Methodist by calling attention to certain distinguishing marks.[87] These represent Wesley's understanding of what a real Christian, one who had grown to the stature of Christ, looked like. Negatively, the perfect person cannot be recognized by one's assent to certain theological opinions or by one's performance of ecclesial practices. Wesley is adamant that a distinction can and must be made between essential and indifferent doctrines and practices. The authority of Scripture, the divinity of Christ, and the doctrine of Trinity are essential. One cannot be a Christian without assenting to these. "But as to all opinions which do not strike at the root of Christianity we 'think and let think.'"[88] This distinction is of consequence for our inquiry because it allows Wesley to recognize holiness outside the bounds of his ecclesial community. Since Wesley insists that the distinguishing mark of a perfect Christian is not found in a certain mode of worship or adherence to particular formulations of the articles of faith, Wesley can acknowledge the sanctity of "that good and wise (though much mistaken man) Gregory López,"[89] a Mexican mystic who credited his virtues to the merits and intercession of the Blessed Mary, queen of heaven. We will consider Wesley's remarkable recognition of López' sanctity in the final chapter of this study. Positively, the distinguishing mark of the perfect person is the love of God that has been shed into the heart by the Holy Spirit (cf. Rom 5:5). The outpouring of God's love into the believer's heart—and this person must first believe before he can receive the Spirit—fills the Christian with happiness in God and hope of eternal inheritance. The perfect Christian "exercises his love to God, by prayer without ceasing, rejoicing evermore, and in everything giving thanks" (cf. 1 Thess 5:16-18).[90] Another distinguishing mark of the perfect Christian is their obedience to God. Such obedience grows in proportion to love; only one who loves God with one's whole heart can love God with one's whole strength. The perfect acts with a single eye and a pure heart because "the love of God has purified his heart from all vengeful passions, from envy, malice, and wrath, and from every unkind temper or malign affliction."[91] The result of this spiritual purgation is that "There is no motion in the heart but is according to his will. Every thought that arises points to him, and is in obedience to the law of Christ."[92]

In addition to giving the Methodists a set of guidelines and marks that can be helpful for distinguishing perfection from presumption, Wesley set forth contemporary examples or exemplars of the doctrine. Maddox is right in saying that "not as though I had already attained" is a fitting motto for anyone who is striving for the Christian perfection that Wesley preached so much about.[93] However it would be disastrous for Christians to interpret this maxim as implying we strive for perfection "not as though *any* had already attained." In his sermon "On the death of John Fletcher," Wesley makes it clear that Fletcher was one who had attained.

> [F]or many years I despaired of finding any inhabitant of Great Britain that could stand in any degree of comparison with Gregory López or Monsieur de Renty. But let any impartial person judge if Mr. Fletcher was at all inferior to them! Did he not experience as deep communion with God, and as high a measure of inward holiness, as was experienced either by one or the other of those burning and shining lights? And it is certain his outward holiness shone before men with full as bright a lustre as theirs.[94]

According to Wesley, Fletcher's sanctity is in no way second to that of other more widely recognized saints, but indeed may actually be greater because he is someone who was personally known by Wesley and not someone whose life has been massaged by hagiographers. Fletcher is a contemporary, a fellow Methodist, and because he is closer, the light of his life outshines that of more distant luminaries. Fletcher's life confirms what Wesley preached, that one can be made perfect here below. His life is a kind of proof of the doctrine of perfection, but his life is not the only one to assume such an evidentiary character. In "A Plain Account" Wesley calls attention to the life of Jane Cooper as another living witness of Christian perfection. The splendor of her life, as shown in her due mixture of intellect and passion, beckons others to seek a more intimate communion with God. We will consider the ecumenical significance of Jane's life in the final chapter of this book. For Wesley, recognition of the perfection of others encourages us to attain perfection for ourselves. So that, for instance, Fletcher's holiness stimulates our own striving for perfection: "As it is possible we all may be such as he was, let us endeavor to follow him as he followed Christ."[95]

Wesley's boldness in pointing out saints below stands in marked contrast with his reticence about naming names of the saints above. However, given his coupling of perfection and glorification and his strong affirmation of the intercession of the saints on our behalf, his silence speaks more to his anti-Catholic tendencies than to a prudent eschatological reserve.[96]

Before concluding these reflections on the recognition of perfection we should assess what role if any miracles play in communal discernment. Wesley was accused of confusing the ordinary and the extraordinary gifts of the Spirit.[97] The distinction between the ordinary and extraordinary gifts is similar to that which Thomas draws between *gratia sanctificans* and *gratia gratis data*, except that Wesley thinks that some of those gifts Thomas ranks among the gratuitous graces, like the gift of persuasion, are part of the Spirit's ordinary operations.[98] In any case, the extraordinary gifts are good, but the best gifts fall under the ordinary operations of the Spirit, chief of these being love. As Wesley says,

> [Love] will lead you to happiness both in this world and in the world to come; whereas you might have all those [extraordinary] gifts, yea, in the highest degree, and yet be miserable both in time and eternity.[99]

On more than one occasion, Wesley's critics asked him to produce miracles as proof of the legitimacy of the Methodist movement. This demand for signs led Wesley to offer his own reflections on the role of miracles throughout church history. First of all, Wesley believed that the gift of miracles was reserved only for a minority of Christians.

> Were all even then Prophets? Were all workers of miracles? Had all the gifts of healing? Did all speak with tongues? No, in no wise. Perhaps not one in a thousand. Probably none but the Teachers in the Church, and only some of them.[100]

Wesley correlates the gift of miracles with the office of teacher and with the abundance of love (whether on the part of the teacher, the community, or both). The correlation is undoubtedly complex, as the twelve apostles received the gift of miracles before they received the gift of sanctification; they healed the sick from the moment that Jesus sent them to the lost sheep of Israel, but they were not born from above until the day of Pentecost. Nevertheless, the correlation between charism, charity, and institution is undeniably present from the beginning of the church. However, with the passage of time, even the apostolic teachers and fathers seem to have become inured to these extraordinary workings of the Spirit, giving rise to the question of why.

Why do we not witness these kinds of wondrous signs anymore? Why were these extraordinary gifts limited to so few for such a short time? Some argued that these extraordinary gifts were originally given as a sign to unbelievers, but with the advent of Christendom, miracles, prophecies, and tongues were no longer needed because the whole world was basically Christian. Wesley rejects this line of reasoning.

> This is a miserable mistake: not a twentieth part of it was then nominally Christian. The real reason was: "the love of many"—almost of all Christians, so called—was "waxed cold."[101]

For Wesley, the turning point in church history was the rise of Constantine. The extraordinary gifts of the Spirit were quenched by the flood of wealth and honors that the emperor wrongheadedly heaped on the church. One of the consistent themes of Wesley's theology is the inverse proportionality between faith and wealth; the more one waxes, the more the other wanes.[102] Nevertheless, Wesley does not discount the possibility of miracles in the modern age. As he states in reply to one of his foes,

> I do not recollect any scripture wherein we are taught, that miracles were to be confined within the limits either of the apostolic or the Cyprianic age; or of any period of time, longer or shorter, even till the restitution of all things.[103]

God still works miracles, even in eighteenth-century England. Indeed, Wesley claimed to have witnessed cures that came about in supernatural ways.[104] Yet, whereas in the first centuries miracles were signs that made manifest the holiness of the apostolic community, in the eighteenth century these signs made manifest the sovereignty of God. To put it another way, in the early church miracles confounded the Jews and Gentiles who denied that Jesus was Messiah and *Kurios*; in the English Church, miracles confounded the deists who denied that God still acted in the world.

Finally, for Wesley, miracles are signs but not knockdown proofs. After all, not all miracles come from God; there are also the lying wonders (τέρατα ψεύδος) of the devil.[105] In addition to demonic signs, there are also the tricks of charlatans and the superstitions of the credulous. All of these false signs call into question the self-attesting character of true signs and highlight the need for spiritual discernment. Furthermore, even authentic miracles do not offer irrefutable evidence for anything. Pharaoh's heart was not softened by Moses' wondrous works; the Pharisees were not persuaded by Jesus' healing of the blind man. Miracles cannot convert the person; only the convicting grace of God can accomplish this mighty work. As Wesley argues, for the unbeliever

> Nothing will ever be an effectual proof to these of the holy and acceptable will of God, unless first their proud hearts be humbled, their stubborn wills bowed down, and their desires brought, at least in some degree, into obedience to the law of Christ.[106]

In sum, miraculous signs are not necessarily signs of holiness. This is the reason why Wesley's editing hand discarded the miraculous from the hagiographies that he presented for Methodists' emulation. Miracles in the life of the saints are unnecessary and potentially confusing evidence. The abundance of these signs in someone's life might be a cause for admiration but not necessarily for imitation. After all, people are called holy not because they work wonders but by being virtuous.[107] The "great and extraordinary work of God" is not the parting of the sea but the conversion of the sinner. This change does not need to be confirmed by yet another miracle. "The proper way to prove these facts is by the testimony of competent witnesses. And these witnesses are ready, whenever required to give full evidence of them."[108] Holiness is not made manifest by miracles but by testimony. Hence, without the company of others holiness remains invisible.

The Wayfarers to Perfection

We began our inquiry into Wesley's doctrine of perfection by describing the essentials of Methodist doctrine by means of the metaphor of a house. The porch of this house is repentance; the door to this house is faith, and the interior of the house is holiness itself. The metaphor expresses both the sense of movement (*via salutis*) and of discrete status (*statūs salutis*) in salvation. Wesley's preaching and teaching of perfection had the purpose of describing the floor plan of this house to get people onto the porch, through the door and into the house. The house of holiness itself stands on two pillars: freedom from sin and perfect love. The journey into this house is by grace mediated through means of grace. It is by grace that persons are rendered fit in this life for glorification in the life to come, and it is also by grace that persons can be signs for the renewal of the church and the transformation of the world. These are the essential characteristics of Wesley's teaching. Entering into the house of holiness is the goal of all Christians: male and female, married and single, lay and clergy. However, the attainment of this goal cannot simply be advanced by teaching and preaching. Wesley knew better than that.

Wesley instituted a complex system of bands, classes, and societies structured to meet the needs of the pilgrim along all the stages of the way of salvation.[109] For those who were altogether outside the way, Wesley instituted the practice of field preaching. The preacher who awakened unbelievers from the slumber of sin was charged to "follow the blow"[110] by gathering these people in small groups known as "trial bands." For those who experienced the forgiveness of sin, Wesley recommended participation in "band meetings." Finally, for those who were going on to perfection or had attained the highest reaches of the house, Wesley formed "select bands" or "select societies." In addition to these groups, Wesley organized "class meetings" and "united societies" whose membership was more soteriologically diverse.

Each of these groups had its own characteristic size and structure suited to its soteriological purpose.[111] For instance, since the class meetings focused on discovering the way of salvation, these groups tended to be larger (twelve to thirty-six members) and had leaders chosen for their spiritual maturity. Other groups like the bands which focused on overcoming sin and the select bands which focused on love of God tended to be smaller (though not always) and allowed for shared leadership. In any case, all groups had a set of rules that guided them; breaking the rules could lead to the placing of the offender in a "penitent band" for a probationary period, or in extreme cases, to expulsion.

The location of each of these groups with respect to the Methodist house of holiness was soteriologically clear. Field preaching occurred in the yard; the trial bands and the penitent bands (backsliders) gathered on the porch; the bands met on the threshold and the select bands inside the house itself. The class meetings and united societies gathered people from all over the house.

Here are a few concluding remarks on the Methodist house of perfection: First, the Methodist house makes room for people in all states of salvation: seekers and penitents, babes and adults, saints and backsliders. The house is modest in size but it is hospitable. The reason for the hospitality of this house (the only condition for entering the porch is the desire to flee the wrath to come) is that the doctrine of Christian perfection is *de fide* for all people. Christian perfection is catholic doctrine in the

Vincentian sense, *quod ubique, quod semper, et quod ab omnibus creditum est*. The complex array of Methodists bands, meetings and societies is structured to form lay practitioners of this doctrine. Second, the Methodist house is held together by a common purpose and a common discipline. Without the common goal of perfection the whole soteriological orientation of the Methodist group is lost. Without the common Methodist discipline, there is no possibility of holding each other accountable and formation becomes impossible. Third, the Methodist house sits in the middle of a yard not far from the church. Without the yard the house has no field of membership from which to draw. Without the church the house has no place to turn people to for the means of grace which are vital for growth in holiness. By this last comment I do not mean to say that the church is only of instrumental significance for the Methodist house. On the contrary, it is when the church becomes instrumental that the Methodist house loses its own peculiar significance and becomes a mere denomination. I will return to this issue later.

"Going on to Perfection"—A Historical Postscript

I close this exposition of Wesley's doctrine of Christian perfection with a brief historical postscript. In *Christian Perfection and American Methodism*, John Peters documents the theological shifts in this doctrine from the time of Wesley to the twentieth century.[112] Peters rightly assures us that the doctrine of Christian perfection was not the invention of Wesley, nor did he claim it was. Long before Wesley, Law, or Taylor called on Christians to lead a devout and holy life, the Greek Fathers had taught the same doctrine. Nevertheless, the antiquity of this doctrine does not suggest that Wesley made no significant contribution to its development; on the contrary, more clearly than anyone else before him Wesley insisted that perfection was a viable and necessary way of life for every Christian. This perfection was only possible through an obedient faith that cooperated with God's grace bestowed chiefly through the sacraments in order to perform works of love; a tried faith which is tested and examined in class meetings and societies. These were the key elements of Wesley's doctrine of perfection, but a strange thing happened when the teaching came overseas to the American colonies.

First of all, the sacramental mediation of grace was largely lost. There simply were never enough ordained ministers of the sacraments to serve the fast-growing Methodist churches. So in the American colonies, despite Wesley's insistence on the duty of constant communion, the Eucharist was never more than an occasional service and the camp meeting became the chief means of grace. One might say that the Methodist house was replaced by the revivalist tent.

Second, the zeal of Methodist preachers to bring the gospel to the frontier led in many cases to the virtual neglect of the doctrine. Among the rough-and-tumble settlers where these Methodist preachers worked the urgent message was not "be perfect," but "repent."

Third, where the doctrine was heeded it became the focus of almost obsessive attention though not in a holistic way. On the one hand, some revivalists emphasized the instantaneous achievement of perfection to the virtual exclusion of any progressive growth in holiness. On the other hand, others concerned about the enthusiastic excesses of those who emphasized instantaneous perfection rejected such a view in favor of a more gradual, and we might say bowdlerized version of perfection. As Peters paints the picture, by the end of the nineteenth century,

> The doctrine of Christian perfection was presented in differing fashion by two Methodistic groups, both claiming Wesleyan authority for their positions. In the sects it was an abbreviated Wesleyanism—in many respects characteristic of his unmodified 1760 views, stressing his instantaneous teaching and neglecting in large part his emphasis on the gradual. In the church it was an uncertain Wesleyanism—in many respects characteristic of his 1745 views, mildly hopeful of the efficacy of a gradual approach but ignoring for the most part his emphasis on the instantaneous.[113]

Peters acknowledges with some chagrin that it is in the "abbreviated Wesleyanism" of the holiness and Pentecostal churches rather than in the "uncertain Wesleyanism" of the mainline Methodist churches that Christian perfection continues to be taught and sought. But rather than despair and write of perfection as a historical oddity, Peters holds out hope that were this doctrine to be rediscovered among the mainline Protestant churches, they would not only be renewed in themselves but find themselves drawn into a closer union with all churches. "It may be discovered," Peters hopes, "that at this exalted level Protestant and Catholic enjoy a highest common denominator. If so, let it be explored and shared gladly."[114] It is in the hope of discovering this highest common denominator that we now turn to Thomas Aquinas' doctrine of perfection.

Chapter Three

Aquinas on Christian Perfection

> [D]uplex est perfectio; scilicet prima, et secunda: prima perfectio est forma uniuscuiusque, per quam habet esse; unde ab ea nulla res destituitur dum manet; secunda perfectio est operatio, quae est finis rei, vel id per quod ad finem devenitur et hac perfectione interdum res destituitur.[1]

With this rich quote, we leave behind the simplicity of the Methodist house of doctrine and enter into the vast cathedral of Thomas' theology. This transition requires that we not only switch metaphors but that we allow the semantic range of the concept of perfection to stretch beyond Wesley's normal bounds. Wesley's chief interest lay in Christian perfection, but for Thomas *duplex est perfectio*: the perfection of the form and the perfection of operation. Thomas teaches the doctrine of Christian perfection within the larger framework of the doctrine of God and creation.

Over the next two chapters we will consider the twofold character of perfection and how it is attained. For this purpose, I will mostly, though not exclusively, as the opening quote shows, focus our attention on the *Summa Theologiae*. It is in this work that we find the angelic doctor's most mature and extensive treatment of perfection. In this chapter, we will begin our exploration of the Thomist cathedral by considering his teaching on the perfection of God, a perfection that can be considered from two aspects, that of being and of person. From there we will move to a consideration of the twofold perfection of the universe, the perfection of its form, and the perfection of its operation. From this cosmic backdrop, we will zoom in to focus our attention on that small portion of the universe that is the immediate concern of this study—the human. In particular, we will consider what it means to be made in the image of God and how this image is both perfect by nature and perfected by the twin operations of knowing and loving. How this perfection is concretely accomplished in Christ will be the subject of the next chapter.

The structure of these two chapters conforms in outline to the structure of the *Summa Theologiae* itself. The perfection of God, the universe, and the first perfection of the image correspond to the *Prima Pars*, the second perfection to the *Secunda Pars*, and the way of perfection, Jesus Christ, to the *Tertia Pars*. This correspondence is no accident. In his magisterial treatise on St. Thomas Aquinas,[2] Jean Pierre Torrell argues convincingly that Aquinas must be understood not just as an academic theologian but also as a spiritual master. A good case can be made for reading the *Summa Theologiae* as something analogous to Bonaventure's *Itinerarium mentis ad Deum* or San Juan de la Cruz' *Subida al Monte Carmelo*.[3] If this is the case, then readers of Thomas must attend not just to the content of his teaching but also to its salutary order.

The Perfection of God

In the *Summa Theologiae*, the question of God's perfection follows Thomas' consideration of God's existence and divine simplicity. As one would expect, given the common doctor's declared intent to unfold his teaching according to the order of the subject matter, the placement of the question of perfection is significant. It follows Aquinas' reflections on the existence of God and the intrinsic necessity of the apophatic moment in theology. Surprisingly perhaps, but wholly in agreement with the church's teaching, Aquinas states that, in this life, we cannot know what God is (*quid sit*) but only what he is not (*quid non sit*), and we attain this knowledge by the way of remotion. We know what God is not by removing or stripping away from our consideration of God those things that are contrary to the existence of God. The Thomist *via negativa* begins by removing composition and motion from the list of attributes that can be predicated of God: God is not a composite; God is not moved, God is not limited, etc. However, lest we read Thomas as a skeptic who would rob theological discourse of any real relation with its subject, namely God, we must note again the order of the opening questions of the *Summa*. The question of the simplicity of God follows the question of the existence of God. Why? Because the *ordo cognoscendi* is based on the *ordo essendi*. Rudi te Velde cogently expresses the relationship between negation and affirmation in Thomas' theology:

> The role of negation does not so much indicate the agnostic awareness on the part of Thomas that all our knowledge of God remains deficient and imperfect. Neither should it be interpreted as a manoeuvre for positing God beyond the reach of our knowledge. On the contrary, the negation is part of how the intelligibility of God is to be expressed from the perspective of his effects. Given the existence of the cause, one must say that the cause *is not* one of its effects. Here lies the root of the *via negativa*. One may say that the negation is part of the intelligible constitution of the cause as knowable from its presence in the effects.[4]

Negation plays a key role in Thomas' theology but it does not play solo. The way of negation is only one movement along the *triplex via* by which humans come to know God. Thus, the negative approach to theology is not by itself sufficient. The removal of unfitting things from our consideration of God permits us to "ascend" from effect to cause (*ordo cognoscendi*), but this movement has its origins on the prior "descent" from cause to effect (*ordo essendi*). Hence, the divine attributes are not merely negative statements void of positive content. As te Velde avers, "God is not a negative transcendence but an excessive transcendence, which means that He is distinguished from all things by being all things in an excessive (unified, concentrated) way."[5] The *via remotionis* of divine simplicity presupposes the *via causalitatis* of the Five Ways and is corrected and completed by the *via eminentiae* of divine perfection.[6]

Aquinas' treatment of God's perfection begins with a question: *utrum Deus sit perfectus*.[7] At first glance, the question might seem superfluous, and yet according to Thomas the issue is not quite so simple. After all, the word "perfect" is derived from the world of matter where it refers to something that is fully made (*per-factum*). Given the etymological origins of the word *perfectum*, its semantic field would seem to be restricted to created, not uncreated reality. Furthermore, what comes first is inchoate and imperfect: first the seed, then the flower. So, if God is first, if he was before anything else, is he not most imperfect of all? Would it not be better to say that God is not perfect but is in a process of perfection?[8]

In other words, the question of God's perfection is not merely rhetorical; there are objections that can be raised against the predication of this attribute to God. Yet, the weight of these objections arises from severe misunderstandings regarding the nature of reality. By introducing a couple of key distinctions Thomas dispatches with the objections and clears the way for the right attribution of perfection to God and to the creature.

First, we need to consider the distinction between material and first principles. The seed is the material principle of the flower; it is in potency to the flower. But the seed is not the first principle of the flower because the seed itself came from another flower. Matter, as a material principle, is in potency, but whatever is in potency can only be reduced to act by something actual. Hence, a material principle is imperfect and not primal; the first principle, however, is most perfect because it is the most actual. Indeed, this correlation of perfection and action is what the word perfection means in Thomas' lexicon. Ultimately, it does not matter whether perfection was attained through some kind of manufacture (*per-factum*) or whether the perfection is original. Something is perfect if it lacks nothing essential to its wholeness and integrity; it is perfect if it is in act: *aliquid esse perfectum, secundum quod est in actu.*[9]

Second, we must consider the distinction between essence and existence. All creatures, from the highest seraph to the smallest pebble, are composites of some kind or another. The invisible creation (the angels) is a composite of essence and existence; the visible creation is a composite of essence and existence, but also of form and matter. God alone is free from all composition. In God, there is no combination of potency and actuality, of essence and existence, of body and soul; God is altogether simple, and this quality absolutely distinguishes God from creation. God alone is pure actuality (*actus purus*), and since existence is the most perfect of acts (*esse est perfectissimum omnium*),[10] God, who is existence itself (*ipsum esse susbsistens*), is most perfect of all.

These two distinctions rule out univocal predication of perfection; there is a real distinction between God's existence and our own. On the one hand, God's *esse* allows no addition because it is not in potency to anything. On the other hand, creaturely existence (*esse commune*) allows specification, not by virtue of an *essentia* being added to it, but by giving existence to an essence and thus "becoming" that particular entity. In creatures, existence is something received, a formal principle, or, one might even say, a gift. In God, his essence is his existence and for this reason God is the most perfect of all and the most gratuitous of givers.

The contrast between God's perfection and creaturely perfection should not blind us to their analogical relation. It is important to observe that from the very beginning of his reflections in the *Summa Theologiae*, Thomas consistently treats the perfection of God in relation to the perfection of things. This is of course a necessity for creatures, whose knowledge of divine things proceeds from creation, but there is more to it than that. The interpenetration of the discussion of divine perfection with reflections on creaturely perfection is no mere epistemological necessity but a theological exigency.

From the beginning, Thomas does not treat God's perfection as something shut up in eternity but as something in which creation participates.

Creatures are perfect to the degree that they are like God. The likeness between a cause and an effect results from a communication of the form from the agent to the patient, but this sharing occurs in many ways (*secundum multos modos communicandi*).[11] Not all things are said to be alike in the same way.

First, some things share in the same form according to the same proportion (*secundum eandem rationem*) and the same mode (*secundum eandem modum*). These things are called identical; their similitude is most perfect (*perfectissima*). Second, some things share in the same form according to the same proportion (*secundum eandem rationem*) but not according to the same mode (*non secundum eandem modum*). These things are only imperfectly alike. Third, some things are said to be similar because they communicate in the same form, even though not according to the same proportion (*non secundum eandem rationem*). These agents are said to be non-univocal, but even here there is a distinction that needs to be made. Some agents communicate their form according to the likeness of the species (*secundum similitudinem speciei*), as when a human being begets another human being. Other agents communicate their form according to the likeness of the genus (*secundum similitudinem generis*), as when something is heated by the rays of the sun. However, if an agent and its effect are not contained in the same species or even in the same genus, indeed if there is an agent who is not contained in any species or genus, then the likeness of the agent will be conveyed to the effect according to a kind of analogy (*secundum aliqualem analogiam*). It is in this way and in this way alone that a creature can be said to be like God.

Talk of the similitude of the human to God is an exhilarating but dangerous idea, so Thomas offers us a word of caution: the perfection of the creature is not achieved through pantheistic assimilation into God's essence. On the one hand, the perfection of the creature, its similitude to the Creator, cannot be understood univocally; the creature is not and can never be God *simpliciter*. On the other hand, when we say that the creature can be perfect we are not simply speaking nonsense. The term perfection can be applied to both God and creatures analogically. Whatever is found to be good or true or otherwise perfect in the creature is found in God in an eminent way. In the words of te Velde,

> The cause is the effect in a more eminent way, insofar as it possesses originally and by way of excess all the perfections of the effects (*via eminentiae*).[12]

Aquinas believes that it is indeed possible to speak of the creature as perfect, to be like God not by assimilation into the divine essence but by the similitude of the creature to its Creator, the effect to its First Cause. Marty explains Thomas' position:

> L'essence de la perfection des créatures est donc dans une ressemblance de Dieu, Parfait, Cause Première, ressemblance qui s'exprime dans les degrés distinct qui composent l'univers.[13]

To summarize, the analogy of God's perfection and creaturely perfection is based on the analogy of *esse*. Whatever is perfect in creation is perfect insofar as it has being (*aliqua perfecta sunt, quod aliquo modo esse habent*), but God as *ipsum esse subsistens* is the cause of all that is. For this reason, no created perfection can be found wanting in him. All created perfections preexist (*praeexistere*) in God in a more eminent mode (*secundum eminentiorem modum*) than in creation because God is the first efficient cause of things (*prima causa effectiva rerum*). In fact, if some created perfection were found wanting in God, then God could not be the cause of its existence, and if that were the case then the perfection of that thing would come from some other first cause (another God or itself). The existence of a self-standing creaturely perfection is absurd; such perfection would entail a sharing in God's incommunicable essence. On the contrary, all created things are like God in that they exist and have God as the primal and universal principle of their being (*primum et universalis principium totius esse*). However, this similarity between divine and creaturely perfection is founded upon a greater dissimilarity: God's existence is by essence (*per essentiam*), whereas creaturely existence is by participation (*per participationem*).

These reflections on the analogical predication of perfection of God and creatures technically conclude Thomas' consideration *de Dei perfectione* but not his inquiry into divine perfection. Instead the angelic doctor invites us to now consider the relation between goodness (*bonitas*) and being (*ens*).[14]

On the one hand, being and goodness refer to the same reality (*secundum rem*) and are interchangeable. Something is good only to the extent that it is perfect, and something is perfect only to the extent that it is actually in existence. For Thomas, existence is that which makes all things actual (*esse enim est actualitas omnis rei*); something is said to have being absolutely (*ens simpliciter*) when it has been reduced from potentiality to substantial existence (*esse substantiale*). This first act (*primus actus*) is perfect because something is perfect to the extent that it exists.

On the other hand, although goodness and being refer to the same reality, they differ notionally (*secumdum rationem*). Substantial existence (*esse substantiale*) can be said to have being absolutely (*ens simpliciter*) and to be perfect and good but only relatively. Something is said to be absolutely good (*bonum simpliciter*) not by its first act (*primus actus*) but by its final act (*actus ultimus*) whereby something attains its final perfection (*perfectio ultima*). So even though being and goodness are convertible, goodness adds something to being—desirability.[15] Because being is good it is desirable; perfection too is desirable: *Perfectum vero habet rationem appetibilis.*[16] To understand why this is so, we need to remember that God is the cause of all that is, but every effect resembles its cause, or in Thomas' formulation, *omne agens agit sibi simile.*[17] Hence, any aspect of desirability in the effect must be present in the cause by participation. To put it another way, whatever good is found in creation is found in God supremely. For this reason God is fittingly called the *summum bonum*;[18] he alone is good *per essentiam.*[19]

Thomas' reflections on the convertibility of being and goodness allow him to draw two significant inferences of immediate importance for our study. First, all things are good: *omne ens, inquantum est ens, est bonum.*[20] This assertion seems incredible—the kind of thing one might expect a monk insulated from the real world by the securities of a university-endowed chair to say. Most people, even many Christians, consider the goodness of creation as something past or ephemeral. However, for Thomas, the goodness of creation is a present reality, a reality that he discerns not by looking at the world through rose-colored glasses but by accepting the world as it is: God's creation. The convertibility of being and goodness assures us that it is good to be, and that to be is to be perfect.

If one finds this inference hard to believe, one will not like the second any better, for Thomas is convinced that all things desire God: *omnia, appetendo proprias perfectiones, appetunt ipsum Deum.*[21] In desiring their own perfection all things tend toward God because whatever perfections they seek are so many likenesses of God's nature (*similitudines divini esse*). Each thing desires God in a manner suitable to its nature, humans and angels in one way, plants and animals in another, inanimate objects in still another way. Nonetheless, all these ways end in God, who as the *summum bonum* of the universe is the last end of all things (*ultimus finis omnium rerum*).[22]

With these thoughts on the goodness and perfectibility of creation in God, it might seem that we have come to the end of Thomas' teaching on divine perfection, but it is necessary to consider God's perfection not only from the perspective of the divine essence, but also from another aspect—the divine persons.

In the *Prima Pars*, after establishing the existence of God, Aquinas begins his reflection on the nature of God by considering those things that belong to the divine substance (ST 1.3–1.13) and to God's operation (ST 1.14–26). Only after he reflects on God's nature from the vantage point of the unity of the divine essence does Thomas explicitly turn his attention to the divine persons in God. Needless to say, the ordering of the doctrine of God in the *Prima Pars* has been the subject of vigorous debate. The objection most frequently raised charges that Aquinas illegitimately privileges the unity of the divine essence over (or perhaps even over against) the plurality of divine persons. The debate over Thomas' alleged essentialism is not without consequence for Christian reflection on the relationship between faith and reason, but these are not the questions of direct relevance for our inquiry. Nevertheless, the question of how we understand the relation between what belongs to the divine essence and what belongs to the divine persons is of relevance to this study.

To plunge to the heart of the issue, in the *Prima Pars* Aquinas offers two statements of what is *perfectissimum.* On the one hand, *Ipsum esse est perfectissimum omnium.*[23] On the other hand, *Persona significat id quod est perfectissimum in tota natura.*[24] The question, to put it bluntly, is: Which is it? And how are these two statements reconciled? Is the former statement a philosophical one, whereas the latter is strictly theological? Are the two statements an example of Thomas' theological *redoublement?*[25] Is the latter implied in the former?[26] My purpose in asking these questions is not to answer them definitively but to bring out the significance of Aquinas' understanding of personhood for understanding his teaching on perfection.

To begin with, it is important to observe that Aquinas' use of the concept *persona* is found almost exclusively within his discussion of the doctrine of the Trinity and Christology. In the former case, the term *persona* is used to explain the plurality of *supposita* in God. In the latter case, it accounts for the union of the two natures of Christ. In any case, Aquinas' use of the term occurs within a strictly theological context. Frankly, this is surprising, as one might expect personhood to be a key anthropological category, and yet this is not the case, at least terminologically, in Aquinas. St. Thomas' use of *persona* is careful and reserved. Indeed, even before he employs this term in reference to God, the word is subjected to a theological *askesis* akin to the one the term perfection had to undergo.

First, *persona* is purified in its etymological origins. Aquinas acknowledges that this term was first given to the masks worn by Greek tragedians as they represented characters on the stage; such a background might suggest that any predication of personhood in God is metaphorical at best. Thomas neatly sidesteps this obstacle by pointing out that the persons represented on stage by the actors wearing these masks were people of rank and honor, so that the name of person was later given off the stage to people who held a high office or post. The word *persona*, as Aquinas explains, came to be applied to *hypostasis proprietate distincta ad dignitatem pertinente*.[27] It is this objective meaning of person, not its etymological derivation that is to be attributed to God because the dignity of the divine nature far exceeds that of all created things.

Second, *persona* needs to be purified in its theological register. Aquinas adopts the definition of person given by Boethius: *persona est rationalis naturae individual substantiae*.[28] Boethius elaborates this definition in his work *De duabis naturae* in order to account for the personal union of the two natures of Christ. In other words, the term *persona* was used in the service of Christology, but the definition itself came from creatures. Of course, it could not be otherwise, but for this reason we need to be able to distinguish between the meaning of persons in general and the meaning of persons in God.

In general, a person is an individual substance (*substantia individua*). This means that a person exists by itself; a *persona* is *per se una*. A person is not an accident of something else, an epiphenomenon of matter, but rather is the subject of accidents. To put it another way, the genus of substance pertains to what is universal; it stands under (*sub-stare*) all accidents; it constitutes the quiddity of a thing. To the genus of substance, the term individual brings singularity. The substance might be universal but the individual is not. As Aquinas explains, "the term *individual* is placed in the definition of person to signify the mode of subsistence (*modus subsistendi*) which belongs to particular substances."[29]

Peculiar to the personal mode of subsistence is incommunicability.[30] Individuality limits the universal substance to a particular instantiation. In angels, what distinguishes one angel from another is the substantial form; this is the reason why each angel must represent on its own a distinct species, or else they would be indistinguishable from one another and hence one. In material creatures, it is designate matter that individuates the substance. It is the concrete stuff that one chair is made out of (its particular atoms) that allows us to distinguish it from another. Even for humans the principle of individuation is matter. The soul is a part of the person but not the whole. According to the common doctor, "an individual substance is something complete existing by itself."[31] However, even though the soul can continue to exist apart from matter (for instance, in between death and the general resurrection), the soul remains incomplete without the body; it is not an individual substance by itself (*per se una*) but the substantial form of the composite human being. In other words, a soul is not a person, any more than a hand is a body.

Moreover, a person is of a rational nature (*rationalis natura*). The key term here is rational, since nature is already included in substance. A chair is an individual substance, but a chair is not a person; neither is a dog. Only an individual subsistence of a *rational* nature can be called a person. A rational nature is one that is not only acted upon but one that has the capacity to act and to be self-aware of its act. Although the term rational is usually associated with discursive reasoning, Aquinas does not limit the definition to its anthropological register, but opens the term to include all intellectual natures: human, angelic, and divine.

By defining a person as a subsisting individual of a rational nature, Aquinas has not exhausted the meaning of personhood. Indeed, if the term person is to be applied to God at all, it is important that the depths of its meaning remain unsounded and even unfathomable. The person eludes comprehensive definition because it is singular and the singular is not definable. Even though Aquinas asserts that the general idea of singularity can be defined,[32] such a definition does not explain this person or that one, and it most certainly does not explain God. By following the *triplex via* and removing (*via remotinis*) from "person" those qualities that are incompatible with its original meaning (*via causalitatis*), Thomas has made space for its analogical use beyond created reality (*via eminentiae*). In sum, *persona* is a perfection of being and as such is applicable to God in a higher way than to any creature.

Further elucidation of Aquinas' understanding of "person" exceeds the scope of this project. Nevertheless, from what we have already considered of the angelic doctor's use of the term *persona*, an important consequence for our study follows: God's perfection is personal.[33] The perfection of God is not a static nature but a dynamic act, the dynamism of *ipsum esse*, but this *ipsum esse* subsists in the three eternal relations of Father, Son, and Spirit.[34] So the two statements are true, yet irreducible to each other: *esse* is the "*perfectio omnium perfectionum*"[35] and *persona* is "*omnia naturarum dignissima.*"[36] It belongs to the perfection of the divine persons to be constituted by the divine essence according to its personal mode of existence (*secundum proprium modum existendi*), and it belongs to the perfection of the essence that there be a plurality of modes of existence (*plures modi existendi*), a Trinity. Aquinas will go so far as saying that "there would not be absolute perfection (*perfectio omnimoda*) in God unless there were in him the procession of Word and Love."[37] Indeed, it is because God is (tri)personal that he is perfect in every way, and that he becomes the perfector of persons; for it is by the indwelling of the divine persons that God comes to abide in the rational creature as in his temple (*habitare in ea sicut in templo suo*) for us and for our sanctification.[38] The perfection of the human in God does not entail the dissolution of individuality but its consummation in the communion of divine persons.

The Perfection of the Universe

We began our study of Thomas' doctrine of perfection by exploring his account of the perfection of God. This starting point was necessary for two reasons. On the one hand, God's perfection is the source of all perfection; all created perfections are nothing more or less than a participation in God's own perfection. On the other hand, the perfection of God is the goal that all things are called to attain insofar as is possible. Hence, God's perfection anchors the great *exitus-reditus* circle that characterizes all created reality; all things come from and return to God, who is all, in all. Although it would be possible from this theological vantage point to dive straight into Thomas' theological anthropology and soteriology and attain the heart of our inquiry, the perfection of the human, such a jump is not desirable for we would miss the cosmological basis and implications of his doctrine of perfection. Indeed, for the angelic doctor, the perfection of the universe and the perfection of the human are so profoundly related that before turning our attention to the latter we must account for the former.[39]

Let us begin by considering Thomas' exposition of the creation account in Genesis. In the treatise on creation, the question is asked whether God completed his work on the seventh day.[40] Scripture's witness on this matter is clear: "On the seventh day God ended his work which he had made; and he rested on the seventh day from all his work which he had made" (Gen 2:2). However, as Aquinas points out, there are some apparent problems with this statement. After all, if God truly ended his work on the seventh day, history should then have come to an end because whatever happens in the world is the result of God's work. In fact, many things have happened since that seventh day: multitudes of individual beings have been born; new souls have been created; whole new species have come into existence. Indeed, how can anyone who believes in the incarnation of the Word and hopes for the advent of the new creation affirm that the old was somehow complete? Besides, even if one wanted to speak of a completion of God's work, it would seem better to say that he ended his work on the sixth day since he made nothing new on the seventh day but only rested.

Against these objections, Aquinas introduces a distinction that we have already encountered but now needs clarification. For the angelic doctor, perfection is not a static achievement. The imperfect is not all on one side of the cosmic scale and the perfect all on the other. Perfection is gradated, but this gradation does not mean that we cannot draw important distinctions, and one that Aquinas returns to time and again is the distinction between first perfection (*perfectio prima*) and second perfection (*perfectio secunda*).[41]

The first perfection is the perfection of form. It is the perfection that a thing has from being whole and lacking nothing of its essential parts. When on the fifth day of creation, God made the fish of the sea and the birds of the air, God gave fins to one and wings to the other according to their own mode of perfection (*secundum modum suae perfectionis*).[42] An albatross with fins for wings would not be perfect, but a whale with two pectoral fins and a fluke is. When God sees the work of this fourth day and declares it good, he is in effect declaring it perfect according to its first perfection, since whatever is good is perfect.[43] Since God rests from creating on the seventh day, one should say that the universe is already perfect on the sixth day as to the completeness of its parts (*secundum integritatem partium universi*). After the sixth day, God does not make any thing totally new. Any new species or individual that comes to exist throughout history is present in the work of the six days either materially (*materialiter*) or causally (*causaliter*). Hence, the seventh day of creation marks the completion of the work of creation, its perfection, and, here is the key, its *perfectio prima*.

The second perfection is the perfection of operation. If in the first perfection God gives creatures their essence and existence, in the second God directs them to their proper end. That a whale has fins instead of wings pertains to its first perfection. That this same whale actually uses its fins to swim rather than to crawl pertains to its second perfection. The second perfection can also be referred to as the final perfection (*perfectio ultima*), because by it the creature's end is attained; the whale swims, the bird flies. On the seventh day when God rests from his work as Creator the movement toward second perfection begins (*ad inchoationem*). God sustains and guides the universe in its self-propagation according to its own matter and principles (*rationes seminales*),[44] but the completion of this operation will not occur till the *eschaton*.

These two perfections are closely related. The perfection of the form is the cause of the perfection of operation "because the form is the principle of operation."[45] However, the second perfection is the reason why the first perfection was granted. It is important to note what the angelic doctor is not saying. He is not saying that the first perfection is static and the second dynamic, nor is he saying that the first perfection is pure essence and the second pure act. A form as such is an act.[46] What Thomas is saying is that perfection is constituted by two distinct but inseparable acts; the first perfection by the *actus essendi*, the second perfection by *operatio*. As Marty observes,

> Saint Thomas lie la notion de parfait à la forme et aux principes d'action. C'est la forme en effet qui constitue l'espèce en te degré de perfection; et

> les *habitus operativi* tels que les facultés, les vertus rendent l'être capable de l'activité correspondant à sa espèce. C'est donc à un univers qui se réfère ici Saint Thomas. Sa perfection est faite des divers degrés des êtres, ordonnés à partir d'un degré suprême.[47]

Still, the question remains, how are we to understand God's rest on the seventh day? If the second perfection is the perfection of operation and God ceased to work on the seventh day, then one might think that God is most imperfect of all. However, what we must understand is that the doubling of perfection we have been considering applies only to finite beings and not to God. In us the act of existence is in potency to operation, the first act to the second, but this is not so in God. Rest in God is not related to potency but to perfection; this relation occurs in a twofold manner. On the one hand, God ceased his work of creation on the seventh day. After the sixth day, God created no new species, as that work was complete not because all the species and individuals that would ever exist had been created by then, but because whatever species or individuals come afterward are already in some sense present in the work of the six days (*aliquo modo*).[48] In other words, God did not cease to create because he had grown tired or run out of ideas, but because the work of creation had reached its assigned terminus. On the other hand, God rested *from* his work on the seventh day. Aquinas draws attention to the preposition *from* (*a* in the Latin), for it tells us that God did not rest *in* his works as if he created out of necessity. God rested *from* his works, meaning in himself. Of course, God rests in himself from all eternity, but by stating that God rested after finishing the work of creation, the Bible is telling its readers that the final perfection of creation is to rest not in ourselves but in God.

The consequence of this duality of God's rest (cessation from creation and rest in God) is that God's blessing over the whole of creation on the seventh day has a double aspect. First, since God rested from creation, God blesses creatures so that they will increase and multiply and in this way preserve the perfection of species. Of course, this work of preservation can only occur thanks to God's ongoing providential care, though the creatures' act of generation is also at work. Second, since God rests in himself, God sanctifies the seventh day "since the special sanctification of every creature consists in resting in God."[49]

From Thomas' exegesis of the Genesis creation account we learn that everything that God created is perfect though not as perfect as it can be—perfection is perfectible; first perfection is given for the sake of second perfection. The perfection of everything that has being by participation has a history; it has a beginning (form) and it proceeds to an end (operation). The perfection of human beings has a temporal axis. Thus, it is possible to speak of the perfection that is proper to different historical ages or conditions (before the law or after the law, state of grace or state of glory), and it is possible to rank these various states with respect to each other. We will examine these theological states later when we look more closely at Thomas' soteriology; for now it is important to reiterate a point made in passing earlier: the perfection of the universe is gradated. Some things are more perfect than others, and they are more perfect both by virtue of their first and/or second perfection. Some forms are more perfect than others. Some species are more perfect than others, and within the same species some have attained greater perfection of operation than others.[50]

At first glance, the presence of degrees of perfection in creation seems problematic. Would it not be better if all parts of the universe stood on equal footing? Why should angelic nature be more perfect than human nature? Why is the value of the sparrow less than that of a human? In order to account for this plurality, Thomas likens the constitution of the universe to that of a house where a diversity of parts is necessary for the integrity and perfection of the whole. A wise builder does not construct the foundation and the roof out of the same materials or in the same order, but in such a way as is fitting for each part's role in holding up the house. So it is with God. As Thomas avers,

> God would not make the whole universe the best of its kind, if he made all the parts equal, because many grades of goodness would then be lacking in the universe, and thus it would be imperfect.[51]

The perfection of any effect resides in its similitude to its cause. The perfection of the universe is attained as it participates in God's own perfection after its own manner. However, no created thing, no species or genus is sufficiently great to manifest all of God's perfections; as Aquinas explains,

> The presence of multiplicity and variety among created beings was therefore necessary that a perfect likeness to God be found in them according to their manner of being.[52]

The diversity and multiplicity of the universe is not the result of chance or extrinsic necessity, but the result of God's loving desire to produce something as perfect as himself, albeit in a created reality.[53] This created perfection is increased by the multiplication of individuals within a species, but also by the plurality of species because the good of the species exceeds the good of the individual. In other words, the diversity of species in the universe is truly something to be celebrated and to be thankful for; diversity is a sign of the goodness of God and creation. A less diverse universe would be a less perfect universe.[54]

The perfection of the universe requires diversity of parts and species, but it is crucial to note that this diversity is ordered. Commenting on Genesis 1:31, where God declares the whole of creation to be not simply good but very good, Thomas explains,

> For each thing in its nature is good, but all things together are very good, by reason of the order of the universe, which is the ultimate and noblest perfection in things (*ultima et nobilissima perfectio in rebus*).[55]

In the universe, both diversity and order are correlative. Without diversity order could not exist, but without order diversity is less perfect than it could be. A stack of accurately cut planks made of the finest oak is perfect in its own manner, but when they are fit together to constitute the frame of a house their perfection is greater; the planks have received a higher form, a second perfection that results from the operation of the builder. A similar thing obtains in the case of the universe. As Aquinas states, "this world is called one by the unity of order, whereby some things are ordered to others."[56] This unity of order brings a perfection to the multiplicity of individuals and the diversity of species that they would otherwise lack; this perfection allows for the parts to work together in a way that perfects the whole and makes it as one song: *uni-versus*.[57]

The order of the universe does not denote a static hierarchy but an ordered diversity where all of the parts work for the good of the whole. The most perfect universe (*perfectio optima*) is one where creatures imitate God not only by being good in themselves but by acting for the good of others. "But no creature could act for the good of another creature unless plurality and inequality existed in created things."[58] Thus, inequality exists for the sake of complementarity and service; one creature filling up another by sharing of its goodness. A plurality of grades of perfection results in a variety of degrees of goodness and allows for the good of the parts to be diffused throughout creation for the sake of the whole.

The perfection of the universe does not occur at the expense of the perfection of the parts. On the contrary, in order for the universe to attain its highest perfection (*perfectio summa*), its constitutive parts must return to their principle of production: God. All creatures approximate God insofar as they exist, according to their *perfectio prima*. However, the perfection of the universe requires that there be some creatures that are like God according to their operation, according to their *perfectio secunda*. Since God has no operations but those of the intellect and the will, the perfection of the universe requires that there be creatures made *ad imaginem Dei*, that imitate God by knowing and loving.[59]

In sum, Aquinas considers the universe to be the highest perfection of creation; it has no boundary at which it terminates and another starts, and it is more extensive and inclusive than any intellectual creature. The universe is the *totum integrale*, and next to it even the most perfect angel appears as only a part. However, by acts of knowing and loving, intellectual creatures draw the disparate parts of the universe out of their isolation into a greater and more perfect unity than they would otherwise have. Because intellectual creatures are capable of the highest good (*capaces summi boni*), they can know not only other created species, but they can also know and love God. Thus, although intellectual creatures are only a part of creation, they are in a sense the whole (*quodammodo omnia*), and without the knowing and loving activity of intellectual creatures in general, humans in particular, the universe would remain incomplete. It is to Thomas' treatment of the perfection of the image of God that we now turn.

The First Perfection of the Human—*Ad Imaginem Dei*

As we have had occasion to observe, the architecture of the *Summa Theologiae* itself expresses the centrality of perfection in Aquinas' theology. The object of the science of theology is God and also humans as they proceed from God and are directed to God.[60] These two objects, the exemplar and the image, constitute the foundation of the *exitus-reditus* schema of the *Summa*. The *Prima Pars* presents the procession of the image from the exemplar; the *Secunda Pars* the movement of the image toward the exemplar; the *Tertia Pars* the union of the image with the exemplar in the person of Christ. So despite the relative scarcity of the term, the image of God in the human is one of the master motifs of Aquinas' theology. In this section, we will examine this doctrine of the image as Thomas develops it in Question 93 of the *Prima Pars* of the *Summa Theologiae*.

Aquinas refers to the image of God as the end (*finis*) or term (*terminus*) of the production of the human. In an important treatise on this subject, Juvenal Merriell argues strongly for reading the word "end" as referring only to the creature's creation (*perfectio prima*) and not to the creature's consummation (*perfectio secunda*).[61] The confusion in terms is understandable given the importance of final causality throughout the *Summa*. However, careful readers should distinguish between "end" as *finis operis* and "end" as *finis operantis*. The former refers to the completion of the creative act that Aquinas began to describe in Questions 90 and 91, namely the procession from God of a being with a rational soul and a material body—the human. The latter extends to include God's purpose for this human, namely beatitude. It is to avoid this ambiguity that Aquinas adds the word *terminus* in apposition to *finis*, because here in the *Prima Pars* he means to discuss the image as *finis operis* and not as *finis operantis*, to which purpose he will devote the *Secunda Pars*.[62]

Leaving open the possibility that Merriell does not allow for sufficient interpenetration and movement among the themes in the different parts of the *Summa*, there is an important issue at stake in Thomas' choice of terms. By first considering the image of God in the human as the *terminus operis* and not as the *finis operantis*, the angelic doctor is underscoring the dignity of the human as creature as well as preserving the gratuity of grace.

Before proceeding to consider Aquinas' doctrine of the image of God as such, we must pause and inquire into the difference between an image and a vestige. This is a key distinction Thomas had treated earlier in the *Summa* during his discussion on the doctrine of the Trinity.

The question is asked: "whether in creatures is necessarily found a vestige of the Trinity."[63] Thomas counters arguments that reject the presence of this mode of representation of the Trinity in the creature by appealing to Augustine, who asserts: "the vestige of the Trinity appears in creatures."[64] Since every effect resembles its cause, everything in the creature must be reduced to the single causal act of the Triune God. However, this mode of similitude does not represent the species of the cause but only its genus. Aquinas' favorite illustration of this generic likeness expresses it well: "such a representation is called a trace (*vestigium*) for a trace shows that someone has passed by but not who it is."[65]

Thomas' reflection on the image draws on this earlier discussion of the *vestigia trinitatis* in order to carefully delineate the contours of the *imago trinitatis*. At the beginning of his inquiry Aquinas avers, citing Augustine, that "where an image exists, there forthwith is likeness; but where there is likeness, there is not necessarily an image."[66] Two significant terms with a long history of theological usage are introduced here: image and likeness. The question that immediately arises, and is implicit in the quote from Augustine, is: how are image and likeness related? Indeed one could say that the chief goal of Question 93 of the *Prima Pars* of the *Summa Theologiae* is the clarification of the scope and applicability of these terms to the creature in relation to God.

Aquinas understands likeness in two ways. First, "likeness may be considered in the light of a preamble to image, inasmuch as it is something more general than image."[67] Inasmuch as something exists it has a likeness to the first being; inasmuch as something is alive it has a likeness to the first life. As Aquinas avers, "every creature is an image of the exemplar type thereof in the divine mind."[68] When someone says that they commune with God in nature, they may not be merely sentimental. The likeness of rocks, animals, and plants to the Creator is real, but it does not attain the level of image; it remains a trace.

Second, "likeness may be considered in another way, as signifying the expression and perfection of the image."[69] This way of understanding likeness corresponds to patristic usage, which reserved the term *homoiosis* for what Aquinas calls "the likeness of glory."[70] This mode of likeness is not an intensification of the former, a greater generic likeness, but a likeness of a different kind, a similitude of species. Thus, whereas the image may become perfected by participating in its exemplar to a greater degree, the vestige cannot participate in its cause in such a way that it becomes an image of anything other than of its exemplar type. Unlike Wesley, Aquinas would not say that all dogs go to heaven; the reason being not that God does not love dogs, but that it is not in the nature of dogs to see God. "Intellectual creatures alone, properly speaking, are made to God's image."[71]

Since the image of God is found in intellectual creatures, Aquinas does not omit angels from his exposition of the doctrine of the image. Indeed, it is on account of his extensive treatment of angels that Thomas receives the title *doctor angelicus*. Regrettably, an examination of Thomas' angelology lies beyond the scope of this work. Suffice it to say that angels are not the only beings made in the image of God. Humans, too, bear this image, albeit less perfectly than angels.[72] It is to a consideration of the image in union with human flesh that we now turn.

The basis for Aquinas' teaching on the image of God in the human is the creation account in Genesis: God said, "let us make man to our own image and likeness" (Gen 1:26). Thomas takes this passage as a *prima facie* affirmation that the image of God is found in all humans, both male and female. The chief interpretive challenge of this biblical passage lies in giving an account of the image that appreciates the natural dignity of the intellectual creature while respecting the Creator-creature distinction. The former challenge we have already addressed by attending to Thomas' distinction between image and vestige. The latter is what we must now allow the *doctor angelicus* to instruct us on as he refines our speech by teaching us the meaning and usage of the simple preposition *ad*.[73]

Aquinas calls our attention to what Scripture teaches concerning the Son of God. Christ is the *imago Dei invisibilis* (Col 1:15). He alone is the perfect image of God, identical in nature to the Father; the image of God exists in Christ as the image of the king in his son. By contrast, the image of God exists in the human in an alien nature, as the image of a king in a silver coin; it bears both a real likeness (*imago*) and an imperfect likeness. The very words of Genesis 1:26 evoke this distinction between perfect and imperfect likeness. In Scripture, God does not make the human in the *imago Dei simpliciter*, but rather the human is said to be made *ad imaginem et similitudinem nostram*. For Thomas, the distinction between *imago* and *ad imaginem* is of tremendous significance. First of all, Aquinas observes: "the preposition *ad* signifies a certain approach (*accessus*), as of something at a distance."[74] Also, the preposition *ad* refers to the *terminus factionis* or as we said earlier, the *finis operis*, so that the sense of this verse is "let us make man in such a way that our image may be in him."[75] In addition, the preposition *ad* points to the exemplar cause, the source of the *finis operantis*. The most concise and powerful rendering of the difference between the imperfect and the perfect image is found in Aquinas' discussion of the image of God in the Son where he says,

> Man is not simply called the image, but *ad imaginem*, whereby is expressed a certain movement of tendency to perfection.[76]

From this grammatical analysis an important consequence follows. The image of God in the human is ordered toward God as its proper end; the image is made for the exemplar.

With this clearer understanding of the difference between the perfect and the imperfect image, we are now ready to inquire into the constitution and "location" of this image of God in creation. Earlier I quoted Thomas as saying that only intellectual creatures are made to God's image. To understand why this is so let us look at one of the most lyric passages in the *Prima Pars*, where Thomas says,

> The image of the Trinity is to be found in the acts of the soul, that is, inasmuch as from the knowledge which we possess, by actual thought we form an internal word; and thence break forth in love.[77]

The image of God in us is not only an image of the divine nature, but of the Trinity of persons. By the procession of the word in the intellect and the procession of love in the will, the rational creature images the eternal processions of the uncreated Trinity.[78] For this reason, the image of God is found only in the intellectual nature, which attains a certain representation of the species of the divine persons, and not in the human body where we can only speak of traces of the Trinity.

To summarize, to be human is to be made *ad imaginem Dei*. It pertains to the first perfection of human beings to be intellectual creatures who are capable of knowing and loving God. The imaging of the Trinity by the person is most perfect when it is most actual, meaning, when the creature actually knows and loves not just anything, but God.[79] This first perfection cannot be lost, for the image of God is present virtually in the habits and even in the powers of the soul, in the same way that the act is present in its principles. As long as the powers of the soul are present, the image of God persists even without actual acts. As Thomas avers,

> The image of God abides ever in the soul; whether this image of God be so obsolete, as it were clouded, as almost to amount to nothing, as in those who have not the use of reason; or obscured and disfigured, as in sinners; or clear and beautiful, as in the just.[80]

This affirmation of the permanence of the image of God in the human under all kinds of conditions is very important, as we will later see, for understanding the nature of the human under the condition of sin. Not only is the image of God in the human perfect and indefectible, it is also perfectible. The first perfection is capable of its second perfection; creation is capable of deification.[81]

The Second Perfection of the Human— *Per Cognitionem et Amorem*

Something of a conundrum arises at this point of our exposition of Aquinas. On the one hand, the perfection of the human becomes reality only in the concrete person. As Marty remarks, "chaque individu humain vaut comme vaut une espèce."[82] The person, not the species, is what is most perfect in all of creation. On the other hand, the species is what is most perfect in the individual: "c'est ne pas cet homme, mais l'homme qui est l'intention de la nature."[83] The individual human is subject to the general law of the species; it achieves individuation through matter. Avicenna solves this conundrum by claiming that the union of the soul to the body leads to the individuation of the soul. In this view, the body is thus the prison of the soul. Aquinas understands the relation of body to soul otherwise. For Thomas, the individuation achieved through matter is not that of the soul but of the whole person, body and soul. The soul is the form of the body, not its prisoner. Thus, the human is for Aquinas the horizon between matter and spirit, a microcosm of creation, who though the weakest of intellectual beings has the power to recapitulate the entirety of the universe. The first perfection of the human is given to it in the act of creation, in its hylomorphic constitution. The second perfection of the human is attained through the act of reflection. As Marty avers,

> La réflexion, puis qu'elle est l'exercice du degré d'être de l'homme, marque comment l'activité de l'homme est similitude de Dieu, quel type de participation de l'Être divin elle réalise. Cette similitude divine tient dans une présence à soi, un agir libre, dont en l'homme la caractéristique propre est la médiation de l'univers matériel.[84]

Thus, the human achieves the perfection proper to its place in the hierarchy of being precisely by its capacity to abstract and interiorize the intelligible species of a thing through the act of knowing. In the *conversio ad phantasma*, in what Marty calls the "retour à l'essence," creation becomes present to the human and the human to him- or herself. According to Aquinas, the principle for this act of interiorization is nothing less than the law of charity.

The way to perfection begins with the ontological constitution of creation which makes it possible to speak of a perfection in the creature, but this perfection is only fully realized in the creature's love for God. This love is first poured into the heart as a supernatural habit, an infused law, but over time through prudent action the law of love becomes more and more interiorized. The composition of the universe with its diversity of species, the hylomorphic structure of the human, the gospel law, and the evangelical counsels have been given to us by God so that we might return to him and be perfect as he is perfect.

In the *Tertia Pars* of the *Summa*, as Thomas reflects on the unity of Christ's two natures, the angelic doctor describes two modes of union whereby human nature is elevated to God. The highest mode of union is that of personal being (*per esse personale*) whereby a divine person assumes a human nature. This mode is unique to the incarnate Word. There is also a union that occurs by way of operation (*per operationem*); this mode of union is proper to the saints who are united with God by knowledge and by love: *unio sanctorum ad Deum [est] per cognitionem et amorem.*[85] In this section, rather than focus our attention on one particular scriptural passage or question of the *Summa*, I will rely on an excellent study of this subject by Michael Sherwin. Sherwin helpfully elucidates the manner in which the union of the image with its exemplar is accomplished through the graced operations of the intellect and the will.[86]

According to Thomas, humans act from knowledge because the will is a rational appetite.[87] On the one hand, the will is a rational *appetite*. As such, the will is both like and unlike other appetites. Like the natural and sensitive appetites, the will is structured to desire something. The will, by its very constitution, desires the universal good and those things that help the agent attain this good. Unlike these appetites, the will's inclination follows a free, rational deliberation. On the other hand, the will is a *rational* appetite; the object of its desire is something apprehended by reason, namely, the good. This *bonum apprehensum* may be somewhat vague and imprecise; it might even be wrong, but it is not completely unknown: *si enim esset omnino ignotum, non quaeretur.*[88]

The relationship between intellect and will in human action is complex. In one sense, the intellect is prior to the will: *omnis actus voluntatis praeceditur ab aliquot actu intellectus*.[89] At every step of the process of a free action, an act of the intellect precedes an act of the will. All moral acts flow from a will that has deliberated about the end and the means to it. For this reason, although a person is called good on account of their good will and not their good understanding, the goodness of their will depends on reason (*bonitas voluntatis dependet a ratione*).[90] In another sense, intellect and will depend on each other: *intellectus aliquot modo movet voluntatem, et aliquot voluntas movet intellectum et alias vires*.[91] By presenting the will with its proper object, the intellect exerts formal causality on the will. All acts of the will (*velle*, *intendere*, *eligere*) presuppose cognition of something good (*velle*) that is attainable (*intendere*) by certain means (*eligere*). However, the will exerts final causality on the intellect. In relation to its act, it can choose to act or not to act. In relation to its object, it can will one means or another. In relation to its end, things are more complex. The will can will both good and evil, but this evil would be willed under some aspect of the good. The indeterminacy of the will with respect to its particular acts results from the fact that no individual act that the will may choose adequately expresses the potentiality inherent in the universal that is apprehended by the intellect.

The will has the power to shape the judgment of reason. However, this power of the will to command the intellect at the level of *exercitium* does not make Aquinas a moral relativist. The first mover of the will is not reason, nor the will itself, but God; it is God who establishes the will's natural inclination to the good; God alone is "the first efficient cause of the will's subsequent efficient causality."[92] Moreover, although Aquinas' account of agency states that every act of the will (except its first act) presupposes an act of the intellect, it avoids the pitfalls of psychological or social determinism. Granted the universal applicability of the primary principles of natural law, human action requires judgment over their particular application and this can happen in various ways in diverse circumstances. One implication of this indeterminacy of the will is that although one can specify a given act as not a fitting good here and now, the ability to sin is not a true correlate of freedom but results from the freedom to do good in various ways.[93]

At this point in our reflection on the relation between intellect and will, it is important to consider the distinction between *specificatio* and *exercitium*. As Sherwin observes, "things both *move* toward their goal and move toward it *in a certain way*."[94] To move toward the goal pertains to the exercise of the act. One can act or not act; act well or act poorly. To act in a certain manner, that is to say, to be an act of one type instead of another (say, an act of burning versus an act of falling) pertains to the specification of the act. This specification follows the form (*specificatio quidem actus est ex forma*),[95] but its exercise comes from an agent (*ab agente*) acting for a purpose (*ex fine*).

The acts of the will and of the intellect are specified by different objects. The act of the intellect is specified by being and truth, the first principles in the genus of formal causes. As Sherwin states, "the first thing that the theoretical intellect apprehends in any act of knowing is being."[96] The apprehension of being by the light of the agent intellect activates the first principles of reason that were habitually "stored" in the intellect, principles such as the principle of noncontradiction, that the whole is greater than the part, and the like. The act of the will is specified by the good, the first principle among final causes. As Sherwin states, "the first thing that the practical intellect apprehends is the good."[97] The light of the agent intellect activates not just the habit of *intellectus* but that of *synderesis* wherein the first principles of practical reason are habitually contained, such as good is to be done and evil to be avoided.[98] However, for a good to be attractive to the will it must be a *bonum conveneniens apprehensum*, that is to say, it must be apprehended as a good that is fitting here and now. Whether a good is specified as convenient or not is a judgment of the intellect (*secundum rationem*), nevertheless the will can direct reason to consider one aspect of the object apprehended by the intellect and to ignore others. In this way, the will shapes the judgment of reason. So, for example, even if all people desire happiness, one can will not to think about happiness. This inclination of the will is affected by a person's disposition. This disposition has been shaped by nature and history. In other words, whether a good appears fitting or not depends on our character (*habitus*) and our state of mind (passions).

Contra Socrates, Aquinas regards intellectual virtue as an insufficient motivator of morally good action: *appetitiva obedit rationi non omnino ad nutum, sed cum aliqua contradictione*.[99] So even though prudence is the intellectual virtue that perfects practical reason, for prudence to rightly order the agent toward what needs to be done, it needs the assistance of the moral virtues: *prudentia realiter est in ratione sicut in subiecto, sed praesupponit rectitudinem voluntatis sicut principium*.[100] In other words, if one would act well one needs not just soundness of mind but rectitude of will and this rectitude is attained with the assistance of the moral virtues and above all, by love.[101]

Love rectifies the will, but love depends on knowledge. Aquinas remains faithful to a key Augustinian insight: *nullus potest amare aliquid incognitum*;[102] we can only love what we know. Love does not belong to the intellect but to the appetite, and as there are different kinds of appetites there are different kinds of love.[103] First, there is the *amor naturalis* that arises not from cognition but from a natural appetite that desires connaturality between the lover and the loved. Second, there is the *amor sensitivus* that arises from the sensitive appetites, a *complacentia* for the sensitive good; with respect to this kind of love the human has a certain degree of liberty (*quid libertas participat*) as this good obeys reason. Finally, there is the *amor rationalis* which arises from a rational appetite (i.e. the will), a *complacentia* for the good absolutely speaking. Knowledge of the beloved spurs the will to desire to know intimately everything about the beloved (*singula quae ad amatum pertinent*) and in this way penetrate into the beloved's very self (*ad interiora eius ingreditur*).[104]

So love depends on knowledge, but the converse is also true: knowledge depends on love. *Amor rationalis* is always freely chosen. One might think that the contrary is the case, and that the intellect would force some loves on us. However, as we just saw, even though the intellect has the power to specify our loves, the will has power over the exercise of the intellect. For instance, love can distract the intellect away from certain immediate things in order to meditate on the beloved.[105] In a fundamental way, "our love is the product of our own choices."[106]

Hence, according to Thomas, love is the primary principle of human action: *Unde manifestum est quod omne agens, que quodcum sit, agit quamcumque actionem ex aliquo amore.*[107] This seems to contradict what Aquinas says at the beginning of the *Prima Secundae*, where he states that the end of human acts is happiness, but strictly speaking happiness is an intellectual operation. Thomas recognizes that if happiness were essentially an act of the will, the act of desiring happiness would make us happy, which is absurd.[108] The act of reaching for the object of our desire is an act of the will, but the act of apprehending what we desire is an act of the intellect:[109] *finem primo apprehendit intellectus quam voluntas, tamen motus ad finem incipit in voluntate.*[110]

Nevertheless, before love becomes a principle of human action, love is a response to the goodness and value of someone's existence: *unusquisque enim amicus primo quidem vult suum amicum esse et vivere.*[111] Before I will any goods to my friend (*amor amicitiae*), before I seek companionship with someone (*amor concupsicentiae*), I am simply glad that this person exists. Sherwin's words on this easily overlooked aspect of Thomas' account of human action are well worth meditating on:

> At its most basic level, love is a response to the goodness of reality, a response to the real as it is or as it could be. Before reason assesses whether a particular good is fully attainable by us, reason first recognizes it as a good that is somehow already in harmony with us. It is part of the

> same creation in which we participate and as such is something we can already celebrate and enjoy.[112]

Love's primal act is an act of simple receptivity to and affirmation of the goodness of creation. The first stage of human action springs from loving contemplation of a being's first perfection. This first stage of action is indeed a fitting end for human operation; a person's active receptivity to the created good is a complete human act. However, a person might follow this simple affirmation by an intention to attain this good, deliberate over the means to do so, and then command the will to make use of the necessary powers to act for that end.

Thus far, our examination of Thomas' understanding of knowledge and will has proceeded by considering the operations themselves and not their object, but the second perfection of the human does not consist in knowing and loving just any intelligible good but in knowing and loving God himself, and for this end humans need the aid of faith and charity. It is to the consideration of the graced elevation of the intellect and the will that we now turn.

The human being considered absolutely, for example, *in puris naturalibus* (not to be confused with the original state), that is, considered solely in its metaphysical structure as *creatura rationalis,* is endowed with love of God.[113] For Thomas, a consideration of the human being in *puris naturalibus* is necessary if one is to secure the gratuity of life with God. Just because God is our Creator does not mean that he needs to be our savior. Nevertheless, as eyes are ordered to light, so are rational creatures capable of grace.

Grace plays a central role in Aquinas' soteriology. By grace, God becomes present to us in a new way.[114] No longer is God simply present according to the common way in which he is present to all creation. By grace, God is at home in the rational creature like he is in his very temple (*sicut in templo suo*). This grace is a *habitus*, a sort of "second nature" that raises and perfects the natural powers of the human so that we might "become participants of the divine nature" (2 Pet 1:4). There are three such kinds of infused habits that perfect the powers of the soul. First, the theological virtues perfect the intellect and the will with respect to God. Second, the infused moral virtues perfect the intellect and the will with respect to means (things ordered) to God. Finally, the gifts of the Holy Spirit (cf. Isa 11:1-2) render the intellect and the will pliable to the guidance of the Holy Spirit. Let us first consider the theological virtues of faith and charity before turning to the other kinds of infused habits.

Faith is the infused habit that perfects the intellect. By faith, we believe those things that God has revealed about himself and our destiny in him.

Faith imparts the light of faith by which certain supernatural principles, the *credibilia* of faith, are rendered intelligible and the way to heaven is clear. As Thomas argues,

> This is also shown from the fact that before the coming of Christ none of the philosophers was able, however great his effort, to know as much about God or about the means necessary for obtaining eternal life, as any old woman knows by faith since Christ came down upon earth. And therefore it is said in Isaiah, "the earth is filled with the knowledge of God."[115]

As a theological virtue that perfects the intellect, faith shares in the firm assent of *scientia* while also sharing in the restlessness of *dubitatio* or *opinio*. In addition to illumining the intellect with the light of faith, faith imparts an inclination of the will to act, to believe. The origin of this act of faith, the person's assent to the *credibilia* of Christianity, cannot be traced back to a single cause.[116] There are many possible exterior causes for the act of faith: seeing a miracle, hearing a persuasive sermon. But these exterior causes are not sufficient causes. After all, not all respond in the same way to the same sermon or sign: *quidam credunt et quidam non credunt*.[117] So in addition to the exterior causes, the act of faith requires an interior cause. This interior cause is not, like the Pelagians supposed, the *liberum arbitrium*. None can freely choose to perform an act that exceeds their nature; the act of faith must originate *ex supernaturali principio*,[118] in addition to the exterior revelation there must be an *interior instinctus*[119] that moves the intellect to assent, namely, God's grace. Hence according to Thomas, *Ipsum autem credere est actus intellectus assentientis veritati divinae ex imperio voluntatis a Deo motae per gratiam*.[120] The intellect, the will, and God's grace all work together to make the act of faith possible.[121]

Charity is the infused habit that perfects the will by making us friends of God. Aquinas' understanding of charity benefits from a close reading of Aristotle's concept of *amicitia*. According to the philosopher, friendship has three preeminent characteristics.[122] First, there is the idea of mutuality. Two friends from their mutual beneficence recognize their common goodwill. Second, friendship is a kind of *habitus*, a second nature; it is not easily lost and abides even when the friends are apart or asleep. Finally, friendship entails an active *communicatio in bono* which is based on a "passive" *communicatio vitae*. At the very least, two friends share a common species (they are both human), but they might also share a profession, a culture, an ethnicity, and so forth. Despite the philosophical provenance of Thomas' thought on *amicitia*, the theological transposition of this concept into *caritas* stretches the Aristotelian categories almost beyond recognition, for by charity, humans become friends of God. By this virtue, even while in this life, humans are united directly with God (as a supernatural end). The perfection of charity achieved by charity is not static; the strength of the bond between God and human effected by charity can increase. The bond of love grows in perfection as charity intensifies its rule over the other virtues, resulting in acts of greater and greater charity. As charity perfects the will, it perfects all moral acts; even the act of *simplex voluntas* is perfected so that reason rests in recognizing that God is and that God is good.[123] To reiterate, the act of charity presupposes the knowledge of faith. Love is not blind: *Deus autem quanto perfectius cognoscitur, tanto perfectius amatur.*[124]

These brief reflections on the perfective operations of faith and charity might lead us to think that we have reached the end of our inquiry into Thomas' understanding of the human's second perfection. If, as St. Paul says, "the only thing that counts is faith working through love" (Gal 5:6); and if, as we have seen, faith perfects the intellect and charity the will, then what more is to be said? However, Thomas insists that the infusion of faith and charity is not sufficient by itself for humans to attain happiness in God. The theological virtues indeed order human actions to God, but this ordering to God as our final end leaves open the particular means to that end. The Gospel Law is universal: "You shall love the Lord your God with all your heart, and with all your soul, and with all your strength, and with all your mind; and your neighbor as yourself" (Lk 10:27). However, what does loving God look like right here and now? The habit of faith by itself cannot answer this question, nor the habit of charity. Discerning how to apply the universal principle in the particular pertains to the virtue of prudence. Sherwin explains the dependence of charity on prudence in the following way:

> If our charitable actions toward our neighbor are going to be rightly ordered toward our ultimate end, they must be specified according to some cognitive scale of values (*regulam*). Since human reason of itself does not obtain such a *regulam*, this cognitive *regulam* [sic] must be infused.[125]

In other words, the perfection of charity requires the infusion of prudence. Prudence is the habit that helps the person judge rightly about what is to be done, which acts or means are fitting for the end. Infused prudence is not a natural aptitude but the work of grace that implants in the soul the habit of judging well about ordering things to God.

To restate, the perfection of the intellect and the will is accomplished by the perfection of the virtues in general and of charity in particular.

Other infused virtues, moral (like prudence) and theological (like faith), are necessary; these prepare the way for the union of charity by removing impediments to perfect love (the work of the moral virtues) and by giving us a dark knowledge and incipient communion with God (the effect of faith and hope). Nevertheless, according to the angelic doctor, in order to attain the fullness of perfection, the theological virtues need, in addition to the aid of the infused moral virtues, the assistance of the gifts of the Spirit.

The gifts of the Spirit work in us a second effect of grace. These gifts perfect the operations of the will and the intellect as these have been elevated by grace. The gifts of the Holy Spirit are dispositions, habits, which render us pliable to the prompting of the Spirit. Without these gifts the Spirit could not move us without doing violence to our *liberum arbitrium*.[126] Indeed, in the saints, *ipsum motum voluntatis et liberi arbitrii Spiritus Sanctus in eis causat*.[127] The distinguishing mark of the gifts of the Spirit is their mode of operation. The infused theological virtues are supernatural *quoad substantiam* but not *quoad modum operandi*, whereas the gifts of the Spirit are supernatural in both of these senses. While the theological virtues, having God himself as their object, are more perfect than the gifts that have the goal of facilitating the operation of the virtues, the gifts are in a sense superior to the virtues, for through them we are ruled by the Holy Spirit. In his treatise *Teología de la Perfección Cristiana*, Royo Marín accurately expresses the rationale behind Thomas' insistence on the need of the gifts of the Spirit for Christian perfection.

> Sólo bajo la influencia del don del entendimiento, que sin destruir la fe—porque no se trata todavía de la visión beatifica—le da una penetración y profundidad intensísimas en los misterios sobrenaturales (*quasi intus legere*)—, y, sobre todo, bajo el don de la sabiduría, que le hace saborear las cosas divinas por cierta connaturalizad y simpatía—*per quandam connaturalitatem*—, alcanzará la caridad su plena expansión y desarrollo en la medida que requiere y exige la perfección cristiana.[128]

The gift of understanding perfects faith and the gift of wisdom charity, but these are only habits. Yet, as we have seen, the second perfection of the human is not the perfection of form but of operation. These supernatural dispositions are truly perfect when they move our intellect and will into action. The gifts of the Spirit produce the fruits of the Spirit. When these fruits reach their maturity, they are called Beatitudes. When the intellect is perfected by faith and directed by the gift of understanding it attains cleanness of heart and is rewarded with the vision of God.[129] When the will is perfected by the gift of wisdom it practices peacemaking and is rewarded with the assurance of divine adoption.[130] Thus, according to Thomas, peacemaking is a manifestation of the second perfection of the human, which makes sense given that the human's first acts of intellect and will are joy in that which exists.

Conclusions

Our study of Thomas' understanding of perfection confirms the centrality of this doctrine in the angelic doctor's thought. Indeed, one might say that the whole of the *Summa Theologiae* is to be understood as a manual of Christian perfection. Our study of this doctrine is not at an end, for we have yet to consider the way of perfection itself; this inquiry will be the subject of the next chapter. However, before we turn our attention to an examination of the concrete way in which humans become perfect in knowledge and in love, let us review some of the key findings of this chapter.

First, the doctrine of perfection is built upon a biblical foundation. Not only are the scriptural quotations copious throughout Thomas' exposition of the perfection of God, the universe, and the image, the angelic doctor is faithful to the methodology he laid out at the beginning of the *Summa*, "nothing necessary to faith is contained under the spiritual sense which is not elsewhere put forward in its literal sense."[131] Even subtle distinctions between first perfection and second perfection are grounded in Aquinas' understanding of the literal sense of the text.

Second, the image of God in the human is perfect according to its *perfectio prima*. According to Aquinas, the human is not an unfinished symphony (one which the composer is obliged to complete). Even under the condition of sin the human remains a complete *opus*. All our created faculties and powers persist after the fall. The problem is that these faculties are now disordered. For Aquinas, sin wounds but does not destroy nature. This affirmation is important, for it means that the most depraved sinner never ceases to be a human made in the image of God, and must be treated as such. The same is true for sufferers of cerebral palsy or people in a vegetative state. The image of God is indelibly inscribed in the rational creature, and neither sleep, nor sin, nor senility can erase its mark on the soul.

Perhaps the most startling result of our inquiry into Thomas' understanding of perfection is that love is grounded in a general receptivity to the goodness of reality. At the outset of the person's journey toward God, there is a primal act of love that affirms and rejoices in the existence of the other. Even before the neighbor becomes my friend, I am simply glad that this person lives; my neighbor's very being is a token for me of the goodness of the created order.[132] This act of *simplex voluntas*, as Aquinas calls it, becomes complicated as it becomes integrated into a complex moral action, and it becomes contradicted as it is enmeshed in a history of sinful aversion from the neighbor. Yet at the heart of human agency lies love of being and receptivity to the real. As humans move from first perfection to second perfection, the obstacles to this receptivity are removed and the way for the affirmation of being in its manifold manifestations is cleared to such an extent that St. Francis rejoices in the existence and operations of brother sun and sister moon.

Doubtless this account of the dignity of the image of God under the condition of sin will strike some as too optimistic. Aquinas' talk of wounded nature, some would argue, does not take the ravages of sin seriously enough. Not withstanding such "hypothetical" objections, Aquinas is no semi-Pelagian. The only cure for the wounds of nature is grace, and there is nothing the human can do without grace to merit the first grace of conversion.

Third, the image of God in the human is perfected through the dynamic interplay of its *perfectio prima* and *perfectio secunda*. The human is a perfect *opus*, albeit one that is open to further depths of interpretation.[133] The image of God should not be considered as some static divine *imprimatur*, but as a moving picture that increases in clarity the more it imitates its exemplar. Merriell says it well:

> Man expresses the divine Trinity not merely as a mirror reflects a thing set to some distance from it, but as an actor who imitates the character he plays by entering into his character's life.[134]

As we saw, human beings have been created to attain a greater and greater degree of likeness to their Creator. We are rendered deiform as by grace our will and intellect is moved to actually know and love God as supernatural end. The approach of the image to its exemplar attains such close proximity that Aquinas does not hesitate to call it deification, *theosis*. Nevertheless, Aquinas always protects the Creator-creature distinction. Only God is perfect by nature; he alone is pure actuality. Humans, however, are perfect by participation. For us, first perfection and second perfection are two distinct acts. It is in our nature to know and love God, but only as the intellect and the will are perfected by the infused virtues and gifts of the Spirit is the soul rendered pliable to the Spirit's immediate guidance, so that all its powers operate perfectly and thereby attain the human's final perfection—beatitude.

Chapter Four

Aquinas on the Way to Christian Perfection

> Quia igitur principalis intentio huius sacrae doctrinae est Dei cognitionem tradere, et non solum secundum quod in se est, sed etiam secundum quod est principium rerum et finis earum, et specialiter rationalis creaturae, ut ex dictis est manifestum; ad huius doctrinae expositionem intendentes, primo tractabimus de Deo; secundo, de motu rationalis creaturae in Deum; tertio, de Christo, qui, secundum quod homo, via est nobis tendendi in Deum.[1]

In the previous chapter we considered how humans are perfect insofar as God made them in his own image. The *perfectio prima* of the human is a gift that is consummated by a second gift, the gift of grace, which perfects the operations of the will and the intellect so that the human actually knows and loves God. This union with God *per cognitionem et amorem* constitutes the *perfectio secunda* of the human. In this chapter, we shift our focus from the first parts of the *Summa* to the final passages of the *Secunda Secundae* and on to the *Tertia Pars*. *Duplex est perfectio*, but there is only one way to perfection: Jesus Christ *via est nobis tendendi in Deum.*

The States along the Way of Perfection

Broadly speaking, Aquinas distinguishes three ways in which the image of God is present in the human: three degrees of likeness.[2] First, the image of God is found in the very nature of the mind, in the human's natural capacity for knowing and loving God. This *imago creationis* is present in all humans and constitutes the first perfection of the human. Second, the image of God is made manifest when the human loves and knows God either habitually or actually yet imperfectly. This *imago recreationis* consists in the conformity of grace; it is present only among the baptized and attains its highest brilliance in mature, holy Christians. Third, the image of God is found in its fullness in those who know and love God perfectly. This *imago similitudinis* consists in the likeness of glory and is found only among the blessed. This last degree of conformity of the image to its exemplar is the goal and purpose of all human beings, their second and final perfection. In sum, human *capacitas* receives its gratuitous fulfillment in divine *conformitas*.[3]

According to the angelic doctor, a particular theological *status* corresponds to each degree of similitude. In this chapter we will consider the states along the way to perfection, including the state of perfection itself. Let us begin by studying the concept of *status*.

The term *status* is derived from the word *standum* from which the English word "stand" comes. A *status* refers to a certain kind of position; an order, so to speak, suitable to the nature of the one standing. A true *status* is characterized by a proper stance. The proper stance for a human is to stand with the head held aloft, back straight, and two feet firmly planted on the ground. Such a stance differs from the one that is proper to the status of a dog. In other words, a *status* is intrinsic and natural. Moreover, a *status* is not easily changed. A *status* receives its name from its stability (*statum*); the one who stands (*stare*) does not move. Economic class and social standing, for instance, are extrinsic and mutable conditions; there are no proper states. Two marks must be attained for a certain life condition to be considered a *status*: immobility (*immobilitas*) and connaturality (*connaturalitas*). For this condition of life to be considered a genuinely human *status*, a further, more fundamental mark must be found: freedom.

> Unde status pertinet proprie ad libertatem vel servitutem, sive in spiritualibus sive in civilibus.[4]

A human *status* pertains to conditions of bondage and freedom. Aquinas applies the term *status* to three realms of human existence: the civil, the spiritual, and the ecclesial. Let us consider each of these in turn.

First, there are civil states, such as being a member of the government. Indeed, the concept of *status* has its antecedents in Roman law,[5] but Aquinas' understanding of the duties of those in political office is not the concern of our present inquiry.

Second, there are the theological states. Aquinas speaks of the *status incipientum*, the *status proficientum*, and the *status perfectorum*.[6] These three states demarcate the diversity of stages of the spiritual life; a diversity that is present according to the various degrees of charity.[7] Elsewhere, Thomas will speak of the *status naturae*, *status gratiae*, and the *status gloriae*.[8] These various "states" have two things in common. On the one hand, these are common states. All those in the *status viae*[9] have fallen from the *status innocentiae*[10] and must be moved by God out of a *status peccati*[11] into a *status gratiae* so that after this life they may enter the *status gloriae*. On the other hand, these states pertain to conditions of *inner* spiritual freedom or servitude. Someone abiding in the state of sin is in servitude to sin and "free" from the demands of justice. Likewise someone in the state of grace is free from sin and in "servitude" of justice. The quotation marks are necessary to call attention to the fact that Aquinas clearly insists that freedom from sin (*libertas a peccato*) is true freedom (*vera libertas*), whereas servitude to sin (*servitus peccati*) is true servitude (*vera servitus*).[12]

Third, there are ecclesial states. These states denote conditions of *outer* spiritual freedom or service.[13] Thomas draws particular attention to the episcopal and religious states because these are, as we shall see, states of perfection.[14] Indeed, Aquinas devotes the last questions of the *Secunda Secundae* to the clarification of the overlap and distinction of the theological *status perfectorum* and the ecclesial *status perfectionis*. The ecclesial state that Thomas does not consider is the state of the laity. The groundwork for such a development is implicitly present in Thomas' reflections on baptism, the life of the Spirit, and especially confirmation, but the *doctor communis* does not bring these together into a coherent vision of lay life. In the judgment of one of Thomas' commentators, "*Die Zeit war nicht reif.*"[15]

With these reflections on the term *status* in mind, let us consider the theological states leading to the *status perfectorum* before turning our attention to the *status perfectionis*. These theological states are the state of innocence, the state of fallen nature, the state of grace, and the state of glory.

The state of innocence is the original state of humanity. On the authority of Scripture, Aquinas asserts that "God made man right."[16] God gave Adam all the faculties befitting his human nature (intellect, will, the five senses, the ability to move, to eat, etc.). Just as important, God's grace sustained these faculties in a proper order. In paradise, the human body was subject to the lower powers, and the lower powers in turn were subject to reason, which was in turn subject to God. The various names by which the state of innocence is called (the primitive state, the state of integrity, the perfect state, the state of nature) unanimously proclaim the state of innocence as one of order and harmony.

The rectitude of this state was given by God as a gift at the moment of creation. God bestowed upon Adam an ease and efficiency of operation unknown to his descendants. In the state of innocence, as Adam subjected himself to the government of God, all creatures subjected themselves to the government of Adam.[17] No need here for bridles or whips, Adam had but to command for animals to obey. Add to this the fact that in the state of innocence, by the grace of original righteousness, the human body was incorruptible;[18] the passions easily avoided the snare of sin and deceit;[19] and the intellect enjoyed a contemplation of God unhindered by exterior things.[20]

From the preceding remarks, one might conclude that Aquinas regarded the original state as perfect *simpliciter*, and yet this is not the case, for the state of innocence is not the state of glory. In Eden, Adam did not enjoy the beatific vision.[21] Had Adam enjoyed the beatific vision he would not have fallen, for those who see God in the light of glory cannot sin. Instead, Adam's knowledge of God was in some kind of middle state between heaven and earth, a state superior to our present knowledge but inferior to the knowledge of the blessed. Adam saw God in an enigma, in his created effects. Adam possessed all the natural virtues, but these could only direct him to a natural end, to his *finis operis* (keeping the Garden of Eden, procreation with Eve, exercising dominion over animals, and the like) and not to the supernatural end of union with God. For this later end he needed the infusion of the theological virtues. So, Adam too was in need of grace if he was to achieve his *finis operantis*, his second perfection, namely loving God not only as Creator but also as friend. In other words, in addition to the grace of original righteousness, human beings needed the assistance of sanctifying grace if they were to attain the vision of God. Consider the following passage from one of Thomas' late works, *De malo.*

> On this point we must note that in general some divine help is necessary for every rational creature, namely, the help of sanctifying grace, which every rational creature needs to enable him to arrive at complete happiness. . . . But over and above this help, another supernatural help was necessary for man because of his composite nature.[22]

This passage introduces a slight nuance and improvement from his earlier treatment of this subject in the *Summa Theologiae*. When Thomas considers what it means for Adam and Eve to have been created in grace, he speaks mostly of the supernatural *auxilium* of original righteousness. Thanks to this supernatural gift, the composite nature of human beings did not burden or hinder the intellect from attaining the summit of contemplation. By this gift, Adam and Eve's powers of reason were subject to God, their passions to reason, and their bodies to their souls.[23] That this ordering is from grace rather than from nature is evident in that it does not remain after the fall. What *De malo* explains with greater clarity than the *Summa* is that the divine *auxilium* of original righteousness is not sufficient to render human beings deiform. In addition to the right ordering of their composite nature, Adam and Eve needed another aid if they were to attain the highest good that they were capable of, namely eternal beatitude in God. This second aid is sanctifying grace. The first *auxilium* is a kind of aptitude (*quasi dispositio*) for the second *auxilium*. In other words, in the original state, Adam and Eve needed and received not one but two supernatural gifts and aids: original justice and sanctifying grace. Had Adam and Eve not rejected these divine aids in favor of the serpent's self-help suggestion, they would have attained the Beatific vision.

Therefore, the *imago creationis* in the state of innocence must be seen as perfectible. In light of this assertion, the *exitus-reditus* schema cannot be understood as a simple return or restoration to the original state (as in Origenism), for that would fail to secure our inability to fall again or our hope of attaining our goal—union with God. The *imago similitudinis* surpasses the *imago creationis* both in its degree and mode of conformity to its exemplar. The perfectibility of Adam follows and presupposes the perfection of his nature.

Having briefly looked at how Aquinas understands the human in the state of innocence, we turn our attention to his treatment of what he calls the state of corrupt nature.[24]

To begin with, I must state in no uncertain terms that for Aquinas sin does not destroy the image of God in the human. The principal effect of original sin was the loss of the original justice with which Adam was endowed and not the erasure of the image.[25] With the privation of its primal rectitude, the original harmony and hierarchy of faculties in the human is destroyed, but not the faculties themselves. As Aquinas avers, "sin does not diminish nature."[26] Since the human is by nature a rational creature, the powers of the soul are neither destroyed nor diminished; they are disordered. The principal effect of sin, then, is to place obstacles in the way of the soul's ability to attain its proper end. Sin diminishes the inclination to virtue and the natural desire for the true and the good. However, sin does not and cannot destroy nature; sin merely wounds nature. Sin does not destroy the image's first perfection but prevents the attainment of its second perfection.

In the state of corrupt or wounded nature the image of God in the human is stained by sin.[27] By loving things that are contrary to the divine law and by cleaving to these very things, the soul defiles itself. The stain of sin on the soul is like a shadow that obscures the splendor of the divine light of wisdom and the natural light of reason. Note well, the light is not extinguished. Even after the fall, humans can do good things; indeed, they can do very good things, like build houses and plant vineyards.[28] Sin does not transform a human into something inhuman or subhuman; even as a sinner the human being is still made in the image of God, and thus still perfect according to the first perfection and perfectible by grace according to the second perfection.

In the state of innocence, Adam needed grace in order to both desire and do the supernatural good and in this way attain the *imago similitudinis*. However, after the fall, our natural powers are unable to properly accomplish many of the operations that pertain to our nature.[29] Under the condition of sin, we need grace for a reason that Adam did not. We need grace to be healed. Grace is God's medicine for restoring health to our wounded nature. Despite the varieties and degrees of grace that Thomas considers, all grace has one cause and one end—God. God alone causes grace, and God alone deifies.

The gift of grace (*donum gratiae*) is nothing less than a kind of partaking (*quaedam participatio*) of the divine nature.[30] The state of grace begins what the state of glory completes. The whole concept of grace is foreign to the pagan world, and only appears, at least latently, in the Old Testament's assurance of God's assistance to the just Israelite. It is in the New Testament, where the notion of divine assistance is identified with the gift of the Holy Spirit, that the concept of grace becomes manifest. The implications of the relation of grace and the Holy Spirit are clarified and taught by the church fathers as the doctrine of divinization. This doctrine arguably achieves its culminating synthesis and formulation in Thomas.

In his study on the doctrine of grace in Aquinas, Morency warns us that in order to understand the greatness of Aquinas' doctrine of God's indwelling of the just through grace, we must eschew three misunderstandings of this teaching.[31] First, we must avoid reading a false mysticism into Aquinas: "St Thomas n'attribue donc à Dieu aucune causalité intrinsèque, matteriélle ou formelle, en quelque sens que se soit."[32] God neither absorbs the person into his essence, nor does he simply take over the person's faculties. In uniting himself to the just, God becomes present to the soul in a manner that is "quasi formelle," with emphasis on the "quasi." When God regenerates a person, he does not communicate to the person a new nature on the order of substance, but a "quasi-nature," an intrinsic accident or *habitus*.[33]

Second, in reading Thomas' teaching on grace, we must avoid falling into naturalism. God is present in all things *per essentiam, potentiam et praesentiam*.[34] This means that God is both the efficient cause of all things and their exemplar. To put it another way, God's presence in the creature and the perfection of the creature in God are related. The more perfect the creature, that is to say, the more the creature resembles God, the more intensive is God's efficient causality on it, and therefore the more God is present to the creature. At the other end of this spectrum, so to speak, from this general presence of God in the creature, there is the uniquely intimate mode of the presence of God with human nature called the hypostatic union. Only the incarnate Word enjoys this profound degree of union with God. In between these two modes of presence (the spatial language here is of course metaphorical), there is a special mode of divine presence in the just where not only God is the exemplar and efficient cause of the human action, but God also comes to inhabit the soul, becoming the principle of its operations through an infused supernatural *habitus*—grace.

When speaking of the various manners in which God is present in the just, we need to distinguish clearly between the effects of this union in the natural and supernatural orders. While it is true that the just can and do enjoy a union with God at the level of nature due to God's common mode of presence in the creature or by the intellectual creature's similitude to God, there is a privileged or graced modality to this union that exceeds the capabilities of nature. As Morency avers,

> Par la grâce, Dieu est donc au plus intime de l'âme non seulement en modelant efficienment en elle sa propre image, et en se l'unissant ainsi par une union de passion et assimilation, mais ainsi en attirant suavement l'âme à soi, et an se l'unissant par une union de finalisation Dieu est le bien infini, présent dans l'âme, qui éveille et entretient en elle le désir de le posséder immédiatement et pleinement, par la connaissance et par l'amour.[35]

For Thomas, grace unites God and the human by being the term of the efficient, exemplary, and final cause of the person's conformity to God. Every effect is related to its origin, and grace, as an effect of God, brings God into the person. It makes us deiform, divine by participation, and orients us to God as our final end. Moreover, by becoming the formal extrinsic (never intrinsic) cause of our actions, grace allows us to attain God himself and maintains us in deep and intimate communion with him.

Third, we must not read Thomas' doctrine of grace in separation from his doctrine of the Trinity. The temporal divine missions of the Son and the Spirit, which are grounded in the eternal Trinitarian processions, establish a new mode of God's presence in creation. This new mode of presence can manifest itself visibly, as in the incarnation of the Word (or the descent of the Spirit as a dove), or it can manifest itself invisibly, as in the Trinity's presence in the just by habitual grace. It is in this last modality of God's presence that we can speak of fitting appropriation of the different degrees and objects of this divine presence by different persons of the Trinity. As Morency explains,

> C'est par un quadruple lien que la grâce se rattache à Dieu: l'union de passion qui peut être attribuée, par appropriation, au Père ; l'union d'assimilation qui peut être attribuée, par appropriation, au Fils ; l'union de finalisation qui peut être attribuée, par appropriation, à l'Esprit-Saint ; l'union d'opération, dont le terme est la Trinité : Père, Fils et Esprit-Saint.[36]

By grace, Christians attain a higher knowledge of God than is possible by natural reason. The natural light of the intellect is assisted by the light of faith so that the person can attain knowledge of God that exceeds the reach of unaided reason (e.g., the Trinity of persons in God), and also to gain greater clarity about those things that natural reason attains but with difficulty and error (e.g., the existence of God). As we saw in the last chapter, for Thomas, the virtue of faith does not raise the human intellect above the human mode of knowing. In this life, even the Christian does not know God as he is; faith unites us to God as to something almost altogether unknown: *quasi ignoto*.[37]

Within the state of grace, there are two exceptional cases where knowledge exceeds the natural mode of knowing: the gift of prophecy and the phenomenon of rapture. The common mode of knowledge for all creatures here below, even in the state of grace, is that of *scientia acquisita*. The light of reason, illumined and strengthened by the light of faith, considers the truths proposed by divine revelation. However, Thomas recognizes a higher mode of knowledge that he associates with the gift of prophecy and the life of contemplation; this knowledge is called *scientia infusa*. In this kind of knowledge, the intelligible species is not abstracted from phantasms but is directly imprinted or infused by God. In this life, humans do not possess this *scientia infusa* in the form of a habit, but the impression of the prophetic light (*lumen propheticum*) might leave a certain disposition (*quaedam habilitas*) to further illuminations.[38] In addition to the knowledge that comes from the gift of prophecy, there is the knowledge that comes from the phenomenon of rapture. Ordinarily, the vision of the divine essence belongs only to the saints in heaven; for this reason it is called the *scientia beata*. However, Aquinas considers the phenomenon of rapture as a genuine, if fleeting, participation in this kind of knowledge. Like Paul or Moses, the person who is raptured participates in the science of the saints but does not possess the habit of this knowledge: *in raptu non fuit beatus habitualiter, sed solum habuit actum beatorum.*[39] In this case, the habit of faith remains but not the act of faith.

To summarize, in the state of grace the perfection of knowledge usually consists in the *scientia acquisita* by faith with the support of the gifts. But the normal, if transitory and uncommon, peak of perfection is reached in infused contemplation (*scientia infusa*) and rapture. Thus, one might say that the perfection of knowledge that is possible in this life is more passive than active; it consists not so much in learning as in suffering divine things.

Having considered the summits of the state of grace, let us turn our attention to the state of glory, our *perfectio ultima*. The final goal of the human is the happiness of heaven. What is happiness? Aquinas rules out any notion of happiness that would be satisfied with created goods. Happiness does not consist in wealth, honors, fame, power, health, pleasure, or even in spiritual goods.[40] What does happiness consist in? "Final and perfect happiness can consist in nothing else than the vision of the divine essence."[41] However the questions arise: Can anyone see God? And if we see it, is it God? On the authority of Scripture Aquinas answers in the affirmative: "When he shall appear, we shall be like to him; because (Vulgate) we shall see him as he is" (1 John 3:2). However, Thomas knows that appeals to authority are the pedagogically weakest kinds of argumentation, so he offers a probable speculative argument to illuminate the teaching of Scripture.

> The ultimate beatitude of man consists in the use of his highest function, which is the operation of the intellect; if we suppose that the created intellect could never see God, it would either never attain to beatitude, or its beatitude would consist in something else beside God; which is opposed to faith.[42]

Nothing less than seeing the divine essence will make us happy. However, Thomas sets strict limits to human knowledge of God. As we have already observed, the common doctor consistently teaches that it is possible to know *that* God is (*an sit*), but it is not possible to know *what* God is (*quid sit*).[43] God is not unknown because he is beyond reason. In himself, God is supremely intelligible (*maxime cognoscibile in se*), but not to us. As the light of the sun exceeds the visual capacity of an owl, God's very intelligibility (*propter excessum intelligibilis*) overwhelms our understanding. Hence, to know God lies beyond the power of the created intellect. The natural light of our intellect is sufficiently strong to attain a natural knowledge of God. We can through consideration of created effects be led to their first uncreated cause, and in this way know that God exists.[44]

However, if we are to know God more profoundly, God himself must raise our intellect beyond its nature (*ultra suam naturam*).[45] As we have already discussed, this elevation happens by grace among the baptized and it is perfected by the light of glory among the blessed.

By the light of glory, the blessed see the divine essence, not a similitude of the essence, not an image, but the essence itself. This light is not a medium in which (*in quo*) God is seen but by which (*sub quo*) God is seen.[46] Even in the state of glory, things are known according to the mode of the knower (*cognitio autem est in cognoscente secundum modum cognoscentis*),[47] but the light of glory elevates the human mode of knowing and renders it deiform so as to be capable of receiving the divine essence.

The degree to which a person sees this divine essence will vary not on account of any natural intellectual predisposition to it, since this vision exceeds the power of nature, but according to the degree of charity. The more one has the virtue of charity, the more one participates in the light of glory. The more one participates in the light of glory, the more this light elevates our intellect and the more perfectly we see God.[48] The reason for this correspondence of charity and vision is that charity increases desire for the thing known, in this case God, and the more we desire union with God, the more we are in some way (*quodammodo*) rendered able and fit (*aptum et paratum*) for this union.

Aquinas clearly teaches that in the state of glory, although we are able to attain God (*attingere*), we are not able to comprehend him: *comprehendere Deum impossibile est cuicumque intellectui creato*.[49] In heaven, we will know God as perfectly as he can be known by us, but not as perfectly as God knows himself. We will not possess the science of God (*scientia divina*) but the science of the saints (*scientia beatorum*). In this unbroken and insuperable act of knowing and loving God we humans attain our final perfection.[50]

The State of the Perfect

So far we have considered the various theological states along the way, from first to final perfection. Each of these states is characterized by a condition of theological freedom or servitude, which limits or empowers human action within that state. A number of questions can be asked at this point. Are perfect freedom from sin and freedom for perfect love possible in this life? And in what theological state can one be perfect? Is the second perfection of the human, the final perfection of knowing and loving God, attainable only in the state of glory? These questions lie at the heart of our study.

To begin with, according to Aquinas, the bar for perfection is quite high. "The perfection of the Christian life consists radically in charity."[51]

As we have seen, charity is the basis of our union with God; it is a friendship, a participation in God's own loving, and a communication of goods and indeed of our very selves. Without charity I am nothing (cf. 1 Cor 13:2), but when charity is present in the soul, all the theological virtues, the moral virtues, and the gifts of the Spirit are present too. For this reason, as Aquinas avers, "Charity is called the mother of the other virtues."[52] When charity is perfect in the soul, all virtues and gifts are also perfect. However, this is a goal to be attained: having some perfect virtues is not enough. The perfection of charity requires the fullness of faith, hope, fortitude, temperance, prudence, and justice. In other words, there is no room for vice in the perfect.[53] Having set the bar for the perfection of the Christian life at this level of excellence, we would expect it to be impossible to attain perfection in this life. But we have the dominical command, "Be perfect as your father in heaven is perfect" (Matt 5:48), and God does not command the impossible.

In order to understand how charity can be perfect in this life, Thomas, not surprisingly, draws a threefold distinction that we need to attend to. First, the perfection of charity may be considered on the part of the beloved, namely God. In this case, perfection would mean that God is loved as much as God is lovable. This perfection is not possible for any creature either in this life or the one to come. Only God can love himself as much as he is lovable. Second, the perfection of charity may be considered on the part of the lover. In this sense, perfection would mean that someone loves God as much as is humanly possible—so that the lover's thoughts and motions actually and not just habitually tend to God. This perfection is not possible for the pilgrim on the way but only for those who have entered heaven. Third, the perfection of charity may be considered on the part of the lover, not as the lover loves God in every act, but as the lover removes obstacles contrary to the love of God. This is the perfection that can be attained in this life. At its lowest level such a perfection consists in removing from our affections those things that kill charity—mortal sin.

All Christians are called, at the very least, not to love anything contrary to God. This degree of perfection is common to all Christians and required for salvation. However, a higher degree of perfection than this is possible in this life. This more perfect perfection consists in removing from the affections not only those things that are contrary to charity, but also those things that hinder a complete dedication to God. In such circumstances, a person moved by love not only refrains from what is hostile to God but sets aside even lawful things so as to dedicate himself more fully to God's service. This is the degree of perfection that is codified in the evangelical counsels. However, the perfection of this life does not consist primarily in keeping these counsels or in experiencing mystical ecstasies. At best these rules and experiences are means to or fruits of perfection. Perfection itself consists in joyful obedience of the law of love.

All humans need to respond wholeheartedly to the call to love God and neighbor. As Thomas states, "The perfection of divine love is a matter of precept for all without exception, so that even the perfection of heaven is not excepted from this precept."[54] To reiterate, a degree of perfection in love is necessary for salvation, and no one dare set a limit on what obedience of the divine precept entails. The Christian's love of God and neighbor cannot settle for the least possible level of perfection and leave the rest as a matter of counsel. Perfection is not optional; it is not something only for monks and mendicants; all Christians without exception are called to be perfect as their Father in heaven is perfect. In attaining this perfection, the counsels are helpful—Aquinas calls them "schools of perfection." The counsels are helpful in removing the hindrances to the concrete practice of charity. However, the counsels are only means to perfection and are not themselves constitutive of perfection.

Perfection of charity is the chief goal of the Christian life. Has anyone attained this goal? Thomas clearly asserts that Jesus and Mary are perfect, but of course their way is quite different from the rest of humanity; they were born perfect.[55] Has anyone started out as beginner and become proficient enough to attain perfection? Thomas' theology as *scientia* focuses on universals, not particulars, but he does think that many people are saints. First, there are the martyrs. Martyrdom is the greatest proof of the perfection of charity.[56] In the martyrs we witness that love which for the sake of the beloved lays aside everything, even life itself. The martyrs exhibit the highest degree of Christlike obedience, being obedient unto death. Second, there are the bloodless martyrs, the saints. While still in this life these saints exhibited such a high degree of virtue that their holiness was widely recognized and allowed for their veneration after death. One interesting characteristic of Aquinas' hagiology is that it allows for differentiation. Just because one is perfect in charity does not mean that one is reduced to homogenous anonymity. On the contrary, some saints are known more for one virtue than for another.[57] In any case, the saints are the "perfect wayfarers."[58] Their perfection in this life consisted not in their freedom from all sin (venial sins are not incompatible with the habit of perfect charity),[59] nor in their indefectibility (the perfect can fall from the state of grace by committing a mortal sin, though this does not happen easily or suddenly),[60] but in their resolve to give God all their time and attention. This is the chief distinguishing mark of the perfect. Christian beginners concern themselves with avoiding sin and resisting concupiscence. More proficient Christians dedicate themselves to making progress toward the good by growing in virtue. The perfect Christian's chief preoccupation is simply union with God.[61]

The State of Perfection

The state of the perfect and the state of perfection are not identical. The perfection of charity is what the theological *status perfectorum* consists in and what the ecclesial *status perfectionis* is constituted for. In order to elucidate the distinction between the state of the perfect and the state of perfection, Thomas reminds us of the parable of the two sons in Matthew 21:28. A father asks his two sons to go work in the vineyard. The first son said he would not go, but then changes his mind and goes. The second son said he would go, but then does not. The first son is the one who is perfect, for without binding himself to do his father's will he goes and does it anyway. The second son is the one who is in the state of perfection; he has bound himself to his father's will and yet has failed to do it. From this parable, Aquinas draws several pertinent conclusions. First, one can be perfect (*status perfectorum*) without being in a state of perfection (*status perfectionis*). One can be a lay person living in the world raising a family and be perfect. Second, it is possible to be in a state of perfection (*status perfectionis*) and be far from perfection (*status perfectorum*). Sadly, there are wicked bishops and lazy monks. Nevertheless, the fact that those in the *status perfectionis* have not attained the *status perfectorum* does not void the former from significance.

> Those who enter the state of perfection do not profess to be perfect, but to tend to perfection . . . hence a man who takes up the state of perfection is not guilty of lying or deceit through not being perfect, but through withdrawing his mind from the intention of reaching perfection.[62]

Within the ecclesial state of perfection Aquinas focuses his attention on two states: the episcopal and the religious. The episcopal state is the highest state of perfection because bishops are in the position of being perfecters. What Aquinas means by perfecter in this case does not have to do primarily with the conspicuousness of the prelates' personal holiness,[63] though Aquinas does insist that since bishops are perfecters they must already have attained a certain degree of perfection *before* their consecration into the episcopal state: "One needs to be perfect in order to bring others to perfection."[64] The perfection of life that is requisite for the episcopal state need not be the full perfection of charity but one that displays a certain capacity for governing the church in peace.[65] Given the high standard expected of bishops, the episcopal state is not one that can ever be lawfully aspired to; it can only be humbly received, not sought.[66]

The religious state is different; monks, nuns, and mendicants are in the position of being perfected. The religious state is a school instituted for the attainment of the perfection of charity.[67] As such, one who enters religion need not be perfect nor act in accordance with perfect charity; for the religious state it is enough to want to attain perfection and to seal this desire with a solemn vow. Life in this school is rigorous; in order to advance one must be willing to sacrifice. The religious makes his whole self available to God and solemnizes this self-immolation by making vows of poverty, chastity, and obedience. Each of these vows schools the religious on the way to perfection. By means of the vow of poverty, the religious offers to God his material goods and withdraws his affections from earthly things. By means of the vow of perpetual continence, the religious offers to God his body by giving up the pleasure of sexual union and the gift of children. By means of the vow of obedience, the religious offers to God something greater than his goods or body: his will. These vows are efficient exercises for removing those things that hinder us from dedicating ourselves fully to the service of God and the exercise of charity.

By singling out religious orders for special mention, Aquinas is not being simply a mendicant apologist but a good spiritual master. Thomas does not merely define perfection and leave us there; he encourages us to enroll in schools of perfection. You do not have to become a Dominican to be perfect (though Aquinas is convinced that the Order of Preachers is the most perfect of schools). There are different schools of perfection, each with their own particular emphasis.[68] Aquinas reminds us that some religious orders were established for those leading an active life and some for those leading the contemplative life. Some orders were dedicated to soldiering, some for preaching, and others for study. It is almost as if Aquinas wants to tell his readers, there is an order out there for each one of them. These Schools have open enrollment for all who would be perfect and a curriculum of exercises to help its students attain this goal.

By this point, readers of Thomas could be forgiven if they regarded the angelic doctor's understanding of perfection as clericalist, but Thomas is not suggesting that all Christians should be monks; diversity is intrinsic to the nature and perfection of the church. As Thomas avers, "*diversitas in membris Ecclesiae ad tria ordinatur, scilicet ad perfectionem, actionem et decorem.*"[69] One might expect a representative of Christendom to say otherwise. One might expect him to say that difference is repugnant to unity, or that diversity is an obstacle to peace. Some people (like Joachim of Fiore) did advance arguments of this sort, but Aquinas was utterly opposed to such views. According to the common doctor, diversity is essential for the perfection of the church, but the diversity that Thomas speaks of is not based on social or ethnic differences but rather on the Spirit who bestows upon the church a diversity of gratuitous graces (*secundum diversas gratias gratis datas*), a diversity of kinds of life (*secundum diversas vitas*), and a diversity of states (*secundum diversitatem officiorum et statuum*).[70] It is important to notice that even though these distinctions correspond to the hierarchical structures of the medieval church, their origin is biblical. Let us consider Thomas' interpretation of a well-known Pauline statement on the theological origins of ecclesial diversity.

> Now there are varieties of gifts, but the same Spirit; and there are varieties of services, but the same Lord; and there are varieties of activities, but it is the same God who activates all of them in everyone. To each is given the manifestation of the Spirit for the common good. (1 Cor 12:4-7)

The diversity of the church results from a variety of gifts. All Christians receive sanctifying grace; they receive the theological virtues and the infused moral virtues so as to be rendered holy and acceptable to God. All Christians by virtue of their union with Christ through baptism receive the gifts of the Holy Spirit.[71] However, not all Christians receive the gift of prophecy or the other gifts of the Spirit that are given to some for the purpose of leading others to God; these graces are for the purpose of building up the church. For instance, when Paul speaks of faith as a gift alongside the gift of healing, he is not referring to the virtue of faith by which we believe in our hearts that God raised Jesus from the dead, but to the gift that permits someone to expound persuasively and rightly on the matters of faith (like announcing the resurrection of the dead in the Areopagos). The virtue of faith is common to all Christians but the gift of articulating this faith is not. Yet, every Christian receives a measure of some charism[72] and is called to aspire to even greater gifts.[73] In other words, for Thomas, the *gratiae gratis datae* are to some extent experienced by all believers and should be desired by all. The question of prophecy in the *Summa Theologiae* is not some theological excursus included for the sake of theological thoroughness but an integral part of Aquinas' virtue ethic. By sanctifying grace the Holy Spirit indwells and perfects the believer; by charismatic graces the Holy Spirit is made manifest so as to confirm the truth of the church's teaching,[74] and in some cases, to confirm the holiness of certain persons.[75]

The diversity of the church results from a variety of kinds of life and activities. The division of life into active and contemplative is not the result of the diversity of ministries but a diversity of intentions on the part of the agent.[76] This diversity of intentions is constituted by the division of the intellect into the speculative, whose end is knowledge of the truth (*cognitio veritatis*), and the practical, whose end is an external action (*exterior actio*).[77] In the words of Gregory the Great, whom Aquinas quotes, "the contemplative life is to cling with our whole mind to the love of God and our neighbor, and to desire nothing beside our creator."[78] The active life pertains to those spheres of activity that are uniquely human; a life dedicated to eating and procreation might be suitable for animals but not for rational creatures, whose proper operations are intellectual. For Thomas, the contemplative life and the active life truly are different, but this division must not harden into separation; these two manners of life are not mutually exclusive. Embracing the contemplative life does not mean that one does not act in charity towards the neighbor, nor does abiding in the active life mean that one has given up on loving God. It is the main intention of someone's actions, his life orientation, so to speak, that distinguishes one manner of life from the other. In other words, Aquinas is not setting up an antithesis between the practical and the theoretical, nor between the moral and the intellectual, but an order. On the one hand, the active life is ordered toward the contemplative because the moral virtues of the active life dispose people to the contemplative life. On the other hand, the contemplative life can overflow into the active.[79] So, it is not simply that the active life is a prequel to the contemplative but that in the contemplative life a return to the active can be a help to deeper contemplation.[80] Indeed, as his reflections on the various kinds of religious life show, a mixed life of action and contemplation is to be preferred to the active life or even to the contemplative life, because by leading such a manner of life one is not only enlightened, but a light that enlightens others *ex plenitudine contemplationis*.[81]

The diversity of the church results from a variety of states. The gratuitous graces, the contemplative life, the state of perfection are all things pertain to some persons in particular, but in a qualified sense they are proper to the habits and actions of all humans. The virtuous life and the "ecclesial" life are inextricably connected. The moral virtues are dispositively related to the gratuitous graces[82] and contemplation,[83] as well as being teleologically related to the various states of life since the goal of all states is the state of perfect (*status perfectorum*)[84] which is greatly advanced by the state of perfection (*status perfectionis*), which as we have seen, is nothing but a school of virtue.[85]

In sum, the final questions on the diveristy of gifts, lives, and states in the *Secunda Secundae* are not propaganda promoting the benefits of joining the Order of Preachers, but a theological meditation on the social character of Christian holiness.[86] Perfection is not God's gift to a particularly pious individual but a gift to and through the church. Granted, the way to perfection is greatly aided by living in an intentional community such as the Dominican order. However, only the church is the primary community and the foundation for the way of perfection. Perfection is not attained through the heroic ascetic practice but through Christ's grace. Only in the church is the grace of God mediated to us in an orderly and dependable way through the sacraments—outside the church there is no Christian perfection. In order to clarify this connection between the perfection of the Christian and the perfection of the church we need to turn to the final part of our inquiry into Thomas' doctrine of perfection: the perfection of Christ.

Jesus Christ, the Way of Perfection

Duplex est perfectio, and there are many states between the creation of the image and its consummation in glory but only one way to perfection: Jesus Christ *via est nobis tendendi in Deum.* The placement of Christology at the end of the *Summa Theologiae* might lead us to think that the person of Christ is vestigial to Thomas' theological oeuvre. Is the *Tertia Pars* an appendix to an otherwise complete opus? Do we not find here the confirmation of the worst suspicions about Scholastic theology, namely that it is little more than half-baptized philosophy? On the contrary, the deferral of Christology to the Third Part of the *Summa* is, in the words of Torrell, "a deliberate decision to reclaim Christ's role in the creature's movement of return toward God and in the fulfillment of the history of salvation."[87] Differently said, Thomas' doctrine of perfection is christocentric.[88] This christocentrism is built into the *Summa Theologiae*, and also plays a central role in Wesley's theology, which described the goal of Christian perfection by means of two biblical images: "to have the same mind that was found in Christ Jesus" (Phil 2:5) and "to walk as he walked" (1 John 2:6). At the same time Wesley and Thomas eschew any semblance of christomonism in theology; their understanding of perfection grounded on the doctrine of the image of God is thoroughly Trinitarian.

Thomas' teaching of Christology is divided into two sections. First, he treats the mystery of the incarnation of Christ. Second, he treats the mysteries of the life of Christ. Let us look at each of these in turn.

The *Tertia Pars* of the *Summa* opens with an extended treatment of the incarnation of the Word. Though Thomas did not state it in these terms, we might say that Questions 1 through 26 of the *Tertia Pars* are not just a treatise *de incarnatione Christi* but *de perfectione Christi*. Unlike in the *Summa Contra Gentiles*, the Christology here is not in the service of apologetics but of spiritual theology. The thrust of these opening questions of the Third Part is not simply to defend the *verus homo, verus Deus* of Scripture against those who argued for *purus homo* or *purus Deus*, but to show how Christ is the way of perfection.

Obviously, this is not the place to unfold Thomas' Christology in detail, but a few observations are pertinent to our study. First, Christ's humanity is perfect by virtue of the hypostatic union. As Wawrykow makes clear in a brief but helpful study on Thomas' Christology, Aquinas condemns two accounts of the incarnation popular at the time, the *homo-assumptus* theory and the *habitus* theory.[89] Instead, Thomas introduces a finely nuanced subsistence theory. A person, as we earlier saw in the last chapter, is an individual substance of a rational nature. In the case of human beings, the rational nature is individuated by matter but subsists by God's granting of *esse*. In our case this *esse* is a created *esse*, but in the case of Jesus, this *esse* is the *ipsum esse subsistens* which the Word shares with the assumed human nature.

> Esse aeternum filii Dei quod est divina natura, fit esse hominis, inquantum humana natura assumitur a filio Dei in unitate personae.[90]

The second christological affirmation for us to keep in mind as we move forward with our study is that Thomas, in agreement with other scholastic theologians, regarded Christ as both a *viator* and a *comprehensor*. That is to say, in addition to the divine knowledge that was his as the eternal Word of the Father, Christ had both beatific knowledge and infused knowledge.[91] Like the saints in heaven, Christ was a *comprehensor* who saw the divine *esse* in the light of glory. Like the saints on earth, Christ had infused knowledge that came not from phantasms but from the direct imprinting of intelligible species on his intellect. Like all of us here below, Christ learned from experience. Unlike his contemporaries, and even some of his own earlier writings, Thomas asserted that Christ also had naturally acquired knowledge. His sensory apparatus and brain are not there merely for show, or for the sake of the completeness of the incarnation; his eyes, ears, and gray matter are there to be used. As Thomas explains, *nihil eorum quae Deus in nostra natura plantavit, defuit naturae assumptae a verbo Dei.*[92]

The third and final christological affirmation that is important for us to consider at this point of our study is that St. Thomas of the Creator[93] regarded everything naturally human as good and assumable by God. In assuming a passible body and soul, even the passions are taken up by Christ: *veram naturam humanam scepisse cum omnibus naturalibus affectibus.*[94] For the Stoics, the passions were evil, a disease of the soul; growth in virtue consisted in being cured of the passions.[95] For Thomas, the passions are an integral part of human nature and worthy of serious consideration. Indeed, when ruled by reason, the passions can aid in the attainment of virtue. For these reasons, Aquinas says that Christ assumed the passions, though he immediately clarifies that they do not rule over him in the same way that they sometimes rule over us.[96]

One important point to take away from these brief remarks on Thomas' Christology is that the angelic doctor emphasizes the humanity of Christ with a vigor that is unusual among other scholastic or even patristic theologians.[97] Everything truly human is assumed by Christ; even those aspects of human nature that we share with other animals like our *natura animalia* are assumed and perfected by Christ.[98] What about sin? No, for Scripture tells us that Christ was like us in every way "yet without sin" (Heb 4:15). But is not a sinless Christ less than truly human? Not for Thomas, because *peccatum non pertinet ad naturam humanam.*[99]

If we can call Questions 1 through 26 of the *Tertia Pars* a treatise *de perfectione Christi*, we might refer to Questions 27 through 59 as *de perfectione vitae Christi.* To phrase it another way, the former questions treat the first perfection of humanity, the latter questions the second. The structure of these questions is in itself a miniature model of the *Summa*; it begins with Christ's entry into the world, followed by his manner of living in the world and concluding with his departure from the world. The chief running thread throughout Thomas' exposition of the life of Christ is that of fittingness or *convenientia.* This is not surprising given the contingency of concrete historical events where questions of "why now?" and "why this way?" are inevitable. However, one interesting feature of Thomas' reflection on this topic is that while he asserts that all things that Christ did or suffered occurred in a fitting way, he is nevertheless very cautious to avoid saying that they had to happen in this way. The *acta* and *passa* of Christ are a matter of *convenientia*, not *neccesitas.*

The manner of Christ's life is of particular significance for our study because it is here that we see the most concrete manifestation of the second perfection of the human—the perfection of operation. In Question 40 of the *Tertia Pars*, Thomas reflects on the particular way in which Christ lived.[100] Elsewhere, the angelic doctor considers what Jesus said and did (teachings and miracles), but here, Thomas' attention is drawn to his manner of life. In particular, he is interested in how Jesus relates to other people, things, and traditions, or to put it another way, he is interested in Jesus as a social animal.

For Thomas, the life of Christ has a kind of double significance for the Christian. On the one hand, everything in Christ's way of life was for us and for our salvation: *conversatio Christi talis debuit esse ut conveniret fini incarnationis*.[101] A few examples might prove helpful. First, consider Jesus' embrace of poverty.[102] It was fitting that Jesus was poor because this manner of life advanced the cause of his coming. His detachment from worldly goods gave Jesus the freedom to travel from town to town without being burdened by worldly affairs. Moreover, with his poverty Jesus stopped the mouths of those who might charge him with preaching for profit. Second, consider Jesus' observance of the law. By keeping the Torah, Christ testified to its divine origin and abiding validity, but in addition to this, he actually fulfilled the Law and brought it to completion in himself. By submitting to circumcision, attending the synagogue, and obeying the commandments, Christ exegeted the christological orientation of the law (*ad ipsum erat ordinata*) and delivered us from subjection to the law as an end in itself. These two characteristics of Jesus' life—his poverty and his Jewishness—are perfectly suited to meet the purpose of the incarnation: our salvation.

On the other hand, every act of Christ was for our instruction: *dominus in sua conversatione exemplum perfectionis dedit in omnibus quae per se pertinent ad salutem*.[103] By learning what conditions of life are fitting for the incarnation, we also learn what conditions of life are fitting for perfection. Consider, for example, Jesus' practice of associating with other people. Christ called disciples; visited homes; attended weddings: Christ led a social life. Yet it seems that he should not have. According to Aristotle, humans are political animals; society is integral to our survival, and those who live by themselves without the benefits of neighbors are either beastlike or divine. So it seems that Jesus, being divine, should have lived alone. Moreover, as Thomas himself established earlier,[104] the contemplative life is more excellent than the active. So again, it seems that Christ should have withdrawn from the world of human interactions to dedicate himself solely to the service of God. Yet Thomas keenly observes that Christ's manner of life was not for his sake but for ours. His association with other people does not satisfy the needs of his life but the ends of the incarnation. By making friends with fishermen and eating with sinners, Jesus opened the way to salvation and also showed us that the most perfect life is not, strictly speaking, the contemplative one, but the mixed life, which out of the fullness of contemplation perfects others by preaching and teaching.

In sum, the double significance of the perfection of Christ's life for us can be stated in this way. Christ's manner of life was perfect in order to show us what perfection is and to lead us to this perfection. Christ is both the efficient cause and the exemplary cause of our perfection. So if anyone would be perfect, he or she must turn to Christ, *quia natura humana in ipsa incarnatione est perducta ad summam perfectionem*.[105]

The perfection of the Christian begins with the humanity of Christ both in its instrumentality and exemplarity. For although God is both knowable and lovable in himself, on account of our intellectual weakness humans need to be led by the hand from sensible things to divine things: *ut dum visibiliter Deum cognoscimus, per hunc in invisibilium amorem rapiamur.*[106] The humanity of Christ is this helping hand in three ways.

First, we are made perfect through the contemplation of Christ. The contemplation of all things pertaining to Jesus in the days of his flesh offers the Christian, in the words of Torrell, "a kind of pedagogy supremely adapted to lead to his divinity."[107] The contemplation of Christ and his life both causes and increases the devotion whereby Christians surrender themselves to God. However, for Thomas, the life of Christ is not all evenly weighted; Christ's exemplarity reaches its greatest intensity at the cross. The Dominican preacher likes appealing to 1 Peter 2:21 in this regard: "Because Christ also suffered for you, leaving you an example, so that you should follow in his footsteps." The mystery of Christ's passion provides us with the perfect example of patience, humility, love, and self-denial. If anyone would be perfect they must contemplate the crucified Christ: *Quicumque enim vult perfecte vivere, nihil aliud faciat nisi quod contemnat quae Christus in cruce contempsit, et appetat quae Christus appetit.*[108]

Second, we are made perfect through the imitation of Christ; the perfection of Christ's humanity in nature and history is our ontological and moral exemplar. As the ontological exemplar, Christ is the source of all grace, the head of the church, and the head of the human race. As the eternal Word, the Son is the primordial principle of the procession of all things from God. Jesus is the image of the invisible God, the firstborn of all creation (cf. Col 1:15), and in this way he is the exemplar of spiritual creatures. However, this exemplar is too far above us: *Hoc autem exemplar Dei prius erat a nobis valde remotum.*[109] Hence, the need for the incarnation of the Word; we need a divine model that is brought down to earth, so to speak. The brightness of all the saints (*splendores omnium sanctorum*), a brightness that originates from the spiritual graces and gifts that God pours on humanity, shines in Christ with incomparable though communicable intensity.[110] In the incarnation of the Word, the primordial exemplar becomes a human exemplar, but the latter only follows on the former.

As the incarnate image, Christ is both the principle and exemplar of all creatures in their procession from God (first perfection) and in their return to God (second perfection). In this way, in the words of John of Patmos, Christ is creation's Alpha and Omega, the *protos* and *eschatos*, the *arche* and *telos* (cf. Rev 22:13).

As the moral exemplar, Christ is the model we imitate and follow: *Christi humanitas sit nobis via tendendi in Deum.*[111] As our way to God, Christ is not a static road but a living way, a running stream. We imitate Christ by imitating his dispositions (humility and charity being chief among these), and also by imitating him as he imitates the one who sent him. Indeed, it is in this obediential relation that the holiness of Christ and the Christian consists: *In hoc est sanctitas hominis quod ad Deum vadat.*[112] Thomas' reflections on John 13:15 ("I have set you an example") deepen this theme.[113] Examples can be powerful motivators of human action: *plus movent exempla quam verba.*[114] However, a merely human example would not be able to provide a suitable basis for universal imitation, least of all for action that is to exceed human nature. Thus, there is need of the example of Christ as an infallible guide to human action. As the *ars patris* Jesus is the *exemplar creationis* and the *exemplar justificationis.*[115] So the exemplarity of Christ is not confined to his incarnation but it extends to the whole of his life.[116] Each event in the life of Jesus, from his nativity to his ascension, even his hidden life, is an *exemplum perfectionis.*[117] No aspect of Jesus' life is void of theological significance and exemplarity: *Christi actio fuit nostra instructio.*[118] This is the reason why Thomas spends an unusual amount of time meditating on the life of Christ.

Third, we are made perfect through participation in Christ. It is in the life of grace, a life nourished and sustained by the sacraments, that the perfection of humanity becomes possible. The sacraments are the *instrumentum separatum* of the divinity whose efficacy derives from the humanity of Christ, the *instrumentum coniunctum* of his divinity. To put it another way, the power of the sacraments comes from God *through* the humanity of Christ: *virtus salutifera derivetur a divinitate Christi per eius humanitatem in ipsa sacramenta.*[119]

In order to understand better the instrumentality of Christ's humanity and its effect on the sacraments, I will rely on Theophil Tschipke's important study of this topic.[120] Tschipke argues that, for Thomas, the humanity of Christ is not a passive instrument. It is not like a copper wire that can bear electricity but is otherwise inert. The humanity of Christ is not simply a channel or conduit for grace; it is an active means.[121] Even though the humanity of Christ is active, the source of its power is extrinsic. The humanity of Christ is not like an explosive whose power to work is intrinsic to its chemical composition; it is more like a chisel—it needs the hand of the artist to guide it and wield it in order to carve a statue out of a block of wood. Just as the form of the statue exceeds the capacity of the chisel to attain by itself, the power to perform miracles exceeds the capacity of the flesh of Christ by itself.

Only by serving as an *instrumentum* can the chisel carve the statue and the touch of Christ's hand heal the leper. However, whereas the chisel, like the sacrament, is an *instrumentum separatum* of the agent, the humanity of Christ is an *instrumentum coniunctum*. In the words of Tschipke,

> Les instruments conjoints se distinguent de ces derniers par ceci, qu'ils ne reçoivent pas l'énergie instrumentale de dehors, mais d'une source qui leur est intérieure.[122]

The source of this interior energy is the divine *esse* which the Son shares with the assumed human nature. However, because the humanity is truly an instrument of the divinity, the action of the latter is in some sense limited or marked by the former in a way analogous to how one's handwriting is affected by one's choice of pen.[123] By virtue of the hypostatic union, the humanity of Christ is perfected not just as a means of grace but as a principle of grace, and not only his humanity but also his operations are elevated and assume the character of proto-sacraments.[124] According to Thomas, the flesh of Christ and the life of Christ are raised by grace to become the *organum divinitatis*.[125] In this way, the humanity of Christ in its first and second perfection is possessed of instrumental force and efficacy and truly becomes the *instrumentum coniunctum* of the divinity. However, as Tschipke states, for Thomas

> La force instrumentale n'est pas donnée à l'humanité du Christ en vue de la perfection de son être, mais pour qu'elle devienne une source divine de salut.[126]

Christ is perfect not for his sake but for ours. By the grace of personal union, the flesh and doings of Jesus are sanctified above and beyond all so that he can become the source of sanctification for all: *Cum ergo sanctificatio Christi fuerit perfectissima, quia sic sanctificatus est ut esset aliorum sanctificatur*.[127] By participating in the sacraments (*instrumentum separatum*) Christians are perfected (*ad perficiendum animam*)[128] by the grace which comes through and from the humanity of Christ (*instrumentum coniunctum*). Perfection in Christ makes the Christian an *instrumentum separatum* of Christ.[129]

Conclusion

In this chapter we have considered Thomas' teaching on the states along the way of perfection. We looked at the various degrees of conformity that the image of God in the human traverses in its journey toward the exemplar. In particular, we looked at the state of the perfect where humans are free to love God and neighbor perfectly. The state of perfection, as an ecclesial state, is an invaluable aid in attaining this freedom, but perfection does not consist in keeping the evangelical counsels; perfection consists in following Christ, our way to perfection. By contemplating, imitating, and participating in Christ we conform to him and become instruments of his divinity for the perfection of the church and the cosmos.

Nevertheless, this talk of states and instruments is insufficiently specific or attentive to the dynamic character of Thomas' doctrine of perfection, which as we learned in the previous chapter is grounded in act: *aliquid esse perfectum, secundum quod est in actu.*[130] As we conclude our study of Thomas' doctrine of perfection, let us consider the *via perfectionis* from the vantage point of the typical *viator*.

A baby girl is born and, without having committed an actual sin, inherits the guilt and penalty of original sin. The church baptizes this child and in so doing both the stain and the punishment of original sin are removed. Regrettably, since concupiscence is not usually removed at baptism, the bent to sinning is still present, and, sooner or later, the child falls into mortal sin without possible recourse to a second baptism, baptism being unrepeatable. Thankfully, the church has been gifted with more than one sacrament. God gave the church the sacrament of penance as a second plank for those who have shipwrecked their faith.[131] Penance has the power to remove any post-baptismal sin, and by it the girl is restored to the same level of virtue she had before falling into sin.[132] Since each of the church's sacraments bestows grace and strengthens the virtues,[133] one might expect this girl to grow steadily in her conformity to the image of Christ and soon reach the summit of perfection that is possible in this life—the perfection of charity. We *should* expect this, especially when we consider that the Eucharist was instituted as the sacrament whose chief effect is precisely the increase of charity and the perfection of the spiritual life.[134] The girl grows into a youth and is strengthened through the sacrament of confirmation. She becomes a woman and decides in which state she will take her stand, lay or religious. The latter is a school of perfection and very helpful in furthering growth in holiness, but since perfection consists in the precepts not in the counsel, she decides without any detriment to her salvation to remain in the lay state and marries. As she raises a family, she continues to grow in grace by practicing charity, confessing her sins, and receiving the Eucharist. Finally, in the dusk of her mortal life, she receives the sacrament of extreme unction that removes any remainders of sin (*reliquiae peccati*) from her soul and prepares her for glorification.[135]

Did this baby grow up into a saint? Not necessarily. The way just described does not work with the mindless efficiency of a people mover that automatically carries both the indolent and the indefatigable to their destination. Most people do not die in an ecstasy of perfect love. How are we to understand the fact that such a clear way of perfection yields so few saints? We must account for two factors in this woman's movement on the way to perfection.

First, we must account for her fervor. The grace that a person receives from a sacrament is dependent upon the fervor or preparation of the person. For instance, the sacrament of baptism though usually producing the same effect on children, when administered to adults will bestow a lesser or greater amount of grace on the baptized in accordance with the lesser or greater devotion with which they approach the sacrament.[136] The same dependence of effect on disposition is evident in the reception of the Eucharist.[137] So, we may assert that the reason that not all people reach the perfection of charity is that not all desire it with the same intensity. Growth in perfection depends on the intensity of desire, but this is not a sufficient answer to our question.

Second, we must account for God's predestination for this woman.[138] I already hinted at this mystery by qualifying the equality of grace dispensed in the baptism of infants. When Aquinas addresses the question of equality of the effect of baptism on the baptized he draws a distinction between the essential effect of baptism and its accidental effect.[139] Its essential effect is spiritual regeneration, the begetting of children of God, but baptism may also have other effects, like absolutely eradicating the bent to sinning. Such an effect is accidental (non-essential) and is not given in proportion to any devotion on the part of the person being baptized but solely according to God's providence. Hence, the evident diversity that we see in the church between beginners, proficient, and perfect does not have its origin primarily in the fervor of the pilgrim. As Aquinas avers,

> He who is better prepared for grace, receives more grace. Yet it is not here that we must seek the first cause of this diversity, since man prepares himself only inasmuch as his free-will is prepared by God, who dispenses his gifts of grace variously, in order that the beauty and perfection of the Church may result from these various degrees; even as he instituted the various conditions of things, that the universe might be perfect.[140]

Thus, it is to God that we must turn in order to explain the variety of states and grades in the church. Certainly, we are confronted here with the mystery of God's predestination, and we cannot expect to understand why God dispenses his gift the way he does. Still, we can hope that God will give this woman the actual grace that she needs to persevere in the life of faith and that even in this life she will love God above all things and the neighbor like herself. If she does not, as long as she did not sin against love we need not despair of her eternal salvation, and yet her life will not shine with the beauty of holiness, which it could have otherwise had.

It would be a mistake to conclude from the story of this soul that Aquinas considers that some of us are simply not called to the perfection of charity. Perfection is a matter of precept, not counsel; holiness is not optional, and we can set no limits to love's claims upon our lives. We cannot even exclude the perfection of heaven as a proper response to God's love. Even so, the perfect, the heroically virtuous, are not self-made people. God alone makes saints. God perfects people like the woman in the preceding story so that he can dwell in them as in his own temple and so that through their lives and deeds some special aspect of the beauty and perfection of the church is made visible and concrete.

Chapter Five

Dialogue on the Beatitudes

We began our study of Wesley's doctrine of Christian perfection by considering the house-like structure of his theology. The Methodist house of religion is no English manor but a simple dwelling with a porch, a door, and an interior. The porch of this house is repentance; the door to this house is faith; the inside of the house is holiness itself.[1] When we turned to Aquinas the scene shifted tremendously. We found ourselves not before a humble if hospitable house, but before a Gothic cathedral that threatened to overwhelm us by its sheer scale. The interior of this cathedral is cavernous; there are such treasures in this place that centuries of Thomist commentators have not surveyed them all. Our study amounted to little more than a cursory walk through.

Looking at Wesley and Aquinas side by side it is easy to feel dizzied by the differences. Methodist house and Thomist cathedral, what can these two possibly have in common? Even when focused on a central doctrine, like perfection, the differences seem to be so great as to render any comparison as fruitless as that of the proverbial apples and oranges. Yet in the same way that both house and cathedral have generic common features (walls, roof, doors, etc.) that allow for comparison, so do Aquinas' and Wesley's respective teachings on perfection. The chief commonality that their teachings share is that they are grounded in the Scriptural Witness as interpreted by the Christian tradition. To be more precise, it is particularly in Jesus Christ's teaching on the Sermon on the Mount that both Wesley and Aquinas sketch their understanding of perfection.

The Sermon on the Mount represents the goal of the Christian life and in that sense defines the purpose for which the Methodist house and the Thomist cathedral were built in the first place—to lead people into union with God. In the case of Aquinas, not only is the Sermon on the Mount of teleological significance in his teaching, but also of structural significance for the *Summa Theologiae*, particularly in the *Secunda Pars*, where the Beatitudes are like so many flying buttresses holding up the infused theological and moral virtues against the gravitational pull of finitude and sin. Given the centrality of the Sermon on the Mount to both the Methodist house and the Thomist cathedral, we will devote ourselves in this chapter to sitting with Wesley and Aquinas as they listen to Jesus' teaching.

Wesley's Discourses upon the Sermon on the Mount

Wesley's interest in the Sermon on the Mount dates to the earliest days of his ministry. His second sermon was based on Matthew 6:33, and between the years 1739 and 1746 he preached over a hundred sermons from different texts in Matthew 5–7.[2] The thirteen discourses on the Sermon on the Mount that we are going to examine in this chapter were composed between 1748 and 1750; this is the time Wesley began the process of integrating the new insights he gained on the doctrine of justification from his contact with the Moravians into the doctrine of sanctification that he had received from Anglican divines such as William Law and Jeremy Taylor. In this sense, Wesley's discourses on the Sermon on the Mount can and should be read as significant pieces of Wesleyan theology. However, these sermons should also be read as Wesley's response to the challenges arising from the growth of rationalism and industrialism in eighteenth-century England.[3] In these discourses, Wesley is proclaiming a robust form of the gospel that challenges the reigning Anglican rationalism yet condemns the growing gap between rich and poor.

Wesley understood the Sermon on the Mount as a coherent and ordered unfolding of the heart of the gospel message. Wesley is not overly interested in matters of whether Jesus spoke these words or on clarifying the relation between the Sermon on the Mount in Matthew and the Sermon on the Plain in Luke. For Wesley, the words in Matthew 5–7 are nothing less than the opening up of the way to heaven. In his *Explanatory Notes on the New Testament*, Wesley comments: "To bless them, to make men happy, was the great business for which our Lord came into the world. And accordingly he here pronounces eight blessings together, annexing to so many steps in Christianity."[4] In the Sermon on the Mount, Jesus teaches humanity "the complete art of happiness."[5]

Wesley's exposition of the Sermon on the Mount consists of a series of thirteen discourses treating holiness, holy works, and the hindrances to both. First, he begins with the Beatitudes. The Beatitudes are the most perfect description of the religion called Christianity (Discourses I–III), this religion is social in its essence (Discourse IV), and is the fulfillment of the Law given by the prophets to the people of Israel (Discourse V). One might say that the Beatitudes fill out the contours of that "short sketch of holiness delivered by God in those ten words of commandments to Moses on Mount Sinai."[6] Second, throughout his exposition of the Sermon on the Mount, Wesley is at pains to distinguish without dividing this inward religion from its outward manifestation. Inward holy tempers lead to purity of intention and purity of intention both consecrates and is exercised by outward works of mercy like almsgiving and works of piety like prayer (Discourse VI) and fasting (Discourse VII), as well as in the works of the common life (Discourse VIII). Purity of intention and the holy tempers are of particular significance in Christian attitudes toward the use of money (Discourse IX). These various works are to be used as means to the end of the Christian life without confusing them for the end itself. Indeed one of the complaints Wesley has against the counsels like voluntary poverty is that these counsels seem to arise from or at least easily fall prey to this very confusion.[7] Third, Wesley examines the inner and outward hindrances to holiness in the Christian life. On the one hand, holiness is hindered by bad habits like that of judging others (Discourse 10). On the other hand, holiness is hindered by the abundance of bad examples of holiness (Discourse XI) and bad instructors of holiness (Discourse XII). The whole series of discourses concludes with a call for self-examination and an exhortation to pursue and exercise the holy tempers rewarded in the Beatitudes (Discourse XIII).

Given the length of these discourses and the extent of topics that they cover, I will not attempt to discuss each sermon individually. Instead, I wish to highlight several aspects of Wesley's exposition that are of particular relevance to the engagement with Thomas on the doctrine of perfection. For this reason, even though I will draw on the series of sermons as a whole, I will focus our attention on the Beatitudes, for these are the leitmotif to which the various discourses turn again and again.

Following both tradition and the Greek New Testament, Wesley interprets the "blessed" statements as declarations of happiness. The eight Beatitudes follow the same pattern: a divine temper is praised as happy and rewarded. Hence, the exposition of each of these Beatitudes also follows this pattern: first, a description of the divine temper that the Lord is commending (often beginning with a clarification of what it is not), then an exposition of the attached reward. From the content of the sermon, its structure, and its original setting, Wesley surmises that the words of Jesus in this passage must apply to all human beings.

> [E]ither all the parts of this discourse are to be applied to men in general, or no part; seeing they are all connected together, all joined as the stones in an arch, of which you cannot take one away, without destroying the whole fabric.[8]

Wesley dismisses the objections of those who would say that some words are meant for the twelve and some for the crowd, or that some words were only applicable to Christians in the apostolic era and others for all the ages. Indeed Wesley intends his exposition to be a refutation of any kind of two-tiered ethic. Every Christian is called by Christ to be perfect, to be holy, to be a city on the hill, to exceed the righteousness of the Pharisees.

Wesley's reflections on the Sermon on the Mount underscore three aspects of the Beatitudes that we need to examine: the relation between happiness and the holy tempers, the descriptive and prescriptive dimension of the eight Beatitudes, and the social character of holiness. Let us examine each of these in order.

First, Wesley associates each of the Beatitudes with a holy temper. As we have seen, the formation of holy tempers lies at the heart of John Wesley's theology.[9] One of the persistent motifs throughout his reflections is that "[t]rue religion is right tempers towards God and man."[10] These tempers or dispositions (Wesley uses these two terms interchangeably) describe inherent characteristics of the person. Tempers are enduring inclinations which both orient the person toward a certain object and are the result of that same orientation.[11] Holy tempers cannot subsist without that faith that works by love. On the one hand, Wesley insists that "right tempers cannot subsist without right opinion: The love of God, for instance, cannot subsist without a right opinion of him."[12] On the other hand, Wesley admits that "right opinion may subsist without right tempers. There may be a right opinion of God, without either love, or one right temper toward him."[13] Hence, living faith or loving faith is necessary for any Beatitude or perfection. Take, for instance, the first Beatitude: "Happy are the poor in spirit for theirs is the kingdom of heaven." Wesley begins by clarifying who are the "poor in spirit." The "poor in spirit" are not those who are outwardly poor because of the circumstances of life, nor are they those who are poor by choice. The "poor in spirit" are those who are humble in the sight of God because they know themselves to be sinners. "Poverty of spirit" is the foundational temper of the Christian life in the sense that it must accompany genuine repentance.

> "Poverty of Spirit," then, as it implies the first step we take in running the race which is set before us, is a just sense of our inward and outward sins, and of our guilt and helplessness.[14]

Second, the Beatitudes are both descriptive and prescriptive. On the one hand, every Christian to some extent has a share of each of the divine tempers praised in the Sermon on the Mount. As Wesley observes, "both poverty of spirit, and every other temper which is here mentioned, are at all times found, in a greater or less degree, in every real Christian."[15] On the other hand, there is an order to the Beatitudes; each stands as a successive step on the way of perfection.

> [The] real Christianity always begins in poverty of spirit, and goes on in the order here set down, till the "man of God is made perfect." We begin at the lowest of these gifts of God, yet so as not to relinquish this, when we are called of God to come up higher: But "whereunto we have already attained, we hold fast," while we press on to what is yet before, to the highest blessings of God in Christ Jesus.[16]

Each of the Beatitudes builds upon the other (mourning follows from poverty of spirit, meekness on mourning, etc.) without displacing the one before it. So, poverty of spirit is not simply the initial disposition that prepares a sinner for repentance, but "a continual sense of our total dependence on him for every good thought or word or work."[17] However, it is not simply that the various tempers are ordered toward each other and abide with each other; the divine tempers increase as they are exercised.[18] This is true even for poverty of spirit, as Wesley states,

> The more we grow in grace the more do we see of the desperate wickedness of our heart. The more we advance in the knowledge and love of God, through our Lord Jesus Christ (as great a mystery as this may appear to those who know not the power unto salvation), the more do we discern of our alienation from God, of the enmity that is in our carnal mind, and the necessity of our being entirely renewed in righteousness and true holiness.[19]

In other words, there are degrees of beatitude corresponding to the growth in grace of the person. A babe in Christ will not have the poverty of spirit of an elder in Christ.

After describing the holy temper of "poverty of spirit," Wesley describes the reward, the new birth. The poor in spirit receive the kingdom of heaven interiorly as their sins are forgiven and they are renewed daily in the image of God. The rewards in the Beatitudes are both future and present, but

Wesley's exposition emphasizes the "now" over the "not yet." For instance, the reward of the kingdom of heaven is awarded the moment the sinner turns to God in repentance and is justified (Wesley does not think that poverty of spirit merits justification, only that it is a disposition requisite for justification). The consolation of those who mourn is not merely a reward to be received in heaven when God shall wipe the tears from every eye, but here and now "they shall be comforted by the consolations of his Spirit."[20] The Christian is "happy in the end and in the way; happy in this life and in life everlasting."[21]

Third, the Beatitudes are essentially social. In the exposition of the Beatitudes there is often a missiological turn when Wesley shifts attention to the manner in which a certain holy temper is perfective of the person and the manner in which that temper is perfective of others. Admittedly, this turn is more evident in some Beatitudes than others but since all the Beatitudes are linked together one might say that the turn is implicit in all. Wesley's words leave little room for doubt on this score:

> It would be easy to show, that some intercourse even with ungodly and unholy men is absolutely needful, in order to the full exertion of every temper which he has described as the way to the kingdom; that it is indispensably necessary, in order to the complete exercise of poverty of spirit of mourning, and of every other disposition which has a place here, in the genuine religion of Jesus Christ.[22]

As an example of the social aspect of the Beatitudes, consider the one associated with mourning. Wesley speaks in very strong terms about the mourning that is the result of temptation and struggle in the Christian life. The mourning that is praised in the Beatitude is, in the first place, that which young Christians experience as "they see temptation and sin—which they fondly supposed were gone never to return—arising again."[23] These mourners, "if they resolutely reject all the comforts of sin, of folly, and vanity,"[24] shall be comforted by a new outpouring of God's love. Yet, after this Beatitude has been achieved, Wesley unfolds a deeper level of mourning: "They still mourn for the sins and miseries of mankind: they 'weep with them that weep.' They weep for them that weep not for themselves, for the sinners against their own souls. They mourn for the weakness and unfaithfulness of those that are in some measure saved from their sins."[25] The same missiological turn is evident throughout Wesley's exposition of the Beatitudes.[26]

The Christianity that the Sermon on the Mount proclaims is a social reality. The holy tempers are exercised primarily though not exclusively in the context of love of neighbor; hence Wesley's great dislike of hermits and solitaries. For a Christian to fly to the desert or enter a monastery is tantamount to lighting a lamp and hiding it under a basket. Yes, religion is a matter of the heart. Yes, a certain amount of mixing solitude and society is necessary for all Christians; we need time apart to enter our closet, shut the door and pray to our Father in secret. However, the setting apart of too much time for contemplation is destructive to many of the holy tempers. "For will any man affirm that a solitary Christian (so called, though it is little less than a contradiction in terms) can be a merciful man,—that is, one that takes every opportunity of doing all good to all men?"[27] Hence, no one can grow in the happiness announced in the Beatitudes without the company of others. Without friends and enemies we are deprived of neighbors to love; how then can one attain that holiness without which it is impossible to see the Lord? For this reason Wesley famously states that: "'Holy solitaries' is a phrase no more consistent with the gospel than holy adulterers. The gospel of Christ knows of no religion, but social; no holiness but social holiness."[28] A Christian without a mission is as worthless as salt that has lost its taste.

Holiness makes a Christian as conspicuous as the sun in the sky; "love cannot be hid any more than light."[29] Wesley forcefully insists throughout his exposition of the Sermon on the Mount, as he does throughout his career, that one's personal salvation is ordered to the salvation of the other. In the language of Thomas, we could say that sanctifying grace and gratuitous grace are ordered toward each other. The saint is not simply good, but a *bonum diffusivum sui*. In the language of Wesley,

> This is the great reason why the providence of God has so mingled you together with other men, that whatever grace you have received of God may through you be communicated to others; that every holy temper and word and work of yours may have an influence on them also. By this means a check will, in some measure, be given to the corruption which is in the world; and a small part, at least, saved from the general infection, and rendered holy and pure before God.[30]

Aquinas' Exposition of the Beatitudes

St. Thomas' *Lectura super Mattheum* dates from the period of the angelic doctor's second Parisian regency (1269–1270).[31] His exposition of the Sermon on the Mount is roughly contemporaneous with his reflections on perfection in the *Summa Theologiae*, *De perfectione*, and *Quodlibet III*. Unfortunately, the text for Thomas' commentary on the Sermon on the Mount is at present not available in English; indeed not even the full Latin text is readily available.[32] Nevertheless, there is sufficient authentic material in the *Lectura*, the *Summa Theologiae*, and *De caritate* for us to learn how Thomas understood the Sermon on the Mount.

The Sermon on the Mount is the supreme exposition of the *doctrina Christi*. After concluding his sermon, Jesus confirms this teaching with miracles (Matthew 8); he instructs the teachers of this message, namely the apostles (Matthew 10), confounds its enemies (Matthew 11), manifests its power (Matthew 13), and finally shows the purpose of this teaching (Matthew 17): the glory of the transfiguration of our bodies and souls into the form of Christ. In short, the Sermon on the Mount marks the launching stage for humanity's journey to the happiness of union with God through Christ.

The structure of the Sermon on the Mount is roughly as follows. Jesus begins by announcing the reward for keeping his teaching—Beatitude (Matthew 5). He then introduces the precepts of his teaching (Matthew 6) and finishes the sermon by showing his listeners how to keep the commandments (Matthew 7). In order to keep the scope of our reflections manageable and textually reliable we will limit ourselves to examining Thomas' commentary on the first eight Beatitudes, which in any case constitute the heart of the Sermon.

Before he begins his verse-by-verse exposition of the text, Thomas offers some introductory remarks on the setting and purpose of the sermon. Among the first things that Thomas considers is the audience of the sermon. For whom is this sermon? Is Jesus speaking only to the disciples or to the crowds also? Thomas links the question of the audience to the relation of the Sermon on the Mount in Matthew to the so-called Sermon on the Plain in Luke 6. Are these two texts different accounts of the same sermon or are they two different sermons? Thomas reviews the merits of various solutions to this question, and though he allows either reading, he seems to favor the one that harmonizes Matthew and Luke into a single event. The Sermon on the Mount is addressed to both the multitude and the apostles, with some parts pertaining to those called to keep the teachings of Jesus (all humanity) and some only to those who are called to both keep and spread these teachings (the apostles). All are called to be poor in spirit; all are called to be peacemakers and to suffer persecution for justice's sake; only the ministers of the gospel are called to be reviled on account of Jesus' name. We will return to this point later in the chapter.

After inquiring into the setting of the sermon, Thomas considers the nature of beatitude in general. He begins by reiterating a chief Aristotelian/Augustinian anthropological axiom: *omnes enim homines appetunt beatitudinem*.[33] The problem is that people often go astray in judging wherein their happiness lies. For this reason, Jesus' preaching begins with the

Beatitudes. By declaring that the poor in spirit are happy, Jesus rejects the opinion of those who found their happiness in exterior things. When Jesus says that the merciful are *beati*, he repudiates the opinion of those who think that happiness lies in the satisfaction of one's desires. Against those who try to satisfy their irascible desires through vengeance, Jesus says that happy are the meek. Against those who look for joy in their concupiscible desire, he declares that happy are those who weep. To those who think that perfect beatitude is found in the active life, he tells them that the peacemakers are happy not because of what they do but because of what they are going to become: children of God. To those who think that happiness is found in the contemplative life, he cautions them that the pure in heart *shall* see God. In other words, the Beatitudes reorient our desire for happiness away fro m those things that are only means to happiness to wherein perfect Beatitude lies, union with God by knowledge and love.

The other general remark that Thomas makes on the Beatitudes regards the form of the Beatitude. All the Beatitudes present a certain merit (poor in spirit) and a reward for this merit (the kingdom of heaven). We will examine Thomas' understanding of merit in the next chapter, but suffice it to say for now that merit is nothing less than a perfect act of virtue. According to Aquinas, virtue operates in two modes: *unum communis quae perficit hominem modo humano; aliud specialis, quam vocat heroicam, quae perficit supra humanum modum.*[34] Each of the virtues rewarded in the Beatitudes can be understood according to these two modalities. Take poverty of spirit, for instance. One can be poor in two ways, by necessity or by humility. However, there are two levels of performance of this act of voluntary detachment or humility. On the one hand, there are those who even if they have riches do not become spiritually attached to them. This poverty of spirit pertains to common virtue. On the other hand, there are those who neither have possessions nor seek them. This poverty of spirit pertains to heroic virtue. As Thomas comments,

> [I]sti dicuntur proprie pauperes spiritu, quia actus donorum, qui sunt supra humanum modum, sunt hominis beati: et quod homo omnes divitias abiiciat, ut nec aliquo etiam modo appetat, hoc est supra humanum modum.[35]

Only those whom the Holy Spirit has drawn away from spiritual and physical attachment to earthly goods are properly called *beati*. Thomas reminds us that Augustine links this Beatitude with the gift of fear (*donum timoris*), which Isaiah listed as one of the gifts of the Spirit which the incarnate Lord would bring to earth, and although it is true that Isaiah listed this gift last and Jesus first, the difference is one of perspective, *quia Isaias praenuntiavit adventum Christi ad terram; Christus autem de terra sursum trahebat.*[36] It is filial fear (*timor filialis*) of God which draws the heart away from worldly possessions and merits the reward of the kingdom in hope (for the reward is only perfect in heaven) and in reality (for the reward begins now): *unde sancti habent quamdam inchoationem illius beatudinis.*[37]

In sum, the Beatitudes pertain to heroic virtue, virtue operating in a supernatural mode according to the guidance of the Spirit. As Thomas states, "*ergo ista merita vel sunt actus donorum, vel actus virtutum secundum quod perficiuntur a donis.*"[38] This relationship between the virtues, the gifts and the Beatitudes is developed systematically in the *Summa Theologiae*, where each Beatitude is the act of an infused virtue which a gift has rendered pliant to the direction of the Holy Spirit. On this relationship the exposition *supra Mattheum* is far less detailed than the one in the *Summa*. However, the reading of the commentary makes it clear that the main source for Thomas' understanding of beatitude is not Aristotle or even Augustine, but Jesus.[39]

In the Sermon on the Mount, the Beatitudes are not simply listed but ranked both in terms of merit and also of reward. This order is already evident from the comparison that Thomas makes between Isaiah's list of the gifts of the Spirit and Jesus' list of the Beatitudes. However, in addition to this textual rationale, Thomas finds an intrinsic reason for this order in the nature of virtue itself. According to the angelic doctor, the purpose of virtue is threefold and the Beatitudes are ordered to realize these three things. First, virtue removes that which is evil (*removet a malo*). By humility, mercy and tears, virtue draws one away from cupidity, cruelty, and depraved desires. Second, virtue accomplishes what is good (*operatur et facit operare bonum*). By hunger and thirst for justice virtue leads one to act well. Third, virtue disposes to what is best (*disponit ad optimum*).[40] By purity of heart and peacemaking, virtue disposes one to know and love God. As is evident from Thomas' categorization, it does not exactly follow the dominical order, but it is expressive of this order and accounts well for how all the Beatitudes depend on each other. Poverty of spirit is not sufficient for beatitude: *immo requiritur mansuetudo, quae temperat circa iras, sicut temperantia circa concupiscentias.*[41] Hunger for justice without mercy will not lead to happiness *quia justitia sine misericordia crudelitas est; misericordia sine justitia mater est dissolutionis.*[42]

All the Beatitudes are ordered toward the rewards of seeing God and being called children of God. As Thomas asks, rhetorically, "*Quid enim agitur per paupertatem spiritus, per luctum, per mansuetudinem, nisi ut mundum cor habeatur? Quid per iustitiam et misericordiam, nisi ut pacem habeamus?*"[43] The ranking among the various Beatitudes is most evident in the final

Beatitudes. For instance, not only is the seventh Beatitude the culmination of the first six, Thomas associates peacemaking with the seventh day of creation, the day of rest and peace. However, just as the promised reward of the eighth day is greater than that of the seventh, the eighth Beatitude is the perfection of all other Beatitudes. As Thomas explains, "*notandum quod haec beatitudo octavo loco ponitur, sicut octava die circumcisio fiebat in qua quaedam generalis circumcisio martyrum praenuntiatur.*"[44] The eighth Beatitude pertains to martyrdom. The kingdom of heaven is given to the poor in Spirit on account of the perfection of their patience, but it is given to the martyrs on account of the perfection of their charity. To put it another way, the poor in Spirit receive the kingdom in hope, the martyrs in reality.

Dialogue on the Sermon on the Mount

Now that we have explored Aquinas' and Wesley's exposition of the Sermon on the Mount it is time to bring them together in dialogue. My goal in this section is not to uncover genetic dependence of one on the other, but rather to see how their respective readings of the Beatitudes compare and how this comparison throws light on the structure and purpose of the doctrine of perfection within the Methodist house and the Thomist cathedral. We will focus our attention on three key features highlighted in Wesley's and Aquinas' readings. First, we will look at how our two figures use key biblical and theological terms in this passage. Indeed, one of the benefits of reading the doctrine of perfection through the prism of a common biblical text is that it gives us the opportunity to understand better our duo's vocabulary of perfection. Second, we will examine the relation between perfection and counsels of perfection as they understand these to be present or absent in the Sermon on the Mount. Finally, we will reflect on how Aquinas and Wesley understand the social character of the holiness which is the subject of beatitude.

We begin by examining the theological lexicon of Wesley and Aquinas. The first term that I want to draw our attention to is the Greek word "*makarios.*" Though more explicitly in Aquinas than in Wesley, both read this term in light of an Aristotelian eudaemonic ethic that posits happiness as that which all desire. This happiness, eternal happiness, is supernatural and hence only possible by grace. Though by nature humans are made to be happy, only God can fulfill this desire. So far, there is a great deal of agreement between Wesley and Aquinas, but a difference arises on the relation between perfection and beatitude. Both agree that while beatitude begins in this life, it will only achieve its completion in the life to come. However, whereas Aquinas reserves the term "beatitude" for the perfect operation of virtue, Wesley applies it to both perfect and imperfect virtue. The difference here is perhaps subtle yet not inconsistent with Wesley's emphasis on a realized eschatology. Wesley insists that even a babe in Christ enjoys a measure of beatitude, even though he admits that only when all of the Beatitudes of the Sermon on the Mount are "transcribed into our hearts . . . graven there by the finger of God" shall we be holy and perfect as God is holy and perfect.[45] For his part, Aquinas affirms that in this life every Christian has a disposition for happiness (*dispositiones ad beatitudinem*), but only in the perfect (*viris perfectis*) is there an imperfect beginning of this future happiness.[46] Nevertheless, for both Wesley and Aquinas, the terms perfection, happiness, and holiness are correlative.

The second term that we need to consider is "tempers," particularly as these are related to the Beatitudes. From the usage to which Wesley puts this term in his discourses on the Sermon on the Mount and elsewhere, tempers are analogous to virtues. They are stable dispositions; they constitute "that fixed posture of soul"[47] that allows for the doing of good and the avoiding of evil with ease. Strictly speaking, tempers are not natural. According to Wesley, "Men may have many good tempers, and a blameless life, (speaking in a loose sense,) by nature and habit, with preventing grace; and yet not have faith and the love of God."[48] There are good tempers found in those whose fallen nature has been quickened by prevenient grace, but these tempers have a different orientation than those which are found among those who are being sanctified. For instance, the "heathen virtue" of patience is not to be confused with the "gracious temper, wrought in the heart of the believer, by the power of the Holy Ghost."[49] Indeed, it is possibly the desire to avoid this sort of confusion of nature and grace that leads Wesley to favor the language of tempers over virtue in the first place.

In linking beatitude to graced dispositions in the life of the Christian, Wesley comes close to Aquinas, yet there are differences. For Wesley, the happiness of beatitude is a holy affection. Wesley speaks of the affections and passions as exertions of the will.[50] As exertions, these affections are transient, but they flow out "like a torrent" from the holy tempers.[51] In the case of the Beatitudes, the happiness flows from the exercising of the holy tempers. For Thomas, Jesus is not here speaking of holy habits but of holy acts. For instance, "meekness is to be taken here as denoting the act of meekness: and the same applies to justice and mercy."[52] The presence of virtue represents a potential for perfection, but perfection itself consists in the reduction of this potential to a perfect act. Nevertheless, in spite of these differences, Aquinas and Wesley are at one in asserting that the attainment of perfection in this life requires more than the possession of faith, hope, and love. Perfection requires the exercise of holy habits. Wesley calls them holy tempers, Aquinas calls them merits or acts, but both agree that God will reward the actualization of these dispositions fully in the life to come and imperfectly in this life.[53]

Before leaving our consideration of the holy tempers and Beatitudes, we must consider the way in which both Wesley and Aquinas understand the connection of the Beatitudes. For both, the Beatitudes are listed in an order beginning with the lowest and ascending to the highest. This ascending order of dispositions in action and their corresponding rewards is basically due to what Thomas calls the connection and equality of the virtues.[54] Without going into detail on this important issue, we can say that for both Wesley and Aquinas, the virtues are connected in such a way that if said humility is lacking, wisdom will also. Like the fingers of the hand, virtues grow proportionally.[55] The consequence of this proportional equality and organic unity reaffirms a point I made earlier in passing. Christian perfection consists in the perfection of love, but love cannot be perfect without the perfection of faith and hope, nor can love be perfect without perfect poverty of spirit, perfect meekness, and so on. So even though it is true that some saints are more renowned for the practice of one virtue or another, there is no room for specialization in moral theology in the sense that some virtues are simply ignored for the sake of others. A person with perfect justice but no mercy would not be a perfect person but a caricature of a person, indeed a monster (Think Inspector Javert, in Victor Hugo's *Les Misérables*). Only when the virtues are united in a harmonious ensemble can we speak of perfect virtue and Christian perfection. Significantly, both Aquinas and Wesley insist that this unity and harmony is not a human achievement but the work of God through Christ. As the Thomist theologian Romanus Cessario states,

> Grace makes the unity of the virtues a possibility for every believer. What the philosophers took as a description of a distinctive few, a moral oligarchy, the Gospel message proposes for all those who, in faith, accept the power of the risen Christ in their lives. According to Christ's own account, the moral hero of the New Testament remains the one whose basic moral disposition toward virtue resembles that of a little child.[56]

The second issue that we need to consider in this section is the relation between the instructions in the Sermon on the Mount and the evangelical counsels. When it comes to the audience for the Sermon on the Mount, Wesley and Aquinas agree that Jesus is speaking to both the multitudes and the crowds. The Beatitudes are for all Christians because all are called to be perfect. Yet, whereas Wesley draws no distinction between what Jesus says to his disciples and what he says to the crowd, Thomas thinks that Jesus is not addressing both in the same way at the same time, but that some of the Beatitudes as well as some parts of the Sermon on the Mount pertain only to those in a state of perfection. The introduction of this differentiated reading of the Sermon on the Mount raises Protestant concerns of an apparent two-tiered Catholic ethic. As appreciative a reader of Aquinas as Stephen Long remarks that,

> Wesley, like Aquinas, made the Sermon on the Mount the centerpiece of his moral theology. But in one respect he produced an advance over Aquinas: Wesley did not read the sermon in terms of the distinction between counsels for the religious and precepts for ordinary Christians. He avoided the "Catholic" tendency of interpreting the sermon as counsels for a religious state and the Decalogue as commandments for the masses.[57]

Given this historic suspicion of Catholic ethics and by implication of the Catholic call to holiness, two questions need be asked: Is Long's reading of Wesley correct? Is his reading of Aquinas correct?

In light of our preceding exposition we can state that Wesley's reading of the Sermon on the Mount is not quite as flat and egalitarian as Long makes it sound. Yes, all the Beatitudes apply to all Christians, but there is a diversity of degrees of beatitude among Christians. The meekness that we see and expect among recent converts is not that which we should see or expect among those that are more mature in Christ. Wesley allows for different "counsels of perfection" for different persons. For instance, what Jesus required of the rich young man, namely that if he would be perfect he must first sell all he has, is not to be read as general rule but as a particular instruction. "For him this was necessary to salvation; to us, it is not so. To sell all was an absolute duty to him; to many of us it would be an absolute sin."[58] Yet, these particular cases aside, one of the consistent themes in Wesley's exposition of the Sermon on the Mount is the insistence on the common way that God has made for humans to attain happiness and holiness. His concern here is to outline the rule, not the exception, for fear of making the way of salvation seem too broad and haphazard. Nevertheless, in his later years Wesley makes allowances for different stages of this journey and indeed for a higher and lower way of salvation itself.[59] We shall return to this subject in the next chapter.

Is Aquinas' reading of the Sermon on the Mount elitist? Although implicit in his reflections on heroic acts of virtue, Thomas' distinction between the perfection that is a matter of precept and that which is a matter of counsel is not as evident in his reading of the Beatitudes as it is elsewhere. Consider, for instance, Thomas' exegesis of Matthew 5:48 in *De caritate*. The words "Be perfect, therefore as your heavenly Father is perfect" are not meant only for the religious but for all Christians because perfection is necessary for salvation. Thomas makes the following observation: "the saying, 'Be ye perfect,' etc., seems to have reference to the love of enemies."[60] The relation between Christian perfection and love of enemies is one that is not as emphasized in Thomistic or Wesleyan literature as it need be, but it is one that Thomas underscored because of its biblical origins. At any rate, the way in which Christians are called to love their enemies allows for degrees. There is a degree of love of enemies, which if lacking renders one unfit for salvation. As Thomas explains, Christians cannot hate their enemies.

> If one regards his enemy with hatred, his enmity toward him predominates in his heart over divine love. Therefore he hates the friendship with such a one more than he loves God.[61]

These words make it clear that the perfection in love to which all Christians are called is incompatible with hatred for enemies. Such an assertion might seem obvious, but notice again the reason that Thomas gives.

> We hate something to the degree that we love the good of which we are deprived by the enemy. Therefore it remains that whoever hates his enemy loves some created good more than God.[62]

Perfection and love of enemies are linked for Thomas because if we are friends of God, we are friends of all who are related to him, even our enemies. When we strike out against those who hate us that shows that rather than losing whatever our foes threatened to take from us (security, freedom, etc.), we prefer to lose God's friendship. As Christians we are called to love our neighbor and to do good even unto those who hate us. Christians are not simply forbidden to hate but are actually commanded to love. Of course, we cannot show our love to everyone in the same way. We have a greater responsibility for those who are nearby than to those who are far away. For Thomas, there is a hierarchy of love that renders us more responsible for those who are close to us by ties of space, time, kin, or simply need. The Good Samaritan was responsible for the welfare of the man who fell among thieves on the road from Jerusalem but not for the one who was robbed on the Via Appia. Yet Thomas insists that these contingent circumstances do not limit the obligation to love.

> We are bound, however, by the affection and the carrying out of the works of charity, by which we love our neighbors and pray for them, not

> to exclude even those who are not joined to us by any special bond, as for instance those who live in India or Ethiopia.[63]

In other words, it belongs to the perfection of charity to which all are called that we love humanity in general all the time and in particular as need arises.

At this point, one might well wonder what is left: is there any perfection greater than this? The perfection that belongs to the precept of charity and the one that belongs to a counsel seem a lot alike but there is an important if subtle difference.

> When man for the sake of God shows toward his enemies that special affection and deeds of love which he devotes to those who are joined to him, this is perfect charity and follows from a counsel. For, it arises from the perfection of charity that charity alone should so move one toward an enemy in the manner that both charity and particular love move one toward a friend.[64]

It belongs to the perfection of the precept to love our enemies in the sense that we do not hate them or we repay evil with good. It belongs to the perfection of counsel to love them as one would love a friend. A Good Samaritan would help a foreigner, even an enemy, who happened to be in need. A Mother Teresa would settle in the foreign country, open an inn, and treat all the needy as she would her own immediate family.

The distinction between counsel and precept is not meant to be an excuse for mediocrity as if one could sign up for Christianity on a pass/fail basis. A pastoral concern underlies this distinction. As Thomas insists, "the perfection of Divine love is a matter of precept for all without exception, so that even the perfection of heaven (*perfectio patriae*) is not excepted from this precept."[65] The distinction is there as both a prompt and a prop. Yes, by God's mercy it is true that our salvation does not depend on actually attaining the holiness of a Mother Teresa, but it does depend on us not ruling out or despairing of attaining or even surpassing such perfection. The moment that we draw a distinction between precept and counsel (Aquinas) or between "two orders of Christians" (Wesley),[66] we must understand our Lord's words from the mount as one sermon with multiple levels of meaning and interpretation. For Wesley, both orders can attain salvation but only the higher-order Christian is purposely going on to perfection. For Aquinas, the perfection that is required for salvation is less perfect than that which is a matter of counsel, and presumably that distinction has implications for purgatory and future glory. Wesley rejects purgatory and so the difference can only be in the degree of glory attained. Yet, since Wesley insists that Christian perfection or entire sanctification is necessary for glorification, it is not clear that the distinction he draws can be sustained. We will return to this topic in the next chapter.

The final issue that we must consider in this comparative reading of the Sermon on the Mount is the social character of holiness. There are two aspects of this issue. First, there is the relation of holiness and mission. Second, there is the relation between perfection and society. We have seen the way in which for Wesley all the Beatitudes had a missiological aspect to them. Growth in holiness connects the Christian more strongly to the world. Christians do not weep for themselves alone but for all who are lost from God. They do not hunger just for their own sustenance but for all who have not tasted that the Lord is good. For Wesley, there is a one-to-one correlation between being perfect and being a perfecter. All Christians, but particularly the perfect, are called to let their light shine. For Aquinas, the correlation between perfection and perfecter is not as strict. All perfecters are in some sense perfect, but not all the perfect are perfecters. The reason for this gap between perfect and perfecter is not because the former hide their light under a bushel but because the latter are institutionally ordered to be dispensers of spiritual corn to God's people.[67] The prelate is a perfecter because he is the teacher of the gospel. The teaching office is the most distinguishing mark of the episcopal state. But are not all Christians teachers? Yes, but in different ways. As Thomas states,

> Instruction is manifold. One leads to the embracing of the Faith; and is ascribed by Dionysius to bishops (*Eccl. Hier.* ii) and can be undertaken by any preacher, or even by any believer. Another is that by which a man is taught the rudiments of faith, and how to comport himself in receiving the sacraments: this belongs secondarily to the ministers, primarily to the priests. A third is instruction in the mode of Christian life: and this belongs to the sponsors. A fourth is the instruction in the profound mysteries of faith, and on the perfection of Christian life: this belongs to bishops 'ex officio,' in virtue of their office.[68]

In other words, lay people have a teaching role but it differs from that of the bishops, who are charged with teaching the *profunda mysteria fidei*. In order to carry out this task, the bishop needs to lead a mixed life of action and contemplation so that he can teach others what he has learned from contemplation (*contemplata aliis tradere*). For Aquinas, it is not the general body of believers that are the salt of the earth but the bishops; they are the real light of the world.

This clarification of Thomas' thought might seem to make the charge of elitism worse, but what must be remembered is that this distinction between the perfect and the perfecters, like the distinction between precept and counsel, is integrally related to the perfection of the church. The point that is important for our current inquiry is the way in which Thomas grounds the pursuit of holiness more strongly in the church than in the school of perfections. The church's perfecters par excellance are the bishops, who as successors to the apostles are charged with the responsibility of propagating the message of the Sermon on the Mount through their teaching and making possible the attainment of beatitude through their administration of the sacraments. The teaching and example of monks or mendicants, or even Methodists, might prove of vital importance to those who are going on to perfection, but these are secondary means and not necessary in the sense that the church is necessary.

Second, there is the social character of holiness. Wesley insists that "'Holy solitaries' is a phrase no more consistent with the gospel than holy adulterers."[69] The chief reason for the impossibility of this juxtaposition is that the exercise of the holy tempers requires the presence of the neighbor. How can we practice meekness without neighbors? How can we practice peacemaking without enemies? "What can be more plain, than that this fundamental branch of the religion of Jesus Christ cannot possibly subsist without society, without our living and conversing with other men?"[70] As we saw when we considered Wesley's theology of the tempers, the tempers become stronger as they are exercised. Life together gives us occasions both for this exercise (we have neighbors to make peace with) and also for accountability (we have friends who correct and encourage). In short, the Methodist societies helped form the tempers by holding us accountable for works of piety and works of mercy.

Now, when it comes to the perfect beatitude of heaven Aquinas states that "the fellowship of friends is not essential to Happiness, since man has the entire fullness of his perfection in God.[71] "Wherefore if there were but one soul enjoying God, it would be happy, though having no neighbor to love."[72] For, "perfection of charity is essential to Happiness, as to the love of God, but not as to the love of our neighbor."[73] Comments like these raise concerns of the kind of anti-social beatitude that Flew descried and decried in Thomas.[74] However, the danger is averted when we read Aquinas more carefully on this score, because in this same article where he insists that friends are not necessary for the enjoyment of beatitude he asserts that "in order that man may do well whether in the works of the active life, or in those of the contemplative life, he needs the fellowship of friends."[75] We need friends so that we might do good unto them and be helped by them. In this regard, we cannot forget the importance that Wesley and Aquinas attached to intentional communities such as Methodist societies and religious orders. In addition to, though not in substitution of, the church, these communities through their common discipline, teachings, and examples provided invaluable assistance for the attainment of holiness. "Hence," as Thomas avers, "a social life is necessary for the practice of perfection."[76] Wesley could not have stated this in stronger terms.

Since society is necessary for the attainment of perfection, does that rule out the solitary life? Wesley says, yes; he allows for seasons of solitude but not a life of solitude. Aquinas says not necessarily. First of all, according to the angelic doctor, at best, solitude is only a means to perfection and not perfection itself. Furthermore, this means is only to be employed by those who excel in the common life. The solitary life is only fitting for those who have attained perfection in charity. Aquinas cites, with approval Aristotle's famous saying that "he who associates not with others is either a beast or a god."[77] The "holy solitary" is either a beast who cannot stand the company of others or a divine man (*divinus vir*) lacking nothing. When rightly pursued, entrance into the solitary life is not the same as lighting a candle and hiding it under a bushel. Thomas insists that "those who lead a solitary life are most useful to mankind."[78] Wesley and we might ask, in what way do solitaries help others? Thomas answers by quoting Augustine,

> To some they seem to have renounced human intercourse more than is right: but these understand not how much such men profit us by the spirit of their prayers, what an example to us is the life of those whom we are forbidden to see in the body.[79]

"Holy solitaries" are not made in the desert but in a school of perfection, in the company of holy friends whose teaching and example prepare the way for contemplation. Hence, to fly to the desert in search of solitude without being first a graduate from such a school of virtue is, in the words of Thomas, "frought with very great danger, unless the grace of God supply that which others acquire by practice, as in the case of the Blessed Anthony and the Blessed Benedict."[80]

To sum up, according to Aquinas, even hermits need friends if they are to be "holy solitaries." Yes, sometimes God takes shortcuts and leads people into the desert without the necessary acquired skills, but these exceptional circumstances when God infuses such a high degree of virtue without preparation are not the norm. Besides, even in those rare cases like Benedict or Anthony, how much time were they really alone? Were they not constantly pursued by disciples, sought out by the sick and attacked by demons? Society and friendship with others and not just friendship with God is necessary for the acquisition, development, and perfection of virtue in this life and the attainment of beatitude in the life to come. Does the common doctor think that the significance of friends is only a terrestrial limitation to become irrelevant in heaven? Not at all, as in heaven "the fellowship of friends conduces to the well-being of happiness."[81] For Thomas, as for Wesley, heaven is a social reality where there is communion of the saints with God, with the angels, with the other saints above and even with us below.

Conclusion

The foregoing exploration and evaluation of how Wesley and Aquinas understood the Sermon on the Mount in relation to their teaching of perfection begins, I hope, to show that house and cathedral are not altogether as dissimilar as they seemed at first sight. In a sense, for both Wesley and Aquinas, Christian perfection is child's play. Perfection must not be confused with the moral seriousness of the sanctimonious; true holiness is happiness. What could be easier than being called to live as children of God, children whose perfect love casts out all fears but one—filial fear? Holiness, happiness, childlikeness (not childishness), and grace; these are some of the common building blocks of the doctrine of perfection as taught by Wesley and Aquinas.

The foregoing exploration also showed that although Wesley and Aquinas use some of the same elements in formulating their doctrine of perfection, they arrange these in contrasting ways. And yet the differences between one and the other are analogous to the contrast between the house and the cathedral. The most important difference between a meeting house and a cathedral is not one of size but one of purpose: the cathedral is where the bishop sits. Everything else in the cathedral (its physical dimensions, the quality of its artwork, the number of side chapels, etc.) is secondary to and derived from the role of the bishop as perfecter in the ecclesial community. In this sense, it is fitting that Aquinas' reading of Matthew and his doctrine of perfection makes room for a distinction between perfecter and perfected, whereas Wesley's does not. Yes, there is room in Wesley's house for degrees of perfection, perhaps even for counsels of perfection, but there is no room for different states of perfection nor for different schools of perfection. In Wesley's schoolhouse of religion, there are appointed leaders but there are no prelates, no contemplatives, and no holy solitaries. The hierarchical arrangements of Methodist bands and societies are not grounded in ecclesial states or sacramental orders but in soteriological states.

Actually, Aquinas' heart is not far from Wesley's; Thomas' ideal for the Christian life does not lead either to the desert or the cloister, but rather to the city and a mixed life of contemplation and action. Though Thomas considers the mendicant orders in general and the Dominicans in particular to be the best schools of perfection, he does not for that reason look down on other religious orders as inadequate or call for their closure. In sum, there is no problem with Wesley understanding the Methodist house of religion as a place where mostly lay men and women are schooled in active works of charity so long as he does not claim that the Methodist way to perfection is the only way.

Another fruit of the comparative reading that we have conducted in this chapter is the conclusion that the structurally sacramental church is essential to perfection.[82] The Methodist house cannot subsist by itself nor (and this is key) should it try to recreate the cathedral inside the house. The Methodist house lives from and for the cathedral. When Methodists forget this connection, things go wrong for the house and the cathedral. In the words of Albert Outler,

> One of our difficulties, I suggest, is that Methodism's unique ecclesiological pattern was really designed to function best *within* an encompassing environment of *catholicity* (by which I mean what the word meant originally: the effectual and universal Christian *community*). We don't do as well by our lonesome as some other denominations appear to do—and for good reason. Preoccupation with self-maintenance distracts us from what is actually our peculiar *raison d'etre*. This is why a self-conscious and denomination-centered Methodist is such a crashing bore to all but his own particular kith, kin and kind.[83]

As a house, the Methodists are theologically and practically *une église manqué*.[84] "We need a catholic church within which to function as a proper evangelical order of witness and worship, discipline and nurture."[85]

House and cathedral belong together. The early Methodists understood this. The church was both the object of their reform and the source of their strength. This connection is clearly seen in the Eucharistic practice of the early Methodist societies. The Methodist revival was to a large extent a Eucharistic revival; it was fed and sustained by the practice of what Wesley called "constant communion." This is not the place to review in detail the ups and downs of the history of the Lord's Supper among the Methodists.[86] Instead I want to point out two features that highlight the connection between house and cathedral in the mid-1700s. Methodists depended on the cathedral for ordained priests and consecrated grounds. These two desiderata were available in the local parish. Indeed the early Methodist practice avoided scheduling society meetings during church hours, so that Methodists could attend the Eucharistic celebration at the local parish or cathedral. As Bowmer tells the story,

> Several times in his *Journal* Charles Wesley mentions that he went to the Sacrament, with the society, at other times with the leaders, and in the early days of Methodism the crowds which attended these Communion services were phenomenal.[87]

As the doors of the local parishes began to close on the Methodists, in part as a reaction against the crowds coming for Eucharist, the Wesleys administered the Eucharist through other venues. They took advantage of an article in canon law which allowed for the administration of the Lord's Supper to the sick in their houses. The visitation of the sick became an occasion for the gathering of substantial numbers of Methodist communicants.[88] The Wesleys acquired the use of several formerly Huguenot chapels which, owing to their complex relation with the Church of England, were consecrated buildings.[89]

I should explain that the history is not as neat as just narrated. There were Eucharistic services that were held in unconsecrated spaces from the earliest days of the Methodist movement, but this was not the Wesleys' preference. True, in later years the Wesley brothers, especially John, rethought the whole necessity of consecrated liturgical spaces.[90] In any case, until very late in the revival the Methodists depended on the Church of England for duly ordained priests.

The relation between the house and the cathedral that existed in early Methodism is one full of ecumenical potential. The potential can become actualized in two ways. First, the potential becomes reality as the house is more house-like and the cathedral more cathedral-like. Second, the potential becomes actualized as the house and cathedral rediscover their mutual relation and complementarity. In this regard, I consider the present state of Wesley's Chapel in London to be a step in the wrong direction. The chapel, as originally designed by Wesley, was to have clear windows, wooden pillars, and plain walls. For the centenary of its completion, the clear windows were replaced with stained-glass windows, the wooden pillars with marble, and the walls with numerous marble and bronze plaques. The result, in my opinion, is not beautiful but gaudy precisely because of the lack of proportion that is an integral component of beauty. The gilding and the plaques literally look tacked on as if they do not really belong to this structure, which makes sense because these elements are not original. In *The Ecumenical Moment*, Wainwright proposes understanding Methodists as an order within the church catholic.[91] As Wainwright suggests, ecclesial unity will require more than reconciled diversity or federalism. Ecclesial unity is costly and may require death in the hope of resurrection.[92] Speaking for Methodists, I would say that it may require a stripping of the proper cathedral elements from our own houses so that we might again be of service to the holy catholic church. We will return to this issue at the end of the next chapter.

Chapter Six

Dialogue on Christian Perfection

Throughout this book I have compared Aquinas and Wesley by employing the metaphors of house and cathedral. The metaphor of the house might be perceived as condescending to Methodists, but such is not my intention. Rather, I employ these metaphors for two reasons. First, these metaphors offer a way to compare theologies that otherwise might seem incommensurable. In comparing Wesley and Aquinas we are not simply considering apples and oranges. After all, whatever else could be said about them, medieval cathedrals and Methodist houses have commonalities; they are both spaces that are set apart for the worship of God; they share a common purpose which is made manifest in particular furnishings such as a lectern or pulpit of some kind. Analogously, Aquinas' and Wesley's doctrines of perfection share common elements which we have already pointed out (their grounding in Scripture) and purpose (the leading of humans to the happiness of God). Second, these metaphors offer us a way of considering the real differences between Wesley and Aquinas. In spite of their various commonalities, a cathedral is not a house, nor is a scholastic theologian a revivalist preacher; there are differences that need to be considered. In a building, walls might be built out of wood or stone according to the availability of materials, the anticipated load on the wall, and the experience of the builders. In this chapter we will conclude our examination of the structural elements of the doctrine of perfection as taught by Wesley and Aquinas.

Our goal in this chapter will be twofold. First, we will consider some of the key commonalities and differences between Wesley and Aquinas.

In this examination we need to observe whether the differences are ornamental (Gothic versus Elizabethan, so to speak), functional (house versus cathedral), or fundamental (anti-Catholic versus anti-Protestant). Second, we will consider how Aquinas and Wesley might help each other shore up their doctrine against perceived or alleged weaknesses. The present comparison of their respective doctrines will not be exhaustive but representative. We will begin by examining the central aspects of their doctrines (image of God, love, and sin) before studying the supporting elements (the life of the virtues, assurance, and merit).

First Perfection and the Image of God

Perhaps the most immediately striking difference between what Aquinas and Wesley teach about perfection is the scope of their respective doctrines. Wesley's doctrine of perfection is a doctrine of *Christian* perfection; it is the perfection of the Christian, not perfection in general, that concerns Wesley. The preacher of perfection formulates and teaches his doctrine within the context of the *via salutis*, which begins with repentance and ends in sanctification. Thomas' doctrine of perfection is set against the larger backdrop of the procession and return of all things to God. The universally inclusive scope of the *exitus-reditus* schema compels Thomas to consider the theological basis of perfection in God and the ontological basis of perfection in creation.

The difference between Wesley and Aquinas at this point is not, I would argue, theological as much as it is vocational, and yet, this difference is not inconsequential. Wesley believes in the first perfection of the human and affirms the doctrine of the image of God in important ways. His reflections on the natural, moral, and political aspects of the image are interesting, and resonate with Aquinas' own reflections. Still, Wesley's lack of sufficient attentiveness to the difference between first perfection and second perfection leave him incapable of affirming the goodness of nature as it exists today. This is a very important point. One does not have to master the history of metaphysics to understand that the distinction between being and operation is important. For one thing, without this distinction it becomes very difficult to affirm the goodness of creation after the fall. Indeed, this is precisely one of the problems that we have seen in Wesley, in whose theology there is a nagging ambiguity in terms of the relation between nature and grace. Wesley tends make right operation the work of grace and wrongful inclinations the work of nature. The result of this parceling out of all good to God and all evil to creation is that nature is left without any proper work. One consequence of the omission of first perfection in Wesley's theology is epistemological. There is in

Wesley's anthropology nothing akin to the Thomist *simplex voluntas* that is content simply to affirm the existence of things. Wesley chiefly looks at humans in terms of their *finis operantis*, with the passion of an evangelist concerned with whether Mr. X is going to heaven or hell. This is a proper thing, and no one should gainsay him for that concern for others' eternal wellbeing that is characteristic of those who mourn. What Wesley does not do is stand in amazement at the *finis operis* of Mr. X, who regardless of his doings and destination is still wondrously made. If he does consider the grandness of the human, it is only to build up steam for the rhetorical turn, "how have the mighty fallen."

I have painted a bleak picture of Wesley's doctrine of creation, too bleak in some respects. The sharp antinomies between nature and grace that I have just sketched are more characteristic of the middle Wesley (the Wesley of the Aldersgate years) than of the late Wesley. In some of his final works Wesley adopts a more positive evaluation of nature and claims that the order and abundance of created order, even under the condition of sin, bears witness to the providential goodness of God.[1] On this point, the angelic doctor affirms and encourages the preacher of perfection to deepen his mature reflections. By underscoring the goodness and perfection of creation as it exists today, the way is opened for recognizing a pattern of holiness which renounces what is worldly while affirming what is natural (sin and evil both being unnatural) and with this recognition the possibility of an authentic form of creation spirituality becomes realizable. As an aside, it seems to me that the development of Wesleyan ecological ethics would find a surer foundation on the doctrine of the first perfection rather than on the eschatological speculation of talking animals.

The Universal Call to Christian (Second) Perfection

Our study has shown that the first perfection that is the image of God in the human is made for the sake of knowing and loving God perfectly. This second perfection will only be fully attained in heaven, but when applied to human beings in this life, Aquinas' *perfectio secunda* and Wesley's Christian perfection are basically synonymous expressions. All human beings are made for God. Moreover, as the renewed image of God, all Christians, clergy and lay, are called to perfection. There is no possibility in the accounts of perfection of Wesley and Aquinas for relegating the goal of perfection to the realm of personal choice or optional counsel. Perfection is commanded by Christ and whoever is not striving for perfection has strayed from the way of discipleship. Faced with this call to perfection, two questions arise: What must I do to be perfect? And, how perfect must I become?

During his ministry, as John Wesley tried to define the demands of perfection, he was at pains to avoid setting the bar of perfection too high or too low. On the one hand, he claimed that "to overdo is to undo."[2] John feared that some of his brother's hymns pushed perfection lyrically out of this world; in his verses, Charles appeared to present a view of entire sanctification more consistent with angelic nature in heaven than with human beings on the way.[3] On the other hand, if the bar of perfection is set too low, a greater danger looms. As Wesley explains to a certain skeptic,

> If there be a mistake, it is far more dangerous on the one side than on the other. If I set the mark too high, I drive men into needless fears; if you set it too low, you drive them into hell-fire.[4]

Like Wesley, Aquinas insists that second (Christian) perfection is the goal of the Christian life. However, the angelic doctor distinguishes between two levels of perfection; the first is necessary for salvation; the second is not. In simple terms, the perfection that is necessary for salvation consists in not rejecting love. The perfection that is a matter of counsel consists in dedicating one's life to love. Is not this understanding of perfection elitist? Does not the distinction between precept and counsel set up a division within the church of average Christians versus real Christians?

We have already looked at the question of distinctions within the church in previous chapters. Let me reiterate the fundamental point: all legitimate diversity in heaven, earth, or the church exists for the sake of better representing the surpassing perfection of God. Hence, the distinction between the perfection that is necessary for salvation and that which is not must not be understood as a concession for lax Christians but as a confession that the incomparable perfection of God is made manifest through different degrees of perfection among his creatures: *Deus in gradibus eius cognoscetur.*[5]

Late in life Wesley admitted to two legitimate orders of Christians and in doïng so acknowledged the hierarchical gradation of heaven and earth. There are higher and lower Christians, higher and lower saints.[6] This hierarchy is not based on ecclesiastical status but on degrees of love.[7] For Wesley, diversity in heaven and earth is ordered in a hierarchy of holiness. In this regard, if Methodists charge Roman Catholics' understandings of sanctity as being elitist, they should expect to be told by Aquinas, "*tua res agitur.*"

Nevertheless, in spite of their common witness on the call to second/ Christian perfection, Wesley still has something to teach Aquinas in this area. Aquinas did not develop a theology of the lay state. His teaching on the virtues and the sacraments provide the building blocks for such a theology but there is no concrete blueprint for their integration. Might not Wesley's rules for the Methodist societies provide one such concrete plan? In the Methodist societies in general, but in the Methodist itinerant connection in particular, we meet with people who are committed to pursuing not only that holiness which is the common goal of all Christians, but the perfection which belongs to the more excellent way of love. In the language of Aquinas, the Methodist societies are schools instituted for the attainment of the perfection that is a matter of counsel. The specific counsels of these societies differ from those of the religious state, but they differ precisely in that these counsels are compatible with the lay state. To repeat, both Aquinas and Wesley insist that all Christians (lay and clergy) are to strive for perfection. However, only Wesley provides an intentional community with and for the church that is organized expressly for the purpose of attaining this perfection. Could this be a way in which the Methodist house complements the Thomist cathedral? Perhaps, but Methodists would first need to retrieve the long neglected practice of mutual admonition and accountability before presenting it to others.

Perfection in Love

For both Aquinas and Wesley the summit of perfection in this life consists in the perfection of charity. Wesley prefers to use the words "perfect love" because, among other reasons, that is the way the English translation of 1 John 4:18 reads. Aquinas on the other hand settles on *caritas*, for that is how his Bible translates agape. In Aquinas' theology, love and charity are related terms with overlapping though distinct fields of meaning. Love denotes a principle of movement that moves the lover to the beloved. "Charity denotes, in addition to love, a certain perfection of love, insofar as that which is loved is held to be of great price, as the word itself implies."[8] Whereas for Aquinas the charity that unites us to God is a habit, for Wesley it is a holy temper. As we saw in the last chapter, these terms are basically synonymous. Leaving aside these terminological differences, which stem in part from their different attitudes toward Aristotle, it is possible to identify important commonalities in Aquinas' and Wesley's understanding of the centrality of love in the second perfection of the human.

First, love is not merely a feeling, but a human response to the divine love poured out of the cross. Charity is not just any kind of love or attraction, but that love by which we love God who is most dear (*carus*) of all. It is in the perfection of this love, whose effect is to unite us with our beloved, that we reach the perfection of Christian life. The love of the newly baptized and the love of the saint are only possible because of the infusion of divine love through grace. However, perfect love is distinguished from imperfect love by its extent (*secundum extensionem*), its intensity (*secundum intensionem*), and its effect (*quantum ad effectum*).[9]

Second, perfect love is attained through conformity to Christ. Wesley insists that to be perfect means "to have the mind of Christ" and "to walk as he walked." Aquinas asserts that even for mendicants who have taken vows of poverty, "perfection consists, essentially not in poverty, but in following Christ." For both, this *imitatio Christi* is not based primarily on emulation of Christ's lifestyle but in obedience to Christ's great commandment: love the Lord your God with all your heart, soul, mind, and strength, and love your neighbor as yourself. Thus, the perfection of the Christian life is not based on a necessary return of the creature to the Creator along the lines of the neoplatonic *exitus-reditus* schema, but on God's command to his people according to Scripture. Perfection in love means perfect obedience, which is the proper and free "reditus" of the rational creature to the Creator.

Third, perfection in love is possible in this life. This affirmation follows from the fact that perfection is a matter of precept. Jesus does not command things that are impossible for us. If Jesus said "be perfect as your heavenly Father is perfect," then somehow perfection must be possible for us, even in this life. Thus, perfection in love is in principle attainable by all people in this life because sufficient grace is offered to all humans for this very purpose. However, the perfection that is possible in this life is not the perfection of heaven. The perfection that is possible in this life is the perfection of the will, the perfection of love. It is not the perfection of the intellect, the perfection of knowing, nor is it the perfection of the body. Hence, perfection in this life is always perfectible and never indefectible. The perfect can fail and even fall, but they can also grow.

If the perfection that is possible in this life is not identical to the perfection of the life to come, how are we to understand their relation? What is the connection between perfection and glorification? Granted that that these two perfections are different (not in kind but in degree), and that perfection in love is possible in this life, must Christian perfection be attained by all in this life? The logic of Wesley's theology pushes in the direction of answering this question in the affirmative. As we saw, Wesley's doctrine of the middle state between earth and heaven presents paradise as the abode of those who die in grace and are awaiting the resurrection of the body; paradise is a place of ripening and growing in grace; it is not a place of purgation. Hence, unlike Catholics, Wesley cannot defer entire sanctification to the afterlife. However, consigning the perfection of the Christian to a sudden stroke of irresistible sanctifying grace at the very moment of death hardly seems congruent with Wesley's understanding of grace and freedom. The only remaining alternative seems to be that every Christian has to be made perfect in love during this life or be thrown into the lake of fire. As Collins rightly observes,

> To be sure so insistent was Wesley that we be free from the *being* of sin before we die—in a way that distinguished his thought from that of Lutherans, Calvinists and Catholics—that he expostulated on one occasion: "Unless we have clean hearts before we die, it had been good we had never been born."[10]

In later years, while not denying that today was the day of salvation, Wesley increasingly pushed the time of sanctification close to the time of death. Collins offers a possible explanation for this deferment of perfection to the end of life:

> The crisis of death, in other words, the realization that time will indeed end, apparently serves as the appropriate catalyst out of which entire devotion to God and the full cleansing power of the Spirit may arise.[11]

Collins is implicitly appealing to the venerable tradition of *ars moriendi* with which Wesley was well acquainted and, in general, approved of. There might well be a connection between the impending end of our mortal life and the crumbling of the barriers that resist the outpouring of God's love. Yet there are problems with this explanation. First, this explanation does not account for what happens to those who die suddenly and unprepared. It is true that Christians should always be prepared, and we should always remember that we are dust and to dust we will return, but I am not sure that *ars moriendi* can be raised to the level of a normative Christian practice; it might be more a matter of counsel than of precept. Second, and more significantly, the postponing of perfection to a near-death experience mitigates the urgency of the "now" and reduces the semiotic significance of sanctification for other believers. In my judgment, to associate entire sanctification with the crisis of death practically ends up in the Reformed understanding of perfection.

Methodists who would follow Wesley seem to be left with an unhappy set of choices: insist on perfection in this life with the attendant consequence that most people will likely end up in hell, admit the possibility of perfection at the moment of death with its overtones of irresistible grace, or allow for postmortem perfection with its risks of spiritual mediocrity in this life. The last of these options (minus the spiritual mediocrity) is the one that is available to Aquinas.

Like Wesley, Aquinas established a close connection between perfection and salvation. However, the perfection that is necessary for salvation is not that of actually or even habitually obeying the great commandment, but that of not doing anything contrary to it. Since such holiness is not heroic such a person would require further purgation after death so as to be made fit for the light of glory. In a sense, the late Wesley's admission of two orders of Christian existence leans in the direction of the Thomistic distinction between ordinary and heroic sanctity (considered further in the next chapter). In any case, for both Wesley and Aquinas entire sanctification in this life is the normal goal of Christian life. In the words of Garrigou-Lagrange,

> Purgatory after death, frequent though it may be, is not according to the order arranged by God for the full development of the supernatural life, since immediately after death it is radical to the order established by Him that the soul should possess God by the beatific vision.[12]

On this final point, the doctrine of purgatory poses a question to the Methodist teaching of Christian perfection and to the Catholic universal call to holiness. Methodist consideration of a doctrine of purgatory requires a theological account of the role of suffering in preparation for the beatific vision beyond what is possible within the confines of the present study.[13] For our present purposes, let us instead consider a related, albeit more limited, question: Does suffering play a role in the eradication of sin from believers?

The question concerning the relation between suffering and sanctification has been hovering around the edges of our discussion of perfect love. The Wesley brothers were not of one mind on this.[14] In a poetical commentary on Hebrews 12:8, Charles writes,

> In sorrow, as in grace, we grow,
> With closer fellowship in pain,
> Our Lord more intimately know,
> Till coming to a perfect man
> His sharpest agonies we share,*
> And all his marks of passion bare.
>
> Partakers of His bitterest cup,
> And burden'd with His heaviest load,
> We fill His after-sufferings up,
> Conform'd to an expiring God;
> And only such our Father owns,*
> And seats on our appointed thrones.[15]

At each asterisk John Wesley handwrote a resounding "NO!" Purgative suffering is not a condition for sanctification or glorification.[16] John is deeply concerned about any strong association of suffering with salvation. Consider his remarks about Madame Guyon, whose unmistakable holiness was marred by her mistaken notion that "God never does, never can, purify a soul, but by inward and outward suffering."[17] For Wesley, only faith is necessary for salvation and any talk of the necessity of darkness or privation is unscriptural, false, and possibly dangerous.[18]

For the angelic doctor, suffering can be therapeutic: *poenae sint quaedam medicinae.*[19] As van Nieuwenhove observes, for Aquinas "just as the will was drawn toward consent to sin by means of pleasure, so it is strengthened in the detestation of sin by means of penances."[20] There is in Aquinas' theology a correlation between a certain kind of suffering and growth in grace. As van Nieuwenhove explains, "If we accept afflictions about which we ourselves cannot do anything, they lose their penal character and acquire instead a satisfactory character."[21] Such a statement should not surprise any reader of the Bible. The author of Hebrews exhorts all Christians to "endure trials for the sake of discipline."[22] God disciplines us by means of suffering "in order that we may share his holiness."[23] Reflecting on the salvific significance of suffering in Aquinas' theology, Stump claims that "if suffering is the chemotherapy for spiritual cancer, the patients whose regimen does not include any are the only ones for whom the prognosis is really bad."[24] And if this claim sounds like so much hyperbole, did not Jesus say: "woe to you who are rich for you have received your consolation"?[25] Hence, the absence of suffering from Christian life might be interpreted as a countersign of our adoption as God's children.

Now is not the time to address the objections, medieval and modern, that have been raised against Aquinas' account of suffering. We will return to his account again in the next chapter, but the point that is important for our purpose at present is to note that for Thomas, perfection is not achieved without purgation.[26] Sin is not simply removed by the presence of its opposite, charity, but also by submitting to satisfactory chastisements. On the relation between suffering and sanctification Thomas is perhaps closer to Charles Wesley than to John.[27]

Freedom from Sin

Perhaps the most controversial element in John Wesley's teaching on perfection is the claim that perfect love excludes all sin.[28] A number of objections have been raised to this teaching from various viewpoints: psychological, pastoral, and theological. However, the issue that all critics seem to circle around is Wesley's definition of sin as a voluntary transgression of a known divine law. Some find such a definition inadequate; it is too limited. For one thing, this definition appears to exclude sins of omission. Others find even this degree of perfection to be unrealistic.

From the outset, it is important to remember that Wesley was not fond of the term "sinless perfection."[29] Indeed, Wesley often had to defend himself against the "scarecrow of *sinless perfection*"[30] that others had erected as evidence of Methodist "enthusiasm" or as a defense for their own antinomian tendencies. The term was open to multiple misunderstandings. Set the bar too high, and perfection is deferred till glory. Set it too low, and the door to enthusiasm and antinomianism is thrown wide open. Yet for Wesley perfect love and freedom from sin are correlative terms. As we become aware that the love of God is being poured into our hearts there is born in us a love for God and for all humankind. Concurrent with this outpouring of divine love there is also an expelling of "the love of the world, the love of pleasure, of ease, of honour, of money, together with pride, anger, self will, and every other evil temper."[31] In short, one love drives out another; holy tempers extinguish evil tempers. Perfection, holiness, and sinlessness belong together. As Wesley states,

> Ye shall then be perfect. The Apostle seems to mean by this expression, τέλειοι, ye shall be wholly delivered from every evil work; from every evil word; from every sinful thought; yea, from every evil desire, passion, temper; from all inbred corruption, from all remains of the carnal mind, from the body of sin; and ye shall be renewed in the spirit of your mind, in every right temper, after the image of him that created you, in righteousness and true holiness. Ye shall be entire, ὁλόκληροι—the same word which the Apostle uses to the Christians in Thessalonica. This seems to refer, not so much to the kind as to the degree of holiness; as if he had said, "Ye shall enjoy as high a degree of holiness as is consistent with your present state of pilgrimage."[32]

Aquinas also holds perfection in charity and freedom from sin together. When love drives away lust, gluttony, and the like, it has attained a degree of perfection that is "sinless" with respect to mortal sin.[33] However, such "sinless perfection" needs to be qualified in two important ways. First, the perfection that is necessary for salvation is compatible with venial sin. Second, the fact that there is in the church the sacrament of penance as a remedy for mortal sin tells us that this perfection can be lost. Thus, the kind of "sinless perfection" which is the common privilege of those living in the state of grace does not mark the highest degree of perfection attainable in this life. The love that removes mortal sin is perfect; the love that removes whatever hinders the perfect act of love of God is more perfect.

So, for Thomas, the perfection that is attainable in this life is not incompatible with venial sins.[34] Even the saints offend for many reasons as a consequence *ex infirmitate praesentis vitae.*[35] What does this mean? It means that although by God's grace it is possible to live without committing mortal sin, and through a vow to devote oneself wholly to the service of God, while we are in this corruptible body perfect virtues are not unerringly and unceasingly translated into perfect acts.[36] To put it another way, freedom from mortal sin belongs to the state of grace, freedom from temporal affairs to the state of perfection, but freedom from infirmities only to the state of glory. These infirmities are not sinful in and of themselves; they are not even venial sins, but they are hindrances to the act of perfect charity by limiting the acts' duration and intensity. A sleepy person cannot pray as attentively as an alert person. Eventually, even the saintly Simeon must say "*nunc dimitis.*" Still, these infirmities are signs of an imperfect act, not of a missing habit.

Observe how closely Aquinas' understanding of the limits of sinlessness in this life parallels Wesley's own teaching: "There may be ten thousand wandering thoughts, and forgetful intervals, without any breach of love, though not without transgressing the Adamic law."[37] Admittedly, Wesley repudiates the distinction between mortal and venial sins,[38] but his rejection is based on a misconception. Wesley correctly apprehends that according to Roman Catholic teaching "there is no perfection here which is not consistent with venial sins."[39] However, he mistakenly believes that "among venial sins they commonly reckon simple fornication."[40] Whatever the basis for Wesley's misunderstanding (Protestant propaganda or Catholic popular piety), this is certainly not the teaching of Aquinas. Indeed, when it comes to the issue of fornication, the angelic doctor insists that the only excuse for such an act would be if it were performed by a person who was mentally unstable (*furiosi*) or disabled (*amentis*).[41] In either case, fornication would not be called a venial sin because given the involuntary nature of the act it would not be called a sin at all.[42]

Such reasoning might perhaps trouble Wesley, but it need not. Thomas is not saying that such an act would not be evil; it just would not be sin. The heart of the matter is that for the angelic doctor, *malum in plus est quam peccatum.*[43] Evil is a broader concept than sin. The former includes any kind of privation of the good for whatever reason (natural, moral, or punitive). The latter is limited to any *voluntary* action that deviates from the eternal law. Looked at in this way, Wesley's "abbreviated" doctrine of sin is remarkably similar to that taught by Aquinas.

> For neither love nor the "unction of the Holy One" makes us infallible: Therefore, through unavoidable defect of understanding, we cannot

> but mistake in many things. And these mistakes will frequently occasion something wrong, both in our temper, and words, and actions. From mistaking his character, we may love a person less than he really deserves. And by the same mistake we are unavoidably led to speak or act, with regard to that person, in such a manner as is contrary to this law, in some or other of the preceding instances.[44]

These mistakes are not sin because they arise from an "unavoidable defect of understanding," or as Thomas might state it, from "invincible ignorance." So, "while all our tempers, and thoughts, and words, and works, spring from love,"[45] we live in harmony with the eternal law. Venial sins and infirmities indeed diminish the beauty of this harmony but they do not destroy it. In Wesley's words,

> Though these are deviations from the holy, and acceptable, and perfect will of God, yet they are not properly sins, nor do they bring any guilt on the conscience of "them which are in Christ Jesus." They separate not between God and them, neither intercept the light of his countenance; as being no ways inconsistent with their general character of "walking not after the flesh, but after the Spirit."[46]

Contra his critics, John Wesley's doctrine of sin is neither weak nor abridged. He is not making perfection attainable by narrowing his definition of sin. By no means is Wesley excluding sins of omission from his definition, nor is ignorance of sin necessarily innocent.[47] Wesley does not reject the idea of unconscious sin, but what he does reject, and rightly so, is the idea of involuntary sin. He uses the language of infirmities, not sins, because these deviations occur without the concurrence of the will.[48] For his part, Thomas uses the language of infirmities, though he frequently uses the term venial sins but only "in reference to an imperfect notion of sin."[49] In either case, these offenses, though not destructive of the communion of the Christian with God, can and need to be atoned for by personal appropriation of the sacrifice of Jesus Christ on the cross.[50]

What about structural sin? For many modern ethicists, both Aquinas' and Wesley's understanding of sin are deficient on this score. Consider, for instance, Lessmann's assessment of Wesley's blind spot:

> Die Heiligungsbewegung verzerrte Wesleys Theologie in zumindest einem Punkt: sie betonte übermäßig den individuellen-individualistischen Aspekt der Heiligung und verlor zunehmend ihren sozialen, gesellschaftsbezogenen Gesichstpunkt.[51]

According to Lessmann and other interpreters,[52] the problem with Wesley's doctrine of sin lies chiefly in the way that awareness of forgiveness for personal sins can anesthetize to awareness of our collective guilt. What does this collective guilt consist in? It varies according to one's social location. For Cobb, it means,

> I participate in the guilt of Southern Whites for our collective crimes against blacks. I participate in the crimes of the United States in its support of repressive regimes in Latin America. I participate in the guilt of Christians for our vilification of the Jews. I participate in the guilt of the human species for what is done to other species.[53]

For many of Wesley's interpreters, the universal scope of the doctrine of unintended consequences, the fallibility of human nature—in short, the tenets of Niebuhrian realism— render all claims of perfection suspect or even demonic.[54] Indeed, it is not clear that Jesus himself would be exempted from the stain of collective guilt. After all, as a man was he not guilty of collective crimes against women? As a Jew was he not guilty of Judea's historic oppression of Samaria? As a human was he not guilty of exploiting the environment?

Consideration of one's complicity in perpetuating oppressive structures and regimes can be an important component of self-examination and confession. Indeed in some contexts such considerations might even be necessary for salvation. But whatever its merits, the doctrine of unintended consequences cannot be given precedence over the doctrine of perfection. Indeed, I would go so far as to say that the qualification (if not outright elimination) of all claims to holiness by appeals to "fallibilism," "structural sin," and "collective guilt" is one of the devil's chief ways of hindering progress to perfection, driving men and women into needless fears and possibly despairing collusion with those very powers. As Wesley points out, one of Satan's most subtle devices consists in pricking our conscience with the awareness of how much remains to be done in this life before we are worthy of the life to come.

> [T]hat subtle adversary often damps the joy that we should otherwise feel in what we have already attained, by a perverse representation of what we have not attained, and the absolute necessity of attaining it. So that we cannot rejoice in what we have, because there is more which we have not. We cannot rightly taste the goodness of God, who hath done great things for us, because there are so much greater things which as yet he has not done.[55]

I will touch on this topic again in the next chapter, but suffice it to say for now that according to Aquinas and Wesley, perfection, even in this life, is characterized by joyous fulfillment, not tragic failure.

Sanctification and the Virtues

According to some Wesleyan theologians, our relationship with God is a "moment by moment" affair.[56] When speaking of salvation, the "now" is all important. Being born again yesterday, so to speak, is of little comfort if I am a child of the devil today, and having peace today is no guarantee for tomorrow. God does not give his saints a lifetime's supply of holiness that the saints claim as their own and draw upon as needed. On this telling, sanctification, justification, and indeed the whole way of salvation is a series of puncticular events. This concentration on the "now" or "today" of salvation emphasizes the immediacy of the operation of God. Faith depends upon Christ from "moment to moment."[57] Our perfection in love requires the intercession of Christ and the presence of the Spirit from "moment to moment."[58] We cannot stand against the power of sin "unless we be endued with power from on high; and that continually, from hour to hour, or rather from moment to moment."[59] It is in this same way that God preserves everything in being, our very breath he deals out "moment to moment."[60]

Dependence on God's continuous outpouring of grace for the sustenance and growth of Christian life is also a feature of Aquinas' theology. However, Wesley's strong emphasis on the "now" of God's work raises two related issues that we must consider: first, the relation between instantaneous and progressive operations of sanctifying grace; second, the relation between grace and the life of the virtues.

The first of these issues can be stated in the form of a question: is entire sanctification instantaneous or is it a gradual process? Wesley's heirs have reflected extensively on this question without coming to a consensus. Most acknowledge that Wesley's soteriology makes room for both instantaneous and gradual dimensions. The debate centers on how one is to understand the relation between these two motifs and whether one motif is more dominant than the other. On the one hand, Maddox is convinced that "while the affirmation of the possibility of entire sanctification may have been *distinctive* of Wesley, the conception of sanctification (as a whole) as the progressive journey in responsive cooperation with God's empowering grace was most *characteristic* of Wesley."[61] On the other hand, Collins acknowledges the importance of this gradual journey; "responsible grace" is indeed an important aspect of Wesley's soteriology, but it is by no means the whole of it.[62] The instantaneous element was not something adopted by the middle Wesley (of Aldersgate) to be laid aside by the late Wesley. According to Collins, the elderly Wesley retains this motif in his soteriology. By insisting on the instantaneous, Wesley "not only highlights the graciousness of God, that it is the Holy Spirit and not men and women, who *makes* the heart entirely holy, but also keeps before the believer the *unconditional* element of faith—that perfection in love may yet occur even if only this ingredient is missing."[63]

At its heart, this debate is not animated simply by a desire to provide the most historically accurate account of Wesley's theology possible but by a judgment over the contemporary state of Methodism. Those who highlight the instantaneous work of grace do so not just because they think that this is the best way to read Wesley, but because they think that this is the best way to defend the sovereignty of grace and to strike a blow against the pervasive moralism afflicting contemporary Methodism. Those who underscore the gradual work of grace do so not just because they think that it is more faithful to the whole tenor of Wesley's theology but because it allows contemporary Wesleyans to affirm human responsibility on the way of salvation.

What is Thomas' view of this issue? Is the work of grace, sanctifying or otherwise, instantaneous or gradual? We might expect that someone who devoted a whole volume of his magnum opus to theological reflection on the virtues would see the work of grace as an exclusively gradual process, but one would be mistaken in thinking so. According to Thomas, "the infusion of grace takes place in an instant and without succession."[64] Sometimes the infusion of grace is preceded by a period of preparation where the disposition for grace grows gradually, as in the case of the Ethiopian Eunuch who, before receiving the Spirit had already spent considerable time pondering the Scriptures and hearing them expounded. Sometimes the infusion of grace and the disposition for grace happen suddenly, as in the case of Paul on the road to Damascus. In either case, "God, in order to infuse grace into the soul, needs no disposition save what he himself has made."[65]

In other words, the time of preparation for grace might vary in duration according to God's own purpose, but the infusion of grace itself takes place in an instant. As the angelic doctor describes it, the way in which grace operates on the soul is analogous to the way in which air becomes luminous immediately upon receiving light. Admittedly, there are in nature counterexamples to this kind of instantaneous operation. Sometimes the work of impressing a new form on ordinary matter takes time, but this work is gradual only because of the limited power of the agent to overcome matter's resistance to the new form. In the case of God, whose power is infinite, such resistance is no impediment, "therefore the justification of the ungodly by God takes place instantaneously."[66] Since grace is infused instantaneously, there is a demarcation in time that distinguishes the life of a person before and after grace. As Thomas explains,

> We must say that there is no last instant that sin inheres (*in quo culpa infuit*), but a last time; where as there is a first instant that grace inheres (*in quo gratia inest*); and in all the previous time sin inhered (*inerat culpa*).[67]

Allowing for some terminological distinctions, Thomas' description of the instantaneous change that grace works in the soul is remarkably close to Wesley's.

> If sin cease before death, there must, in the nature of the thing, be an instantaneous change; there must be a last moment wherein it does exist, and a first moment wherein it does not.[68]

A few words of caution are in order lest we bring Aquinas and Wesley too quickly together on this question. First of all, the immediate context for Thomas' remarks on the instantaneous work of grace concern the justification of the ungodly and not the entire sanctification of believers. Second, though Thomas belonged to the Order of Preachers he was not an eighteenth century revivalist. He teaches and preaches within the context of Christendom where the work of justification is associated with baptism, not with an altar call or adult conversion experience. Third, and most significantly for Thomas, the work of justification is instantaneous because it consists in the infusing of a new form, or perhaps we should say forms, since at this time the theological virtues and the gifts of the Spirit are also infused. In principle, Wesley agrees. However, knowing that sin remains in the believer, Wesley expects God to act again in a manner very analogous to justification in order to raise the believer to a higher level of sanctification. In response to the perfectionist controversies Wesley perhaps lightened the theological load of this teaching but he did not explicitly abjure it altogether.

The late Wesley thinks of perfection as both the uprooting of the unholy tempers remaining after justification and the maturation of the seeds of the holy tempers imparted in the new birth. Thomas expects progress in holiness, and distinguishes those who are beginners and are mostly concerned with avoiding mortal sin from those who are proficient and are mostly concerned with growing in virtue, from those who are perfect and are mostly concerned with union with God.[69] Like the late Wesley, Thomas does not think that attaining perfection in love consists in the granting of a new form but in the removing of the remains of an old one, namely the *fomes peccati* and the *reliquiae peccati*.[70]

> God heals the whole man perfectly; but sometimes suddenly (*subito*), as Peter's mother-in-law was restored at once to perfect health, so that "rising she ministered to them" (Luke 4:39), and sometimes by degrees (*successive*), as we said above (44, 3, ad 2) about the blind man who was restored to sight (Mark 8). And so too, He sometimes turns the heart of man with such power, that it receives at once perfect spiritual health, not only the guilt being pardoned, but all remnants of sin being removed as was the case with Magdalen (Lk. 7); whereas at other times He sometimes first pardons the guilt by operating grace, and afterwards, by co-operating grace, removes the remnants of sin by degrees.[71]

In sum, for Aquinas, perfection can be the work of an instant (*subito*) or it can occur by degrees (*successive*). On the one hand, the forgiveness of sins is always instantaneous; God never half pardons someone. On the other hand, the removal of the remains of sin can be instantaneous but it need not be; God sometimes half heals someone as in the case of the blind man whose eyes Jesus touched twice.[72] The difference stems not from the condition of the patient, as if some were more apt for healing, but from the mode of divine operation which sometimes works without our willing and sometimes through our willing (but never against our willing). Indeed, this distinction between two modes of divine action, which Thomas calls *gratia operans* and *gratia cooperans*, helps undo the Gordian knot that has tied the Maddox and Collins debate over *ordo* and *via*. The elucidation of this claim will need to wait for a later section when we look at the nature of merit. However, for now, let me simply say that for Aquinas it is the primacy and sufficiency of grace that makes room for responsible grace.

The second issue raised by Wesley's emphasis on the "now" of grace concerns the role of the virtues in Christian life. This issue can be phrased in a series of questions: What is the relation between the "moment to moment" presence of God and the holy tempers or virtues which renew human nature? Is there a genuine *verbum hominis* to *and with* the *verbum divinum*?[73] Or does Wesley's description of Christian existence as a "moment to moment" affair eclipse the salutary significance of exercising the holy tempers? Indeed, does not the emphasis on the "now" turn the Christian into a spiritual hypochondriac constantly concerned about their spiritual temperature?[74] Rather than addressing these questions one by one, we will consider them by looking at the nodal point that brings them all together—backsliding.

Since Wesley and Aquinas agree that the perfection that is attainable in this life allows both increase and decrease, they admit the possibility of backsliding along the way of salvation. No matter how far one has walked in the Spirit, it is possible to fall from grace. No matter how mature one has grown in Christ, it is possible to lose this perfection. The possibility of falling from grace probably comes as no surprise to anyone who reads the newspapers with their far-too-frequent accounts of the peccadilloes (and the *magna peccata*) of public figures; indeed it sometimes seems that people are more attracted to disgraced heroes than to saints. Be that as it may, what is startling in Thomas' account is that all that separates a person who has attained the highest summit of perfection from plummeting into a state of spiritual death is one mortal sin. Now, the angelic doctor acknowledges that this kind of fall is a rare occurrence.

> A man who is in the state of perfection, does not suddenly go so far as to commit a mortal sin, but is disposed thereto by some previous negligence, for which reason venial sins are said to be dispositions to mortal sin. . . . Nevertheless, he falls and looses charity through the one mortal sin if he commits it.[75]

One mortal sin can undo a lifetime of vigils, fasting, and service, and yet it does not seem that it should be so. After all, charity is a habit, and one does not lose a habit by one contrary act. Rather, a habit is only lost by acquiring an opposite habit and it takes more than one spiteful thought to turn a loving person into a hateful person. However, charity is not the kind of habit that can be acquired through practice. Charity is infused by God's action and depends on communion with God for its permanence. As Thomas observes,

> [J]ust as the light would cease at once in the air, were an obstacle placed to its being lit up by the sun, even so charity ceases at once to be in the soul through the placing of an obstacle to the outpouring of charity by God into the soul.[76]

These words sound harsh yet they are echoed by John Wesley.

> The holiest of men still need Christ as their Prophet, as "the light of the world." For he does not give them light but from moment to moment; the instant he withdraws, all is darkness.[77]

According to Wesley, God pours his love into our hearts so that our hearts might be poured out in love towards God and neighbor. Sin closes the heart to the fountain of grace. According to Aquinas, all moral virtues and gifts of the Spirit are ruled by charity, the *vinculum perfectionis*; sin severs this bond. It is this incompatibility of sin and charity that excludes any kind of flawed sanctity from being regarded as perfect or holy. A saint can become a backslider but a backslider is not a saint. A holy person can fall into adultery and an adulterer can repent and be restored to grace, but a holy adulterer is an oxymoron.[78] Sin closes the door on God's love and without love *nihil sum.*[79]

In sum, the insistence on the "now" of grace, far from undermining the life of the virtues, vouchsafes its supernatural character. When Wesley says that the grace of Jesus Christ is given to none but "from moment to moment" he is not trying to say that Christian existence is ephemeral but that all Christian tempers, habits, and virtues are gifts from above. Aquinas says very much the same thing, though in a more nuanced way, by drawing a distinction between habitual and actual grace (to be examined when we consider the role of merit in sanctification). For both Wesley and Aquinas, the holy tempers/infused virtues do become a kind of second nature in us, but this second nature is only possible by participation in God's own nature. In other words, the ultimate ground for the stability of Christian life comes not from any virtue, acquired or infused, but from communion with God in whom there is no shadow of turning.

Perfection and Assurance

So far, our assessment of Wesley's and Aquinas' understanding of perfection has considered those structural elements that are common to both doctrines: the universal call to second perfection, the centrality of love and freedom from sin, and the significance of the infused virtues. Throughout this examination I have tried to show how these elements are used in *analogous* ways in their respective teachings on perfection. I underscore the term "analogous," because as in any analogy there are differences and proportions, but I would argue that these differences and proportions are commensurate with those that distinguish a house from a cathedral. In the final two sections of this chapter, I wish to turn our attention to two contrasting elements that seem to stretch the analogy beyond reasonable proportion: Wesley's doctrine of assurance and Aquinas' teaching on merit.

According to Wesley, one of the ordinary privileges which God grants those whom he has justified is the gift of assurance. All Christians can know how things stand between God and them; they can know that all is well with their soul because the Holy Spirit witnesses with their spirit that they are children of God. For the believer, grace can be perceived by means of the spiritual *sensorium*, which though dormant in fallen nature becomes activated when one is born again. The actual perception of grace is the basis for faith (the conviction of things unseen) and love (we love as we become aware of God's love for us).

In a thorough study on the perceptibility of grace in Wesley's theology, Daniel Luby expresses deep appreciation for Wesley's doctrine of assurance.[80] "By encouraging us to expect and seek in our prayer ever more affecting awareness of God's love for us, and greater sensitivity to the manifold ways in which that love is expressed, Wesley is inviting us to foster a more conscious devotion to the Holy Spirit, whose ministry alone can make us more aware of and sensitive to divine love."[81] However, Luby's reception of Wesley is not uncritical.[82] Indeed, he singles out two key areas of concern in Wesley's understanding of assurance that are of relevance for our discussion. The lesser fault could be described as methodological or terminological. Wesley does not draw sufficiently clear distinctions between the various ways in which grace and freedom intersect. In particular, his lack of attention to the distinction between actual and habitual grace leaves Wesley open to the charge of illuminism.[83] We have already raised this issue in terms of the relation between the "now" of grace and the life of the virtues and suggested that Wesley's thought on this issue would indeed benefit from the conceptual clarity of Thomas' account of grace. "The more serious flaw in Wesley's thought on the perceptibility of grace lies in his approach to faith. Wesley appears to be wed to the Enlightenment's epistemological demands for empirical, tangible evidence in the form of "immediate" perception as a requirement for credibility."[84] One consequence of this epistemic empiricism is an inadequate account of the darkness of faith. Faith is not sight; we see in a mirror dimly, but Wesley appears to consider any experience of uncertainty or night as a mark of personal failure.[85]

The role of suffering in sanctification is an area that deserves further exploration in Wesley and Aquinas beyond what we have already accomplished in this study. Instead, I want to turn our attention to the related issue of personal certainty. The issue can be stated in two questions: Is assurance of sanctification possible? If it is possible, is such assurance desirable? For Wesley, the answer to both these questions is "yes."

In his "A Plain Account of Christian Perfection," Wesley insists that one can know that one is sanctified. How can we know?

> We know it by the *witness* and by *the fruit* of the Spirit. And first, by the *witness*. As, when we were justified, *the Spirit bore witness with our spirit*, that our sins were forgiven; so, when we were sanctified, he bore witness, that they were taken away. Indeed, the witness of sanctification is not always clear at first; (as neither is that of justification;) neither is it afterward always the same, but, like that of justification, sometimes

> stronger and sometimes fainter. Yea, and sometimes it is withdrawn. Yet, in general, the latter testimony of the Spirit is both as clear and as steady as the former.[86]

The Spirit works in similar ways in both justification and sanctification. As Collins points out, in both justification and sanctification there is a direct witness (the Holy Spirit) and an indirect witness (the fruit of the Spirit) of our relation before God.[87] The difference between sanctification and justification is not that the Spirit is given in the former but not the latter (as some later interpreters of Wesley would claim when linking entire sanctification to the baptism of the Spirit) but in the object of the witness and the ripeness of the fruit of the Spirit. In justification, the Spirit bears witness that our sins are forgiven. In sanctification, the Spirit bears witness that our sins are removed. In justification, the fruit of the Spirit is love, joy, peace, longsuffering, and the like. In sanctification, the fruit of the Spirit is the same, but riper, more mature, more resistant to the effects of adversity. The intensity of the witness of our sanctification can fluctuate; indeed at first it might not be clear at all that the root of sin has been removed. Yet, Wesley expects that over time the witness of our sanctification grows in clarity and strength until one attains the full assurance of faith. This full assurance, this *plerophory* "is the true ground of a Christian's happiness."[88] In short, for Wesley, full assurance of our sanctification is possible and desirable.[89] Where do things stand with Aquinas?

From the early days of his career, Thomas rejects the possibility that Christians can be aware of their present state of grace, or, what amounts to the same thing, that they can perceive charity. As the angelic doctor states in *De veritate*,

> One who has charity can surmise that he has charity from probable signs (*ex aliquibus probabilibus signis*), as when he sees that he is ready to undertake spiritual works, and that he effectively hates evil, as also through other things of this sort which charity affects in a man. But one cannot know with certainty that he has charity unless it be revealed to him by God.[90]

This answer seems to be contrary to our common experience. After all, what is more evident to a person than one's own likes and dislikes? Most people, if fortunate, have had the opportunity to tell someone "I love you," and that proclamation is made with the greatest conviction, "I know I love that person." Yet, when we probe the epistemic basis of these declarations we need to make certain distinctions. As Thomas says, "anyone who knows, knows that he knows. . . . But the perfection of charity does not consist in certitude of knowledge but in strength of affection (*in vehementia affectionis*)."[91] When I declare my love, I perceive that I have affection toward the object of my love, but what is not clear is precisely the strength or source of that affection (as the tragic ending of many marriages tell us all too clearly).

The gap between the act of love and the perception of this act increases when knowledge of the object of love decreases. In the case of God, since he is never comprehended, it is not possible for someone to know that they are united to God in charity. Thus, "the act of love which we perceive in ourselves, insofar as it is perceptible, is not an adequate indication of charity, because of the similarity between natural love and infused love (*propter similitudinem dilectionis naturalis ad gratuitam*)."[92] Yes, with God all things are possible, and God might reveal to someone that he or she loves with perfect charity, but this certain knowledge is neither necessary for salvation nor even especially desirable. "In fact, it is generally more advantageous not to know, because thus solicitude and humility are preserved (*quia per hoc magis sollicitudo et humilitas conservatur*)."[93]

As I stated earlier, Thomas consistently insists that certain knowledge of being in the state of perfect charity is neither necessary nor likely for the Christian. He reiterates this judgment in the *Summa*, where he considers the question of whether humans can know that they have grace.[94] In answer to this question, Thomas develops with great detail the ways in which we might know that we have received God's sanctifying grace (*gratia gratum faciens*). The first way in which we might know that we have received the gift of charity is by revelation.

> God by a special privilege (*ex speciali privilegio*) reveals this at times to some, in order that the joy of safety (*securitatis gaudium*) may begin in them even in this life, and that they may carry on toilsome works with greater trust and greater energy, and may bear the evils of this present life (*et confidentius et fortius magnifica opera prosequantur, et mala praesentis vitae sustineant*).[95]

The classic example of this special privilege is Saint Paul, who, for the sake of his mission, was entirely sanctified at the moment of his conversion.[96] By his own testimony, Paul received assurance of this grace as a consolation for the thorn in his flesh (cf. 2 Cor 12:9). This assurance does not pertain to present salvation but to final salvation. Hence it is fitting that only those who lead holy lives receive this consolation. As Thomas observes in *De caritate* (written around the same time as the *Secunda Pars* of the *Summa*),

> Although every one is bound to live without mortal sin, it is not for every one to have complete assurance in this matter; but only for the perfect who have completely overcome sin (*licet quilibet teneatur esse sine peccato mortali, non tamen omnium est huiusmodi rei securitatem habere; sed perfectorum, qui peccata totaliter subiugaverunt*).[97]

The second way in which we might know if we have received grace is from our knowledge, but in this way, it is not possible to know for sure that we have received grace. No one can understand a conclusion that does not know the principle. Analogously, since God is God, he cannot be comprehended by us and for this reason, "his presence in us and his absence cannot be known with certainty" (*eius praesentia in nobis vel absentia per certitudinem cognosci non potest*).[98] Garrigou-Lagrange explains Thomas' position well: "Grace is the seed of glory. In order to know its essence intimately, we must first have seen the divine essence of which grace is the participation."[99]

Finally, it is possible to know things by conjecture, and in this way it is possible to have awareness of God's grace in the soul. As Thomas states, "whoever receives [grace] knows, by experiencing a certain sweetness, which he who does not receive it, does not experience" (*quia scilicet ille qui accipit, per quandam experientiam dulcedinis novit, quam non experitur ille qui non accipit*).[100] As we experience greater and greater delight in the worship of God, as we are increasingly repulsed by the evil things of this world, our conviction of grace increases, "yet this knowledge is imperfect" (*ista tamen cognitio imperfecta est*);[101] it is only conjectural, "the object or end of grace is unknown to us on account of the greatness of its light" (*Obiectum autem vel finis gratiae est nobis ignotum, propter sui luminis immensitatem*).[102]

In sum, for Aquinas it is possible to know for certain that one has been sanctified, and it would be a great consolation and encouragement to know that one has been made perfect, but this certitude is not a common benefit of the children of God, but a special privilege extended only to a few for the sake of their perseverance in their mission from God. Hence assurance of sanctification has a role in the doctrines of perfection of both Wesley and Aquinas, but it is not exactly the same role. Both underline the significance for Christian life of knowing God by a certain sweet experience. Both allow for certain knowledge of one's status before God. Both admit that there are benefits and risks to such knowledge. However there is a difference. If there is one place in the comparison between Wesley and Aquinas that can best be understood by appealing to Otto Hermann Pesch's distinction between sapiential and existential modes of theology, the doctrine of assurance is that place. Wesley is simply much more interested in the believer's present status before God than Aquinas; indeed, to the extent that the angelic doctor speaks of assurance and awareness of grace he appears to do so more for the sake of the *ordo disciplinae* rather than out of an inner necessity in the *via salutis*.

Holiness and Merit

The final area that we need to consider in this dialogue between Aquinas and Wesley on the doctrine of perfection is merit. If I may phrase this *locus theologicus* in terms of a question: what is the role of merits in Christian perfection? This question is important not for the sake of the comprehensiveness of our treatment but because, in taking up this issue, we go to the heart of one of the recurring themes of our study, namely the relationship between divine action and human action.

John Wesley's attitude toward the role of merits in salvation is unambiguous; he repudiates any notion of meriting our salvation or being justified by works. Wesley repeatedly asserts that only the merits of Christ appropriated by faith are of any saving significance. For a number of his opponents, Wesley's insistence on holiness as necessary for our final salvation smacked of "popery." Indeed, in the "1770 Minutes," Wesley appears ever so cautiously to crack a window to the value of merits in salvation.

> As to merit itself, of which we have been so dreadfully afraid: We are rewarded according to our works, yea, because of our works. How does this differ from, "for the sake of our works?" And how differs this from *secundum merita operum*? which is no more than, "as our works deserve." Can you split this hair? I doubt cannot.[103]

The context for this statement is a discussion of the conditions for acceptance before God. In the midst of this discussion, Wesley claims that God accepts people "not by the merit of their works but by works as a condition."[104] This assertion leads to the clarification of works and merit cited above. The three phrases whose nuanced differences Wesley finds so hard to tease out are various possible translations of Matthew 16:28, which speaks of the day when the Son of Man returns in glory with his angels "to render unto every man according to his work."[105]

All this hairsplitting smacked of "popery" to his Calvinist foes and they said so, giving occasion for Wesley to clarify his thoughts on this matter. In a letter in response to one of his critics, Wesley explains his thoughts on merit by drawing a distinction between merit in the proper sense and merit in the improper sense.

> [T]here is no merit, taking the word strictly, but in the blood of Christ; that salvation is not by the merit of works; and that there is nothing we are, or have, or do, which can, strictly speaking, deserve the least thing at God's hand.[106]

For Wesley, "in a strict sense," no work merits but the work of Christ. Even works after justification, acts that are empowered by grace do not, "strictly speaking," deserve any kind of reward. This is the sense in which Wesley abjures all usage of the word. There is, however, another way of applying the term "merit."

> [T]ake it in a looser sense, and though I never use it, (I mean, I never ascribe it to any man,) yet I do not condemn it.[107]

In its "looser sense," Wesley defines merit "as nearly equivalent with rewardable."[108] Scripture often speaks of merit in this "improper sense." Some works are rewardable and can thus be considered meritorious.

Interpreters of Wesley have been somewhat at odds over these statements on merit from the pen of the elderly Wesley. For Gunter, "these statements inclined more in the direction of moralism than anything Wesley had ever preached or published."[109] Indeed, Gunter is convinced that not only was the language of the "1770 Minutes" on merits unguarded but that it went "farther in the direction of works' righteousness than [Wesley] really believed acceptable."[110] Collins, reading of the controversy surrounding these Minutes, is more generous. Contra the critics, Collins insists that "it was really unfair to read Wesley's soteriological thought through the interpretive lens of Trent."[111] According to Collins, Rome understands merit only in the strict sense, whereas Wesley recognizes a loose sense as well.

> Wesley's understanding of merit in the loose sense, then does not underscore autonomous human achievement; on the contrary, it doubly highlights the graciousness of divine activity: once in the giving of grace; the other in the rewarding of its fruit.[112]

Collins does not seem aware of it, but his description of Wesley's understanding of merit "in a looser sense" is very close to that of Aquinas.

> Now it is clear that between God and man there is the greatest inequality: for they are infinitely apart, and all man's good is from God. Hence there can be no justice of absolute equality between man and God, but only of a certain proportion, inasmuch as both operate after their own manner. Now the manner and measure of human virtue is in man from

> God. Hence man's merit with God only exists on the presupposition of the Divine ordination, so that man obtains from God, as a reward of his operation, what God gave him the power of operation for, even as natural things by their proper movements and operations obtain that to which they were ordained by God; differently, indeed, since the rational creature moves itself to act by its free-will, hence its action has the character of merit, which is not so in other creatures.[113]

According to Thomas, humans have no right to a reward *simpliciter* but only *secundum quid*. Humans do not merit by virtue of any natural equality between their effort and the reward, but only because God has gracefully determined to reward those works that are done under the power of the Holy Spirit. This is not the place to unfold the content of Thomas' doctrine of merit but we need at least to consider the twofold purpose of this doctrine. First, according to Wawrykow, the teaching on merit displays the goodness of God, who invites human beings to share in his eternal felicity. Second, the teaching "discloses the special dignity and perfection of the one who merits."[114] For Thomas, merit and the second perfection of the human are integrally connected. In Wawrykow's words, "Because people are free to act and are able to reach their end through their acts, they are of greater perfection than agents simply moved to their acts."[115] Or in Aquinas' words: *nobilius habetur id quod habetur per meritum quam id quod habetur sine merito*.[116] Human attainment of perfection by grace (there is no meriting without grace) is more perfect with merit than without it.[117]

As paradoxical and counterintuitive as it might sound to Protestant ears, by using the term "merit" Aquinas secures Wesley's "orienting concern."[118] First, humans have a real role to play in their salvation. It is by meriting that the words of one of Wesley's favorite sayings are fulfilled, namely, that "he that made us without ourselves will not save us without ourselves."[119] Second, salvation is all of grace. It is by meriting that the gratuity of grace is preserved because all the good we do is all of grace.

> Deus non sine nobis nos iustificat, quia per motum liberi arbitrii, dum iustificamur, Dei iustitiae consentimus. Ille tamen motus non est causa gratiae, sed effectus. Unde tota operatio pertinet ad gratiam.[120]

Charles Journet observes that expressions like "fitness for heaven," "spiritual fruitfulness," and "merit" are basically synonymous.[121] If so, Wesley ought not to be chided for not using the word "merit," nor Aquinas for insisting on it. As Journet wisely remarks,

> The very word [merit] is a source of contention; when we use it in talking to Protestants, they are put off and refuse to listen. It is better, in fact, not to use the *word* but to explain the *thing*. Perhaps they will find they have believed it all the time.[122]

Protestant fears of merit as Pelagian stem to a large extent from a misconception of divine causality. Many Protestant theologians have set up an insuperable dialectical opposition between divine action and human action: when God works the human is passive and when the human works God is passive. Even those who insist on divine-human synergism in salvation usually understand this relation as one where God works first and then waits for the human to respond, or God performs ninety-nine percent of the work and the human picks up the remaining one percent. In short, despite their many differences, many Wesleyans and Calvinists understand God's causality as operating on the same level of human causality. This is not how Aquinas understands the issue.

In order to comprehend Thomas' understanding of divine-human action we must briefly consider his division of grace into two sets of categories: operative and cooperative, habitual and actual. In his classic study on the nature of grace and freedom, Lonergan concisely and precisely sums up Thomas' understanding of these categories.

> When the will is *mota et non movens, solus autem Deus movens, dicitur gratia operans*. On the other hand, when the will is *et mova et movens, dicitur gratia cooperans*. In habitual grace divine operation infuses the habit, to become cooperation when the habit leads to free acts; in actual grace divine operation effects the will of the end to become cooperation when this will of the end leads to an efficacious choice of means.[123]

With this distinction between *gratia operans* and *gratia cooperans* the Gordian knot tying the instantaneous versus gradual debate is undone.[124] On the one hand, as operating grace, all divine operation is instantaneous. The infusion of virtue in habitual operating grace and the reducing of the will to action in actual operating grace take place in an instant. On the other hand, as cooperating grace all divine operations are gradual. The exercise of virtue and willing of acts are not instantaneous, not because of any deficiency in God, but because our willing and doing are temporal acts.

Does this mean that operating grace is irresistible and cooperating grace is resistible?[125] Such a question would be ill posed for Thomas because it would reduce the operation of God to the level of a created cause which would sometimes override human refusal and sometimes not. When Aquinas speaks of God's action as the first cause of all created actions, he does not mean that it is first in a temporal sequence but that it is first in a causal hierarchy, first in dignity, and first in importance.[126] In Thomas' theology the prefix "pre," as in prevenient grace, is first and foremost ontological not chronological. All the operations of grace—infused and actual, operating and cooperating—are prevenient because grace belongs to an order superior to natural causality. God is the first cause of our being and of every operation of our being including our willing and doing.[127] This is why for Aquinas salvation is one hundred percent the work of God and one hundred percent the work of humans: "our merits are from God and Christ as first cause, and from us as second cause—God gives us in Christ the power to assent to him."[128]

If this talk of God working on and through our will sounds a lot like predestination, that is because that is precisely what it means. For Thomas, predestination is that aspect of the doctrine of providence that concerns the ordering of intellectual creatures to share in his eternal life. We will misunderstand Thomas' doctrine of predestination if we read the prefix "pre" in predestination as relating to a temporal rather than causal priority. As we just saw, God's causality and human causality operate on different planes. As with merit it is not possible to examine Thomas' doctrine of predestination within the confines of this study, but it is really Thomas who makes us consider the question of predestination when we take up the issue of merit.

Wesley does not deny that the Bible teaches a doctrine of predestination. He claims that predestination must be understood in two senses. On the one hand, the Bible presents a doctrine of predestination for an earthly mission. This predestination is unconditional. As McGonigle avers, according to Wesley,

> God elected certain men and women to do a particular work in the world, and such election is absolute and unconditional. Examples of this are Cyrus who was chosen of God to bring about the rebuilding of the temple in Jerusalem, and Paul, called of God to preach the gospel. This election had nothing to with eternal salvation, for Jesus elected his twelve apostles, yet by his own admission one of them had a devil.[129]

On the other hand, the Bible presents a doctrine of predestination for salvation. This predestination is conditional. As McGonigle states, for Wesley, "predestination means foreordination based on foreknowledge of faith."[130] If God predestines someone to salvation it is because he has foreseen his or her faithful response to God's summons. Likewise if he predestines someone to damnation it is because he has foreseen that they will refuse his divine overtures. For Wesley, "God's foreknowledge of man's salvation is not dependent on God's foreordination. He 'foreknows,' not because he decreed it but because he is omniscient."[131] This understanding of predestination corresponds to that which the scholastics called *post praevisa (de) merita* and stands in contrast to the version held by Calvinists who taught that predestination occurred *ante praevisa (de)merita.*

Wesley's understanding of predestination as *post praevisa (de)merita* is shared by Aquinas in his early works, for instance in his *Commentary on the Sentences*. However, by the time of the *Summa*, Thomas' understanding of predestination shifts. As Paluch observes,

> Nous voyons donc qu'après une interprétation de la réprobation proche du cadre *post praevisa demerita* dans les *Sentences*, Thomas tend à rejoindre celle qui pourrait être nommée *simul ac praevisa demerita*. On pourrait penser qu'une telle solution le rapproche aussi de la fameuse *gemina praedestinatio* et de l'interprétation calviniste mais ce n'est qu'une apparence. Il ne s'agit pas d'éliminer la responsabilité humaine au nom de la cohérence métaphysique dans l'interprétation de l'action divine. Nous avons vu que la liberté des puissances humaines est fortement soulignée. *Simul ac praevisa demerita* n'est pas une version mitigée d'*ante praevisa demerita*. Son interpretation essaie de conciler ces deux données dans une solution qui paraîtmétaphysiquement plus neutre, c'est-à-dire qui semble les tenir les «deux bouts de la chaîne.[132]

As it happens, both the Arminian and Calvinist answers to the question of grace and freedom are two faces of the same coin. Both solutions hinge on reducing God to one actor performing on the world stage, doubtless the most powerful one, the star, but one among many nonetheless. However, as Paluch rightly observes, "En Dieu n'y a ni *ante* ni *post*."[133] These words are well worth meditating on, for they point out the temporal fallacies that underlie most accounts of predestination. However, even when the *ante* and *post* are understood ontologically rather than chronologically, two problems remain, *les deux bouts de la chaîne*. Affirm the *ante* and the door to double predestination, fatalism, and God's responsibility for sin is opened. Affirm the *post* and God's immutability is assailed because it appears that the creature can affect God. Thomas' solution to this problem opens a third way. This way is emphatically not a synthesis of the first two but rather presents the least unsatisfying solution to this issue in order to avoid the aforementioned dangers. In the end, the question of predestination is not a logical problem to be overcome dialectically but a saving mystery to be approached apophatically. In the words of Paluch,

> La *profondeur* du mystère de la prédestination et sa portée pour la foi chrétienne ne sont pas à charger dans l'image d'un Dieu *arbitraire* qui ne choisit pas tel ou tel pour le salut. C'est notre liberté qui peut *vraiment* rejeter Dieu. En d'autres termes : nos difficultés avec le mystère de la prédestination ne sont pas constituées par le problème d'un amour divin limité mais par celui de notre compréhension limitée et par celui des limites de notre propre amour. La prédestination est le mystère lumineux d'un Dieu qui nous donne tout gratuitement, qui est toujours de notre côte dans notre effort pour le suivre.[134]

Continuing these reflections on predestination in Wesley and Aquinas would take us beyond the limits of our present inquiry. Some might say that we have already left the boundaries of the doctrine of perfection, properly speaking. Perhaps so, yet, it was important to take up the question of predestination in connection with the doctrine of perfection in order to offer some explanation for the puzzling fact that, though Aquinas and Wesley insist that perfection is the ordinary end of Christian life, few Christians seem to attain it in this life. Yes, God's grace is universal and it is sufficient to turn a sinner into a saint, yet too frequently this grace is not made efficacious but rather is tragically rejected.

The parable of the talents offers a clear illustration of a doctrine of predestination that could, I think, be accepted by Methodists. The distribution of talents displays the mystery of divine love which gives to each according to the capacity that it gave to each in the first place. Everyone receives, even if not equally. This mystery escapes elucidation by way of excess; it is too luminous, too sublime. In the words of Charles Wesley, "in vain the first born seraph tries to sound the depths of love divine."[135] The burying of the talents displays the mystery of sin which spurns both nature and grace for the sake of the void. Everyone receives and many reject what they receive. This mystery, too, escapes elucidation, not by way of excess but by way of deficiency; it is too dim, too subrational. In any case, I hope that this short theological excursus has shown that predestination cannot simply be treated as a historical artifact, a relic of the conflicts of yesteryear between Wesley and Whitefield or between Molina and Bañez, but as an abiding structural element of a sound doctrine of Christian perfection.[136]

Wesleyan Thomism? Thomistic Wesleyanism?

In this chapter we have considered the structural elements of the Methodist house and the Thomist cathedral. Our investigation has shown that Wesley and Aquinas used some of the same materials in similar ways: the importance of beatitude, the centrality of love, the universality of the call to perfection, the importance of the life of the virtues and the social character of holiness. In addition to these common building blocks, we considered those elements that were in one doctrine but were missing or even rejected by the other. In particular, we examined the role of assurance and merit and found that these elements play a significant structural role in their respective places; they are not merely decorative.

All along in this comparison I have been suggesting that house and cathedral complement each other, and they complement each other precisely because they are different. Hence, the cause of ecclesial unity would not be furthered by stripping medieval metaphysics from the Thomist cathedral. The result would not be a more hospitable space for Methodists but an empty shell that is home to none. Likewise, it would be a mistake to tack scholastic elements directly on the Methodist house so as to make it more appealing for Catholics. The result would not be a cathedral but a tacky, pretentious, ungainly structure. On the contrary, ecumenical rapprochement is furthered when the Thomist cathedral and the Methodist house are true to their original plans. The differences between house and cathedral exist for the sake of the beauty and perfection of the church catholic. By Methodist theology being house-like and Thomist theology cathedral-like the church as a whole is built up and renewed.

All this talk of building and materials is obviously metaphorical, and must not be given undue conceptual weight. Wesley and Aquinas are more artists than engineers; their work is more contemplative than constructive. They are not trying to assemble disparate parts into a coherent whole, but to find a coherent way of proclaiming the exemplar of perfection revealed in Scripture, Jesus Christ. Hence, the relative neglect of merit in Wesley and of assurance in Aquinas signals less the repudiation of each other's vision than their obedience to God's particular mission for each of them.

Our exploration of Thomas Aquinas' and John Wesley's doctrine of perfection suggests that engagement of these two figures is rich in possibilities for ecumenical and theological inquiry. In the introduction to this study I appealed to the way in which Jacques Maritain understood Aquinas as a speculatively practical theologian whose work is foundational for and complemented by St. John of the Cross, a practically practical theologian. Maritain called the former "the great Doctor of the highest incommunicable wisdom . . . the Doctor of Light";[137] the latter he called "the great Doctor of this supreme incommunicable wisdom . . . the Doctor of Night."

Is there room for Wesley next to the Thomist sun and the Sanjuanist moon? I think so, if we understand Wesley as a practically practical theologian of the active life; the Doctor of *Walking* in the Light. Yes, at times Aquinas and Wesley speak a different language (first perfection); at times they use the same language in different ways (Beatitudes, assurance). At times they appear to contradict each other (the perceptibility of grace, merit). Yet, there is a fundamental agreement in their theological work that comes not from knowledge of each other but from knowledge of God's revelation. Hence, I believe that we can without too much difficulty or presumption claim for Wesley and Aquinas what Maritain said of the Doctor of Light and the Doctor of Night. When it comes to Wesley's and Aquinas' understanding of perfection, "accidental and *reducible* divergencies between witnesses confirm the veracity of their testimony, by showing that their agreement was not premeditated."[138] In other words, their doctrines of perfection stand on more sure ground precisely because they did not read or depend on each other's formulation. Furthermore, their agreement is all the more significant "because the former is not at all interested in playing the role of scholastic theologian, but only in singing what he knows divinely."[139] Wesley and Aquinas "had different missions to perform," but "both bear witness to the same living truth."[140]

The common witness of Wesley and Aquinas to perfection is not without consequence for their respective heirs. Indeed, one of the purposes of this study has been to take Wesley and Aquinas out of the museum of great figures of history, where their works are displayed in separate rooms, unstudied, and unreconciled in order to suggest the vitality and viability of their thought for contemporary Christian theologians and their respective communities. Alone, Wesley is not a complete catholic theologian.[141] Alone, Methodism is, as Outler averred, *une église manqué*.[142] Alone, the communities constituted by the heirs of Wesley "suffer from defects."[143] However, Methodism's peculiar providential purpose might not lie in being a sister church but precisely in being an ecclesial community in service to and for the church catholic, in being a house for the cathedral.

There is room in the Methodist meeting house for a Thomistic Wesleyanism. That is to say, there is room for one who engages in theological reflection in a speculatively practical mode, whose intellect strengthened by faith seeks to bring greater conceptual clarity to the truths of revelation, someone like John Fletcher whose introduction of scholastic distinctions into Wesley's theology, far from being a departure from the spirit of Methodism, clarified Methodism's catholic spirit.

There is room in the scholastic cathedral for a Wesleyan Thomism. That is to say, there is room for one who speaks not to budding theologians (*incipientes*)[144] but *ad populum*:[145] a simplifier, a practitioner who does not only define perfection but leads others to perfection, someone like

John Paul II who took the cathedral into the world and reiterated the call to holiness not just with words but with exemplars.

Such examples might strike some readers as fanciful or illicit, as no more than a theological dressup game where one clothes historical figures according to one's own fancies. It might be so. Examples of mismatched Wesleys and ill-suited Aquinases abound. However, sometimes the clothes make the man a better man and the woman a better woman. A particular set of clothes might show off one's amiable assets and conceal one's flaws better than another. Such is the case with Wesley and Aquinas when it comes to perfection. Reading Thomas can help Methodists be better Wesleyans. Conversely, reading Wesley can help Thomists be better Catholics.

Chapter Seven

Prospects for Christian Perfection

In a relatively recent reflection "On the Ecumenical Situation,"[1] the then Cardinal Ratzinger contrasted two modes of ecumenism. The classical model of dialogical (or consensus) ecumenism attempted "to perceive how positions that are apparently opposed may be compatible at a deeper level and, in doing so, of course, to exclude everything that derives only from certain cultural developments."[2] For various reasons, this mode of ecumenism has been pushed to the sides by a new paradigm that is centered on the practice of charity rather than on the search for truth. Ratzinger is rightly suspicious of playing logos and ethos off each other, but he admits that the classical paradigm had limitations, not the least of which was its frequent inversion of the relationship between truth and consensus which led to the confusion of theological inquiry with diplomacy. Nevertheless, despite their apparent limitations, Ratzinger believes that the path of ecumenism requires the patient practice of both modes of ecumenism. The more humble, chastened way of ecumenism which Ratzinger proposes, I would like to refer to as kneeling ecumenism.

Kneeling Ecumenism

Kneeling ecumenism presupposes the sitting ecumenism of the classical paradigm and the walking ecumenism of the new paradigm. It is not a synthesis of the first two paradigms, or a third model. Instead, kneeling ecumenism represents a modality which is to permeate all postures of ecumenism (sitting and walking) by drawing attention to the primacy of prayer and the ministry of the saints. If the description of kneeling ecumenism sounds remarkably like the "spiritual ecumenism" of *Unitatis Redintegratio* and *Ut unum sint*, that is no accident, for my understanding of ecumenism has been deeply shaped by these documents. However, by placing kneeling ecumenism next to sitting and walking ecumenism I am suggesting that kneeling represents not only the spiritual posture that should underlie all ecumenism but a distinctive mode of ecumenical reflection itself, a paradigm that understands the saints as objects of and partners in ecumenical efforts.

In general this study has been an exercise in sitting ecumenism. We proceeded in a dialogical mode, comparing Aquinas and Wesley, searching not so much for consensus but for truth, or better yet for consensus in the truth. However, reflection on the doctrine of perfection encourages us to move beyond sitting to walking ecumenism, of course, but specially to kneeling. In this final chapter I want us to move toward this modality by engaging in an exercise of recognition of perfection beyond one's own ecclesial bounds. In general, I want to suggest that the doctrines of perfection according to Wesley and Aquinas give us concrete criteria for the recognition of sanctity, a grammar of holiness which helps us discern how to kneel and before whom.

Historically, Wesley's and Aquinas' doctrines of perfection played a powerful role in shaping the criteria which were applied to the recognition of holiness. In the case of Wesley, the legacy was not all positive. An exaggerated understanding of the significance of second blessings and an overreliance on personal testimony all led to what John Peters calls an "abbreviated Wesleyanism"[3] that downplayed the role of the sacraments in sanctification, thereby completely misunderstanding John Wesley's theology of grace. In the case of Aquinas, his treatise on the virtues became central to the Roman Catholic understanding of heroic sanctity as this was described by Prospero Lambertini in his classic *De servorum Dei beatificatione et beatorum canonizatione*.[4]

To this day, both Methodists and Catholics experience difficulties when it comes to recognizing perfect Christians. On the one hand, the unhappy experiments in "self-canonization" during the revivals of the eighteenth and nineteenth centuries made most Methodists give up on any ecclesial recognition of sanctity. On the other hand, the process of canonization as envisioned by Lambertini and developed by centuries of application does not readily allow the discernment of new patterns of holiness that speak more directly to the needs of the church in the twenty-first century.

The saints have a vital role to play in ecumenism. The saints are not static, saccharine portraits of perfection but living icons of the church's ministry of reconciliation; they are the perfect ecclesial bridge builders.[5]

There is in the saints no opposition between orthodoxy and orthopraxy, love of God or love of neighbor, evangelism or mission. Whether active in contemplation, contemplative in action, or active out of the fullness of contemplation, the saints are always ready "to serve the present age"[6] because they already represent the coming kingdom. As John Paul II said, "the most convincing form of ecumenism is the ecumenism of the saints and of the martyrs. The *communio sanctorum* speaks louder than the things that divide us."[7] In the words of Geoffrey Wainwright,

> The prayers and witness of the saints—about membership in whose company there is apparently an increasing ecumenical consensus—must surely be allowed to influence our growing mutual recognition and our progress to greater ecclesial unity on earth.[8]

The prayers of the perfect and the fruitfulness of ecumenism are deeply connected.[9] Yet, until we learn to recognize saints within and without our respective communions the ecumenical significance of sanctity will be more potential than actual. Kneeling ecumenism requires exemplars. Toward this end, I want us to consider Gregorio López' sanctity from the perspective of John Wesley and Jane Cooper's claim to perfection from the vantage point of Thomas Aquinas.

Why Gregorio López? Why Jane Cooper? These are not household names. Their lives attracted the attention of their contemporaries but have since largely fallen into oblivion within their respective traditions only to be sporadically exhumed by historians and graduate students. Moreover, the forms of sanctity that they embodied are those that are now considered passé. They were single; they were contemplatives; they were frail, simple figures. Our age admires the active life; the physically powerful and psychologically complex. We are drawn to tragic heroes and repulsed by do-gooder saints. Yet, as G. K. Chesterton observes, "it is the paradox of history that each generation is converted by the saint who contradicts it the most."[10] Jane Cooper, Gregorio López, and others like them may be the signs of contradiction that our age needs.

Wesley and Gregorio López

Gregorio López was born in Madrid on July 4, 1542. Very little is known about his family origins or his time in Spain. His biographers and critics have variously speculated that he was a secret Jew, a Lutheran, an "*iluminado*," or even the son of Philip II.[11] What is known with some degree of certainty is that around the age of twenty, Gregorio set out for the New World and established a hermitage in New Spain at Atemajac. It is important to note that, at that time, Spain was not a hospitable place for those seeking a life of solitude. Fears of Lutheranism and solifidianism cast a shadow over any kind of life that favored interior devotion over external observance. By the end of the sixteenth century, New Spain became a refuge for those escaping the persecution of the *alumbrados* in the Old World. However, by his own testimony, Gregorio traveled to México not to escape the supervision of the Church, but in obedience to the command of Christ whose voice he heard while visiting the shrine of Guadalupe in Extremadura.

Gregorio López is known to have written several books, his most famous being an exposition on the book of Revelation (*Comentario al Apocalipsis*) and a practical medical guide (*Tesoro de Medicinas*). However, it was not for these writings that he was best known but for the splendor of his interior life. One of the beneficiaries of his spiritual direction was Father Francisco Losa, who became his constant companion and biographer. By the time of his death in 1596, Gregorio had gained a reputation for sanctity to which Losa's biography of his life (*Vida que el siervo de Dios Gregorio López hizo en algunos lugares de Nueva España*, written two years after López' death) contributed in no small measure.

Losa's biography of López is intentionally hagiographical. It is roughly divided into two parts. The first part is an account of the life of Gregorio López cast in the same mold as Saint Athanasius' *Life of Anthony*. Like St. Anthony the Great, Gregorio's life in the desert is spent in spiritual combat. Again and again, the devil attacks Gregorio, sometimes by tempting him spiritually, at times by assaulting him physically, but López proves the victor in these contests thanks to his practice of prayer and mortification. Like St. Anthony, Gregorio does not experience absolute solitude in the desert; whether out of curiosity or devotion, many flee into the wilderness to meet him. Eventually, Gregorio discovers that the true desert is found within and he is thus able to take the desert with him as he travels through many towns in México, dispensing spiritual advice to those willing to hear it. Such is the first part of Losa's hagiography. The second and much more extensive part of Losa's account considers the virtues of Gregorio. In addition to discussing Gregorio's humility, patience, and inward poverty, Losa spends most of his time discussing two things: the extent of Gregorio's knowledge (a knowledge that was not acquired from learning but through infused contemplation), and his practice of continuous prayer. Losa dedicates six entire chapters to the latter.

Losa's account of López' life went through numerous editions and translations. The reasons for the popularity of this hermit's story are not surprising. On the one hand, biblical commentaries, especially those on the Apocalypse, were popular at that time (they still are). López' writing of a commentary on this book from the vantage point of an apocalyptic event, the discovery of the New World, was bound to be noticed. On the other hand, mystic literature was also on the ascendancy, and along comes a mystic who is writing not from an interior castle but from a wilderness not unlike that encountered by the founders of the hermitical life in Egypt. Indeed the mystical experiences of López are so highly valued that Miguel de Molinos rhapsodizes on Gregorio as an incarnate seraph and a deified man.[12] In any case, by the end of the seventeenth century, Losa's *Vida* has gone through several French editions and an English edition translated by Abraham Woodhead, which John Wesley read, abridged, and serialized.[13]

From Wesley's diary, we know that from October 28, 1735 to December 14, 1735 he spent a significant amount of time reading Losa's biography. Given Wesley's intelligence and the relative brevity of this book it is not hard to suppose that he either read Losa over and over again or that he read it very, very carefully. Whatever the case, we do know that after laying the book aside for some years he rereads it on August 31, 1742.

It is not hard to imagine the reasons for Wesley's attraction to this text. Though he does not explicitly say so, Wesley was surely drawn to read López the first time out of a perceived affinity between López' journey to New Spain and his own journey to Savannah; both coming to a new world, both living among a new people, both seeking to establish primitive Christianity in their own way. However, what most attracted Wesley to López and what led him back to that foreign mystic were two things: López' practice of self-denial and his experience of an uninterrupted communion with God.

From Wesley's journal entries and letters, it is clear that Wesley considered López to be an exemplar of Christian perfection. López lived in constant awareness of God's love, for him "all is midday now."[14] According to Losa, López credited the source of this communion to his participation in the Eucharist and to the indwelling of the Holy Trinity.[15] Wesley was convinced that this abiding sense of the presence of God was the perfection to which all Methodists are to aspire. For this reason, when speaking to a young member of the Methodist societies, Wesley encourages the young man to seek "an open intercourse with God, such a close, uninterrupted communion with him, as G. López experienced."[16] On another occasion, bemoaning the worldliness of those Methodists whose *contemptus mundi* was compatible with a life of luxury, Wesley sarcastically wonders: "And this they call 'retiring from the world'! What would Gregory López have called it?"[17]

At times Wesley despairs of actually finding some living witnesses of the holiness that Gregorio López exemplified. When he does find such persons, as in the case of John Fletcher, the highest tribute Wesley can bestow is to claim that his holiness is in no way inferior to that of Gregory López.[18] Fletcher experienced "as deep communion with God, and as high a measure of inward holiness" as López, and "his outward holiness shone before men with full as bright a luster" as the Spanish mystic did.[19]

As an exemplar of Christian perfection, Gregorio López' holiness is a mark of how high a degree of perfection is attainable in this life. Thus when Wesley criticizes Swedenborg's account of heaven, Wesley complains that "his account of it has a natural tendency to sink our conceptions both of the glory of heaven and of the inhabitants of it, whom he describes as far inferior in holiness and happiness to Gregory López."[20]

It might sound strange to modern ears, but even in his poverty, Gregorio was a truly happy man. His happiness was the fruit of that perfect love which he practiced toward God and neighbor, and this happiness was also a consequence of his apparent unawareness of personal sin. When Losa asked López whether sinless perfection is possible in this life, López replied,

> When those whom God has enabled to love him with all their soul, do with his assistance all that is in their power, and that with deep humility, it is possible for them to remain without committing sin; as clearly appears, in that our Lord, who commanded nothing which was impossible to be performed, commanded this, "Thou shall love the Lord thy God, with all thy heart, mind, soul, and strength." But he who does this, not only does not sin, but grows daily in all holiness.[21]

To this assertion Losa replied, "But how can this be, when the Scripture says, 'The just man sins seven times a day?' "[22] López, in turn, explained to Losa that Christians cannot take this text as literally applying to them. Wesley does not think that this explanation sufficiently addresses the question and so he adds the following note:

> Observe what kind of perfection the papists hold! The true answer is, there is no such word in the Bible. Solomon's words are, the just man falleth seven times; not into sin, but trouble.[23]

Readers of Wesley know that Proverbs 24:16 was a frequent proof text used by critics of the doctrine of Christian perfection. Be that as it may, it is certainly the case that López' lack of awareness of personal sin troubled his biographer and hindered his cause for canonization. Indeed, in order to safeguard both Catholic doctrine and López' sanctity, Losa limited such claims of "sinlessness" to refer to mortal sin, or dismissed them as lapses of memory.[24]

For Wesley, not only was López an exemplar of Christian perfection but also of the universality of the gospel. The life of López is a sign that Christian holiness is not limited by denominational boundaries. As Wesley explains,

> Persons may be quite right in their opinions, and yet have no religion at all; and, on the other hand, persons may be truly religious, who hold many wrong opinions. Can any one possibly doubt of this, while there are Romanists in the world? For who can deny, not only that many of them formerly have been truly religious, as Thomas à Kempis, Gregory López, and the Marquis de Renty; but that many of them even at this day, are real inward Christians? And yet what a heap of erroneous opinions do they hold, delivered by tradition from their fathers![25]

In short, Wesley's recognition of López' sanctity is a remarkable witness to that catholicity of Spirit which Wesley preached and, at his best, practiced.[26] Indeed, without much exaggeration, one could say that such Protestant recognition of holiness among Catholics was particularly Wesleyan.[27]

Wesley's reception of López is not uncritical. Wesley is critical of López' biographer "of which Gregory himself was in no wise worthy."[28] In particular, Wesley complains that Losa "ascribed all [López'] virtues to the merits and mediation of the Queen of Heaven."[29] However, the larger issue is Wesley's suspicion of Catholic hagiography in general. To state it bluntly, Wesley considered Catholic hagiographers as uninformed and untrustworthy. They are uninformed because they rely on hearsay or gossip to stitch together a portrait of a person that they did not know.[30] They are untrustworthy because they so misunderstand the nature of sanctity that they crowd the saint's life with all sorts of miracles in order to confirm their subjects' holiness, rather than focusing exclusively on their virtuous life in Christ. Indeed, a survey of Wesley's abridgment of Losa's account shows that Wesley systematically omits mention of postmortem miracles by López. These miracles proved an important part of Losa's text as they served to underscore the true holiness of the servant of God. However, instead of focusing on the saint as a thaumaturge, Wesley highlights his personal virtues as being the true signs of his holiness. In trimming the miracles from Losa's account of López' life Wesley discards what he considers to be unnecessary and potentially confusing evidence. After all, people are called holy because they are virtuous, not because they are workers of wonders. The abundance of these signs in someone's life might be cause for admiration, not imitation. In other words, for Wesley, López' sanctity is made known through the miracle of his life, not the miracles of his relics.

Wesley is also critical of certain aspects of López' life. For him, Gregorio is "that good and wise (though much mistaken) man."[31] López was after all a Catholic, hence some of his beliefs and practices were of necessity not scriptural. However, it was not López' Marian devotion that most unsettled Wesley, but his practice of solitude. Wesley's abridgment of Losa's text, though lacking extensive editorial comments, contains several footnotes decrying Gregorio's longing for eremitical life. For example, regarding López' desire to spend his days serving God in a hermitage, Wesley observes:

> It is absolutely certain that this resolution is not to be justified on Scripture-Principles; and consequently, López is not to be imitated in this; however God might wink at the times of ignorance.[32]

Time and time again, Wesley makes it clear that God's way does not lead through the desert, and that if López is assaulted by tribulations while in the desert it is precisely because he has strayed from God's path.[33] As Wesley writes in a letter to Miss Loxdale, "I do not wonder at the horrid temptations of Gregory López, because he was in a desert, that is, so far out of God's way."[34]

If Wesley is sharply critical of López' flight *to* the desert, he is deeply appreciative of López' flight *from* the desert. Indeed, Wesley appears to read the life of López as an evangelical conversion story beginning in the unfaithful wanderings of the desert and ending in faithful discipleship in the city. Wesley is particularly fond of López' repudiation of his biographer's longing for solitude. López charges Losa to go become a hermit in Mexico City![35] True perfection could not be attained in the solitude of the hermitage but only in the bustle of the city. Losa heeded this advice and in his own words:

> Losa returned thither, and his whole manner of life was entirely changed. Whenever he went thro' the city, whether to collect or distribute charity, he felt an inward recollection and prayer, which not all the noise and hurry of the city could interrupt, as if he had been fifty years in that holy exercise.[36]

It is worthy of note that at this point in the narrative, Wesley's account of this episode corresponds very closely to the original with little in the way of abridgment or alteration. The point that Wesley wants to make (the lesson that he thought López learned from his time in the wilderness) is that there is no wisdom to be found in the desert. Communion with God is helped, not hindered, by living in communion with others. López sums up this insight in a simple testimony, "I find God alike in little things and in great."[37] For this reason, "No created thing was capable of either interrupting or abating his continual love of God and his neighbor."[38] One might say that López was active out of the fullness of contemplation (to use the Thomistic phrase) for he "employed himself wholly in contemplation, in order to confirm himself still more in the love of God and of his neighbor."[39]

For Wesley, as for López, contemplation is Christian when oriented toward action, but action is only fruitful when born from contemplation, and it is in this correlation of action and contemplation that his holiness was made manifest in a "continual act of love."[40] It is in the practice of perfect love in the city and not in the raptures or revelations of the desert that the summit of perfection is reached.[41]

Aquinas and Jane Cooper

According to Wesley, Jane Cooper was "a pattern of all holiness, and of the wisdom which is from above."[42] "She was both a living and a dying witness of Christian perfection,"[43] and for this reason John Wesley included a substantial excerpt of one of her writings in his "Plain Account of Christian Perfection." When John looked around to see who among the Methodists might be the equal of Gregorio López in sanctity he had no doubt that he had found such a person in "that saint of God, Jane Cooper; all sweetness, all gentleness, all love."[44] "There was the due mixture of intellect and passion" in her that kept away the excesses of both enthusiasm and rationalism.[45]

So highly did Wesley prize this woman's life that he published an account of it from extracts from her diary and letters so as to confirm the viability of the doctrine of perfection and to present an exemplar for imitation. This work is not the only one of its kind that Wesley produced; it stands next to other accounts of holy lives both ancient and contemporaneous that Wesley presented for the consideration and imitation of the Methodists. But unlike some of those other lives, which Wesley by his own admission heavily edited so as to clear the gold from the dross (see for example his preface to the life of Madame Guyon), the life of Jane Cooper is presented without apology. His only regret is that "the greatest part of her letters are lost; particularly those of which she took the most pains in writing."[46]

Jane Cooper was born in 1738 in Hingham, a small town about fifteen miles West of Norwich. By her own account, Jane's religious upbringing was unexceptional: "Ever since I can remember, I was desirous of happiness; but I did not seek it in God. I thought if I was religious, I should go to heaven."[47] When she was confirmed at age sixteen she experienced a turning point of sorts; she had a strong premonition that she would die at the age of twenty-four and resolved to lead a more devoted life. Looking back on this moment, Jane avers, "I reflected on those who were put apprentice seven years to learn a trade, and thought I ought to use like application, to learn the business of eternity."[48] However, this resolution and others like it soon wore off, though in the midst of these failures, Jane claims to have found succor and strength in the sacrament of communion.

At the age of twenty, Jane left her home in Hingham to work as a servant for a small family in London. It was in London that she came into significant contact with Methodists and under their preaching her eyes were opened to her predicament: works of piety without living faith in Christ are to no avail. After one particular sermon she recalls, "I went home, and was, for five or six weeks, in a most unhappy situation. Before, I was not bad enough to come to Christ; now, I was too bad to receive him."[49] While in prayer, she heard a voice inwardly assure her of the forgiveness of her sins. Naturally, Jane felt much joy at this testimony, and yet doubts soon returned; it all seemed to be a fool's dream. Yet after many groans and prayers, she became more assured of her forgiveness than before and felt at peace in a hitherto unknown way. By her own admission, "For some time after, I felt no sin, and thought I never should any more: how far it was owing to my own unfaithfulness, I cannot tell, but it was not long, before I found my inward parts were very wickedness."[50] However, the conviction of her inward sinfulness did not destroy her confidence in God, but rather made her cling all the more closely to Christ.

Jane Cooper's sojourn in London was good for her soul but bad for her health. She left the family she worked for to enter into service for a genteel woman who treated Jane more as companion than servant. It is during this time of relative leisure that Jane's practice of spiritual counseling began in earnest, mainly through the letters she exchanged with several friends and acquaintances. Nevertheless, in spite of all the personal freedom that her new situation offered her, Jane's health continued to worsen. In the spring of 1762 her physical condition had deteriorated to such a degree that she quit her job and retired to Norwich. During this time she is said to have "lived as an angel below"[51] ministering to the needs of many while abiding in constant communion with God. By then, her reputation for holiness was such that she had frequent visits from people who came seeking spiritual counsel or simply longing to see what sanctity looked like. Such visits could prove a burden for Jane, who desired nothing more than a life of prayer, but it was a burden that she gladly bore.[52]

Among Jane's visitors was John Wesley, whom she had known and exchanged letters with for several years. Just a few days before her death, Wesley visited Jane one last time, and witnessed her "praising God in the fires."[53] On this final interview, Wesley asked Jane if she believed herself to have been saved from sin. Jane replied,

> Yes. I have had no doubt of it for many Months. That I ever had was because I did not abide in the Faith. I now feel, I have kept the Faith: And "perfect love casteth out all fear."[54]

A couple of days after this visit, Jane uttered her last words: "My Jesus is all in all to me. Glory to him through time and eternity";[55] a little while later she died "without a sigh or groan."[56] On Wednesday, November 25, 1762, John Wesley "buried the remains of Jane Cooper, a pattern of all holiness, and of the wisdom which is from above; who was snatched hence before she had lived five-and-twenty years. In good time! God, who knew the tenderness of her spirit, took her away 'from the evil to come.' "[57]

What would Aquinas say of someone like Jane Cooper? Would he recognize her sanctity? Would he honor her as an exemplar of perfection? No doubt, Thomas would insist on honoring her as a human being who is made in the image of God; Jane Cooper is worthy of the honor of being called a person. She is perfect according to what Thomas calls the first perfection, the perfection of being, and the angelic doctor might want us to linger and meditate on this perfection for a while, for it truly is a mystery that Jane exists and that Jane is Jane. However, after pondering the depths of Jane's first perfection, the question remains: is Jane Cooper perfect according to the second perfection, the perfection of operation?[58]

According to Thomas, only the pope by virtue of his office has received the charism to speak with certitude on whether a person now stands in the glory of God with the angels.[59] The perfection that is possible in this life consists in the perfection of charity, but charity is a supernatural gift that even the bearer has no certain knowledge of. So if even I cannot be sure that I am in the state of grace, how much less can I speak of someone else's perfection? However, even if the theologian cannot speak to someone's second perfection (not even one's own) on the basis of an inerrant spiritual instinct, the theologian and indeed any Christian can speak to someone's second perfection on the basis of probable signs. So, what are the probable signs that Thomas would look for in ascertaining whether Jane Cooper was a perfect wayfarer (*viator perfectus*)?

One thing that Thomas would look for would be any miraculous signs. The angelic doctor is convinced that God works miracles through his saints in order to confirm their holiness. So even though the working of miracles is, strictly speaking, a gratuitous grace given to the individual for the benefit of others, this gift can be a probable sign of a greater gift, the gift of sanctity.[60] In the case of Jane Cooper, we are told that her prayers had led to the regeneration of at least one individual,[61] but we do not read of any miracles that she performed during her life. Nevertheless, the absence of miracles in life is not a definitive mark against her. A more certain mark of Jane Cooper's holiness would be postmortem miracles, so if he truly wished to know whether Jane Cooper's life ended in the perfection of charity, Thomas might offer private prayers to her, seeking her intercession before God. As Thomas observes,

> [I]t happens sometimes that prayers addressed to a saint of lower degree are more efficacious, either because he is implored with greater devotion, or because God wishes to make known his sanctity.[62]

The other thing that Thomas might look for would be any signs of sanctity in Jane Cooper's life. The life of the person is a much more significant and definitive mark of holiness than the working of miracles while living. After all, the latter is at best a confirmation of the former. Indeed, Thomas believes that it is a good thing that God does not work miracles through all the saints, for if he did then people might be deluded into thinking that what makes someone holy are not the moral virtues but deeds of power.[63] Hence, the most important sign of someone's second perfection is the holiness of their life before God and neighbor. To put it in other words, the gift of sanctification is nobler than the gift of prophecy, tongues, or miracles. In fact, according to Aquinas, the conversion of a sinner into a saint is God's greatest work, greater even than the creation of the universe.[64] Thus, in inquiring into Jane Cooper's perfection of operation, Thomas would consider the story of her life. Two questions come up in this connection. Was Jane's life free from vice? And did her life shine with virtue? Let us look at each of these in turn.

Was Jane's life free from vice? As we have already seen, toward the end of her life Jane Cooper was convinced that she had been saved from sin, meaning that God had removed from her all inclination to sin.[65] Is Jane's declaration that she has been saved from sin consistent with the perfection of charity? Or does her very act of voicing this conviction belie it by giving way to pride? In the *Summa*, Thomas avers that "it is presumptuous to think oneself perfect."[66] Is Jane Cooper a witness of perfection or presumption? According to Aquinas, "presumption does not denote excessive hope, as though man hoped too much in God; but through man hoping to obtain something unbecoming to him."[67] Presumption pertains not so much to the end longed for but to the manner of attaining it. For instance, if someone expects to be saved while abiding in sin, that hope is but presumption. In considering whether Jane Cooper's conviction is grounded on truth rather than on wishful thinking, Thomas might consider three questions: First, is it presumptuous for Jane to expect to be completely saved from sin in this life? Second, if it is not presumptuous for her to hope for this, is it presumptuous to believe that she has attained such salvation? Third, if it is not presumptuous to believe that she has been saved to the uttermost, is it presumptuous to tell others? Let us consider these questions one by one.

First, is it presumptuous to expect to be saved from sin in this life? As we have seen, God's grace can transform a life so thoroughly that such a life is rendered holy, without blemish. Hence, it is not unbecoming for Jane Cooper to expect to be saved from sin, since God has called her to be holy as he is holy. Jane never claimed to have been cleansed from sin without repentance or living faith; such a statement would be presumptuous indeed. It is only as she nears the dusk of her brief life after undergoing physical and spiritual struggle that Jane Cooper receives the gift of entire sanctification. Admittedly, the attainment of such holiness as Jane claims is unusual. However, Thomas might suggest that its rarity does not necessarily argue against her state but against ours, who having received liberally of God's grace fall short of the hope of our calling.

Second, is it presumptuous to claim that one has been saved from sin? As we have already seen, for Thomas, it is not possible to know with certitude that one is in the state of grace. My assurance of being moved by the theological virtue of charity is conjectural; it is based upon significant but uncertain signs. However, although it is not possible to know that one loves with charity, it is possible to know that one sins.[68] Indeed, such self-knowledge is essential to salvation since without awareness of sin, there is no confession of sin and hence no remission of sin. Yet one can consider one's past actions and present attitudes in search for sins and vices, and pass this self-test with flying colors only to flunk the next encounter with the neighbor. As Jane Cooper's own struggle with sin shows, self-examination can become an exercise in self-delusion; hence, the aid of good confessors or schools of mutual accountability is indispensable in the pursuit of holiness.

Jane's assurance comes from being presently aware of God's presence, but according to Thomas, this moment-by-moment awareness is not the basis for hope's certainty. As he understands it, "Hope does not trust chiefly in grace already received, but on God's omnipotence and mercy."[69] The certainty of sanctification is for Thomas a statement of hope but the certitude of this hope comes not from the immediate perception of grace (which is impossible for Thomas except in the rare case of special revelation through the gift of prophecy), but from faith in God's power and goodness. In other words, for Thomas, the certainty of hope does not rest primarily in its subject (Jane) but in its object (the Triune God). This emphasis on the objective aspect of hope and assurance does not negate the value of personal experience. Hope looks chiefly to God, but experience also has a role to play; through experience one can discover that what one previously thought impossible can indeed be done. In this way, experience can give rise to hope; the goal is attainable.[70] In any case, whether Jane had or lacked certain knowledge of her state before God, she could and should have had conjectural knowledge of this state by means of signs, such as delighting in divine things, despising worldly things, and the like.[71]

Third, is it presumptuous for Jane to proclaim that she has been saved from sin? Suppose Aquinas grants that Jane Cooper was freed from sin to the extent that is possible in this life; let us also say that he accepts that she had some knowledge of her status before God; should Jane announce her holiness to others? Would not Aquinas consider such a declaration presumptuous? Not necessarily, for as Thomas explains,

> It is requisite for man's perfection that he should know himself; but not that he should be known by others, wherefore it is not to be desired in itself. It may, however, be desired as being useful for something, either in order that God may be glorified by men, or that men may become better by reason of the good they know to be in another man, or in order that man, knowing by the testimony of others' praise the good which is in him, may himself strive to persevere therein and to become better.[72]

From her writings, it is clear that Jane wanted to know whether the remains of sin had been rooted out from her. In her own words, "I knew not whether he had destroyed my sin: But I desired to know."[73] But why did she seek such knowledge? Why did she long for assurance of her sanctification? Her answer is clear: "that I might praise him."[74] Though Jane Cooper's letters and diary are inward looking, it would be a mistake to see them as self-centered. The chief subject of her letters is not her love for God, but God's love for her and for all humanity. Jane does not write to earn praise for herself but for God, whose grace can save human nature to the uttermost. Thus, her claim to be free from sin is not necessarily a mark of presumption. Not all saints are alike. Some, like Saint Paul, emphasize the real and unbridgeable difference between God's holiness and their own.[75] One may indeed be a saint and regard oneself the chief of sinners. Others, like Saint Thérèse of Lisieux, attain a state of holiness where they experience no awareness of personal sin.[76]

Did Jane lead a heroically virtuous life? In antiquity, the term heroic virtue was employed by Aristotle in the *Nicomachean Ethics* to describe an eminent degree of virtue. During the middle ages, this concept was appropriated by scholastic theologians, Aquinas among them, to describe a life of distinctive holiness, a life where the gifts of the Spirit perfect the operations of the cardinal and theological virtues.[77] The distinction between heroic and ordinary virtue is not a distinction in kind, but in degree.[78] A person with an ordinary degree of virtue is like the moon; she indeed shines but with a borrowed light. A person with a heroic degree of virtue is as the sun; she shines from herself.[79]

Jane Cooper acquired *fama sanctitatis* among those who knew her. She was a "burning and shining light" in the eyes of many.[80] But was she a sun or a moon? Were the gifts of the Spirit working in her in such a way that she was sensitive to God's promptings (*per specialem instinctum*) in an extraordinary manner?[81] Barring a sudden inspiration from the gift of prophecy, Aquinas could only offer a probable opinion on this issue after an examination of Jane Cooper's life.

Admittedly, there is not much material to examine. On the one hand, Jane's life was brief and it seems fitting that spiritual maturity and natural maturity be traveling companions. On the other hand, as Wesley himself acknowledges, most of Jane's writings are lost. What little we know of her life is due to Wesley's efforts of preservation. However, the lack of literary evidence is not necessarily a problem; Jane Cooper would not be the first or last person whose magnum opus is her own life. St. Thérèse of Lisieux was only twenty-our when she died; she too produced one enduring work, her autobiographical *Story of a Soul*, and yet she is now considered a doctor of the church; in other words, neither lack of years nor shortage of publications is an impediment to attaining and ascertaining perfect holiness.

Was Jane's life heroically virtuous? Even a cursory examination of Jane Cooper's life as contained in her letters is bound to impress upon the reader one thing: Jane was a woman who suffered greatly and gracefully. Time and again, Jane speaks of the trials that she is experiencing. Yet Jane endures these sufferings with a fortitude that arises from confidence that "there is not one tree of the Lord's planting, but must be purged that it may bring much fruit."[82] "Every trial is sent in mercy."[83] Those who would see the light of Mount Tabor must be willing to endure the darkness of

Gethsemane. Jane's desire was to "drink deep into the Spirit of a crucified Saviour."[84] Day by day, Jesus teaches her the lesson of the cross. He "chastens in order to make us partakers of his holiness."[85] We are made perfect through sufferings,[86] and Jane encourages her friends to be thankful "for this special mark of his love."[87]

Jane's correlation of suffering and sanctification is very similar to Thomas' view of this issue. As we saw in the previous chapter, for Thomas, sufferings that are voluntarily accepted lose their penal character and assume a medicinal value. If this is the case, a life full of suffering can be evidence of one's special standing before God. Thomas might read Jane's attitude toward suffering as a sign of heroic fortitude. By the gift of fortitude, "a man's mind is moved by the Holy Ghost, in order that he may attain the end of each work begun, and avoid whatever perils may threaten."[88] If Jane's life manifested her possession of the virtue of courage in a heroic degree, then it might be the case that her assurance of sanctification did not come from presumption as we discussed in the previous section. It would come from God, who by the gift of fortitude infuses a certain confidence (*infundit quandam fiduciam*) of the security of heaven into the human mind so that all fears of being overwhelmed by adversity are cast aside.[89] Nevertheless, in spite of what we have just been considering regarding Jane's graceful overcoming of adversity, it is not therein that her claim to sanctity truly lies, for what makes virtue heroic is not the greatness of its achievement but the goodness of its achievement.[90] According to Aquinas, Jane's life would not be heroic because she struggled mightily but because she loved mightily.[91]

Patterns of Perfection

At the beginning of this chapter, I argued that an encounter between Wesley and Aquinas on the doctrine of perfection opens the door for a new mode of ecumenical reflection, a kneeling ecumenism that shifts our focus from holy doctrine to holy ones. The preceding exercise suggests that there is sufficient common ground in Wesley's and Aquinas' theology to allow for a certain kind of mutual recognition of at least some of the other's saints. To put it yet another way, the Methodist doctrine of Christian perfection and the Thomistic Christian doctrine of perfection are rich enough to not only empower the performance of holiness within their respective tradition but to allow for the recognition of perfection in the other's house of worship. The process of singling out Jane Cooper, Gregorio López or others for ecumenical recognition does not mean that these are the only saints. For Methodists as for Catholics, one can never say that there are too many saints in the church. As Joseph Ratzinger avers, "Saint Paul told us unequivocally that we are called to holiness: 'This is the will of God, your sanctification' (1 Thess 4:13). Because of this, the number of saints is, thanks to God, incomparably greater than the group of individuals given prominence through canonization."[92] The question for the church is "whether the standards generally in effect until now ought not to be made more complete today by means of new emphases, in order to place before the eyes of Christendom those figures who, more than anyone else, make the Holy Church visible to us, in the midst of so many doubts about her holiness."[93]

What pattern of holiness is in the greatest need of recognition today? This is the question that we need to consider. Is the pattern of holiness that we discerned in López and Cooper one that makes the Church visible today? The whole argument of the study so far has been to answer this question in the affirmative. However, some recent scholarship into the nature of sanctity has answered the question negatively. For these theologians the beauty of holiness is made manifest most clearly through the tragedy of existence. To substantiate this claim, let us consider three contemporary accounts of tragic sanctity: those by Lawrence Cunningham, Theresa Sander, and Edith Wyschogrod. Obviously, this selection is not exhaustive but it is representative of a strand of theologians who are interested in saints but to a large extent dismissive of the exemplars that the church holds up for recognition.

In *The Meaning of Saints*, Lawrence Cunningham makes a passionate case for the recognition of a form of sanctity uniquely suited to our present age.[94] Yes, there are always those perennial saintly personalities, like Padre Pio the Italian miracle worker, whose appeal is not lessened by the fact that their way of life appears to be untouched by modern influences.[95] But Cunningham insists that our time calls for a new pattern of holiness, a hidden sanctity that can penetrate through the indifference and hostility of modern society toward religion in order to transform the world from within.

According to Cunningham, when God disappears from view behind extreme forms of oppression, "it is the saint who makes God appear."[96] This viewpoint is shared and sharpened by Theresa Sanders, who states,

> In this time of frost, when God-language is under interrogation and the future of theology itself is uncertain, saints may function as minor suns, stand-ins for a God whose meaning, not to mention presence is unclear.[97]

Contra Cunningham, Sanders claims that the saint does not actually bring God closer, rather the saint "is the one who experiences most keenly the absence of God."[98] The saints only become visible when God becomes eclipsed. In other words, sanctity shines through tragedy.

The conjunction of tragedy and sanctity is clear not only in the work of Sanders and Cunningham but also in that of Wyschogrod.[99] For her, there are two patterns of holiness: the contemplative and the compassionate. Yet the more relevant of the two is the second. The saint is the one "whose adult life in its entirety is devoted to the alleviation of sorrow."[100] Such a person is a not the product of a particular community or school of perfection, but a kind of moral idiot savant who "apprehends in a direct and immediate fashion . . . the trace of transcendence in the other."[101]

Hidden, secular, and sorrowful, these are the attributes of the modern saint. This pattern of holiness is not found primarily in the official canons of the church but in works of contemporary fiction: Albert Camus' doctor in *The Plague*, the whiskey priest in Graham Greene's *The Power and the Glory*, the unnamed curé in George Bernanos' *Diary of a Country Priest*. These figures help us discern a pattern of holiness that is characteristically modern. As Cunningham explains, in our time, "sanctity reveals itself as a surprise, a surprise either at the kind of person who shows us a saintly life or surprise at where that person comes from."[102] These literary figures are admittedly fictional, but then there is much in hagiography that is fictional. In any case, a "hagiographer" (real or literary) can "create characters so real and compelling that they can offer clear lessons in the way we should or could live our lives."[103]

These accounts of tragic sanctity are not without appeal. However, they are deficient on several counts. First of all, they are insufficiently attentive to the ways in which the modern moral framework presupposes practices inimical to the recognition of sanctity.[104] In the words of David Matzko, modernity "requires an account of morality which does not depend upon local exemplars but reaches beyond the limits of local practice and tradition altogether."[105] Second, in their indifference to the distinction between history and fiction, the significance of the saints is limited to the inspirational realm. In such a realm, the saints are void of any properly theological significance; they do not confirm any doctrine nor bring any new perspectives on Christian life, far less do they have any liturgical significance; they do not remember to pray for us. Only the hardest of hearts could fail to be moved by the pattern of holiness illustrated by Dostoevsky's Zosimas. Only the softest of heads would consider offering a prayer to a fictional starets.

The Perfect Cure for Tragedy

If the tragic pattern of sanctity is not the moral panacea hoped for by postmodern theologians, then where should one turn to find relief from the contradictions of contemporary existence? The cure for the modern malaise which Cunningham, Sanders, and Wyschogrod diagnose is not found in discerning or designing a new pattern of holiness, but in remembering old ones like Gregorio and Jane. Granted, the pattern of holiness embodied by these two is now considered obsolete: the happy contemplative. Yet, in the words of G. K. Chesterton, "the saint is a medicine because he is an antidote. Indeed that is why the saint is often a martyr; he is mistaken for poison because he is an antidote."[106] Jane Cooper, Gregorio López, and others like them may be the antidotes to the poisons of modernity and postmodernity, which inject cynical question marks into all witnesses of holiness and perfection.

In order to substantiate the claim that López' and Cooper's pattern of perfection is very much in need in recognition, I want us to briefly reconsider Thomas Aquinas' distinction between first perfection and second perfection. *Duplex est perfectio.*[107] The first perfection is the perfection of form. The second perfection is the perfection of operation. In the first perfection, God gives creatures their being. In the second perfection, God directs creatures to their proper end. In the case of human beings, it pertains to their first perfection to be made after the image of God. As intellectual creatures capable of knowing and loving God, humans are perfect according to the perfection of form.[108] By way of operation (*per operationem*), by actually knowing and loving with the assistance of grace, humans attain their second perfection, which consists in union with God (*unio sanctorum ad Deum [est] per cognitionem et amorem*).[109]

With these distinctions freshly in mind, let us return to Cunningham et al. It turns out that the sanctity that these theologians prescribe is not heroic but antiheroic.[110] Like the characters in Camus' *The Plague*, these theologians talk about saints, but what really interests them is being human.[111] What interests them is not the second perfection of the human but the first perfection. Take Wyschogrod's description of the saint as one who is especially sensitive to the transcendence of the other. Is not this sensitivity similar to the receptivity to the goodness of creation that is the natural basis for all human action? Or consider Cunningham's search for holiness in the humdrum rhythms of modern life. Is not this longing for the canonization of the quotidian satisfied by insisting that every human life is perfect simply by virtue of existing? Indeed, one might say that part of the genius of people like Dostoevsky lies in the fact that they are able to make manifest through fiction what is true though hidden in reality; that every human being by virtue of being human bears the noblest of titles: person. Finally, look again at Sanders' suggestion that the saints make God appear in places where he might not otherwise be evident. Is not this affirmation confirmed in the doctrine of the image of God, the image which is the basis of the first perfection of the human?

In short, what unites these disparate theologians together is not their interest in particular saints but in the common sanctity of humanity. Such an affirmation is important. However, where they err is in thinking that the heroic sanctity of the second perfection is opposed to the universal dignity of the first. To strive for sanctity is not less ambitious a goal than simply being human, but rather it is the fulfillment of what being human is all about. In other words, the most compelling apology for the dignity of human existence is the saint.[112]

Show and Kneel

In his study of Christian holiness, W. E. Sangster describes a reredos in a Methodist church in Buckinhamshire entitled "The Adoration of the Lamb."[113] The screen depicts the scene of the communion of saints around the throne of God. Kneeling in front of the lamb are of course the Virgin and the Apostles, but also a great cloud of witnesses: St. Augustine, St. Patrick, St. Francis, Luther, John Bunyan, John Henry Newman, John Wesley, and others. For Sangster, this work of liturgical art illustrates his conviction that in the face of ecclesial disunion, "the saints are the chief hope of reunion."[114] All Christian communities insofar as they are connected with the true vine will give rise to perfect Christians: saints. Indeed, as Sangster avers, "It could be a telling part of the answer of any Christians to those who would unchurch them, simply to say: 'Look at our saints.'"[115]

Every year at annual conferences throughout many parts of the world, Methodist bishops ask members aspiring for full connection the following question: "Do you expect to be made perfect in love in this life?" Posing this question presupposes that Methodism as a whole is a viable way for someone to go on to perfection, but this supposition begs the question: Where are they? Who are the ones who have said "yes" and gone on to perfection? To ask a different but related question, can a Methodism that is unwilling or unable to recognize exemplars of entire sanctification truly claim "to spread scriptural holiness throughout the land"? In this study, I have suggested that the answer to this question is no and that unless Methodists are willing to recognize and remember the names of those who have attained perfection, we have our trust betrayed.

If Methodists want, in the words of Charles Wesley, "to serve the present age,"[116] General Conferences might want to shift their attention from amending paragraphs in the *Book of Discipline* or adding pages to the *Book of Resolutions* to writing hagiography and compiling a common calendar of saints. In the words of Saint Paul, "we know that the whole creation has been groaning in labor pains until now" (Rom 8:22). Neither the introduction of new political programs, or social initiatives will ease these pains, "for the creation waits with eager longing for the revealing of the children of God" (Rom 8:21). The whole of the universe is waiting for the second perfection of the human by grace; creation longs for saints. Hence, the ecumenical recognition and remembrance of saints is an ecclesial act that has cosmic implications. By recognizing and remembering persons like Gregorio López and Jane Cooper we begin "a strict account to give."[117]

By recognizing and remembering persons like López and Cooper, exemplars of the second perfection, the first perfection comes into clearer view. Paradoxically, one of the problems with tragic accounts of Christianity is that they are not dramatic enough. It might be that, as Karl Jaspers states: "*Das Sein erscheint im Scheitern.*"[118] Perhaps, it is in suffering and failure that the glory of being, its *perfectio prima*, becomes decisively manifest. However, the presence of God is decisively made manifest in the saints. It is in persons like Jane and Gregorio, that is to say, in persons who have been schooled by the church into their second perfection, that God appears, for it is in and through the body of Christ that God is made visible to and for the world.

By recognizing and remembering persons like López and Cooper, the church is reminded that whatever wisdom the tragic holds only extends, at best, to the first perfection of the human, the perfection of being. Gregorio and Jane were not unacquainted with suffering or failure. For them, the way of perfection traversed deserts, literally and metaphorically. At times, the Oracle of Delphi's injunction to know yourself (*gnothi seauton*) is fulfilled through the doomed struggle of the human against finitude and fate. It is indeed possible to learn through suffering, but suffering has no lessons to teach concerning the second perfection of the human. Sufferings played a part in the sanctification of Gregorio and Jane but their perfection did not consist in suffering. In recognizing them and others like them, the church remembers that the noblest human act is not sorrow but joy: *fruitio est nobilissimus actus patriae*.[119]

By recognizing and remembering saints, we engage in that exchange of gifts longed for by John Paul II and reiterated by the Methodist-Catholic dialogue. We cannot tell our ecumenical partner, "look at our saints," if we have no concrete candidates for this category. Nor can we tell our ecumenical partner, "look at our saints," if our partner considers the very idea of saints outside their institutional communion to be an oxymoron. Of course, John Paul II insists that "The saints come from all the

Churches and Ecclesial Communities which gave them entrance into the communion of salvation."[120] In ecumenical dialogue the presence of saints on each side of the table, so to speak, confirms the fact that this dialogue has a common basis and goal, for after all, "all the saints belong to one communion."[121] Geoffrey Wainwright states the correlation between the saints and ecumenism well: "To recognize saints of another community is also in some way to recognize their home community, and vice versa."[122] One of the conclusions of this study is that through their teaching of perfection Aquinas and Wesley offer us a grammar of holiness that can form the basis for writing ecumenical hagiographies, recognizing perfection outside our church and going on to perfection in communion with our "separated" brethren. "As intimacy grows in the Universal Church and there is eagerness to share the common treasure, a questing soul in one branch will say to a questing soul in another, 'Show me your saints.'"[123] Who knows, we might even kneel together.

Aquinas on Women and the Image of God

As the image of God in the human is indefectible and perfectible, the question could be asked, are all women made in the image of God? The short answer is "yes." "The image of God belongs to both sexes, since it is in the mind, wherein there is no sexual distinction."[1] However, this answer does not by itself suffice to counter the criticism that Thomas' theological anthropology is andropocentric. In considering how the first perfection of the image of God in the human attains its second perfection by actually knowing and loving God, let us go on an excursus to explore Thomas Aquinas' theological account of women.

Aquinas' understanding of gender and the image of God is informed by his reading of Scripture ("man is the image of God, but woman is the image of man," [1 Cor 11:7]) and Aristotle ("the female is a misbegotten male," [*De generatione* 2:3]). From these two texts Thomas draws a distinction between a primary and a secondary signification to the image of God. The angelic doctor states that

> In a secondary sense the image of God is found in man, and not in woman: for man is the beginning and end of woman; as God is the beginning and end of every creature.[2]

The sense of this passage seems to be that the male-female relation is in some kind of analogous correspondence to Creator-creature relation. Man is the beginning of woman, in that according to Genesis 2:22, she came from the side of Adam. The same passage presents man as the end of woman in that she fulfills her first *finis operantis* in being a helper to the man.[3] Thus, Aquinas appears to introduce here a distinction between the thing represented by the image and a certain mode of representation that is different for the man than for the woman.

In her magisterial survey of Western thought on womanhood, Sister Prudence Allen argues that at the level of nature Thomas' understanding of the male-female polarity closely parallels that of Aristotle.[4] Men are a more perfect reflection of the image of God, the first principle of human beings. Women in comparison are derivative, passive, and less capable of intellectual and moral virtue. The relation between men and women at this level is analogous to the relation between God and prime matter: man represents actuality; woman represents potentiality. Such is the relation between male and female at the level of nature. More accurately, Sister Prudence argues that this is only part of the story at the level of nature. Humanity was originally created male and female; God actually intended to create two sexes.

By Aristotelian logic, the sexual polarity of men and women should be overcome at the resurrection. Women are the result of an imperfect generation. For Aristotle, the begetting of a woman is a sign that nature has gone. Hence, in a perfect world there would be no women. Aquinas strongly disagrees with this conclusion. Two sexes are better than one. As Sister Prudence explains, for Thomas, "the variety of two sexes within one species is a greater perfection than if there had been only one sex, even if the female is less perfect than the male."[5] The differences between the sexes are real but not so great as to call for the categorization of men and women into different species.

To clarify, the lesser perfection of women pertains to the state of the actualization of the state of human nature in the female body. But women are just as capable as men of receiving the theological virtues; they are just as capable of receiving the gift of infused contemplation; they are going to be risen in female bodies, and after the resurrection the difference in perfection will not be determined by the gender of the body but by the merits of the person. After all, the Blessed Virgin Mary is the most perfect of saints.[6]

In Sister Prudence's reading, "St. Thomas, by incorporating the intellectual framework of sex polarity as first articulated by Aristotle, put forward a Christian philosophy of sex identity that presented a sex polarity on the level of nature—which moved into a sex polarity on the level of grace."[7]

Pia Francesca de Solenni advances Sister Prudence's reading by arguing that Aquinas' epistemology opens the way for "an integrated, non-dualist anthropology."[8] Thomistic anthropology provides a solid foundation for the development of an adequate Christian feminism. The basis for this startling claim is Aquinas' teaching on the nature of the mind. The human act of knowing has two aspects. By the act of *intellectus*, the mind grasps the truth that is received through the senses. This act is characterized by a certain kind of receptivity. "It knows being because being has been impressed upon it through the senses of the body."[9] By the act of *ratio*, the mind moves from something that is more known to something that is less known. This act is characterized by a certain kind of activity. "It comes to know through a discursive process of reducing the unknown to terms which the *intellectus* already knows."[10]

De Solenni sees a parallel between the dichotomy of *intellectus* and *ratio* in the human act of knowing with the dichotomy of male and female in human nature. Both male and females are made in the image of God and as such the powers to understand (*intelligere*) and reason (*ratiocinari*) will be present in both of them but not in the same way. Women "personify" the receptivity of *intellectus*, whereas men the activity of *ratio*.[11] The implications of paralleling mental faculties with gender characteristics are profound. First, male and female are not the same. Of course, the association of men and women with different aspects of *mens* is not an absolute determination but an indication of what it means to be male or female. Yet, the dichotomy between the sexes like the dichotomy between *intellectus* and *ratio* is real. "If women tend to embody the virtues of *intellectus* (and man to embody the virtues of *ratio*), the natural receptivity that is witnessed in so many feminine roles would be understood as connected to *intellectus* and the way in which woman is in the *imago Dei*."[12] Second, male and female are made for each other. It is by the virtue of *intellectus* that the mind receives the forms about which the mind reasons, and it is the intellectual vision of truth that is the goal of all human acts of knowing. The intellect perfects reason. In the case of men and women there is a profound complementarity. Woman is made from man but man is made perfect by woman.

> Adam, alone, was apart from God. Eve's complementarity replaces the lack caused by Adam's loneliness and, therefore, brings Adam closer to God, who is the source of all goodness and perfection. The creation of Eve provides Adam with a Beatrice who leads his vision to the highest good.[13]

According to de Solenni, a Thomistic anthropology allows us to treat women as both fully human and truly feminine. In this way, de Solenni's account overcomes the deficiencies of other feminist accounts. For despite the varied nature of the latter (and they are legion: feminisms of equality, feminisms of difference, antiessentialist feminisms, deconstructive feminisms, etc.), none of these are able to account for the fundamental complementarity of men and women.[14] Contrary to their intentions, all these other feminisms in their well intentioned attempt to disengage the female subject from the strictures of the reigning paradigms end up severing women (and men) from the relations that help us know who and whose we are. The paradoxical result is that "we are left with individuals who are exactly the same: nondescript."[15]

To reiterate, "woman and man possess the same *mens*, with the same aspects of *intellectus* and *ratio*. They differ only in their bodies which play an essential role in human knowing."[16] The application of Thomistic anthropology to the philosophy of woman allows us better to understand woman's nature and purpose. By better understanding women, we better understand Mary who is the archetype of human (male and female) response to God. "An understanding, therefore, of woman is essential to both man and woman for their ultimate end and happiness."[17]

In sum, Aquinas never denies the presence of the image of God in the woman; women are made *ad imago Dei* and as such women are both perfect and perfectible. Nevertheless, according to the angelic doctor, even *in statu innocentiae* there is inequality among humans as regards intellectual virtue, bodily strength, age, and sex. However, for Thomas, inequality is essential for the perfection of the universe. To be more specific, one of the aspects of what it means for men to be in the image of God is that they must exercise mastery not just over animals but also over other humans, including women! Obviously, we cannot in the framework of this excursus give an approximately comprehensive overview of Aquinas' understanding of women, or of the significant cultural factors (like flawed Aristotelian biology) that influenced his thinking. Suffice it to say that on this issue Thomas' synthesis is incomplete and in need of constructive work.

Notes

Introduction

1 A detailed history of these dialogues and of the whole Methodist-Catholic encounter is ably narrated by David Chapman in his study *In Search of the Catholic Spirit: Methodists and Roman Catholics in Dialogue* (Peterborough, England: Epworth Press, 2004).

2 "All the faithful are invited and obligated to holiness and the perfection of their own state of life. Accordingly let all of them see that they direct their affections rightly, lest they be hindered in their pursuit of perfect love by the use of worldly things and by an adherence to riches which is contrary to the spirit of evangelical poverty," *Lumen Gentium* in *Vatican Council II,* vol. 1: *The Conciliar and Post Conciliar Documents* (Northport, N.Y.: Costello Publishing, 1998), 402.

3 *Christian Home and Family* (Denver, 1971), §52. Even though this doctrine has sometimes been misapplied in overly individualistic ways, "our traditional shared concern for sanctification has been a source of strength," *Growth in Understanding* (Dublin, 1976), §22.

4 *The Grace Given You in Christ: Catholics and Methodists Reflect Further on the Church* (Seoul, 2006), §56.

5 The 2006 *Methodist Statement of the World Methodist Council on the 1999 Joint Declaration on the Doctrine of Justification* underscores the centrality of the doctrine of Christian perfection in Methodist soteriology and sketches the outlines of this doctrine (§4.4). However, the exposition of the doctrine in an ecumenical context lies beyond the purview of the statement, which rightly focused on the Roman Catholic and Lutheran consensus on justification.

6 George Croft Cell, *The Rediscovery of John Wesley* (New York: University Press of America, 1935), 361. The present "orientalism" of Methodist ventures into ecumenical soteriology is surprising when one considers that earlier in the twentieth century George Croft Cell memorably described Wesley's doctrine of salvation

as a "necessary synthesis of the Protestant ethic of grace with the Catholic ethic of holiness." Admittedly, Cell's remark originated from a partisan spirit, not a Catholic one. His intent was to show the superiority of Wesley to both the Protestant Reformers and the Catholics, in what cannot inaccurately be described as a Hegelian *Aufhebung*. For Cell, Wesley's theology is the necessary synthesis of the Catholic thesis and the Protestant antithesis, which will itself be surpassed, according to Cell, by Schleiermacher's.

7 Cf. Randy Maddox, *Responsible Grace: John Wesley's Practical Theology* (Nashville: Abingdon, 1994), 180–81; Theodore Runyon, *The New Creation: John Wesley's Theology Today* (Nashville: Abingdon, 1998), 91.

8 Albert Outler, ed., *John Wesley* (New York: Oxford University Press, 1964), 9–10; emphasis in original.

9 Cf. Steve McCormick, "Theosis in Chrysostom and Wesley: An Eastern Paradigm on Faith and Love," in *Wesleyan Theological Journal* 26 (1991): 38–103.

10 Kenneth Collins, *John Wesley: A Theological Journey* (Nashville: Abingdon, 2003), 195–99.

11 David Ford, "Saint Makarios of Egypt and John Wesley: Variations on the Theme of Sanctification," in *Greek Orthodox Theological Review* 33, no. 3 (1988): 285–312; D. Stephen Long, *John Wesley's Moral Theology: The Quest for God and Goodness* (Nashville: Kingswood Books, 2005), 134, n. 15.

12 Collins, *A Theological Journey*, 196–97.

13 This contrast comes from Albert Outler, who states in his introduction to Wesley's "Sermon on Christian Perfection" that "Protestants, convinced of the *simul justus et peccator*—and used to translating *perfectio* as some sort of perfected perfection—were bound to see in the Wesleyan doctrine, despite all of its formal disclaimers, a bald advertisement of spiritual pride and, implicitly, work righteousness. Even the Methodists, working from their own unexamined Latin traditions of forensic righteousness, tended to interpret 'perfection' in terms of a spiritual elitism—and so misunderstood Wesley and the early Eastern traditions of τελειότης as a never-ending aspiration for all love's fullness (perfecting perfection)" (*The Works of John Wesley*, ed. Albert Outler [Nashville: Abingdon, 1984] 2:98: "The Principles of a Methodist Farther Explained"). When possible I will rely on this critical text of the "Bicentennial Edition" edited by Outler; henceforth referred to as WJW. Otherwise, I will use the "Jackson Edition" of the *The Works of John Wesley*, ed. Thomas Jackson (Grand Rapids: Baker Book House, 1984), henceforth referred to as WW. For "A Plain Account of Christian Perfection," I will be using *John and Charles Wesley: Selected Prayers, Hymns, Journal Notes, Sermons, Letters and Treatises*, ed. Frank Whaling (Mahwah, N.J.: Paulist Press, 1981).

14 The ecumenical significance of sanctity is affirmed by the 1981 Honolulu Report, which issued the following challenge: "We call upon all our sisters and brothers in Christ to join in more ardent pursuit of these higher levels of Christian experience and more effective ways of expressing our faith, hope and love in and to the world for which Christ died. In this way we shall be drawn into an actual communion in Christ and, as we may hope, more readily thereafter into communion *in sacris*, full sacramental fellowship" (*Authority, Moral Decisions, Family* [Honolulu, 1981] §31).

15 Unless otherwise stated, all Latin texts from Thomas Aquinas are based on the Leonine Edition: *Sancti Thomas de Aquino opera omnia iussu Leonis XIII*. For the English translation of the *Summa*, I use *The Summa Theologica of St. Thomas Aquinas*, translated by Fathers of the English Dominican Province (Allen, Tex.: Christian Classics, 1948). Other English translations of Thomas' will be noted as they are cited.

16 In Joseph Pieper's words, "the *Summa Theologica* can only be the work of a heart fundamentally at peace"; Joseph Pieper, *The Silence of St. Thomas: Three Essays* (New York: Pantheon, 1957), 4. Pieper also observes that the objectivity and serenity that characterize Thomas' writing, instead of being recognized as integral to the origin and understanding of his theological task, have been and continue to be mistaken for rationalism or scientific neutrality. This misrecognition of Thomas is all the more perplexing when one considers that Aquinas has a stronger sense of the significance of the apophatic moment in theology than many of his critics and certainly more so than Wesley.

17 Wesley rarely mentions Aquinas by name, but he clearly is acquainted with him. In one occasion he complains of "the profound reverence that [Romanists] have for Thomas Aquinas, a more vehement defender of the decrees than their grand saint, Augustine." Wesley considers Aquinas a teacher of double predestination, a very bad thing indeed in Wesley's book (WW 14:281). In an address to the clergy, Wesley exhorts those who would be ministers of the church to be intellectually prepared for their task by, among other things, seeking to understand "metaphysics; if not the depths of the Schoolmen, the subtleties of Scotus or Aquinas, yet the first rudiments, the general principles, of that useful science" (WW 10:492).

18 Otto H. Pesch, "Existential and Sapiential Theology—the Theological Confrontation between Luther and Aquinas," in *Catholic Scholars Dialogue with Luther*, ed. Jared Wicks (Chicago: Loyola University Press, 1970), 61–81; cf. *Theologie der Rechfertigung bei Martin Luther und Thomas von Aquin: Versuch eines systematisch-theologischen Dialogs* (Mainz: Matthias-Grünewald-Verlag, 1967), 935–48.

19 Jacques Maritain, *The Degrees of Knowledge*, trans. Phelan Gerald, vol. 7. *The Collected Works of Jacques Maritain*, ed. Ralph McInerny (Notre Dame, Ind.: University of Notre Dame Press, 2002).

20 Wesley nowhere defines exactly what he means by "practical divinity," but the following description may stand in lieu of a definition. Practical divinity is "all agreeable to the oracles of God; as is all practical, unmixed with controversy of any kind, and all intelligible to plain men; such as is not superficial, but going down to the depth, and describing the height, of Christianity; and yet not mystical, not obscure to any of those who are experienced in the ways of God. I have also particularly endeavored to preserve a consistency throughout, that no part might contradict any other; but all conspire together to make "the man of God perfect, thoroughly furnished unto every good word and work" (WW 14:222); see also Frank Baker, "Practical Divinity—John Wesley's Doctrinal Agenda for Methodism," *Wesleyan Theological Journal* 22, no. 1 (1987): 7–16; Randy Maddox, "John Wesley: Practical Theologian?" *Wesleyan Theological Journal* 23, no. 1–2 (1988): 122–47.

21 "Existential theology is the way of doing theology from within the self-actuation

of our existence in faith, as we submit to God in the obedience of faith. Its affirmations are so formulated that the actual faith and confession of the speaker are not merely necessary presuppositions but are reflexively thematized. Sapiential theology is the way of doing theology from outside one's self-actuation in the existence in faith, in the sense that in its doctrinal statement the faith and confession for the speaker is the enduring presupposition, but is not thematic within this theology. This theology strives to mirror and recapitulate God's own thoughts about the world, men, and history, insofar as God has disclosed them" (Pesch, "Existential and Sapiential," 76).

22 According to Maritain: "It is important to understand that, with respect to that most eminent of actions, to wit, the passion of things divine and contemplative union with God, there is not only a speculatively practical science which is the science of the theologian, but that there is also a practically practical science which is not so much interested in telling us what perfection is, as leading us to it. This is the science of the master of spirituality, the practitioner of the soul, the artisan of sanctity, the man who stoops to our wretched hearts, which he wants at all costs to lead to their supreme joy" (*The Degree of Knowledge*, 335–36). These two modes of science are distinct; they have their own vocabulary and syntax which are fitting to their particular end: "whereas speculative language, because it considers the pure object of the intellect, is an essentially ontological language, practical and mystical language (if it is to be accurate) must, of necessity, be predominantly psychological and affective, because it considers things in relation to, and even as inviscerated in, the acting subject" (357). Precisely because of the irreducible difference of these two modes of knowledge, they need and complement each other. On the one hand, the speculatively practical science is not a sufficient guide for moral action; it needs the aid of a practically practical science to prepare it for concrete action. On the other hand, the practically practical science presupposes the principles arrived at by speculatively practical science. Without these theological principles the guide of souls would herself be blind and founder.

23 Pesch, "Existential and Sapiential," 64. Daniel Luby warns us about the need to not let Wesley dictate the terms of the discussion between Catholics and Methodists. "Wesley's theology of grace is terminologically imprecise making a comparison to Roman Catholic theology vague and imprecise. For this reason, Roman Catholic theology must not limit itself to Wesley's terms in its encounter"; Daniel Joseph Luby, *The Perceptibility of Grace in the Theology of John Wesley: A Roman Catholic Consideration* (Rome: Pontifical University of St. Thomas, 1994), 198. I agree with Luby that Wesley's theological language does not have the terminological precision of scholastic theology but I would argue that Wesley's theology is "vague and imprecise" in a manner befitting its kind of science, namely "practical divinity." So it is not simply that Methodists and Catholics must avoid reducing the debate to Wesley's conceptual categories. They must avoid limiting the discussion to Thomas' language as well. Both practical and speculative modalities of languages have their role to serve in theology, and the encounter between Wesley and Aquinas must be as bilingual as possible.

24 WJW 9:227, "The Principles of a Methodist Farther Explained."

25 Brian Shanley provides a concise yet detailed account of this reception with a

focus on twentieth-century Thomism in *The Thomist Tradition* (Boston: Kluwer Academic, 2002), 1–20; see also Romanus Cessario, *A Short History of Thomism* (Washington, D.C.: Catholic University of America Press, 2005); Randy Maddox helpfully sketches this history in his chapter "Reclaiming an Inheritance: Wesley as Theologian in the History of Methodist Theology," in *Rethinking Wesley's Theology for Contemporary Methodism* (Nashville: Kingswood Books, 1998), 213–25.

26 Maximin Piette, *John Wesley in the Evolution of Protestantism* (New York: Sheed & Ward, 1937).

27 Piette, *Evolution of Protestantism*, 480.

28 "A Catholic believes that every man who has followed his conscience will find himself eventually in heaven, with the saints, and able to do God's work, in and through his providence. As I have come to know Wesley I have believed him to be there and have prayed to him—not publicly as the Church prays through those declared to be saints—but privately as I pray for and to those who have been close to me"; John M. Todd, *John Wesley and the Catholic Church* (London: Hodder & Stoughton, 1958), 192.

29 Luby, *The Perceptibility of Grace.*

30 Thomas Rigl, *Die Gnade Wirken Lassen: Methodistische Soteriologie im ökumenischen Dialog* (Paderborn: Bonifatius, 2001).

31 An exception to this general attitude is R. Newton Flew's *The Idea of Perfection in Christian Theology: An Historical Study of the Christian Idea for the Present Life* (London: Oxford University Press, 1934). Newton's essay in *Theologia Spiritualis* begins with a simple question: "What is the Christian ideal for the present life" (xi)? It is noteworthy that for Flew this question arises from dismay at the spiritual unpreparedness of the church's response to the brutal realities of the Great War (xiii). In carrying out his pastoral work Flew stumbled, as he put it, on John Wesley's ideal of perfect love as a necessary corrective to the Reformation emphasis on justification by faith alone with its tendency toward antinomianism; furthermore the ideal was a theological resource for challenging the devaluing of the human that preceded, accompanied, and followed the First World War. Though a Methodist preacher, Flew did not limit his study of perfection to a study of Wesley, indeed he is critical of certain aspects of Wesley's teaching; rather he sets out to display the catholicity of this doctrine by examining how perfection has been taught, sought and encouraged by Christian teachers throughout the centuries, and one of the figures whose thought he considers is St. Thomas Aquinas.

32 Long, *John Wesley's Moral Theology.* In brief, according to Long, Wesley's worldview resembled far more closely that of Aquinas than that of Locke or Hume. I will consider certain aspects of Long's argument in the chapter where I examine how Wesley and Aquinas interpret the Sermon on the Mount.

33 George H. Gallup and Timothy Jones, *The Saints among Us: How the Spiritually Committed Are Changing Our World* (Harrisburg, Pa.: Morehouse Publishing, 1992), 123.

34 From Charles Wesley's *Short Hymns* (1762, 2:140) as cited by S. T. Kimbrough Jr. in "Charles Wesley and the Poor," in *The Portion of the Poor: Good News to the Poor in the Wesleyan Tradition*, ed. M. Douglas Meeks (Nashville: Kingswood Books, 1995), 166.

Chapter 1

1 Harald Lindström, *Wesley and Sanctification: A Study in the Doctrine of Salvation* (Nashville: Abingdon, 1946); Maddox, *Responsible Grace*; Kenneth Collins, *The Scripture Way of Salvation: The Heart of John Wesley's Theology* (Nashville: Abingdon, 1997); *The Theology of John Wesley: Holy Love and the Shape of Grace* (Nashville: Abingdon, 2007).

2 Maddox, *Responsible Grace*, 20.

3 Scholars of Wesley dispute the significance of Aldersgate in Wesley's life. Some raise its importance to the highest levels and speak of it as Wesley's conversion from moralism to Christianity. Others downplay the event as an interesting but not too significant moment in Wesley's pilgrimage. Heitzenrater persuasively argues that the issue at stake in Aldersgate was not belief versus unbelief but assurance. Aldersgate marked a decisive step in Wesley's pilgrimage; it is only after Aldersgate that he strongly linked true faith and full assurance. However, this is the very connection that the "late Wesley" undoes when he distinguishes between two orders of Christians: servants and children; cf. Richard Heitzenrater, "Great Expectations: Aldersgate and the Evidences of True Christianity" in *Aldersgate Reconsidered*, ed. Randy Maddox, 49–91 (Nashville: Kingswood Books, 1990).

4 In saying this I am siding with Maddox' interpretation of Wesley over Collins. In *Responsible Grace*, Maddox underscores the maturing growth of Wesley's thought after the perfectionist controversies which moved his theological formulations decisively beyond the 1738 positions on a range of issues: faith and assurance (124–28), sin (75–81, 163–65), nature (92–95), instantaneous sanctification (151–54), and perfection (180–90). For his part, in *The Scripture Way of Salvation*, Collins underscores the continuity of the middle and late Wesley to such an extent that the late Wesley is basically a mature middle Wesley (144–52). We will have occasion to consider these interpretive issues in more concrete terms later in this work.

5 WJW 2:87, "Catholic Spirit."

6 WJW 2:89, "Causes of the Inefficacy of Christianity."

7 WW 10:23, "Predestination calmly considered."

8 Maddox observes that Wesley rejected the nominalist separation of God's goodness and God's willing (Maddox, *Responsible Grace*, 54). By emphasizing the unity of God's being, that is to say his divine simplicity, the glory of God no longer refers primarily or exclusively to the maximization of God's power but rather to the manifestation of *all* of God's attributes. This emphasis on the unity of the divine attributes is thus tremendously important and has far-reaching consequences. See for example Theodore Jennings' chapter, "Transcendence, Justice, and Mercy: Toward a (Wesleyan) Reconceptualization of God" in *Rethinking Wesley's Theology for Contemporary Methodism*, 65–82; From "Wesley's insight that justice and mercy belong to the very being of God, and so are not to be thought as in some way added to, or in potential conflict with, the absoluteness of the divine being" (65), Jennings argues that "the being of God is constituted as a relationship to the violated and humiliated" (65). Whether one agrees with Jennings' inference or not (and there are in my opinion deep

problems with it), the significance of the premise of the doctrine of the divine unity for our understanding of God is incontestable.

9 Maddox, *Responsible Grace*, 50.

10 Maddox, *Responsible Grace*, 51; emphasis in original. An interesting question to consider is whether Wesley affirmed the impassibility of God. On the one hand, he affirms the language of the "Anglican Articles of Religion," which refers to God as having no passions (cf. WJW 4:63). Indeed, when Wesley edited the Anglican Articles of Religion for the use of the American Methodists he left untouched the impassibility language of the first article (Maddox, *Responsible Grace*, 51). On the other hand, as Maddox insists, Wesley "retained a place for affections in God" (Maddox, *Responsible Grace*, 51). So, "If 'passions' were equivalent to 'affections,' then the American Methodists were not betraying Wesley when they deleted the phrase denying passions to God from the Articles of Religion which he sent them" (idem). It is debatable whether this omission was motivated by the repudiation of the classical belief in God's impassibility or by fear that the American Methodists would misunderstand the teaching or by a desire to return to the exact wording of the Augsburg Confession from which the first Anglican Article of Religion came. Maddox appears to lean toward the first of these explanations in that he sees a tension between Wesley's doctrine of responsible grace, and the classical doctrine of divine impassibility. As we will see later this tension only arises when divine action and human action are exclusively seen to occur on the same plane.

11 WJW 4:40–47, "On the Omnipresence of God."

12 WW 10:42, "Predestination calmly considered." As Wesley comments on 1 John 4:8: "God is often styled holy, righteous, wise, but not holiness, righteousness, or wisdom in the abstract, as he is said to be love: intimating that this is his darling, his reigning attribute, the attribute that sheds an amiable glory on all his other perfections"; John Wesley, *Explanatory Notes on the New Testament* (London: Epworth Press, 1976), 914.

13 WJW 1:581, "Sermon on the Mount, VI."

14 WJW 3:560, "Free Grace."

15 WJW 7:491, *A Collection of Hymns for the People Called Methodist.*

16 WJW 2:87, "Catholic Spirit."

17 WJW 4:333, "The Love of God."

18 Cf. WJW 4:64, "The Unity of Divine Being."

19 WJW 3:91, "Spiritual Worship."

20 WJW 4:233, "On Guardian Angels."

21 WJW 3:281, "On Working Out Our Own Salvation."

22 WW 11:7, "Serious Thoughts Occasioned by the Late Earthquake in Lisbon."

23 WJW 4: 195, "On Faith."

24 WJW 2:361, "On Eternity."

25 WJW 1:150, "Awake, Thou That Sleepest."

26 WW 8:352, "Advice to the People Called Methodists."

27 In this connection, there is a parallel between Wesley's doctrine of the divine attributes and the one presented by that little book on God's perfections; Thomas Aquinas, *The Ways of God for Meditation and Prayer* (Manchester, N.H.: Sophia Institute Press, 1995). Each chapter of the book introduces an attribute

of God for our meditation and prayer. So for example, regarding the foreknowledge of God, the author begins with what becomes the refrain of the book, "In God, there is another perfection" (11). He then proceeds to describe the attribute that we are to meditate on, in this case God's foreknowledge, "He foresees with prudence all future things, good or bad. Before they happen, he knows them and sees the good or the evil that will result from them" (11). After the meditation on God comes the invitation to the imitation of God. "Let us also foresee all our doings, our words, our desires, our works, and let us consider the good and the evil that may result for us from them, as well as the scandal or edification that others will receive from them" (11–12). The book has been erroneously credited to Aquinas but it is written in the spirit of the angelic doctor. As Raissa Maritain says in the introduction to the 1946 edition, "If it is not written by the hand of St. Thomas, it is, in any case, the faithful interpreter of his doctrine and its elevated spirit as well as its candor render it worthy of being placed under the name of the angelic doctor" (vii–viii). I would add that this book, though not written by Wesley's hand either, is a faithful interpretation of the Wesleyan doctrine of the divine attributes.

28 WW 7:566, *A Collection of Hymns for the People Called Methodist.*

29 In discussing Wesley's account of God-language, Maddox helpfully shows Wesley's dependence on the doctrine of analogical predication as explicated by Peter Browne, whose book *Limits of Human Understanding* Wesley abridged (Maddox, *Responsible Grace,* 49).

30 "A Plain Account of Christian Perfection," 373.

31 WJW 3:6, "Of Good Angels." What Wesley means by this phrase is not explained at this point but is elucidated by his description of the effects of the fall of Adam, of which we will say more momentarily. Suffice it to say that angels have an ease of movement of thought, will, and action that is not possible for us earthly creatures.

32 WJW 3:6, "Of Good Angels."

33 WJW 3:72, "On Perfection."

34 WJW 3:6, "Of Good Angels."

35 WJW 3:6, "Of Good Angels."

36 WJW 3:6, "Of Good Angels."

37 WJW 4:232, "On Guardian Angels." A similar point is made in his sermon "Of Good Angels" (WJW 3:15). "The grand reason why God is pleased to assist men by men, rather than immediately by himself, is undoubtedly to endear us to each other by these mutual good offices, in order to increase our happiness both in time and eternity. And is it not for the same reason that God is pleased to give his angels charge over us? Namely, that he may endear us and them to each other; that, by the increase of our love and gratitude to them, we may find a proportionable increase of happiness when we meet in our Father's kingdom."

38 WJW 4:232, "On Guardian Angels."

39 Charles Wesley, *Hymns for Ascension Day* (Madison, N.J.: Charles Wesley Society, 1994): hymn VI, stanzas 2, 3, 6.

40 Consider Wesley's sermon "The More Excellent Way." In this sermon Wesley suggests that there are higher and lower places in the kingdom of heaven. The

degree of glorification attained in heaven will depend on the degree of perfection attained on earth. Wesley considers it no small loss to have a lower place than one might have had had one chosen the better part (WJW 3:226). However, if there is the possibility for growth in heaven unto eternity, having a lower place is not a loss but merely a temporary setback. If on the contrary, Wesley believes that the places in the hierarchy of heaven to be at some point fixed then such a belief would come very close to Thomas' conviction that "every rational creature is so led by God to the end of its beatitude, that from God's predestination it is brought even to a determinate degree of beatitude" (*Summa Theologiae* 1.62.9. Henceforth, this work will be referred to by the abbreviation ST).

41 ST 1.62.9.ad2. On the influence of Jesus' life and work on angelic beatitude consult José Antonio Riestra, *Cristo y la Plenitud del Cuerpo Místico: Estudio sobre la cristología de Santo Tomás de Aquino* (Pamplona, Spain: Ediciones Universidad de Navarra, 1985): 181–98. The impact of Christ's work on angelic life is debated among theologians, even among those of the Thomistic persuassion. Riestra argues that for Aquinas the incarnation has no direct bearing on the angelic beatitude. Nevertheless, the incarnation does add to the accidental glory of the angels. First, angelic understanding was strengthened: "Baste pensar que la visión beatífica de Cristo en cuanto hombre es más perfecta que la que pueda poseer cualquier criatura . . . De ahí que, al contemplar plenamente todas las obras divinas y sus razones, pueda iluminar a ángeles y hombres" (194). Second, angelic joy increased: "Bajo este aspecto, los méritos de Cristo alcanzan a los ángeles, pues si bien éstos, en cuanto al premio esencial—la visión beatífica—no eran viadores, sí tienen esta condición, en cierto modo, en lo que respecta al premio accidental, es decir en cuanto ejercen su ministerio sobre los hombres" (197).

42 WJW 2:7, "Original, Nature, Properties, and Use of the Law."

43 WJW 2:7, "Original, Nature, Properties, and Use of the Law."

44 WJW 2:6, "Original, Nature, Properties, and Use of the Law."

45 Early in his life Wesley toyed with the notion of casting holiness as "angelical obedience" (cf. WJW 4:348–50, "In Earth as in Heaven"), but he appears to have quickly dropped this idea as unworkable.

46 Maddox, *Responsible Grace*, 71.

47 Maddox rightly points out that Wesley at times speaks of the soul as possessing an ethereal body in the intermediate state between death and resurrection (Maddox, *Responsible Grace*, 71). As I said when considering Wesley's talk of angelic bodies, I think that Wesley's theology would be helped by a more conceptually rigorous metaphysic such as that developed by Aquinas. Consider the alternative. What if we give conceptual weight to Wesley's talk of an ethereal body? What do we mean by this ether? Is it not simply very light matter? Furthermore, once you make the soul possess some kind of spatial dimension the question of its location inevitably pops up. Is the soul resident in the pineal gland as Wesley thought or in the heart? This kind of physicalist approach to theological anthropology is ridden with pitfalls. The situation does not markedly improve when we adopt a more modern scientific account such as the one proposed by Mark Mann in *Perfecting Grace: Holiness, Human Being, and the Sciences* (New York: T&T Clark, 2006). In attempting to construct an account of holiness that is credible in a scientific age, Mann jettisons

all spirit/body duality in favor of an anthropological model of "nonreductive materialism" based on "supervenience." As Mann explains, "According to this model, consciousness is a property that *emerges from* human physiology and neurology and then is able to supervene upon those properties from which it emerges in certain, limited ways" (123). The materialism that Mann argues for might be nonreductive in one sense (human freedom is nonreducible to biochemical processes) but it is still materialism and is still reductive in that it reduces the invisible to be only a high level manifestation of the visible. Mann does not say so, but in a model such as he proposes, it would make sense to refer to God as the consciousness that emerges from and supervenes over the cosmos. However, such a God is not the God of Abraham, Isaac, and Jacob. It is not the God of the philosophers. In fact, it is not even the God of the deists. It is basically an epiphenomenon of nature.

48 WJW 3:460, "What Is Man?"
49 Wisdom 2:23, cited WJW 1:184, "Justification by Faith."
50 WJW 7, A *Collection of Hymns for the People Called Methodists*.
51 WJW 1:184, n. 5, "Justification by Faith."
52 WJW 2:188, "The New Birth"; emphasis in original.
53 WJW 2:438, "The General Deliverance."
54 WJW 2:440, "The General Deliverance."
55 WJW 4:296, "The Image of God."
56 WJW 2:439, "The General Deliverance."
57 WJW 4:294, "The Image of God."
58 WJW 4:294, "The Image of God."
59 WJW 4:294, "The Image of God."
60 WJW 2:439, "The General Deliverance."
61 WJW 4:295, "The Image of God."
62 WJW 4:24, "What is Man?"
63 Long, *John Wesley's Moral Theology*, 45; For a lucid Thomist interpretation of the problems that arise from the adoption of freedom of indifference into theological anthropology and ethics see Servais Pinckaers, *The Sources of Christian Ethics* (Washington, D.C.: Catholic University of America Press, 1995), 327–53. Pinckaers persuasively argues that for Thomas, "free will was not a prime or originating faculty; it presupposed intelligence and will. It was rooted, therefore, in the inclinations to truth and goodness that constituted these faculties" (331). By contrast, nominalists like William of Ockham raised the freedom of the will to the status of a prime faculty antecedent to knowing and willing. This elevation, or rather, this separation of freedom from nature, turned the moral universe of Thomas Aquinas upside down and "gave birth to twin forces forever at enmity, voluntarism and rationalism" (341). In other words, Ockham's passion for freedom expressed most succinctly in the concept of freedom of indifference ended up reducing freedom to mere arbitrariness.
64 WJW 4:295, "The Image of God."
65 In his sermon, "The End of Christ's Coming," Wesley nuances his understanding of liberty and appear to concur with those who doubt that paradisiacal humanity would choose evil knowing it to be such. What cannot be doubted, according to Wesley, is that in the original state "the human might mistake evil

for good. [The human] was not infallible; therefore not impeccable" (WJW 2:476). Why were Adam and Eve not infallible if their understanding was perfect? Wesley does not explain but kicks the answer up (or down) the ontological ladder. *Unde malum*? From Satan. The devil "was the first sinner in the universe; the author of sin; the first being who by the abuse of his liberty introduced evil into the creation" (WJW 2:476). He "was self-tempted to think too highly of himself. He freely yielded to the temptation, and gave way first to pride, then to self-will" (WJW 2:476). How could the devil be self-tempted to think too highly of himself? Was not his understanding perfect? Where did his understanding go wrong? On this point, Wesley is silent, but might be helped by the angelic doctor. According to Aquinas, the devil erred not in *that* he desired to be as God but in *how* he desired to be as God. "Not that he desired to resemble God by being subject to no one else absolutely; for so he would be desiring his own *not-being*; since no creature can exist except by holding its existence under God. But he desired resemblance with God in this respect—by desiring, as his last end of beatitude, something which he could attain by the virtue of his own nature, turning his appetite away from supernatural beatitude, which is attained by God's grace. Or, if he desired as his last end that likeness of God which is bestowed by grace, he sought to have it by the power of his own nature; and not from divine assistance according to God's power" (ST 1.63.3). In effect, Satan's sin and Adam and Eve's sin stem from the same mistake: all sought to grasp by nature what could only be received by grace.

66 WJW 2:441, "The General Deliverance."

67 Cf. WJW 1:184, "Justification by Faith."

68 Kenneth Collins, *The Theology of John Wesley: Holy Love and the Shape of Grace* (Nashville: Abingdon, 2007): 56.

69 WJW 2:9, "Original, Nature, Properties, and Use of the Law."

70 WJW 2:10, "Original, Nature, Properties, and Use of the Law."

71 Cf. Long, *John Wesley's Moral Theology*, 202.

72 WJW 4:295, "The Image of God."

73 WJW 2:440, "The General Deliverance."

74 WJW 2:441, "The General Deliverance."

75 WJW 2:441, "The General Deliverance."

76 Maddox, *Responsible Grace*, 246–47, 252–53.

77 Consider Wesley's speculation on the state of animals in the new creation: "May I be permitted to mention here a conjecture concerning the brute creation? What if it should then please the all-wise, the all-gracious Creator, to raise them higher in the scale of beings? What if it should please him, when he makes us 'equal to angels,' to make them what we are now? Creatures capable of God? Capable of knowing, and loving, and enjoying the Author of their being? If it should be so, ought our eye to be evil because he is good? However this be, he will certainly do what will be most for his own glory" (WJW 2:448, "The General Deliverance").

78 WJW 2:449, "The General Deliverance."

79 Theodore R. Weber, *Politics in the Order of Salvation: Transforming Wesleyan Political Ethics* (Nashville: Kingswood Books, 2001), 391–420.

80 Cf. Weber, *Politics in the Order of Salvation*, 399.

81 By these comments I do not mean to discount the possibility of human animal interactions that are very different from those we ordinarily experience today. In the church's history we have the stories of St. Francis of Assisi preaching to the birds and St. Anthony of Padua to the fishes. In both cases the animals respond to the preaching of the gospel, but, and this is key, they respond in animal ways, confirming what Aquinas states, admittedly in a very different context, regarding the modalities of perfection, namely, that "every perfection is received in the subject capable of perfection, according to its mode" (ST 1.62.5). Besides such examples of transformed human animal interactions from the pages of hagiography, we have those that occur in the pages of Scripture, where we are told that Balaam's donkey spoke, as did the serpent. However, I think that even the most charitable reading of these stories does not allow us to draw any substantive conclusions regarding the true nature of snakes and donkeys.

82 According to Weber, "The wholistic use of *image of God*—by contrast with a reductionist focus on the *moral* image—requires us to understand the perfection of individuals in the context of the perfection of human kind. It forces attention to the corporate character of human existence and the social nature of the self, and thereby raises even more questions than exist already concerning the prospect of being 'made perfect in love *in this life*'" (Weber, *Politics in the Order of Salvation*, 418; emphasis added).

83 WJW 1:204, "The Righteousness of Faith."

84 WJW 1:184, "Justification by Faith."

85 Weber, *Politics in the Order of Salvation*, 418.

86 WJW 2:185, "Original Sin."

87 Maddox, *Responsible Grace*, 90. Wesley considered the doctrine of original sin to be one of the central doctrines of Methodism and checks against Deism. However, while his insistence on the importance of this doctrine was consistent, his interpretation of it was not. For instance, the late Wesley appeared to have grown increasingly uncomfortable with the Augustinian notion of inherited guilt and came to believe that any such guilt was forgiven at birth through the universal work of God's prevenient grace (Maddox, *Responsible Grace*, 75). No human suffers eternal damnation for the sin of Adam and Eve. Yet Wesley believed that the corruption of human nature was inherited by all of Adam's heirs and for this reason no one is innocent before God, not even the infant. Hence, the suffering of children in this life is justly deserved because they were, in a sense, "in the loins of Adam" when he sinned (Collins, *The Theology of John Wesley*, 67). As disagreeable as these words sound to contemporary ears, Lindström is surely right in saying that "Wesley is trying to reconcile an individualistic approach with the collective view: to combine the idea of personal responsibility and personal cooperation, where man's eternal destiny is at stake, with a conception of the situation of the natural man which emphasizes the idea of saving grace. On the one hand, he maintains that through Adam all mankind are implicated in sin and guilt. . . . On the other hand, the participation in Adam's sin and guilt which original sin involves does not amount to guilt in the full sense. For this the personal consent of the individual is also necessary" (Lindström, *Wesley and Sanctification*, 35–36).

88 Cf. WJW 2:442, "The General Deliverance."

89 WJW 2:443, "The General Deliverance"; emphasis in original.

90 Methodists debate the extent of this corruption in Wesley's theology. On the one hand, Wesley can sound as dark a note as Calvin or Luther on the human condition under sin. On the other hand, for the Eastern Fathers whom Wesley read and was influenced by, "the Fall did render us prone to sin, but not incapable of co-operating with God's offer of healing. As a result we only become guilty when we reject the offered grace of God, *like* Adam and Eve did" (Maddox, *Responsible Grace*, 74). The difficulty that these contrasting views represent for the interpretation of Wesley's theology is most evident when considering the work of prevenient grace on fallen humans. According to Maddox, "Prevenient Grace is not a new endowment given into human possession, it is an accompanying effect of God's initial move towards mercifully-restored Presence in our lives. With God's approach our faculties are increasingly empowered, to the point that we can recognize our need and God's offer of renewed relationship, and respond to it" (Maddox, *Responsible Grace*, 90). According to Collins, "for Wesley, it is prevenient grace that restores the very elements required for responsible personhood and accountability in the first place" (Collins, *The Theology of John Wesley*, 81). Is the human predicament after the fall like that toad, which because it grew up inside the trunk of a tree, had the full possession of its five senses but no possibility of using them (cf. WJW 4:168–76)? Or, is the human predicament after the fall that these senses are not atrophied but simply nonexistent? To switch metaphors, does the human under the condition of sin need medicine or an organ transplant? I would say that at his best Wesley believes that the image of God in the human has been defaced but not effaced. The healing presence of grace presupposes the abiding existence of a nature capable of grace. Otherwise, we might as well say that prevenient grace could bring chairs to repentance by graciously giving them the capacity to hear the word of God.

91 WJW 2:178, "Original Sin."

92 Collins, *The Theology of John Wesley*, 63.

93 One of the first persons to theologically narrate the human predicament in the terms set forth in 1 John 2:16 was Augustine. However, Wesley truly made this Augustinian description his own. As Outler comments, "Wesley repeats the text tirelessly, and its suggestion to him that sin is overreach of what in themselves are innocent appetites (as in the animals) reinforced his notion of our human responsibility in all sin" (WJW 1:226, n. 64).

94 WJW 2:180, "Original Sin."

95 "A Plain Account of Christian Perfection," 311.

96 "A Plain Account of Christian Perfection," 311. The "late" Wesley nuanced this last claim by introducing a distinction between two kinds of wandering thoughts: those that wander from God and those that wander from the point at hand. As Collins explains, "Since the first thoughts constitute practical atheism for Wesley, a heart of unbelief, believers can, at least, expect to be free from this. But they can never be released from wandering thoughts in the second sense, from those that stray from the point they have in mind" (Collins, *The Theology of John Wesley*, 301).

97 WJW 1:241, "The Fruits of the Spirit."

98 WW 12:448, "Letter to a Young Disciple."

99 "A Plain Account of Christian Perfection," 358.

100 WJW 1:439, "The Great Privilege of Those That Are Born of God."

101 WJW 1:319, "On Sin in Believers"; emphasis in original. Wesley clarifies this important distinction of modes of sin inhering in the Christian in the following way, "By 'sin' I here understand inward sin: any sinful temper, passion, or affection; such as pride, self-will, love of the world, in any kind or degree; such as lust, anger, peevishness; any disposition contrary to the mind which was in Christ" (WJW 1:320, "On Sin in Believers").

102 WJW 7:557, Wesley, *A Collection of Hymns*.

103 WJW 2:182, "Original Sin."

104 Maddox points out that Wesley's occasional description of entire sanctification as the "rooting out" or "destruction" of inbred sin, whatever its provenance, is problematic. "The particular problem that Wesley became quite sensitive to was that talk of the "destruction" of sinful affections could connote the impossibility of their return . . . When Wesley was pressed directly on this point he offered an alternative account that in the soul of an entirely sanctified person holy tempers (i.e., enduring affections) are *presently* reigning to the point of "driving out" opposing tempers (although these may return)" (Maddox, *Responsible Grace*, 188). Maddox is right that the language of "destruction" is easily misunderstood. However, I think that Wesley rightly held on to the possibility of such a work of grace occurring. Furthermore, it is not clear to me that for Wesley the holy tempers "drive out" the unholy ones. One could just as well say that the greatest obstacle to growth in holiness is the presence of unholy habits and that the strengthening of the holy habits is premised on the death of the evil habits. Finally, the possibility of instantaneous sanctification and the assurance of such a gift are to a large degree premised on the spiritually discernable eradication of inbred sin.

105 As Maddox states, "Wesley believed that the Christian life did not have to remain a life of constant struggle. He believed that both Scripture and Christian tradition attested that God's loving grace can transform our lives to the point where our own love for God and others becomes a "natural" response. Christians can aspire to take on the disposition of Christ, and live out that disposition within the constraints of human infirmities. To deny this possibility would be to deny the sufficiency of God's empowering grace—to make the power of sin greater than that of grace" (Maddox, *Responsible Grace*, 188).

106 "A Plain Account of Christian Perfection," 328ff.

107 WJW 3:71–87, "On Perfection."

108 WJW 3:75, "On Perfection."

109 WJW 3:74, "On Perfection."

110 "A Plain Account of Christian Perfection," 348.

111 In his 1965 dissertation *John Wesley's Concept of Perfect Love: A Motif Analysis*, David Cubie brings Wesley's understanding of love into critical dialogue with Anders Nygren's work in *Agape and Eros* (Philadelphia: Westminster Press, 1953). Cubie rightly rejects Nygren's opposition of eros and agape and shows how these two kinds of love are held together in Wesley's doctrine.

112 WJW 4:355, "The One Thing Needful."

113 WJW 11:45, "An Earnest Appeal to Men of Reason and Religion."
114 WJW 2:38, "The Law Established through Faith, II."
115 Collins, *The Theology of John Wesley*, 21; emphasis in original.
116 WJW 2:389, "God's Approbation of His Works."
117 WJW 2:372, "On Eternity," 20. Wesley's citation comes from Augustine's *Confessions*, III.xi.
118 WJW 3:94, "Spiritual Worship."
119 WJW 26:182, "Letter to John Smith".
120 WJW 2:425–26, "God's Love to Fallen Man"; emphasis in original.
121 WJW 2:425, "God's Love to Fallen Man."
122 Cf. WJW 2:510, "The New Creation": "Hence will arise an unmixed state of holiness and happiness far superior to that which Adam enjoyed in paradise."
123 WJW 1:442, "The Great Privilege of Those That Are Born of God."
124 WJW 11:45, "An Earnest Appeal to Men of Reason and Religion."
125 WJW 4:336, "The Love of God."
126 WJW 4:355, "The One Thing Needful."
127 WJW 2:39, "The Law Established through Faith, II."
128 Lindström, *Wesley and Sanctification*, 175.
129 Lindström, *Wesley and Sanctification*, 173.
130 WJW 4:333, "The Love of God."
131 WJW 4:331, "The Love of God."
132 WJW 4:333, "The Love of God."
133 Lindström, *Wesley and Sanctification*, 178.
134 Lindström's contrast between the ecumenical work of the "Faith and Order" and "Life and Work" commissions is characteristic of this opposition (*Wesley and Sanctification*, 194). Basing himself on Wesley's talk of unity of affections and opinions, Lindström places Wesley solidly in the latter group. There is much in Wesley to warrant such a move. However, Lindström underestimates the significance of the essentials of Christian doctrine in Wesley's theology. If, as Lindström states (*Wesley and Sanctification*, 182), love is ordered love, if love is ruled by law and measured by reason, then "Life and Works" must be based on "Faith and Order."
135 Lindström, *Wesley and Sanctification*, 183, n. 5.
136 Wesley's clear distinction between love of God and love of neighbor is problematic for Cobb. According to Cobb, "There is no doubt that according to the Bible we should love God with our whole being. But there is some doubt as to whether any biblical writer ever meant that peculiar state of being Wesley describes. Does this love take up *all* the affections and fill the *entire* capacity of the soul? If so, how could there also be love of neighbor"; John Cobb, *Grace and Responsibility* (Nashville: Abingdon, 1995), 61.
137 "A Plain Account of Christian Perfection," 302–3.
138 WJW 4:384, "On Love."
139 Cf. Lindström, *Wesley and Sanctification*, 190–94.
140 WJW 2:140, "Satan's Devices"; cf. Lindström, *Wesley and Sanctification*, 195.
141 WW 14:321.
142 WJW 4:192, "On Faith."
143 WJW 4:191, "On Faith."

144 WJW 4:197, "On Faith."
145 WJW 3:15, "Of Good Angels."
146 WJW 2:510, "The New Creation"; emphasis added.
147 WW 1:165.
148 Lindström, *Wesley and Sanctification*, 196.
149 In *Character and the Christian Life: A Study in Theological Ethics* (San Antonio, Tex.: Trinity University Press, 1975), Stanley Hauerwas is concerned that Wesley's interpretation of the Christian life "can very easily be taken in a moralistic sense suggesting that by a rather mechanical stacking of one good act (work) on another we are somehow made better" (219). While approving of Wesley's emphasis on holiness, Hauerwas wants to understand sanctification not as end in itself but as being conformed to Christ through character formation. As Hauerwas avers, "To be sanctified is to have our character determined by our basic commitments and beliefs about God. It is a willingness to see and understand ourselves as having significance only as our agency is qualified under the form of Christ and the task he entrusts us. Christian character is the formation of our affections and actions according to the fundamental beliefs of the Christian faith and life" (203). Wesley would heartily agree, hence his emphasis on the role of the holy tempers in Christian life. Indeed I would suggest one of the reasons that Methodist theology is so easily prone to the moralistic interpretation that Hauerwas rightly decries is the lack of sufficient attention on the part of Wesleyan theologians like Lindström to the formative significance of the holy tempers in the life of grace.
150 On Wesley's moral psychology see Randy Maddox' chapter "A Change of Affections: The Development, Dynamics, and Dethronement of John Wesley's Heart Religion," in *"Heart Religion" in the Methodist Tradition and Related Movements*, ed. Richard Steele, 3–31 (Lanham, Md.: Scarecrow Press, 2001).
151 Maddox, "A Change of Affections," 5.
152 Maddox, "A Change of Affections," 13.
153 Maddox, "A Change of Affections," 15.
154 Maddox, "A Change of Affections," 16.
155 Maddox, "A Change of Affections," 16.
156 WJW 4:66, "The Unity of the Divine Being."
157 WJW 1:489, "Sermon on the Mount, II."
158 WJW 2:188, "The New Birth."
159 WJW 1:489, "Sermon on the Mount, II."
160 WJW 3:309, "On Zeal."
161 WJW 3:312, "On Zeal."
162 WJW 3:314, "On Zeal"; emphasis in original.
163 WJW 3:314, "On Zeal."
164 WJW 2:429, "God's Love to Fallen Man."
165 WJW 2:432, "God's Love to Fallen Man."
166 "By occasion of this they attained many holy tempers which otherwise could have no being: resignation to God, confidence in him in times of trouble and danger, patience, meekness, longsuffering, and the whole train of passive virtues" (WJW 2:432, "God's Love to Fallen Man").
167 WJW 2:431, "God's Love to Fallen Man."

168 WJW 3:320, "On Zeal."

169 "A Plain Account of Christian Perfection," 362; emphasis in original.

170 Thomas Rigl, *Die Gnade wirken lassen: Methodistische Soteriologie im ökumenischen Dialog* (Paderborn: Bonifatius, 2001), 75.

Chapter 2

1 WJW 2:156, "The Scripture Way of Salvation."

2 WJW 1:118, "Salvation by Faith."

3 Luby, *The Perceptibility of Grace,* 106. Luby makes a strong case for the fundamental agreement of Wesley's thoughts with Roman Catholic doctrine on the supernatural character of grace, its gratuity, provenience, necessity, and resistibility. As we will see, even in the area of merit, despite Wesley's explicit demurrals, there is room for reflecting on the relation between works and their reward in terms of merit *de congruo* and *de condigno.*

4 Thomas Lessmann underscores this relation in his study *Rolle und Bedeutung des Heiligen Geistes in der Theologie John Wesleys* (Stuttgart: Christliches Verlagshaus, 1987). In Lessmann's judgment, "Das Wirken des Heiligen Geistes steht in Zentrum der Theologie Wesleys. Die Pneumatologie ist aufs engste mit der Gnadenlehre verknüpft. Zugespitzt kann man sagen, daß Wesley eine Pneumatologische Gnadenlehre hat. Der Person des Heiligen Geistes kommt darin die bedeutendste Aufgabe zu. Der Heilige Geist macht Sünder und Ungläubige zu Nachfolgern Christi und läßt sie dann in das Ebenbild Gottes hineinwachsen, indem Er in ihnen wohnt, sie antreibt und führt" (130).

5 Lessmann, *Rolle und Bedeutung,* 128.

6 Luby, *The Perceptibility of Grace,*111.

7 Luby, *The Perceptibility of Grace,* 114.

8 Luby, *The Perceptibility of Grace,* 117.

9 WJW 3:545, "Free Grace."

10 WJW 1:382, "The Means of Grace." I add the emphasis to show that Wesley was troubled by those like Molther who played Christ's grace over against the instituted means of grace. In such a context the declaration that "Christ is the only means of grace" became a justification for enthusiastic stillness and antinomianism.

11 WJW 3:545, "Free Grace."

12 WJW 3:207, "On Working Out Our Own Salvation." Compare these words with those of Garrigou-Lagrange on Thomas' distinction between sufficient and efficacious grace. "This [efficacious] grace, which is always followed by its effect, is refused to us, as we said, only if we resist the divine, *auxilium praeveniens*, sufficient grace, in which efficacious help is offered us, as fruit is in the flower. . . . Now man is sufficient of himself to fall; drawn from nothingness, he is by nature defectible. He is sufficiently assisted by God so that he falls only through his own fault, which thus deprives him of new help"; Reginald Garrigou-Lagrange, *Christian Perfection and Contemplation: According to St. Thomas Aquinas and St. John of the Cross* (Rockford, Ill.: Tan Books & Publishers, 2004), 95.

13 WJW 19:332, Journal 5, August 23, 1743; emphasis in original.

14 WJW 19:332, Journal 5, August 23, 1743; emphasis in original.

15 WJW 19:332, Journal 5, August 23, 1743. Luby observes that, "If grace is

cooperant, rather than irresistible, then the importance of perceiving this grace in some way begins to emerge; since in order for cooperation with someone or something to be genuine, one must be aware of the person or thing with which one is cooperating" (Luby, *The Perceptibility of Grace*, 82). By way of anticipation on what Thomas will say, we will need to consider his distinction between *gratia operans* and *gratia cooperans*; cf. Bernard Lonergan, *Grace and Freedom: Operative Grace in the Thought of St. Thomas Aquinas* (Toronto: University of Toronto, 2000).

16 WJW 1:309, "The Witness of Our Own Spirit."

17 Luby, *The Perceptibility of Grace*, 88.

18 Lindström, *Wesley and Sanctification*, 46.

19 WJW 1:263, "The Spirit of Bondage and Adoption."

20 WJW 1:263, "The Spirit of Bondage and Adoption."

21 Harald Lindström draws this distinction in *Wesley and Sanctification*, 40–44.

22 Cf. Ted Dorman, "Forgiveness of Past Sins: John Wesley on Justification, a Case Study Approach," *Pro Ecclesia* 10, no. 3 (2001): 275–94.

23 WJW 2:184, "Original Sin."

24 WJW 1:264, "The Spirit of Bondage and Adoption."

25 WJW 2:164f, "The Scripture Way of Salvation."

26 "A Plain Account of Christian Perfection," 336.

27 WJW 3:203, "On Working Out Our Own Salvation."

28 WJW 2:490, "The General Spread of the Gospel."

29 WJW 2:490, "The General Spread of the Gospel," §12; WJW 3:208, "On Working Out Our Own Salvation."

30 WJW 3:208, "On Working Out Our Own Salvation."

31 According to Luby, "By 'growth in grace,' Wesley means growth in our awareness of the depths of God's love for us and growth in our consciousness of the ethical implications of that love, and as a consequence, growth in our intimacy with God" (Luby, *The Perceptibility of Grace*, 107). However, on this point at least, Luby's analysis seems to me too narrow. Luby does not sufficiently account for the role of the holy tempers in the Christian life. Grace does not simply bring a new perspective from which new motivations arise. Grace brings new habits. As Wesley states: "In the moment we are justified. The seed of every virtue is then sown in the soul" (WW 8:285).

32 WW 11:388.

33 "A Plain Account of Christian Perfection," 335.

34 WJW 2:169, "The Scripture Way of Salvation."

35 WJW 2:167, "The Scripture Way of Salvation."

36 WJW 2:167–68, "The Scripture Way of Salvation."

37 WJW 2:169, "The Scripture Way of Salvation."

38 WJW 2:167, "The Scripture Way of Salvation."

39 "A Plain Account of Christian Perfection," 335.

40 In *The Limits of "Love Divine": John Wesley's Response to Antinomianism and Enthusiasm* (Nashville: Kingswood Books, 1989), Stephen Gunter nicely captures the difference between Wesley and his Moravian friend on the relation between Christ and the sacraments: "Wesley's presuppositions were those of a high church evangelical; Molther was a quietist evangelical. Molther was adamant

that a person came through Christ to the ordinances of the church; Wesley preferred to emphasize the path through the ordinances of the church to Christ. Molther taught that one should be a believer prior to studying scripture, attending communion, or performing good works; according to Wesley all these were avenues by which one could come to faith. For Molther the Sacrament was a privilege only for believers who were absolutely certain of their standing before God; for Wesley it was a means of grace facilitating their certainty. For Molther there are no 'degrees' of faith; either one was a believer or one was not converted. For Wesley people could believe and still not have the certainty of the 'witness of the Spirit'. Molther instructed his hearers to 'wait' until God made them holy; Wesley preached the 'pursuit of holiness'" (90–91).

41 WJW 1:381, "The Means of Grace"; emphasis in original.

42 WJW 1:396, "The Means of Grace"; emphasis in original.

43 For instance, Wesley insists on the efficacy of baptism for spiritual regeneration. As Geoffrey Wainwright states in *Worship with One Accord: Where Liturgy & Ecumenism Embrace* (Oxford: Oxford University Press, 1997): "Because God has commanded the sacrament and promised this blessing, the sacrament will always be effective, whenever it is properly used, i.e., administered to people who have come to repentance and faith, or to the infants of believers who stand within the covenant" (113). For Wesley the presence of faith is essential for the efficacious reception of the sacrament because only by faith can our minds perceive the inward grace in the outward signs. As Luby observes, "the perception of grace in Wesley's thought is given a quasi-sacramental cast. We are to perceive the love of God extended to us for our salvation primarily in the Scriptures, in prayer, in the Eucharist, and so on. As our lives become more and more informed by the constant use of the means (which of course presupposes an ecclesial context), we become able to perceive the hand of God even in the providential occurrences of everyday existence" (Luby, *The Perceptibility of Grace*, 190).

44 As Geoffrey Wainwright states in *Worship with One Accord*, "The Wesleys are very hesitant about explaining *how* the sacraments work; but *that* the sacraments work, they rejoice to confess" (112).

45 *Hymns on the Lord's Supper* (Madison, N.J.: Charles Wesley Society, 1995), LIV.2.

46 *Hymns on the Lord's Supper*, LIV.4.

47 Wesley's appropriation of this tradition is admittedly ambiguous. As he states: "Can anything be a greater help to universal holiness than the continually seeing the light of his glory? It is no wonder, then, that so many wise and good men have recommended, to all who desire to be truly religious, the exercise of the presence of God. But in doing this some of those holy men seem to have fallen into one mistake. . . . They put men wholly unawakened, unconvinced of sin, upon this exercise at their very entrance into religion; whereas this should certainly not be first, but one of the last things" (WJW 3:123, "On Dissipation").

48 WJW 9:268, "A Plain Account of the People Called Methodists."

49 WJW 1:393, "The Means of Grace."

50 WJW 1:394, "The Means of Grace."

51 WJW 1:395, "The Means of Grace."
52 WJW 1:395, "The Means of Grace."
53 WJW 4:174, "On Living without God."
54 WJW 4:175, "On Living without God."
55 Gregory Clapper coins this term in order to suggest that Wesley's theology overcomes the *aporiae* which arise when "right belief" and "right action" are set against each other. As he explains in *John Wesley on Religious Affections* (Metuchen, N.J.: Scarecrow Press, 1989), "Wesley's vision of Christianity contains an important place for both right belief and right action. But 'orthodoxy' and 'orthopraxis' do not exhaustively describe what was essential to his vision of Christianity. What is missing is what I term the *orthokardia*—the right heart. This is a vision of Christianity which cannot be conveyed by stressing only beliefs and action, yet neither is it conveyed by focusing on self-contained inner states or 'feelings.' Without such a 'right heart,' there is no Christianity on Wesley's terms" (154). It is important to observe that Clapper is not suggesting that the real Christian is the one who feels the right way. In this sense, the term *orthokardia* is to be preferred over *orthopathy*. This last term is used by Theodore Runyon in *The New Creation: John Wesley's Theology Today* (Nashville: Abingdon, 1998) to denote "the new sensitivity to and participation in spiritual reality that mark genuine faith" (149). Runyon focuses on right experience as the mark of genuine Christianity. This is not the place to engage his interesting (though not unproblematic) proposal. Obviously neither *orthokardia* nor *orthopathy* are terms that Wesley ever used. In that sense, I am not obliged to use them either. But if I were to choose one I would choose the former over the latter because the former gives us a way of expressing something that, as we have seen, is integral to Wesley's theology, namely the role of the holy tempers in shaping our perceptions and affections.
56 WW 8:299, "Minutes of Several Conversations between the Rev. Mr. Wesley and Others."
57 WJW 4:144, "On the Wedding Garment."
58 WJW 9:178, "The Principles of a Methodist Farther Explained."
59 WW 13:138, "Letter to Mr. John Blackall."
60 Note though that in some of Wesley's early sermons he appears to affirm the Reformed understanding of the relation between death and perfection. In the introduction to his sermon "The Trouble and Rest of Good Men," Wesley states: "But as perfect holiness is not found on earth, so neither is perfect happiness: some remains of our disease will ever be felt and some physic be necessary to heal it. . . . Death shall destroy at once the whole body of sin, and therewith of its companion pain" (WJW 3:533). This theological stance is also evident in his sermon "On Mourning the Dead" (WJW 4:237–43), but it is quietly and irrevocably abandoned in later sermons.
61 WJW 2:490, "The General Spread of the Gospel," §12; WJW 3:208, "On Working Out Our Own Salvation."
62 WJW 4:385–86, "On Love."
63 W. E. Sangster does observe that something like purgatory seems to be creeping back into Protestantism, even if the name itself is rejected because of its association with merit and extra-biblical testimony in Catholic thought, but

the need for a process of perfection beyond death seems manifest to many. In the words of Baron von Hügel, "Purgatory and Hell may be refined, but they must be there. The majority of souls can't go straight to Heaven"; cited by W. E. Sangster, *The Path to Perfection: An Examination and Restatement of John Wesley's Doctrine of Christian Perfection* (Nashville: Abingdon, 1943), 69.

64 Cf. "The More Excellent Way" (WJW 3:266); "On Faith" (WJW 3:497).

65 WJW 3:265, "The More Excellent Way."

66 WJW 3:265, "The More Excellent Way."

67 WJW 3:266, "The More Excellent Way."

68 WJW 3:266, "The More Excellent Way."

69 WJW 3:266, "The More Excellent Way."

70 According to Aquinas, in heaven some will see God better than others: "Of those who see the essence of God, one sees Him more perfectly than another. This, indeed, does not take place as if one had a more perfect similitude of God than another, since that vision will not spring from any similitude; but it will take place because one intellect will have a greater power or faculty to see God than another. The faculty of seeing God, however, does not belong to the created intellect naturally, but is given to it by the light of glory, which establishes the intellect in a kind of 'deiformity,' as appears from what is said above, in the preceding article. Hence the intellect which has more of the light of glory will see God the more perfectly; and he will have a fuller participation of the light of glory who has more charity; because where there is the greater charity, there is the more desire; and desire in a certain degree makes the one desiring apt and prepared to receive the object desired. Hence he who possesses the more charity, will see God the more perfectly, and will be the more beatified" (ST 1.12.6).

71 "A Plain Account of Christian Perfection," 331.

72 WJW 2:105, "Christian Perfection."

73 WJW 9:35, "The Character of a Methodist."

74 WJW 22:72, "Letter to the Editor of Lloyd's Evening Post."

75 Cf. WJW 4:319–28, "Public Diversions Denounced."

76 Cf. WJW 4:271, "On the Sabbath."

77 Notice the politically conservative cast of, among other things, Wesley's correlation of pomp and power in his sermon "On Dress." Some might ask, why is the aristocracy exempted from Wesley's strict dress code but not the people called Methodists? Here is Wesley's reply: "Yea, it may be doubted whether any part of Scripture forbids (at least I know not any) those in any nation that are invested with supreme authority to be arrayed in gold and costly apparel; or to adorn their immediate attendants, or magistrates, or officers with the same. It is not improbable that our blessed Lord intended to give countenance to this custom when he said, without the least mark of censure or disapprobation, 'Behold, those that wear gorgeous (splendid) apparel are in kings' courts.' What is then the meaning of these Scriptures? What is it which they forbid? They manifestly forbid ordinary Christians, those in the lower or middle ranks of life, to be adorned with gold, or pearls, or costly apparel" (WJW 3:250). In other words, Christians are not called to upward mobility but to remain as they are and live, dress, and act in a manner befitting their social station.

78 Cf. WJW 9:527–30, "Thoughts upon Methodism."

79 Cf. WJW 9:534–37, "Thoughts upon a Late Phenomenon."
80 Benedict XVI, *Deus Caritas Est* (Vatican City: Libreria Editrice Vaticana, 2006), 40.
81 The words in this statement are inspired by the lyrics of Fred Pratt Green's hymn "Rejoice in God's Saints" (*The United Methodist Hymnal*, 708), where the phrase "a world without saints forgets how to praise" occurs twice.
82 Benedict XVI, *Deus Caritas*, 36.
83 Benedict XVI, *Deus Caritas*, 42.
84 Cited in John R. Tyson, *Charles Wesley on Sanctification: A Biographical and Theological Study* (Grand Rapids: Francis Asbury Press, 1986), 290.
85 Cited in Tyson, *Wesley and Sanctification*, 291.
86 Clement of Alexandria, *Stromata* in *The Ante-Nicene Fathers*, vol. 2: *Fathers of the Second Century*, ed. Alexander Roberts and James Donaldson (Peabody, Mass.: Hendrickson), 538.
87 WJW 9:32–42, "The Character of a Methodist."
88 WJW 9:34, "The Character of a Methodist."
89 WJW 19:294, Journal 5, August 31, 1742.
90 WJW 9:37, "The Character of a Methodist."
91 WJW 9:38, "The Character of a Methodist."
92 WJW 9:38, "The Character of a Methodist."
93 Maddox, *Responsible Grace*, 190.
94 WJW 4:627, "On the Death of John Fletcher."
95 WJW 4:627, "On the Death of John Fletcher."
96 I find myself in fundamental agreement with Wainwright's evaluation of Wesley's rationale for not naming names in *Methodists in Dialogue* (Nashville: Kingswood Books, 1995): "Wesley's discouragement of the practice of calling on the saints for their prayers may be due to a reluctance to name names in the case of the departed, even with persons of conspicuous sanctity whose bliss might be reasonably supposed. An even stronger motive here, however, may be the association of the invocation of the saints with a cult of relics and a treasury of merit that Wesley found to reproach in the Roman Catholic Church" (245). Wainwright suggests that dialogue between Methodists and Eastern Orthodox Churches might prove a helpful mediating entry into these questions. For good or ill, a study of Thomas Aquinas' doctrine of perfection cannot avoid the question of merit, and we will need to consider this theological locus in the final sections of the next to last chapter.
97 WJW 11:141–70, "A Farther Appeal to Men of Reason and Religion, Part I." The main apologetic goal of this appeal is to defend Methodists from the charge of enthusiasm. Wesley's opponents charged him of two offenses: confusing the ordinary and extraordinary gifts of the Holy Spirit and teaching that the Spirit works without means. To the first charge Wesley defends himself by appealing to Scripture, the Fathers, and the Church of England in order to show that the anointing of the Holy Spirit is one of the ordinary gifts of the Holy Spirit. Wesley repeatedly asserts that "till a man 'receives the Holy Ghost' he is without God in the world; that he cannot know the things of God unless God reveals them unto him by his Spirit; no, nor have one holy or heavenly temper, without the inspiration of the Holy One" (WJW 11:170). To the charge

that he teaches the immediate inspiration of the Spirit, Wesley responds: "So I do, or I mean nothing at all. Not indeed such inspiration as is *sine mediis*. But all inspiration, though by means, is immediate. Suppose, for instance, you are employed in private prayer, and God pours his love into your heart. God then acts immediately on your soul; and the love of him which you then experience, is as immediately breathed into you by the Holy Ghost, as if you had lived seventeen hundred years ago. Change the term: Say, God then assists you to love him. Well, and is not this immediate assistance? Say, His Spirit concurs with yours. You gain no ground. It is immediate concurrence, or none at all. God, a Spirit, acts upon your spirit. Make it out any otherwise if you can" (WJW 11:171–72).

98 Cf. WJW 3:264, "The More Excellent Way."

99 Cf. WJW 3:264, "The More Excellent Way."

100 WJW 1:160, "Scriptural Christianity."

101 WJW 3:263–64, "The More Excellent Way."

102 In this correlation of poverty and grace Wesley shared a portion of the spirit of Domingo de Guzmán. Once, or so the story goes, Domingo visited Rome where the Pope, displaying the splendor of the new work on the Vatican, observed to Domingo, "no longer can Peter say: silver and gold have I none," to which Domingo replied, "neither can he tell the paralytic: rise, take up your mat, and walk"; cf. Chesterton, *Saint Thomas Aquinas: "The Dumb Ox,"* 43.

103 WJW 9:219, "The Principles of a Methodist Farther Explained."

104 WJW 9:214, "The Principles of a Methodist Farther Explained."

105 WJW 9:219, "The Principles of a Methodist Farther Explained."

106 WJW 9:218, "The Principles of a Methodist Farther Explained."

107 Historically, Christians have held the saints' virtue and the saint's power to work miracles in a kind of dialectical tension. In *Making Saints: How the Catholic Church Determines Who Becomes a Saint, Who Doesn't, and Why*, 2nd ed. (New York: Simon & Schuster, 1996), Kenneth Woodward argues that during the middles ages (with the exception of Saint Francis) the saints held up by Rome as exemplary were not of great interest to ordinary Christians. "In the first place, the great mass of believers were not interested in saints as moral examples, but as spiritual patrons who protected the populace against storms and plagues. Second, the moral, ascetical, and intellectual virtues exemplified by the papally canonized could not be easily cultivated outside the cloister or convent" (70). "In sum, the development of canonization as a papal process meant a shift in focus from popular concern with miracles to elite concerns with virtue. To be sure, proof of miracles remained necessary for verifying a candidate's reputation for holiness, but only a thorough examination of the life could establish the presence of virtue" (71). The distinction between the saint as moral exemplar and the saint as thaúmaturge raises questions that I cannot address at this point regarding church authority and popular piety. In any case, as I have been arguing, Wesley is far more interested in the former kind of saint than in the latter. As we shall see, Aquinas too, though he does not diminish the significance of miracles by any means, emphasizes the moral exemplarity of the saint. Indeed, his treatise on the virtues was for a long time the basis for the examination of virtuous characters of candidates being considered for beatification. We will touch on these issues again in the last chapter of this book.

108 WJW 9:220, "The Principles of a Methodist Farther Explained."

109 Cf. Thomas Albin's chapter "'Inwardly Persuaded': Religion of the Heart in Early British Methodism," in *"Heart Religion" in the Methodist Tradition and Related Movements*, 33–66 (Lanham, Md.: Scarecrow Press, 2001). For a detailed study of the development of the class meeting, consult David Lowes Watson, *The Early Methodist Class Meetings* (Nashville: Discipleship Resources, 1985).

110 WW 1:416.

111 Albin, "Inwardly Persuaded," 42–52.

112 John L. Peters, *Christian Perfection and American Methodism* (Nashville: Abingdon, 1956).

113 Peters, *Christian Perfection and American Methodism*, 193.

114 Peters, *Christian Perfection and American Methodism*, 200.

Chapter 3

1 *De veritate* 1.10.ad.s.c.3. For the English version, I am using *Truth*, translated by Robert Mulligan (Indianapolis: Hackett Publishing, 1954).

2 Jean-Pierre Torrell, *Saint Thomas Aquinas: Spiritual Master,* vol. 2, translated by Robert Royal (Washington, D.C.: Catholic University of America Press, 2003).

3 Torrell, *Spiritual Master,* 341.

4 Rudi Te Velde, *Aquinas on God: the "Divine Science" of the Summa Theologiae* (Burlington, Vt.: Ashgate, 2006): 75; emphasis in original.

5 Te Velde, *Aquinas on God*, 80.

6 Te Velde, *Aquinas on God*, 78.

7 ST 1.4.1.

8 As an aside, it is interesting to observe that the objections of Hegel and other process philosophers are both anticipated and accounted for. In the words of Te Velde, "What Thomas tries to think by means of the formula *ipsum esse per se subsitens* is, in fact, the most concrete; not concreteness as a result that a simple form is received into something else, a material substrate, but the full *concretio* of being itself which is, as it were, 'individualized' and distinguished from everything else by the fact that it subsists through itself" (Te Velde, *Aquinas on God*, 84). God is not the *esse formale* of the universe becoming concrete by composition throughout history; "rather, the divine essence is the full and unrestricted actuality (*actus purus*) of being, which, by nature, tends to communicate its actuality to other things by letting them share in being" (Te Velde, *Aquinas on God*, 81).

9 ST 1.4.1.

10 ST 1.4.1.ad3.

11 ST 1.4.3.

12 Te Velde, *Aquinas on God*, 76.

13 François Marty, *La Perfection de l'homme selon Saint Thomas d'Aquin: Ses fondements ontologiques et leur vérification dans l'ordre actuel* (Rome: Gregorian University Press, 1962), 41. Marty sets out to show how the ontological structure of perfection is confirmed in the present order. He starts by observing that Thomas' notion of perfection is polyvalent and closely related to both truth and the good. On the one hand, truth is perfective (*perfectivum*) in the order

of knowledge; it perfects the intellect; it provides it with the *ratio boni*. On the other hand, the good is perfective in the order of being; it both renders perfection as its own reality and makes another perfect by inserting itself in this reality; in short, it makes the Good desirable. What does this mean? Simply put, truth and the goodness are correlative: "le vrai se présent comme bon, et le bien peut être reconnu comme vrai" (8). This correlation becomes identity only in God. In other words, properly speaking only God is perfect, however, this perfection is not closed in on itself: in it the creature too can be perfect by participation.

14 ST 1.5.1.

15 ST 1.5.2.ad1.

16 ST 1.5.3.

17 ST 1.6.1.

18 ST 1.6.2.

19 ST 1.6.3.

20 ST 1.5.3.

21 ST 1.6.1.ad2.

22 ST 1.6.3.

23 ST 1.4.1.ad3.

24 ST 1.29.3.

25 In *Trinity in Aquinas* (Naples, Fla.: Sapientia, 2003), Gilles Emery unfolds a law of redoublement that accounts for the otherwise strangely structured doctrine of God in the *Prima Pars*. "In order to speak the Trinitarian mystery, it is necessary always to employ two words, two formulas, in a reflection in two modes that joins here the substantial (essential) aspect and the distinction of persons (relative properties)" (178). There is a fitting order to this approach. "The understanding of the divine person presupposes the knowledge of the essence *because it integrates it*. . . . One cannot conceive of the person without the substance or without the nature belonging to the very *ratio* of the divine person" (179).

26 In *Explorations in Metaphysics: Being-God-Person* (Notre Dame, Ind.: University of Notre Dame Press, 1994), Norris Clarke makes a powerful case for the fundamental relationality of being: "To be is to be substance in relation" (216). For this reason the perfection of being and the perfection of personhood coincide. As Clarke explains, "to be a person is not something added on to being from without, but is really only the perfection of being itself, being come to its own, so to speak, allowed to be fully what it tends to be by nature when not restricted by the limitation proper to the material mode of being, i.e., the self-dispersal over space that is characteristic of matter. In a word, when being is allowed to be fully itself as active *presence*, it necessarily turns into luminous *self-presence*—self-awareness, or self-consciousness—one of the primary attributes of person. To be fully is to be personally" (218). Clarke's understanding of being as relational or even of being as love is winsome and congenial to the work of contemporary theologians like von Balthasar and Zizioulas. However, as Clarke himself acknowledges, the metaphysics of being as relation diverge from Thomas' metaphysics in important ways. "If being is intrinsically self-communicative and relational at all levels, including the divine, then it would follow that either (1)

God must necessarily, rather than freely, communicate the divine goodness in creation—which Aquinas as a Christian thinker could not subscribe to; or else (2) God's own inner being must be intrinsically relational, involving more than one person—and then we have a philosophical deduction of the doctrine of God as Trinity of distinct Persons, which Christian tradition has always held to be "strict mystery," inaccessible to any argument of natural or purely philosophical reason, and knowable in this life only by a divine revelation" (222). I cannot consider at this point how Clarke addresses this objection or whether his response adequately resolves the two aforementioned departures from Thomas' thought. I think that it is possible to read the metaphysics of "being as relation" proposed by Clarke as deepening Thomas' own account in ways that overcome the limitations of classical ontotheology and its critics (cf. Te Velde, *Aquinas on God*, 86). However, followers of Thomas must surely insist that such an account of the relationality of existence at all levels is only possible in the light of revelation.

27 ST 1.29.3.ad2.

28 ST 1.29.1.Pr.

29 ST 1.29.1.ad3; emphasis in original.

30 The incommunicability of the person must not be confused with a kind of *Ichgeschlossenheit* of being. The person is an individual substance *per se una*, but this individuality makes the person uniquely distinct and as such capable of relation. As Stephen Hipp states at the end of his study, "*Person*," in *Christian Tradition and the Conception of Saint Albert the Great: A Systematic Study of iIts Concept as Illuminated by the Mysteries of the Trinity and the Incarnation* (Münster: Aschendorff Verlag, 2001): "The person is an absolute reality, a being of nature, which tends, *on account of its nature*, to share itself with other distinct individuals. And its distinctness is a presupposition to such interaction. Indeed, like all beings, the person is intrinsically active and self-communicating, but what is communicated to other persons is everything but its distinctive character; a person never communicates its personality to another individual, for the persons *as such* according to first act would be participated by several and no longer be one" (517–18; emphasis in original). On the uniqueness of the person, see also Victorino Rodríguez y Rodríguez, "Estructura metafísica de la persona humana" in *Atti del IX Congresso Tomistico Internazionale III: Anthropologia Tomistica* (Vatican City: Libreria Editrice Vaticana, 1991), 113–28. In the same volume the following articles are also helpful: Mauricio Beuchot, "La noción de persona en santo Tomás algunas notas," 138–48; Alejandro Saavedra, "Fundamentación metafísica de la dignidad de la persona humana," 162–71.

31 *De potentia* 3.9.2.ad13.

32 ST 1.29.1.ad1.

33 I might in passing point out some implications of this argument for current discussions on the nature of personhood. First of all, Aquinas' understanding of God is neither essentialist nor personalist. Second, although the term "person" is borrowed from creatures and applied to God only analogically, the fact remains that Aquinas almost exclusively reserves this term for the divine persons in God, so that the term "person" is hardly to be found outside of his discussion of Trinitarian theology and Christology. Given the current currency

of the word "person" in anthropology and ethics, Aquinas' technical limitation of this term to theology proper might strike the modern thinker as either problematic or promising.

34 As Te Velde helps us understand, God is not perfect because he is *ipsum esse* but because he is *ipsum esse per se subsitens*. Without the perfection that comes from subsisting in itself, God, as *ipsum esse*, would be indistinguishable from the being of all things (*esse formale*). By saying that God is perfect, we affirm that "God is not merely being without essence but being that has fully and completely 'essentialized,' and, as such, God possesses the whole infinite fullness of being" (*Aquinas on God*, 81). By the light of faith we can go further and say that this perfect fullness of being subsists in three eternal relations, three persons.

35 *De potentia* 7.2.9.

36 *De potentia* 9.3.

37 *De potentia* 9.5.ad23.

38 ST 1.43.3.

39 Cf. Oliva Blanchette, *The Perfection of the Universe According to Aquinas: A Teleological Cosmology* (University Park: Pennsylvania University Press, 1992). The universe is the highest perfection of creation—this is Blanchette's argument in a nutshell. According to Blanchette, Aquinas did not settle on one single metaphor or representation of the universe, rather he deployed a series of distinct though complimentary analogies (12–16). At times, Aquinas speaks of the universe as a house; like a house, the universe has certain dimensions and is put together in a certain way and a certain diversity of things needs to come together in a certain way or the whole house collapses. But this analogy is somewhat static, elsewhere Aquinas compares the universe with an army; not only is there as in a house a certain ordination of different parts (*ordinationem distinctorum*) but an active coordination of the whole, a *communicatio ad totum*. Aquinas finds this to be a better analogy than the one of the house, but its dynamism is not sufficiently expressive of the relational character of the universe, so Aquinas turns to a consideration of the universe as a household. In a household the very nature of the communication and the affinity that hold the house together are based on the mutual relation of the parts to each other, a relation that is not contingent as in the choice of a general for an army but intrinsic to the nature of the parts themselves and grounded in familial love. The picture of the universe that emerges from this collage of analogies is one of ordered diversity.

40 ST 1.73.1.

41 ST 1.73.1; *De veritate* 1.10.ad.s.c.3.

42 Cf. ST 1.4.1.

43 ST1.6.3: "Unumquodque enum dicitur bonum, secundum quod est perfectum"; cf. ST 1.5.5.

44 *Scriptum super sententiis* 2.15.1.ad7.

45 ST 1.73.

46 ST1.75.5.

47 Marty, *La Perfection de l'homme*, 50; emphasis in original.

48 ST 1.73.2.

49 ST 1.73.4.

50 The perfection of the universe through diversity actually requires that some parts be imperfect with respect to other parts. As Blanchette explains, "As the order of perfection rises, each being thus is more perfect in itself and participates more intimately in the order of the universe or has greater affinity with it. Beings in the upper parts of the universe are like the sons in the order of the household" (*Perfection of the Universe,* 146).

51 *Summa contra Gentiles* 2.44.16. I am using the version translated by A. C. Pegis et al. (Notre Dame, Ind.: University of Notre Dame Press, 1975). Henceforth, this text will be referred to as SCG.

52 SCG 2.45.2.

53 According to Aquinas, all created things seek to imitate the divine essence but they do so in different ways and degrees. This means that a diversity of creatures can more fully express God's majesty and perfection than if the universe were one undifferentiated substance. In other words, Thomas considers the multiplicity and diversity of the universe to be good and not simply the cause of an ontological fall; they make possible a rich representation of the inexhaustible perfection of the First Cause, but only because this diversity is itself ordered; there are degrees of perfection among the species and within a species.

54 Aquinas carefully distinguishes between multiplicity and diversity. As Blanchette states: "What Saint Thomas understands by multiplicity as distinct from diversity can be called material diversity as opposed to formal diversity . . . formal diversity constitutes a difference of species. Material diversity constitutes a multiplicity within a species" (*Perfection of the Universe*, 140). For Aquinas the diversity of the universe is not an obstacle to its perfection, a fall from a primal simplicity. On the contrary, it is through a rightly ordered diversity that the universe attains its *telos*, its perfection. "What was lacking in Origen, as Manicheaism," Blanchette avers, "was an appreciation of perfection and goodness understood as order in a whole, a *complementum* made up of parts" (124). The more diverse the universe the more it is capable of representing the perfection and goodness of God.

55 SCG 2.45.10.

56 ST 1.47.3.

57 For Aquinas, Blanchette avers, "The perfection of the universe cannot consist of sheer diversity. There has to be an order between the diverse things and such an order requires a certain continuity. Things too unlike one another or to remote from one another do not tend to unite; they remain alien one to another and do not constitute a uni-verse" (*Perfection of the Universe,* 192). Multiplicity within a species itself is ordered toward an end. As Blanchette explains, "The end of the natural process, as Saint Thomas understood it, is not just the multiplication of human beings as such, something that might conceivably go on indefinitely, but a multiplication up to a certain number of them—'certus numerus electorum'" (263).

58 SCG 2.45.4.

59 Besides the principle of diversity, the perfection of the universe requires a principle of continuity that holds together the relatively most perfect beings with the least perfect. The integrating principle that brings an order and unity to the hosts of beings is the intellectual being. Each created being is what it is and

nothing more, but created intelligences can partially overcome this limitation and isolation through the act of knowing. In the intellectual act, a conformity is established between the knower and the known, a *communicatio ad totum* which makes the less perfect participate in the perfection of the more perfect, and in this mediating function the human being plays a central role. As incredible as it may sound given the vastness of the cosmos and the minuteness of the human, according to Thomas the human being has a vital role in the perfection of the universe. As Blanchette explains, "By reason of its place in the universe, last in the order of intelligences but at the summit in the order of generation, human being has an irreplaceable part to play toward the perfection of the universe; if all lower infrarational beings are ordered to it, it is also through it, as well as in it, that they attain their perfection as parts of the universe" (*Perfection of the Universe*, 282).

60 ST 1.1.1.

61 D. Juvenal Merriell, *To the Image of the Trinity: A Study in the Development of Aquinas' Teaching* (Toronto: Pontifical Institute of Medieval Studies, 1990), 163ff.

62 Cf. Merriell, *To the Image of the Trinity*, 164.

63 ST 1.45.7.

64 Augustine, *The Trinity* (book 6, chap. 10).

65 ST 1.45.7.

66 ST 1.93.1.

67 ST 1.93.9.

68 ST 1.93.2.ad4.

69 ST 1.93.9.

70 ST 1.93.4.

71 ST 1.93.2.

72 ST 1.93.3.

73 Cf. Merriell, *To the Image of the Trinity*, 176–77.

74 ST 1.93.1. The Latin *accessus* can refer both to the right to approach (a potential or *capax*) and to the act of approaching itself.

75 ST 1.93.5.ad4.

76 ST 1.35.2.ad3.

77 ST 1.93.7.

78 ST 1.93.6.

79 ST 1.93.8.

80 ST 1.93.8.ad3.

81 In this connection I should mention the A. N. Williams book *The Ground of Union: Deification in Aquinas and Palamas* (New York: Oxford University Press, 1999). The title of this book expresses a double entendre. The ground of union refers to the subject matter of the book: the study of Thomas Aquinas' and Gregory Palamas' understanding of union with God, *theosis*. But the title also offers an ecumenical proposal: if Aquinas' and Palamas' teaching on *theosis* are compatible, then from this doctrine Eastern and Western Christians could find further common ground for rapprochement on other theologically dividing issues. In both of these respects, this book can be read alongside other studies, which posit the presence of a doctrine of *theosis* in Luther, Calvin and even Wesley. Williams' study makes a persuasive case for a Thomist-Palamite

theological convergence on *theosis*. They share a common lexicon (participation, union, light, grace, etc.), they share common concerns (maintaining the ontological Creator-creature distinction), and a common goal (a genuine divine-human encounter occurs in divinization). In these both Aquinas and Palamas show themselves to be faithful heirs of the patristic tradition, though surprisingly on Williams' account, it is Aquinas who sticks to the tradition more closely. Williams is equally convincing in showing how the compatibility of Aquinas' and Palamas' understanding of divinization is not hindered by their respective theological methods. Admittedly, the differences are glaring. The structure of the *Summa* with the fixed form of the article, and particularly the citing of authorities in the objections, allows for a potential conflict among the Fathers unthinkable in the East, even if Aquinas is at pains to answer these objections in a way that vindicates the Fathers. Still, Williams makes a strong case for considering these differences as largely superficial, more a matter of emphasis than substantial disagreement. On the one hand, Aquinas' doctrine of deification emphasizes the vision of God, and his theological method is intent on bringing as much clarity as possible on what this means. On the other hand, Palamas emphasizes the divine darkness. His multiplication of images and cognates for deification are meant to remind us of the poverty of our language in the face of God. Nevertheless, both are at one in affirming humanity's participation in God. In this respect, Williams rightly affirms that both the *Summa* and the Palamite corpus must be read as mystical theology.

82 Marty, *La Perfection de l'homme,* 136.

83 Marty, *La Perfection de l'homme,* 151.

84 Marty, *La Perfection de l'homme,* 197.

85 ST 3.2.10.

86 The following analysis on the nature of intellect, will, and their acts of knowledge and love is greatly indebted to Michael Sherwin's excellent book, *By Knowledge & by Love: Charity and Knowledge in the Moral Theology of St. Thomas Aquinas* (Washington, D.C.: Catholic University of America Press, 2005). The primary purpose of Sherwin's study is to show how Aquinas' understanding of the primacy of the intellect at the level of specification and the primacy of the will at the level of exercise overcome the weaknesses of theologies of moral motivation. However, for the purposes of this present inquiry I am not as interested in whether Sherwin's case is compelling or not (though I think it is), but in his fine exposition of Aquinas.

87 ST 1–2.6.Pro: "voluntas est rationalis appetitus."

88 *Scriptum super sententiis* 1.6.1.3.

89 ST 1–2.4.4.ad2.

90 ST 1–2.19.3.

91 *De veritate* 22.6.

92 Sherwin, *By Knowledge & by Love,* 27.

93 *De malo* 6. For the English translation, I am using *On Evil*, translated by John A. Oesterle and Jean T. Oesterle (Notre Dame, Ind.: University of Notre Dame Press, 1995): "Si ergo consideremus motum potentiarum animae ex parte obiecti specificantis actum, primum principium motionis est ex intellectu: hoc enim modo bonum intellectum movet etiam ipsam voluntatem. Si autem

considеremus motus potentiarum animae ex parte exercitii actus, sic principium motionis est ex voluntate. Nam semper potentia ad quam pertinet finis principalis, movet ad actum potentiam ad quam pertinet id quod est ad finem; sicut militaris movet frenorum factricem ad operandum, et hoc modo voluntas movet se ipsam et omnes alias potentias."

94 Sherwin, *By Knowledge & by Love*, 43; emphasis in original.

95 *De malo* 6.

96 Sherwin, *By Knowledge & by Love*, 55.

97 Sherwin, *By Knowledge & by Love*, 55.

98 ST 1–2.94.2: "Bonum est faciendum et prosequendum, et malum vitandum."

99 ST 1–2.56.2.ad3.

100 ST 1–2.56.2.ad3.

101 Cf. ST 1–2.47.1.ad1: "amor movet ad actum prudential."

102 ST 1–2.27.2.s.c.

103 Cf. ST 1–2.26.1.

104 ST 1–2.28.2.

105 Cf. ST 1–2.28.3.

106 Sherwin, *By Knowledge & by Love*, 74.

107 ST 1–2.28.6.

108 Cf. ST 1–2.3.4.

109 Sherwin, *By Knowledge & by Love*, 82.

110 ST 1–2.3.4.ad3.

111 ST 2–2.25.7.

112 Sherwin, *By Knowledge & by Love*, 95.

113 The relation between grace and nature in Aquinas' theology is hotly contested by contemporary theologians. Hütter lays out some key features of this debate in "*Desiderium Naturale Visionis Dei–Est autem duplex hominis Beatitudo sive felicitas*: Some Observations about Lawrence Feingold's and John Milbank's Recent Interventions in the Debate over the Natural Desire to See God," in *Nova et Vetera* 5, no. 1 (2007): 81–132. I cannot enter into details on this debate but I do want to point out that for Aquinas nature and grace are not two different degrees of instantiation or intensity of the same gift but two different gifts: a *donum primum* (being) and a *donum secundum* or *ultimum* (sanctifying grace). Creation is the first gift but it is not, strictly speaking, the first grace. Regarding the differentiation between these two gifts, Hütter argues that it is indispensable "to acknowledge the proper difference that obtains *realiter* between nature and grace, in order to do justice to the specific gratuity of the grace of predestination, the *donum ultimum*, but moreover, and presently more importantly, to develop a coherent account of the relative and limited integrity of the principle of nature, which preserves the proper gratuity of the first gift, the *donum primum*, and hence does justice to the double gratuity entailed in the economy of salvation" (131). Another way of stating this imperative in the terms that we have been employing in this dissertation is by calling for a more sustained reflection on the integrity of *perfectio prima* in relation to its gratuitous superfulfillment in *perfectio secunda*.

114 ST 1.43.3.

115 *The Aquinas Catechism*, translated by L. Shapcote (Manchester, N.H.: Sophia

Institute Press, 2000), 4. Faith plays a central role in Thomas' understanding of the nature of theology; As Bruce Marshall persuasively argues in "*Quod scit una uetula*: Aquinas on the Nature of Theology" (*The Theology of Thomas Aquinas*, ed. Rik Van Nieuwenhove and Joseph Wawrykow [Notre Dame, Ind.: University of Notre Dame Press, 2005]): "Even the humblest believer in Christ knows more about God and how to lead a good life than the most profound philosopher was able to know without faith in Christ" (1). Wisdom can be attained in two ways: *per modum congnitionis* and *per modum inclinationis.* In the first way, "a person can with effort learn to be a skilled judge of what truth claims Christians ought to accept or reject, and what actions they ought to regard as right and wrong, based on the articles of faith which God has revealed" (25). In the second way, the person knows "by a connatural apprehension of the first truth attested in the language of scripture and creed" (14). This second way of knowledge is both easier and surer than the first. It is easier because it does not require years of leisure and study. One can understand Christian perfection not only by spending years reading and thinking with others but by simply being perfect. It is surer knowledge because it is not arrived at by the tortuous and error-prone path of ratiocination but rather by suffering divine things. Clearly, the second way is superior to the first and yet they are not opposed to each other. The science of the theologian derives from and is in the service of the simple faith of the old woman. As Marshall aptly avers, "The theological master simply strives to make explicit, to recapture *in modo cognitionis*, what the faithful heart of any old woman already knows" (26).

116 *Lectura super Ioannem* 6.5: "multipliciter pater trahit ad filium, secundum multiplicatatem modum trahendi absque violentia in hominibus."

117 ST 2–2.6.1.

118 ST 2–2.6.1.

119 *Lectura super Ioannem* 6.5; cf. Max Seckler's *Instinkt und Glaubenswille nach Thomas von Aquin* (Mainz: Matthias-Grünewald-Verlag, 1961). Thomas developed this concept in critical engagement with Augustine, as the angelic doctor sought to counteract the semi-Pelagian doctrines of conversion that were popular in the Middle Ages. According to Seckler, for Aquinas "Die allgemeine Mitwirkung Gottes in seiner Schöpfung, die auf Rückher hin entworfen ist, konkretisiert sich im Menschen im inneren Instikt" (102). Without this *instinctus* the preaching of the gospel would fail; "Dieser Instinkt ist es, der dem Menschen Auge und Ohr öffnet, der ihn innerlich ruft, inh zum Guten bewegt" (103).

120 ST 2–2.2.9. For a lucid articulation of Thomas' account of the role of faith in the act of conversion see Reinhard Hütter's "St. Thomas on Grace and Freedom in the *Initium Fidei*: The Surpassing Augustinian Synthesis" in *Nova et Vetera* 5, no. 3 (2007): 521–53. Regarding Augustine's account of the beginning of faith, Hütter contrasts the Pelagianism that emerges from Erasmus' theologically erroneous reading to the determinism that comes out of Luther's philosophically erroneous reading (540). The common doctor surpasses both Luther and Erasmus by reading the late Augustine through a metaphysics of being that places God's operations above the orders of necessity and contingency (546). "By way of his metaphysics of being, as it accounts for divine transcendental causality 'all the way down,' St. Thomas offers a salutary way of preserving

St. Augustine's fundamental insight that grace and free will do not need to come into a conflictual competition in the mystery of the *initium fidei*" (552). Central to the preservation of human freedom and divine agency in the act of conversion is Thomas' understanding of nature's openness to *gratia operans*. As Hütter avers, "Because it comes on the way of being (*esse*), operative grace, by way of the divine *instinctus*, is closer to the human will than the will to itself. Consequently, operative grace neither competes nor conflicts with the exercise of created freedom, or *electio humana*, as St. Thomas calls it. Rather, divine instrumentality and created freedom are two sides of one and the same reality" (551). We will return Thomas' understanding of operating and cooperating grace in the final sections of the next to last chapter when we discuss the question of merit.

121 Sherwin, *By Knowledge & by Love*, 145: "On the level of specification, the intellect determines the propositional content of faith; on the level of exercise, the will moves the intellect to determine the content of faith in one way as opposed to another. The *lumen fidei* empowers the intellect to do the former, while the *instinctus fidei* empowers the will to do the latter."

122 Sherwin, *By Knowledge & by Love*, 149.

123 Cf. Sherwin, *By Knowledge & by Love*, 157.

124 ST 1–2.67.6.ad3.

125 Sherwin, *By Knowledge & by Love*, 177.

126 ST 1–2.58.1. For a thorough analysis of Thomas' doctrine of the gifts consult Santiago Ramírez, *Los Dones del Espiritu Santo* (Madrid: Biblioteca de los Teólogos Españoles, 1978).

127 *Lectura super Romanos* 8.3.

128 Antonio Royo Marín, *Teología de la Perfección Cristiana* (Madrid: Biblioteca de Autores Cristianos, 1958), 199; emphasis in original. Royo's study is in effect a manual of perfection. One might call it, utilizing Maritain's terminology (cf. *Degrees of Knowledge*, 335), would call it a practically practical theology of perfection. Theology of perfection "es aquella parte de la sagrada teología que, fundándose en los principios de la divina revelación y en las experiencias de los santos, estudia el organismo de la vida sobrenatural, explica las leyes de su progreso y desarrollo y describe el proceso que siguen las almas desde los comienzos de la vida cristiana hasta la cumbre de la perfección" (Royo Marín, 34). On the foundation of Aquinas, the Spanish mystics, and leaning on Garrigou-Lagrange's own work on the subject, Royo unfolds a theology of perfection that is to serve as a guide for priests and lay people to attain and help others attain the goal of Christian perfection. The book is nothing if not thorough. With scholastic attention to order and detail, Royo defines the scope of this science, describes its source, and provides us with the fundamental principles for the theology of perfection. He then sketches in sharp outlines the unfolding of this theology in the life of the Christian, not omitting the question of intrinsically extraordinary mystical phenomena like levitation or stigmatization. Royo insists that the mystical state is a normal stage in the life of grace; it constitutes the summit of Christian perfection. In other words, all Christians are called, at least remotely, to be mystics. But what does mysticism mean? The phenomenon is notoriously difficult to define, particularly when its specifically Christian and theological

foundation are sought. As Royo understands it, "El constitutivo esencial de la mística que la separa y distingue de todo lo que no lo es, consiste en la actuación de los dones del Espíritu Santo al modo divino o sobrehumano, que produce inmediatamente una experiencia pasiva de Dios o de su acción divina en el alma" (239). What distinguishes Christian mysticism from Christian ascetism or non-Christian forms of spirituality? The Christian mystic's passive obedience to the action of the Trinitarian God. The Christian who has attained the mystical state is like Mary at the annunciation; she lets it be according to God's word, and this obedience is possible for the Christian because of the gifts of the Spirit which God has liberally poured into the person who has walked through the dark night of the senses and of the spirit. The way of salvation ends in mysticism.

129 ST 2–2.8.7.

130 ST 2–2.45.6.

131 ST 1.10.ad1.

132 Sherwin, *By Knowledge & by Love*, 93.

133 On this theme see C. E. O'Neill's essay "L'Homme ouvert à Dieu (*Capax Dei*)," in *Humain à l'image de Dieu*, ed. Pierre Büchler (Genève: Labor et Fides, 1989), 241–60. O'Neill gives special emphasis to the image's dependence on God for the fulfillment of its natural potential. As he states, "L'homme est *capax Dei*, ouvert à Dieu, parce que Dieu l'a crée comme celui auquel il peut se donner en tant que but de sa vie de créature. La ressemblance à Dieu, qui appartaient à l'homme en raison de la création, est susceptible d'un approfondissement tojours croissant à mesure que l'homme, toujours réceptif par rapport à Dieu, se donne d'une façon plus totale à celui qui est le bien suprême" (250).

134 Merriell, *To the Image of the Trinity*, 245.

Chapter 4

1 ST 1.2.Pr.

2 ST 1.93.4.

3 Cf. Klaus Krämer, *Imago Trinitatis: Die Gottebenbildlichkeit des Menschen in der Theologie des Thomas von Aquin* (Freiburg: Herder, 2000). "Thomas deutet diesen dynmischen Prozeß als eine zunehmende Angleichung (*conformitas*) des menschlichen Willens an das angestrebte göttliche Ziel. Hierbei handelt es sich um eine intentionale Angleichung, die zu einer unio spiritualis führt. Sie est zum unterschieden von der ontologischen conformitas, die nur verwirklicht werden kann, wenn die capacitas des menschlichen Erkenntnißvermögens durch die Gnade so erweitert wird, daß Gott selbst zu Erkenntnißform des erkennenden Verstandes werden kann" (418).

4 ST 2–2.183.1.

5 Cf. Jordan Aumann, *The Pastoral and Religious Lives* in St. Thomas Aquinas, *Summa Theologiae*, vol. 47 (Chicago: Blackfriars, 1973), 3.

6 ST 2–2.183.4.

7 Cf. ST 2–2.24.9.

8 ST 1.106.1.ad3.

9 ST 1.13.11.

10 ST 1.94.2.

11 ST 1–2.113.5.
12 ST 2–2.183.4.
13 ST 2–2.184.4.
14 Thomas also recognizes the clerical state which he intended to treat within the sacrament of ordination in the Third Part of the *Summa*; cf. ST 2–2.184.Pr.
15 P. Heinrich Christmann, *Stände und Standespflichten*, in *Summa Theologica: Deutsch-lateinische Ausgabe*, vol. 24 (Salzburg: Gemeinschaftsverlag, 1952), 347.
16 ST 1.95.1.
17 ST 1.96.1.
18 ST 1.97.1.
19 ST 1.94.4.
20 ST 1.94.1.
21 ST 1.96.1.
22 *De malo* 5.1.
23 ST 1.95.1.
24 ST 1–2.109.2.
25 ST 1–2.82.1-2.
26 ST 1–2.85.2.
27 ST 1–2.86.1.
28 ST 1–2.109.2.
29 ST 1–2.109.3: "In the state of perfect nature man did not need the gift of grace added to his natural endowments, in order to love God above all things naturally, although he needed God's help to move him to it; but in the state of corrupt nature man needs, even for this, the help of grace to heal his nature."
30 ST 1–2.112.1.
31 Robert Morency, *L'Union de Grâce selon saint Thomas* (Montréal, Canada: Les Éditions de L'Immaculée Conception, 1950).
32 Morency, *L'Union de Grâce*, 235.
33 Morency, *L'Union de Grâce*, 50, 86.
34 ST 1.43.3.
35 Morency, *L'Union de Grâce*,159.
36 Morency, *L'Union de Grâce*, 253.
37 ST 1.12.13.ad1.
38 ST 2–2.171.2.ad2.
39 ST 2–2.175.3.ad2.
40 ST 1–2.2.
41 ST 1–2.3.8.
42 ST 1.12.1.
43 ST 1.3.Pr. The first questions in the *Summa* comprise a short treatise on apophatic theology; therein is considered not how God is (*quomodo sit*), but how God is not (*quomodo non sit*). A turning point in this mode of proceeding occurs in Question 12 of the Prima Pars on how we know God; the Angelic Doctor does not abandon the *via negativa*, but he turns our attention from God *secundum seipsum* to God *in cognitione nostra*.
44 ST 1.12.12.
45 ST 1.12.5.ad3.
46 ST 1.12.5.ad2.

47 ST 1.12.4.

48 ST 1.12.6: "Unde qui plus habebit de caritate, perfectius Deum videbit, et beatior erit."

49 ST 1.12.7.

50 Cf. Krämer, *Imago Trinitatis*: "Unter den Bedingungen der gloria patriae kommt das Bild Gottes im Menschen somit zu seiner Vollendungsgestalt. Auf den vollkommenen und ununterbrochenen Akt der Gotteserkenntnis in der visio folgt die Liebe als vollkommene Freude an der nicht mehr zu überbietenden Anwesenheit und Nähe des geliebten und ersehnten Gutes" (428).

51 ST 2–2.184.1.

52 ST 2–2.23.8.ad3.

53 For a thoughtful though finally dissenting judgment on the strict connection of the virtues in the saints see Jean Porter's "Virtue and Sin: The Connection of the Virtues and the Case of the Flawed Saint," *Journal of Religion* 75, no. 4 (1995): 521–39.

54 ST 2–2.184.3.ad2.

55 Cf. ST 3.27 on Mary's sanctification.

56 ST 2.2.124.3.

57 ST 1.2.66.3.ad2.

58 ST 2.2.24.8.ad1.

59 ST 2.2.24.8.ad2.

60 ST 2.2.24.12.ad1.

61 ST 2.2.24.9.

62 ST 2–2.184.5.ad2.

63 Cf. ST 2–2.185.3: "[H]e who has to choose or appoint a bishop is not bound to take one who is best simply, i.e. according to charity, but one who is best for governing the Church." Indeed, Thomas states that "nothing hinders one from being more fitted for the office of governing who does not excel in the grace of holiness" (ST 2–2.185.3.ad3). However, there seems to be some dissonance between this emphasis on the institutional qualifications of the bishop and Thomas' insistence elsewhere on the bishop's perfection in charity; cf. ST 2–2.185.1.ad2: "[P]erfection of life is a prerequisite of the Episcopal state, as appears from our Lord asking Peter if he loved Him more than others, before committing the pastoral office to him . . . one needs to be perfect to bring others to perfection." It is from this perfection of charity that "bishops bind themselves to things pertaining to perfection, when they take up the pastoral duty, to which it belongs that a shepherd *lay down his life for his sheep*, according to John 10.15" (emphasis in original). "The perfection of the episcopal state consists in this that for love of God a man binds himself to work for the salvation of his neighbor" (ST 2–2.185.4). How perfect does someone have to be to be fitted for the episcopacy? On this matter, Thomas is not explicit, but if his teaching is not to fall into incoherence, the perfection that is required is that which is a matter of precept, not that which is a matter of counsel. So, for instance a bishop is not bound to live in gospel poverty, because, as Thomas avers, "No one is bound to works of supererogation, unless he binds himself specially thereto by a vow" (ST 2–2.185.6). Returning to the issue that began this little excursus, the bishop need not be more perfect than others in terms of charity: "it suffices

that he perceive nothing in himself which would make it unlawful for him to take up the office of prelate. Hence although Peter was asked by our Lord if he loved Him more than the other, he did not, in his reply, set himself before the others, but answered simply that he loved Christ" (ST 2–2.185.3).

64 ST 2–2.185.1.

65 ST 2–2.185.3.

66 On the relation between the perfection of episcopal and the state of perfection, see Noel Molloy's article "Hierarchy and Holiness: Aquinas on the Holiness of the Episcopal State," *The Thomist* 39, no. 2 (1975): 198–252. According to Molloy, "The most profound reality of the states of perfection is the inner sanctity which animates them, but the states are essentially ecclesial and as such are incorporated into the external structure of the Church as a sign to the world of her inner sanctity" (225). Sanctity grounds all states in the church. However, the differences between the states are not merely functional. Molloy argues that what distinguishes the perfection of the episcopal state from that of the religious state is that whereas the latter is oriented toward the perfect love of God the former presupposes this love but is oriented toward the perfect love of neighbor. The chief, but not only, way in which bishops practice this love is through their teaching.

67 ST 2–2.186.1.

68 ST 2–2.188.

69 ST 2–2.183.3.

70 ST 2–2.179.Pr.

71 *Lectura super I ad Corinthios* 12.2: "Sicut enim nullum membrum est in corpore quod non participet aliquo modo sensum vel motum a capite, ita nullus est in Ecclesia qui non aliquid de gratiis spiritus sancti participet." Admittedly, it is not clear from this quote whether Aquinas is speaking only of *gratia gratum faciens* or if he is also speaking of *gratia gratis data*. On balance, the context of 1 Corinthians 12 suggests that he is speaking of both.

72 See, for instance, his discussion in ST 2–2.177.2 on whether the grace of *sermonis sapientiae* pertains to women. Thomas does not deny that women may indeed receive the grace of prophecy, the grace of wisdom and knowledge but that these are to be used only for private rather than public teaching (*secundum privatam doctrinam, non autem secundum publicam*).

73 *Lectura super I ad Corinthios* 12.3: "Cum multa sint dona spiritus sancti, ut dictum est, *aemulamini*, id est desiderate, *charismata meliora*, id est gratias potiores, ut scilicet magis desideretis ea quae sunt meliora, puta prophetiam quam donum linguarum."

74 *Lectura super I ad Corinthios* 12.2: "Uno modo ut inhabitans Ecclesiam et docens et sanctificans eam, puta cum aliquis peccator, quem non inhabitat spiritus sanctus, faciat miracula ad ostendendum, quod fides Ecclesiae quam ipse praedicat, sit vera." For this purpose, even sinful people who lack the habit of charity are given the gifts of uttering words of wisdom or even more of performing miracles so that by these signs their words if not their lives may be vindicated.

75 *Lectura super I ad Corinthios* 12.2: "Alio modo manifestatur per huiusmodi gratias spiritus sanctus, ut inhabitans eum cui tales gratiae conceduntur." For

instance, Aquinas provides us the example of Stephen whose signs and miracles showed that the Holy Spirit dwelt in him.

76 ST 2–2.180.3.s.c.: "Sed contra est quod vita hic dicitur operatio cui homo principaliter intendit."

77 ST 2–2.179.2.

78 ST 2–2.180.1.s.c.

79 As Aquinas states in ST 2–2.182.2: "Potest tamen contingere quod aliquis in operibus vitae activae plus meretur quam alius in operibus vitae contemplativae, puta si propter abundantiam divini amoris, ut eius voluntas impleatur propter ipsius gloriam, interdum sustinet a dulcedine divinae contemplationis ad tempus separari." In this connection, Aquinas recalls the example of Paul who, out of the abundance of his love for Christ, wished to be cut off from Christ if by such a separation the Jewish people might be restored (cf. Rom 9:3).

80 ST 2–2.182.4.ad3: "Unde et illi qui sunt magis apti ad activam vitam, possunt per exercitium activae ad contemplativam praeparari, et illi nihilominus qui sunt magis ad contemplativam apti, possunt exercitia vitae activae subire, ut per hoc ad contemplationem paratiores reddantur."

81 ST 2–2 188.6: "Et hoc praefertur simplici contemplationi. Sicut enim maius est illuminare quam lucere solum, ita maius est contemplata aliis tradere quam solum contemplari."

82 Cf ST 2–2.172.4: "Et ideo prophetia potest esse sine bonitate morum, quantum ad primam radicem huius bonitatis. Si vero consideremus bonitatem morum secundum passiones animae et actiones exteriores, secundum hoc impeditur aliquis a prophetia per morum malitiam. Nam ad prophetiam requiritur maxima mentis elevatio ad spiritualium contemplationem, quae quidem impeditur per vehementiam passionum, et per inordinatam occupationem rerum exteriorum."

83 Cf. ST 2–2.180.2: "Dispositive autem virtutes morales pertinent ad vitam contemplativam. Impeditur enim actus contemplationis, in quo essentialiter consistit vita contemplativa, et per vehementiam passionum, per quam abstrahitur intentio animae ab intelligibilibus ad sensibilia; et per tumultus exteriores. Virtutes autem morales impediunt vehementiam passionum, et sedant exteriorum occupationum tumultus."

84 Cf. ST 2–2.184.Pr. The state of perfection is the state *ad quem alii status ordinantur.*

85 Cf. ST 2–2.186.3: "status religionis est quoddam exercitium et disciplina per quam pervenitur ad perfectionem caritatis."

86 Von Balthasar underscores this point in *Thomas und die Charismatik: Kommentar zu Thomas von Aquin Summa Theologica Quaestiones II–II*, vol. 23: *171–182* (Deutsche Thomas-Ausgabe. Einsiedeln, Freiburg: Johannes Verlag, 1996): "So wird grundlegend für alle drei Einteilungsglieder auch der soziale Charakter gesichert, der für Charismen und Ämter klar ist, aber in der Ethik der Lebensformen nicht immer ganz deutlich hervortritt. Ja, nach dem vorigen Text [Aquinas commentary on 1 Cor 12] wäre die active und contemplative Lebensform je die 'Ausführung' einer bestimmten kirchlichen Funktion" (254).

87 Jean-Pierre Torrell, *Saint Thomas Aquinas*, vol. 2: *Spiritual Master* (Washington, D.C.: Catholic University of America Press, 2003), 105.

88 According to Wainwright, "Christliche Vollkommenheitslehre wird christologish zentriert sein. Jesus Christus ist 'der Urheber und Vollender des Glaubens' (Hebr 12:2); als solcher ist er unser Lehrer und Vorbild in Sachen Vollkommenheit" (*Theologische Realenzyklopädie*, 35:282).

89 Joseph Wawrykow, "Hypostatic Union," in *The Theology of Thomas Aquinas*, eds. R. van Nieuwenhove and J. Wawrykow, 222–51 (Notre Dame, Ind.: University of Notre Dame Press, 2005).

90 ST 3.17.2.ad2; cf. Wawrykow, "Hypostatic Union," 242.

91 For a comprehensive study of the different modes of Christ's knowing and loving the reader should consult Jacques Maritain, *De la grace et de l'humanité de Jésus* (Bruges, Belgium: Desclée de Brouwer, 1967); for a defense of Thomas' interpretation of the earthly Jesus' beatific knowledge, I refer the reader to a series of articles written by Thomas Joseph White on this subject: "The Voluntary Action of the Earthly Christ and the Necessity of the Beatific Vision," *The Thomist* 69 (2005): 497–534 and more recently "Jesus' Cry on the Cross and His Beatific Vision," *Nova et Vetera* 5, no. 3 (2007): 555–81; for an opposing interpretation, see Thomas Weinandy's "Jesus' Filial Vision of the Father," *Pro Ecclesia* 13, no. 2 (2004): 189–201 and "The Beatific Vision and the Incarnate Son: Furthering the Discussion," *The Thomist* 70 (2006): 605–15. Weinandy detects a hint of both Nestorianism and monophysiticism in the traditional view. On the one hand, the Beatific vision of the Son seems to deny Jesus a naturally human mode of knowing because from the beginning Jesus knows all things by the light of glory, hence the charge of monophysticism. On the other hand, the Beatific vision appears to render the divinity of the Son as an object separate from his humanity that the human Jesus regards as a transcended object over him, hence the charge of Nestorianism. White's refutation of these charges is, in my opinion, cogent and convincing. The key to his argument is that the earthly Jesus possessed the Beatific in a mode uniquely his own, which differs from that of the saints in heaven. In any case, both White and Weinandy agree that Thomas taught that the earthly Jesus possessed the Beatific vision and rejected alternate accounts (like those which posited that Jesus knew all things only by infused science) as inadequate because they failed to affirm the unity and distinction of natures in Christ.

92 ST 3.9.4.

93 This memorable epithet by Chesterton is cited in Paul Gondreau's essay on "The Humanity of Christ, the Incarnate Word," in *The Theology of Thomas Aquinas*, ed. Rik van Nieuwenhove and Joseph Wawrykow (Notre Dame, Ind.: University of Notre Dame Press, 2005), 264.

94 ST 3.12.1.

95 Gondreau, "The Humanity of Christ," 269.

96 ST 3.15.4: "Huiusmodi passions aliter fuerunt in Christo quam in nobis." For a helpful discussion of Thomas' account of the passions see Servais Pinckaers, "Reappropriating Aquinas's Account of the Passion," in *The Pinckaers Reader: Renewing Thomistic Moral Theology*, ed. John Berkman and Craig Steven Titus (Washington, D.C.: Catholic University of America Press, 2005). Pinckaers makes a strong case for how a recovery of Thomas' understanding of the passions would help moral theology overcome the dehumanization of emotions

that took place in Kantian philosophy. For Kant, following Descartes, passions and emotions were perceived as threats to human freedom conceived as liberty of indifference. Thomas, on the contrary, "conceives emotions as a constitutive element of human agency ordered to beatitude in God by means of the virtues and the gifts, as internal or personal principles of action" (277). As these emotions are purified by the virtue of charity, the way is opened for a genuine spiritual experience in which pleasure is transposed into joy.

97 Gondreau, "The Humanity of Christ," 264.

98 ST 3.18.2: "Filius Dei cum natura humana assumpserit etiam ea quae pertinent ad perfectionem naturae animalis."

99 ST 3.15.1.

100 ST 3.40.

101 ST 3.40.1.

102 ST 3.40.3.

103 ST 3.40.2.ad2.

104 ST 2–2.182.1.

105 ST 3.1.6. On this subject see also Luc-Thomas Somme, *Fils adoptifs Dieu par Jésus Christ: La filiation divine par adoption dans le théologie de Saint Thomas d'Aquin* (Paris: Librairie Philosophique J. Vrin, 1997) and *Thomas d'Aquin, la divinisation dans le Christ* (Géneve: Editions Ad Solem, 1998). Somme exposits Aquinas' understanding of the divine indwelling and deification through a comprehensive reading of Thomas' written corpus. The result of this approach is an argument that is not as coherent or synthetic as I would like, but this deficit is more than made up for by the wealth of quotations from Thomas' often neglected scriptural commentaries. Somme's principal thesis is clear: Aquinas' doctrine of grace cannot be separated from his Christology: "La théopoiésis serait alors déjà une certaine huiopoiésis" (*Fils adoptifs*, 384). The incarnation of the Son of God is the instrumental and exemplary cause of our own divine filiation; the *unigenitus* is also the *primogenitus*, the firstborn of a multitude of divinely adopted brothers and sisters, yet with this difference: Jesus is Son by nature, but we are sons and daughters by grace. The union of the divine and human natures in Jesus occurs at the ontological level; the divinization of his human nature results by virtue of the hypostatic union. Our case is different, our union with God is operative or affective not ontological, and our divinization is the effect of grace, the grace of adoption. For further reflections on Thomas' doctrine of divinization the reader should consult Williams, *The Ground of Union*. Williams argues that although direct references to deification in the *Summa Theologiae* are few, their scarcity belies their significance. The central principles of the doctrine of theosis are introduced in I–II.62. But one text of surprising significance for understanding how the doctrine of deification is developed in the *Summa* turns out to be the famous Five Ways. The Five Ways are not only telling us "that God is," but also something about "who God is." On the one hand the Five Ways establish the aseity of God, the uniqueness and distinction of God over against the creature. On the other hand the Five Ways assert the real relation between the uncreated and creation. If God is first mover then there must be a moved. If God is first and final cause then there must be something caused. "In seminal form, the Five Ways not only argue God's existence, but

also the existence of Thomistic doctrine of theosis" (41). At the heart of Aquinas' understanding of deification and consistent with his radical theocentrism is the doctrine of the image of God. The faculties of knowing and loving in the created image of God mirror the eternal processions in the Trinity of Word and Spirit, and as these faculties are actually directed toward God, they participate in God's very knowing and loving. The whole *Summa*, Williams' argues, but especially the doctrine of deification may be read as a sustained meditation on the relation of this divine will and intellect with their created analogues, a relation that allows for increasing degrees of likening to God. In this growing conformity, the virtues are the motive force directing the created will and intellect to the actual knowing and loving of God. Of these virtues, charity is the most deifying as it connects all other virtues and directs them to attaining their supernatural end in God. Charity can effect our likening to God, because it is nothing less than a participation in God's own charity, namely the Holy Spirit. For Thomas, then, deification is intricately related to the work of the Spirit, but also to the person of the Son. Christ is not only divine by means of the hypostatic union, but also by participation. In this way, Christ is the fullest representation of deification, and he recapitulates in himself the story of the creature's return to God.

106 ST 2–2.84.ad2.
107 Torrell, *Spiritual Master,* 110, n. 26.
108 *Expositio in Symbolum Apostolorum* 4.
109 *Lectura super I ad Corinthios* 11.1.
110 *Lectura super I ad Corinthios* 11.1.
111 *Lectura super Ionannem* 5.28. Cited in Gondreau, "The Humanity of Christ," 263.
112 *Lectura super Ionannem* 13.1.
113 Cf. Torrell, *Spiritual Master,* 116ff.
114 *Lectura super Ionannem* 13.3.
115 *Lectura super Ionannem* 13.3.
116 Cf. Torrell, *Spiritual Master,* 118.
117 ST 3.40.2.ad1.
118 ST 3.40.1.ad3.
119 ST 62.6.5.
120 Theophil Tschipke, *L'humanité du Christ comme instrument de salut et de la divinité* (Fribourg, Suisse: Academic Press Fribourg, 2003).
121 Tschipke, *L'humanité du Christ,* 132.
122 Tschipke, *L'humanité du Christ,* 135.
123 Tschipke, *L'humanité du Christ,* 157.
124 Tschipke, *L'humanité du Christ,* 160.
125 ST 1–2.112.1.ad1.
126 Tschipke, *L'humanité du Christ,* 166.
127 ST 3.34.3.
128 ST 3.63.1.
129 ST 3.64.4.
130 ST 1.4.1.
131 ST 3.84.6.

132 ST 3.89.2–3.
133 ST3.62.1–2.
134 ST 3.79.1.
135 ST 3.65.1.
136 ST 3.69.8.
137 ST 3.79.8.
138 I will consider this topic in more detail in the final section of chapter 7.
139 ST 3.69.8.
140 ST 1–2.112.4.

Chapter 5

1 WJW 9:227, "The Principles of a Methodist Farther Explained."
2 WJW 1:467.
3 Tore Meistad, *Martin Luther and John Wesley on the Sermon on the Mount* (Lanham, Md.: Scarecrow Press, 1999), 86–87.
4 Wesley, *Explanatory Notes on the New Testament*, 28.
5 Wesley, *Explanatory Notes on the New Testament*, 28.
6 WJW 1:473, "Sermon on the Mount I."
7 WJW 1:477, "Sermon on the Mount I." Thomas explicitly refutes the identification of perfection and poverty. Possession of things does not diminish perfection, because "our Lord does not mean that poverty itself is perfection, but that it is the means of perfection" (ST 2–2.188.7.ad1). Poverty is not perfection though it is along with chastity and obedience a means to it, even if the least of such means.
8 WJW 1:473, "Sermon on the Mount I."
9 Kenneth Collins, "John Wesley's Topography of the Heart: Dispositions, Tempers and Affections," *Methodist History* 36, no. 3 (1998): 162–75; Randy Maddox, *Responsible Grace*, 131–32. Maddox and Collins sketch the topic of the tempers in similar hues, though Collins chides Maddox for identifying some tempers with certain kinds of affections. The distinction that Maddox is trying to draw "between those [tempers] that are stable orienting dispositions and those that are responsive motivating affections" (132) is not unlike that which Thomas draws between the habits which regulate the irascible passions and those that regulate the concupiscible passions. The nuanced distinctions that Maddox and Collins are attempting to grapple with in Wesley's understanding of religious affections and tempers are precisely the sort of analysis that would benefit from the greater precision of Thomas' psychology.
10 WJW 4:66, "The Unity of Divine Being."
11 Collins, "John Wesley's Topography of the Heart," 163.
12 WW 10:348, *Some Remarks on "A Defense of Aspasio Vindicated."*
13 WW 10:348, *Some Remarks on "A Defense of Aspasio Vindicated."*
14 WJW 1:479, "Sermon on the Mount I."
15 WJW 1:479, "Sermon on the Mount I."
16 WJW 1:479, "Sermon on the Mount I."
17 WJW 1:482, "Sermon on the Mount I."
18 WJW 1:498, "Sermon on the Mount II."
19 WJW 1:482–83, "Sermon on the Mount I."

20 WJW 1:485, "Sermon on the Mount I."
21 WJW 1:474, "Sermon on the Mount I."
22 WJW 1:536, "Sermon on the Mount IV."
23 WJW 1:484, "Sermon on the Mount I."
24 WJW 1:485, "Sermon on the Mount I."
25 For instance on the Beatitude that speaks about those who hunger, Wesley says, "the more they are filled with the life of God, the more tenderly will they be concerned for those are still without God in the world" (WJW 1:486, "Sermon on the Mount I").
26 WJW 1:499, "Sermon on the Mount II."
27 WJW 1:535, "Sermon on the Mount IV."
28 WW 14:320, "Preface to Hymns and Sacred Poems."
29 WJW 1:539, "Sermon on the Mount IV."
30 WJW 1:537, "Sermon on the Mount IV."
31 Jean-Pierre Torrell, *Saint Thomas Aquinas*, vol. 1: *The Person and His Work* (Washington, D.C.: Catholic University of America Press, 1996): 56.
32 Portions of Thomas' commentary on Matthew (5:11–6:8 and 6:14-19) were replaced with passages from the Dominican Petri di Scala's commentary. A complete text was discovered by the commission working on the Leonine edition but only a few fragments from this text have been edited and published. For more information consult Torrell, *The Person and his Work*, 339.
33 *Lectura super Mattheum* 5.2
34 *Lectura super Mattheum* 5.2
35 *Lectura super Mattheum* 5.2
36 *Lectura super Mattheum* 5.2
37 *Lectura super Mattheum* 5.2
38 *Lectura super Mattheum* 5.2. Rochus Leonhardt in *Glück als Vollendung des Menschseins: Die beatitudo-Lehre des Thomas von Aquin im Horizont des Eudämonismus-Problems* (Berlin: de Gruyter, 1998) appears to be of a different opinion. He states that "Die in den beatitudines aus Mt 5 bennanten verdienstlichen Handlungen gehen allerdings nicht direkt aus diesen göttlichen Tugenden hervor, sondern entstammen entweder der unmittelbar den Gaben des Heiligen Geistes (vgl. Jes 11,2), oder sie werden durch diese dona Spiritus Sancti vervollkommnet" (122–23). Leonhardt is right that Thomas applies the term "beatitude" to those acts which flow from the virtues in their normal graced dynamic. However, one cannot set limits on virtue, as if one should only strive for a certain degree of virtue and no more. As Thomas says, "the love of God and of our neighbor is not commanded according to a measure so that what is in excess of the measure be a matter of counsel" (ST 2–2.184.3). On the contrary, when it comes to love, "even the perfection of heaven is not excepted from this precept" (ST 2–2.184.3.ad2). Given the connection between the virtues, I think it more congruent with Thomas' overall understanding of perfection to assert that although heroic virtue is not necessary for beatitude it cannot be regarded as a matter of excess either. Leonhardt is not alone in his bracketing of heroic virtues from his understanding of perfection; see for instance Thomas Osborne's article "Perfect and Imperfect Virtues in Aquinas," *The Thomist* 71, no. 1 (2007): 39–64. In his defense of Thomas' account of the connection of the virtues Osborne

sets aside "those virtues which are not an ordinary part of the moral life, such as heroic virtue" (51). What I find interesting is that Osborne does not even need to defend his decision to bracket the heroic degree of virtue from this discussion of perfect virtues. The only explanation that Osborne offers for this omission is that he is following the commentatorial tradition. Perhaps, but it is also the case that some of the most assiduous exponents of that tradition insist that heroic virtue is a normal part of, indeed the culmination of, the graced development of Christian virtue. Garrigou-Lagrange goes to the heart of the issue, "The word 'normal' should not make us forget the word 'summit,' and vice versa. To understand it clearly, we must remember that Christian life requires of all souls heroism of virtue (according to the preparation of the mind); that is, in the sense that every Christian must be ready, with the help of the Holy Ghost, to accomplish heroic acts when circumstances require them" (Garrigou-Lagrange, *Christian Perfection and Contemplation*, 177). For this reason, Garrigou-Lagrange asserts that, for the angelic doctor, "Christian charity should in its daily progress tend normally to the heroic degree, which permits the prompt and even joyful performance of the most difficult acts for God and our neighbor" (*Christian Perfection and Contemplation*, 177–78).

39 On this point, I find myself in agreement with Leonhardt: "Nicht durch das Studium der *Nikomanischen Ethik*, sondern in erster Linie durch das Zeugnis der Heiligen Schrift und die vorwiegend durch das augustinische Denken repräsentierte theologische Tradition ist Thomas dazu veranlaßt worden, die beatitudo als ein zentrales Thema der christlichen Theologie aufzufassen, bildet sie doch in Mt 5 das Hauptmotiv der doctrina Domini. Allen anderen Vorstellungen vom Glück, die des Aristoteles eingeschlossen, werden vom biblisch-christlischen Zeugnis her beurteilt und davon ausgehend entweder grundsätzlich verworfen oder relativiert" (*Glück als Vollendung*, 125).

40 *Lectura super Mattheum* 5.2.

41 *Lectura super Mattheum* 5.2.

42 *Lectura super Mattheum* 5.2.

43 *Lectura super Mattheum* 5.2.

44 *Lectura super Mattheum* 5.3.

45 WJW 1:530, "Sermon on the Mount III."

46 ST 1–2.69.2.

47 Cf. *Explanatory Notes on the New Testament*, 757.

48 WW 8:293, "Minutes of Some Late Conversations."

49 WJW 3:171, "On Patience."

50 Cf. WJW 2:401, "On the Fall of Man"; WJW 2:438–39, "The General Deliverance"; WJW 2:474–75, "The End of Christ's Coming"; WJW 3:6, "Of Good Angels."

51 Cf. *Explanatory Notes on the New Testament*, 757.

52 ST 1–2.69.ad3.

53 In *Los Dones del Espiritu Santo* (Madrid: Biblioteca de los Teólogos Españoles, 1978), Santiago Ramírez teases out the important terminological distinctions that form the basis of Thomas' teaching on the Beatitudes: "La bienaventuranza *formal* consiste en un acto u operación perfectísimo, no sólo porque la bienaventuranza es ya una gran perfección y la meta de nuestras aspiraciones, sino porque

el acto es ante todo una perfección" (138). A Beatitude is a perfection because it is an act. The Bible mentions many Beatitudes; there are many acts, but perfect beatitude, the happiness of heaven, is only one: "Por lo tanto, las bienaventuranzas evangélicas son en la vida presente bienaventuranzas incoadas" (138).

54 ST 1–2.66.

55 ST 1–2.66.1.

56 Romanus Cessario, *The Moral Virtues and Theological Ethics* (Notre Dame, Ind.: University of Notre Dame Press, 1991): 145.

57 D. Stephen Long, *John Wesley's Moral Theology*, 202.

58 *Explanatory Notes on the New Testament*, 94.

59 WJW 3:265–66, "The More Excellent Way."

60 *De caritate*, 11.ad4. For the English version, I am using *On Charity*, trans. L. H. Kendzierski (Milwaukee, Wisc.: Marquette University Press, 1960).

61 *De caritate*, 8.

62 *De caritate*, 8.

63 *De caritate*, 8.

64 *De caritate*, 8.

65 ST 2–2.184.3.

66 Cf. WJW 3:265–66, "The More Excellent Way."

67 Cf. ST 2–2.185.1.ad3.

68 ST 3.71.4.ad3.

69 WW 14:321.

70 WJW 1:535, "Sermon on the Mount IV."

71 ST 1–2.4.8.

72 ST 1–2.4.8.ad3.

73 ST 1–2.4.8.ad3.

74 R. Newton Flew, *The Idea of Perfection in Christian Theology: An Historical Study of the Christian Idea for the Present Life* (London: Oxford University Press, 1934), 243.

75 ST 1–2.4.8.

76 ST 2–2.188.8.

77 Aristotle, *Politics* 1.1; cited in ST 1–2.4.8.ad5.

78 ST 1–2.4.8.ad4.

79 ST 2–2.188.8.ad4.

80 ST 2–2.188.8. In this connection I should mention Wainwright's reflections on the parallels between Methodists and Benedictine monks. As Wainwright observes, "Given their time and place in eighteenth-century England, the Wesleys would not have known any living examples of monasticism. And Benedictism is not necessarily, or properly, struck by their strictures. The vocation of a hermit is reckoned to be exceptional, and the regular form of Benedictism is cenobitic or communitarian, with ample opportunities for the service, in one form or another, of humankind. Benedictism may therefore be considered, with no obstacle on the Methodist side, as a possible expression of that love of God and love of neighbor in which the Wesleys judged holiness to consist" (*Methodists in Dialogue*, 90). One could say that the disciplined practice of works of piety and works of mercy which characterized the early Methodists witnesses to the spirit of the Benedictine motto: *ora et labora*.

81 ST 1–2.4.8.

82 For a Methodist perspective on this important ecclesiological affirmation, I refer the reader to Wainwright, *Methodists in Dialogue*. For instance, considering how Wesley's hymns delicately describe the interactions between God's action and our response in salvation, Wainwright suggests "If one were to reflect more fully than John Wesley did on the theological implications for ecclesiology of this view of the appropriation of salvation, it would land Wesley rather on the 'Catholic' side in the debates concerning the instrumentality of the Church, in which some contemporary ecumenists have located the 'basic difference' between Roman Catholics and Protestants" (104).

83 Albert Outler, "Do Methodists Have a Doctrine of the Church?" in *The Doctrine of the Church*, ed. Dow Kirkpatrick (Nashville: Abingdon, 1964), 27; emphasis in original.

84 Outler, "Do Methodists Have a Doctrine?" 25.

85 Outler, "Do Methodists Have a Doctrine?" 27.

86 For a readable and helpful account, the reader should consult John Bowmer, *The Sacrament of the Lord's Supper in Early Methodism* (London: Dacre Press, 1951).

87 Bowmer, *The Sacrament*, 62; emphasis in original.

88 Bowmer, *The Sacrament*, 63.

89 Bowmer, 66–67.

90 Cf. WJW 9:531–33: "Thoughts on the Consecration of Churches and Burial Grounds." Charles was willing to preside over the Eucharist in unconsecrated churches and spaces, but he insisted, to John's dismay, that he should be buried in consecrated burial grounds rather than in, for instance, Bunhill Fields where their mother Susannah was buried. So when Charles died he was buried in the Marylebone churchyard, which as it happened had not been duly consecrated (WJW 9:531, n. 1).

91 Geoffrey Wainwright, *The Ecumenical Moment: Crisis and Opportunity for the Church* (Grand Rapids: Eerdmans, 1983), 189–221.

92 Wainwright, *The Ecumenical Moment*, 220.

Chapter 6

1 Consider for instance Wesley's description of God's presence in creation even apart from the order of grace in one of his late sermons (1788), "On the Omnipresence of God": "God acts in heaven, in earth, and under the earth, throughout the whole compass of his creation; by sustaining all things, without which everything would in an instant sink into its primitive nothing; by governing all, every moment superintending everything that he has made; strongly and sweetly influencing all, and yet without destroying the liberty of his rational creatures" (WJW 4:32). Aquinas could have written this statement! The act of existence of these things, an act initiated and sustained by God, is the first perfection of created things. See also Wesley's sermon on "The Wisdom of God's Counsels" where he argues that God's wisdom is made manifest in the present ordering of the universe and even in the government of states (WJW 2:552–53).

2 WW 12:207, "Letter to Miss Furley." Wesley had to assure that Miss Furley

that her nervous constitution did not mark an impediment from attaining perfection.

3 Cf. WW 2:131, "Letters to his Brother Charles." On this topic see also Michael Christensen's article "Theosis and Sanctification: John Wesley's Reformulation of a Patristic Doctrine" in *Wesleyan Theological Journal* 31, no. 2 (1996): 71–94. Christensen argues that John Wesley's understanding of sanctification was deeply influenced by the writings of Clement, Origen, Ephrem, and Pseudo-Macarius. Nevertheless, whereas Charles basically affirmed the doctrine as received from the Fathers, John reformulated the doctrine in two key ways. First, he lowered the bar for full salvation from *theosis* to perfect love. Second, he shifted the means of attainment from discipline to faith. Christensen's reading of the Wesleys is sound but his exposition of the Fathers is derivative, thereby rendering his overall argument weak. The contrast that he draws between *theosis* and sanctification and between discipline and faith are more revealing of contemporary Protestant categories than about the church fathers' understanding of these issues. Contra Christensen, the doctrine of *theosis* as taught by the tradition never loses sight of the Creator/creature distinction. The right understanding of this distinction was what Gregory Palamas labored to preserve by his discussion of the uncreated energies of God; on this topic see Williams, *The Ground of Union.* In Palamite theology the essence-energies distinction safeguards divine transcendence and the authenticity of the divine self-communication.

4 WW 11:451.

5 ST 3.183.3.

6 WJW 3:265–66, "The More Excellent Way."

7 According to Wesley: "The most glorious stars will undoubtedly be those who are the most holy; who bear most of that image of God wherein they were created. The next in glory to these will be those who have been most abundant in good works; and next to them those that have suffered most according to the will of God" (WJW 2:431, "God's Love to Fallen Man").

8 ST 1–2.26.3.

9 ST 2–2.184.2.ad3.

10 Kenneth Collins, *The Scripture Way of Salvation: The Heart of John Wesley's Theology* (Nashville: Abingdon, 1997), 180; emphasis in original.

11 Collins, *The Scripture Way of Salvation*, 180; Cf. Kenneth Collins, "John Wesley and the Fear of Death as a Standard of Conversion," in *Conversion in the Wesleyan Tradition*, ed. Kenneth Collins and John Tyson, 56–68 (Nashville: Abingdon, 2001).

12 Garrigou-Lagrange, *Christian Perfection and Contemplation*, 238. Garrigou-Lagrange sets out to overcome what he terms the "mystical problem," namely the separation of mysticism from theology. According to this Dominican scholar, the church has long believed that "the perfect mystical life is the culminating point of the normal development of life of grace" (27). If a person is to be perfect, he must be rendered pliable to the inspiration of the Spirit, but this availability and openness to God can only be attained after the person undergoes the passive purifications of his or her soul and senses. Dionysius' *via unitiva*, Teresa's *quinta, sexta y séptimas mansiones*, and John of the Cross' *noche obscura* are all normal

stages in the development of every Christian life. If we are to understand the ways in which God draws us to himself we must keep in mind that there is a very important difference between "the intrinsically extraordinary" (i.e., the miraculous) and the "extrinsically extraordinary," which is the normal life of grace. Not all Christians are called to work miracles but all are called to be perfect. And even though actual sanctity may be rare it is not for that reason to be considered extraordinary but the normal conclusion to living in grace. In other words, the normal Christian is the saint! According to Garrigou-Lagrange, this "traditional thesis" has been displaced by the "modern thesis" which regards the mystical union as a privileged state granted only to a few exceptional and perhaps eccentric souls. The result of this "modern thesis" is tragic both for theology and for the Christian life. On the one hand, the separation of theology from mysticism leads to a defective Christian anthropology and soteriology; the bar is set too low. No longer do we expect the church to nurture saints; we are pleased if we do not turn out scoundrels. On the other hand, the divorce of mysticism and theology has led to vacuous forms of spirituality obsessed with cultivating feelings rather than attaining God. Garrigou-Lagrange wants his readers to return to the "traditional thesis" and to strive for the perfection that God holds out to us as a promise, and in this cause our Dominican doctor finds allies in Thomas Aquinas and John of the Cross. The former is the *doctor communis*, the perfect theologian, a master of dogmatic, moral, ascetical, and mystical theology who received a high degree of the gift of *sermo sapientiae*. The latter, the *doctor theologiae mysticae*, the perfect mystic who has been tested by the church (and what tests!) and drank deeply from the streams of theological wisdom coming from Teresa of Ávila and St. Thomas Aquinas.

13 As Maddox observes, Wesley's rejection of the doctrine of purgatory has a twofold motivation. First, Wesley, like many Protestants then and now, thought that purgatory was a place where sinners could repent. Wesley rightly considered such postmortem pardon as incompatible with Scripture. Second, John Wesley, as opposed to Charles Wesley, saw little salutary value to suffering; cf. R. Maddox, *Responsible Grace*, 250.

14 Cf. John R. Tyson, *Charles Wesley on Sanctification: A Biographical and Theological Study* (Grand Rapids: Francis Asbury Press, 1986): 261–68.

15 Cited in Tyson, *Wesley on Sanctification*, 266.

16 Cf. Tyson, *Wesley on Sanctification*, 266.

17 WW 14:277, "Preface to an Extract of the Life of Madame Guyon."

18 Cf. Robert Tuttle, *Mysticism in the Wesleyan Tradition* (Grand Rapids: Zondervan, 1989). Tuttle's book argues that though Wesley was deeply influenced by Protestant and Catholic mystics he, over time, was able to sift the gold from the dross and discard the dark night of the soul in favor of the substitutionary atonement of Christ as the basis of our justification and assurance before God. Tuttle advances some solid textual evidence in support of his thesis but flounders upon an objectionable definition of mysticism which regards the mystical as fundamentally separate from genuine Christian existence. True mysticism, on Tuttle's terms, has too low a doctrine of sin and too high a doctrine of salvation. Indeed, Tuttle finds any talk of union with God to be theologically suspect of confusing the creature with the Creator (cf. *Mysticism*,

151). In any case, despite the weaknesses of his treatment of mysticism, Tuttle rightly observes that Wesley rejects any role for darkness as a stage on the way to perfection (cf. *Mysticism*, 137). On the one hand, for Wesley, "God afflicts those God loves and the love for God is revealed by granting them the grace to bear such afflction" (145). On the other hand, Wesley "insists that God afflicts but that he never brings darkness. We may suffer but darkness is never the will of God, who is always willing to give more light" (147). What Wesley is critical of, then, is not suffering but darkness, not divine chastisement but divine abandonment. He is opposing those who consider "the being in *orco*, as they phrase it, an indispensable preparative for being a Christian" (WW 1:74). The preference for darkness rather than light and abandonment over assurance was for Wesley dangerously alluring: "I think the rock on which I had the nearest made shipwreck of the faith, was, the writings of the Mystics; under which term I comprehend all, and only those, who slight any of the means of grace" (WW 12:27). One could define mysticism in this way but then one would have to refrain from applying the term mystic to persons like St. John of the Cross and Pseudo-Dyonisius whose theology and practice were strongly sacramental.

19 *Lectura super Epistolam ad Hebraeos* 12.2.

20 Rik van Nieuwenhove, "Bearing the Marks of Christ's Passion," in *The Theology of Thomas Aquinas*, ed. Rik van Nieuwenhove and Joseph Wawrykow (Notre Dame, Ind.: University of Notre Dame Press, 2005), 289.

21 Van Nieuwenhove, "Bearing the Marks," 289.

22 Hebrews 12:7.

23 Hebrews 12:10.

24 Cf. Eleonore Stump, *Aquinas* (New York: Routledge, 2005), 469.

25 Luke 6:24.

26 According to Garrigou-Lagrange (*Perfection and Contemplation*), the fullness of Christian perfection requires the passive purifications described by St. John of the Cross as the dark night of the soul. For Thomas, the supernatural character of faith makes mystical contemplation the normal blossoming of this virtue when informed by charity and empowered by the gifts of the Spirit. Infused contemplation such as properly belongs to the mystical state belongs to the category of sanctifying grace and not to the various gratuitous graces (*gratia gratis datae*). This mystical knowledge that comes by way of faith is of a different and higher order than even the natural knowledge of the highest angel. Indeed, the only contemplation which surpasses that of infused faith is the beatific vision. Not that the life of grace is fundamentally different from the life of glory; they are actually integrally related because the life of grace is the *inchoatio vitae aeternae*. Garrigou-Lagrange means to dispel what he considers to be an erroneous reading of Thomas on perfection. When one reads in the *Summa Theologiae* that Christian perfection consists chiefly in the perfection of the virtue of charity one might not unreasonably think that Aquinas considers perfection to be attained through activity, through energetic cooperation with God's grace. But Garrigou-Lagrange insists that such an active cooperation with God's grace is only a beginning. Yes, perfection is a precept, as Thomas explains, and every Christian must strive for the perfection of charity in this life because whoever does not advance falls back. But the full perfection of charity presupposes the

passive purifications of the senses and the spirit described by St. John of the Cross in his poems on the *Noche obscura* and by St. Thomas in his doctrine of the gifts of the Spirit and the inhabitation of the Holy Trinity. Whereas the theological virtues (and the infused moral virtues) dispose the powers of the soul to act in accordance with the dictates of reason illumined by faith, the gifts of the Spirit render the soul docile to the inspiration of the Spirit. Contra Tuttle's reading of the mystics, these purgations are not self-imposed. The mystic is not flagellating herself in the dark night but rather she is being crucified (Tuttle, *Mysticism*). The point that the Sanjuanistas are trying to convey is beautifully illustrated by the encounter between Aslan and Edmund in C. S. Lewis, *Voyage of the Dawn Treader* (New York: Macmillan, 1952). Readers may recall that when Edmund tired of living as a dragon he tried to peel away his scaly skin by digging at it with his claws, but his attempts failed and left his skin scalier than ever. It was only when Edmund allowed Aslan to dig into his flesh with his claws that Edmund's scales fell off for good and he became a child again. In a sense, Edmund's attempts to purge himself of his dragon nature correspond to the ascetic way or to the active night. I say so in a sense, given the negative evaluation that they receive from Lewis. However, Aslan's clawing of Edmund's skin corresponds very closely to the passive purification of the *noche obscura del alma*. In this night, the person is passive and it is God who is active in stripping away the remains of the Christian's carnal nature.

27 I say "perhaps" because John can also speak very positively about the medicinal value of suffering; see, e.g., David Dunn Wilson's book, *Many Waters Cannot Quench: A Study of the Sufferings of Eighteenth-century Methodism and Their Significance for John Wesley and the First Methodists* (London: Epworth Press, 1969). Wilson argues, persuasively I think, that the early Methodists were a people who suffered both externally from persecution and internally from the struggle of flesh and spirit. Much of Wesley's pastoral practice was directed to encouraging his followers to press on to the goal of holiness through suffering. Yes, suffering can be a sign that one has strayed from the way, but it can also be a salutary sign. As Wilson avers, "Wesley shows that reward is the natural outcome of Christian suffering; as a seed eventually produces a flower, so Christian suffering produces reward. Wesley stresses an important truth by his insistence that the reward of the Christian sufferer begins here and now. God rewards the Christian, first of all, by giving him a true insight into the temporary nature of his pain, reminding him that it cannot finally destroy [him] because he is in God's hands. . . . Perhaps even more important, God gives the Christian sufferer a sense of joy in his affliction" (142–43). Wilson's study of Wesley's understanding of suffering comes very close to Aquinas' on the following point: "As long as suffering is allowed to remain under the dominion of evil, to separate embittered man from his God, it will continue to destroy the sufferer. However, once suffering is offered to God for His use, it becomes swallowed up in the sufferings of Christ and works mightily for the glory of God in the world and in the sufferer himself" (196). In any case, in light of Thomas' reflections it might be possible to approach John's writings and Charles' hymnody with a new set of eyes. Contra Tyson, Charles' hymns need not be read as the work of a theologian struggling with disease and depression (cf. Tyson, *Wesley on*

Sanctification, 262, 267). Nor need we agree with Tyson that "Although his basis images and constructs were rooted in the Bible, Charles extended those metaphors of suffering and sanctification in ways that went beyond their biblical basis" (Tyson, *Wesley on Sanctification*, 267–68). It is precisely in the Bible's account of Jesus' passion that we learn that there is a "necessary" connection (a divine **δει**) between suffering and sanctification.

28 Cf. WJW 2:160, "The Scripture Way of Salvation."

29 Cf. WW 10:350, "Some Remarks on 'A Defense of Aspasio Vindicated.'"

30 WJW 9:181, "The Principles of a Methodist Farther Explained"; emphasis in original.

31 WJW 2:158, "The Scripture Way of Salvation."

32 WJW 3:179, "On Patience."

33 Cf. ST 2–2.184.2.

34 ST 2–2.24.8.ad2.

35 ST 2–2.184.2.ad.2.

36 *De virtutibus* 2.10.

37 WW 12:394.

38 WW 10:444.

39 WW 12:239.

40 WW 12:239.

41 ST 1–2.88.6.ad2.

42 Cf. ST 1–2.19.6. In this passage Thomas alludes (implicitly) to the story of Jacob lying with Leah: "If a man's reason errs in mistaking another for his wife, and if he wish to give her her right when she asks for it, his will is excused from being evil: because this evil arises from ignorance of a circumstance, which ignorance excuses, and causes the act to be involuntary."

43 ST 1–2.21.1.

44 "A Plain Account of Christian Perfection," 349–50.

45 "A Plain Account of Christian Perfection," 349.

46 WJW 1:241, "The First Fruits of the Spirit."

47 In this regard, I concur with Cox' rejection of Sangster's critique. "William Sangster is wrong when he said Wesley rejected the idea of unconscious sin. Wesley knew that people have sin in them as believers even when they do not know it. One of Wesley's emphasis was that one should be fully wakened to his sinfulness"; Leo Cox, "John Wesley's Conception of Sin," *Bulletin of the Evangelical Theological Society* 5, no. 1 (1962): 18–24.

48 WJW 1:124, "Salvation by Faith."

49 ST 1–2.88.1.

50 Consider Wesley's remarks on this subject: "Not only sin, properly so called, (i.e., a voluntary transgression of a known law,) but sin, improperly so called, (i.e., an involuntary transgression of a divine law, known or unknown,) needs the atoning blood" (WW 11:396, "A Plain Account of Christian Perfection"). Thomas for his part associates such forgiveness with the sacraments, particularly with the Eucharist, which as spiritual nourishment heats up the ardor of charity. In the words of Ambrose, which Aquinas cites, *iste panis quotidianus sumitur in remedium quotidianae infirmitatis* (ST 3.89.4).

51 Thomas Lessmann, *Rolle und Bedeutung*, 141.

52 John Cobb offers a similar analysis in *Grace and Responsibility*: "Historically, the thrust of Wesley's theology was to move Christians toward emphasis on personal voluntary sins. It would be easy for us simply to follow that trajectory, abandoning the earlier ideas of collective guilt" (82).
53 Cobb, *Grace and Responsibility*, 83.
54 Cf. Long's discussion of fallibilism and perfection in *John Wesley's Moral Theology*, 216–42.
55 WJW 2:141, "Satan's Devices."
56 Cf. A. Skevington Wood, *Love Excluding Sin: Wesley's Doctrine of Sanctification* (Ilkeston: Moorley's Bible & Bookshop, 1980), 19.
57 WW 12:22.
58 WW 10:327, "Preface to a Treatise on Justification."
59 WW 12:397, "Letter to Mrs. Elizabeth Bennis."
60 WJW 4:136, "On Worldly Folly."
61 Maddox, *Responsible Grace*, 190; emphasis in original.
62 Collins, *The Scripture Way of Salvation*, 187.
63 Collins, *The Scripture Way of Salvation*, 179; emphasis in original.
64 ST 1–2.113.7.
65 ST 1–2.113.7.
66 ST 1–2.113.7.
67 ST 1–2.113.7.ad5.
68 WW 8:329, "Minutes of Several Conversations."
69 ST 2–2.24.9.
70 Both the *fomes peccati* and the *reliquiae peccati* remain after baptism; they differ in that the former are habits whereas the latter are dispositions; Cf. ST 3.86.5.
71 ST 3.86.5.ad1; emphasis in original.
72 Cf. ST 3.44.3.ad2.
73 The problem that I am trying to elucidate here is one that von Balthasar saw present in Karl Barth's theology. For Barth the Creator-creature relation is akin to that of headlights and reflectors. The reflector lights on the car reflect light only when the car behind shines its own headlights, "the creature indeed responds, but not really with its own light and word" (H. U. von Balthasar, *The Theology of Karl Barth* [San Francisco: Ignatius Press, 1951], 393).
74 The danger of a reductive "punctiliarism" in a Wesleyan doctrine of grace is adverted to by Geoffrey Wainwright in *Methodists in Dialogue*, 157. Wainwright suggests that the notion of "habit" as developed among scholastics would help Wesley to both affirm the real transformation that grace effects in the life of the believer and avoid Pelagianism. As I argued in the previous chapter this is precisely the role that the language of tempers serves in Wesley's theology.
75 ST 2–2.24.12.ad1.
76 ST 2–2.24.12.
77 "A Plain Account of Christian Perfection," 350.
78 On this point, Jean Porter has written a very interesting piece titled "Virtue and Sin: The Connection of the Virtues and the Case of the Flawed Saint," *Journal of Religion* 75, no. 4 (1995): 521–39, which examines what Thomas' account of holiness would make of someone like Martin Luther King Jr., who though an

adulterer, was, so claims Porter, a saint. While insisting on the value of Thomas' doctrine on the connection of the virtues, the fact of King's holiness leads her to ultimately strongly limit the applicability of Thomas' moral theology. In her view, "the example of King, and of other flawed saints, offers nearly conclusive evidence that Aquinas was wrong to say that the life of charity is inconsistent with serious sin" (538). Porter claims that "If King's recurrent vices had included deliberate cruelty, for example, it would be much harder to consider him to be a saint, flawed or not" (538). However, she avers that "It is significant that King's worst failings appear to have been sexual, because many of us are ambiguous about the moral status of "sexual sins" (537). Porter's account of flawed sanctity makes sense within the modern view that displaces much of the responsibility for personal sin on structural evil, but not, as she admits, within Aquinas' moral universe. Martin Luther King Jr. might well be a saint but that would be in spite of his flaws and not because of them. Yes, he showed admirable or even heroic prudence and courage, and even love for all people (if not always to his wife), yet surely he would have been a holier man had he not lapsed into adultery. The fact that his mission does not appear to have been seriously hindered by this vice does not point to the relative insignificance of this sin with respect to cruelty, as Porter claims, but to the mercy and power of God.

79 1 Corinthians 13:2.

80 Luby, *The Perceptibility of Grace.*

81 Luby, *The Perceptibility of Grace,* 229.

82 Luby, *The Perceptibility of Grace,* 225.

83 Luby, *The Perceptibility of Grace,* 159.

84 Luby, *The Perceptibility of Grace,* 225.

85 Luby, *The Perceptibility of Grace,* 226. In this connection it is important to mention Wesley's surprising 1766 letter to Charles, where Wesley speaks despondently regarding his spiritual state. Wesley says it more much more powerfully than I can, so let me simply quote from his letter. The italics are in the original, the bold represents those portions of the text written in shorthand in the original letter. "I do not feel the wrath of God abiding on me; nor can I believe it does. And yet (this is the mystery) **I do not love God. I never did.** Therefore **I never** believed in the Christian sense of the word. Therefore **I am only an** honest heathen, a proselyte of the Temple, one of the **φοβούμενοι τὸν Θεόν**. And yet to be so employed by God! And so hedged in that I can neither get forward nor backward! Surely there never was such an instance before, from the beginning of the world! If I **ever have had** *that faith*, it would not be so strange. But **I never had any** other **ἔλεγχος** of the eternal or invisible world than **I have** now; and that is **none at all**, unless such as fairly shines from reason's glimmering ray. **I have no** direct witness, I do not say that **I am a child of God**, but of anything invisible or eternal. And yet I dare not preach otherwise than I do, either concerning faith, or love, or justification. And yet I find rather an increase than a decrease of zeal for the whole work of God and every part of it. I am **φερόμενος**, I know not how, that I can't stand still. I want all the world to come to **ὃν οὐκ οἶδα**. Neither am I impelled to this by fear of any kind. I have no more fear than love. Or if I have **any fear, it is not that of falling** into hell but of falling into nothing" (*The Letters of John Wesley,* ed. John Telford

[London: Epworth Press, 1931], 16). This is a fascinating letter and much could be said about it, but let me point out the obvious. Wesley lacks assurance of his salvation but at the same time he is convinced of his vocation and he is zealous for his mission. John's language is very similar to that of many of the saints who have undergone the dark night of the soul (e.g., St. John of the Cross and Blessed Teresa of Calcutta). Wesley does not fear hell. He fears the void. He is borne along but cannot clearly perceive by whom. His only light is that of "reason's glimmering ray." Is Wesley unconsciously drawing on the language of the mystics to describe his condition? Is he undergoing the passive purifications that his theology rejected as necessary? Frank Carver opens some interesting avenues for further investigation of this topic in his brief study, "Growth in Sanctification: John Wesley and John of the Cross," *The Tower: The Journal of Nazarene Theological Seminary* 3 (1999): 33–70. On the subject of the 1766 letter Carver suggests that "If Wesley had read *The Dark Night* discriminately on its own apart from the later mystics, he may have understood better the work of God in his own heart and been able more genuinely to help others without appealing so much to an artificial distinction between 'darkness' and 'heaviness'" (58). Lamentably, we cannot consider Carver's suggestion at this point. At any rate, the 1766 letter and other writings like it—see, e.g., his December 15, 1772 letter to Charles where he cries out *Vitae me redde priori!* (cited in Carver, *Growth in Sanctification*, 58)—should alert us that suffering and darkness of faith played a larger role in Wesley's personal spirituality than he accounted for in his public theology.

86 "A Plain Account of Christian Perfection," 352–53.

87 Collins, *The Scripture Way of Salvation*, 182–84.

88 WJW 3:549, "Free Grace."

89 One of the questions that has been disputed among Methodist scholars is whether justifying faith may be present without the full assurance of faith. On the one hand, Maddox says "yes" (*Responsible Grace*, 124–27). The early Wesley linked faith and assurance so tightly that Christian and perfect were almost synonymous, but the late Wesley came to see that it was possible to believe without perceiving God's pardon. Such a person does not have the "faith of a son" but the "faith of a servant." In other words, faith without assurance is not the fullness of faith but it is Christian faith all the same. On the other hand, Collins says "no" (*The Scripture Way of Salvation*, 131–36). Wesley never loosens the connection between justifying faith and assurance. The distinction between the faith of the servant and the faith of a son is not one of degrees of faith but of theological states. The person with filial faith is "justified." The person with servile faith is "accepted." According to Maddox, accepted and justified are basically synonymous terms, but not so according to Collins. What is the difference between acceptance and justification? Frankly, Collins is fuzzy on details. Acceptance marks a middle state between being children of the devil and children of God. A person who is accepted is no longer under the wrath of God but their sins are not forgiven. I find Maddox's interpretation more coherent than Collins'. It seems to me that Collins has given too much speculative weight to a practical distinction that Wesley used for the consolation or exhortation of his followers. What could it possibly mean to say that God accepts us but does not

forgive us? Collins says that a person who has been accepted is not under wrath; presumably that only holds as long as they keep away from sin, but then what is the difference between the state of acceptance and the state of all humanity under prevenient grace? Yes, Wesley held hope for the salvation of the honest heathen who died outside the visible church, but such hope is grounded on the mercy of God, not on an alternate *via salutis*. For the honest heathen to enter the kingdom he must be forgiven and born from above.

90 *De veritate* 10.10.

91 *De veritate* 10.10.ad5.

92 *De veritate* 10.10.ad1.

93 *De veritate* 10.10.ad7.

94 ST 1–2.112.5.

95 ST 1–2.112.5.

96 As Henri Bouillard states in *Conversion et Grâce chez Saint Thomas* (Paris: Aubier, 1941): "La conversion de saint Paul est miraculeuse, non parce qu'elle a été soudain, mais parce qu'elle a atteint un haut degré de charité du premier coup et no pas progressivement comme chez le commun des hommes" (148).

97 *De caritate* 11.ad10.

98 ST 1–2.112.5.

99 Garrigou-Lagrange, *Christian Perfection and Contemplation*, 56.

100 ST 1–2.112.5.

101 ST 1–2.112.5.

102 ST 1–2.112.5.ad3.

103 WW 10:337–38.

104 WW 10:337–38.

105 So reads Wesley's translation in his *Notes on the New Testament*.

106 WW 10:433.

107 WW 10:434.

108 WW 10:434.

109 Gunter, *The Limits of "Love Divine,"* 252.

110 Gunter, *The Limits of "Love Divine,"* 253.

111 Collins, *The Scripture Way of Salvation*, 204.

112 Collins, *The Scripture Way of Salvation*, 203.

113 ST 1–2.114.1.

114 Joseph Wawrykow, *God's Grace and Human Action: "Merit" in the Theology of Thomas Aquinas* (Notre Dame, Ind.: University of Notre Dame Press, 1995), 241.

115 Wawrykow, *God's Grace and Human Action*, 241.

116 ST 3.19.3.

117 Indeed, the presence of grace makes even the smallest of acts meritorious. In the words of Garrigou-Lagrange, "it is more meritorious to accomplish easy things with great charity than to perform very difficult acts with less charity. Thus many tepid souls carry their cross without great merit, whereas the Blessed Virgin merited more by the easiest acts of charity than all the martyrs together in their torments" (Garrigou-Lagrange, *Christian Perfection and Contemplation*, 133, n. 12).

118 Cf. Maddox, *Responsible Grace*. Maddox considers the abiding concern of Wesley's work to be the preservation of the tension between grace and freedom: "without God's grace, we *cannot* be saved; while without our (grace-empowered,

but uncoerced) participation, God's grace *will not* save" (19). Thus, the orienting concern of Wesley's theological oeuvre is rightly called "responsible grace."

119 WJW 2:490, "The General Spread of the Gospel"; WJW 3:208, "On Working Out Our Own Salvation." Wesley wrongly credits Augustine for this saying. Best say that the saying is in the spirit of Augustine. Thomas knew a different version of this saying and quoted it against those who would diminish the human's responsibility in salvation by advocating a form of quietism that forsakes the assistance of the sacraments (cf. ST 3.84.5), but sometimes he argued against those who would interpret this saying in ways that diminished the primacy of divine agency (cf. ST 1–2.111.2.arg2). In other words, Aquinas and Wesley both understood that this kind of thinking while a strong tonic against antinomianism could have the side effect, if not used properly, of semi-Pelagianism.

120 ST 1–1.111.2.ad2.

121 Charles Journet, *The Meaning of Grace* (Princeton, N.J.: Sceptre Publishers, 1960), 71.

122 Journet, *The Meaning of Grace*, 69.

123 Bernard Lonergan, *Grace and Freedom*, 147.

124 Collins rightly notices the limitations of strictly synergistic understanding of grace. As he avers, "Those scholars who champion this view no doubt take comfort in the notion that this paradigm has a role for both divine and human action while it ever gives *priority* to the former. However, the notion of divine *priority* in and of itself is simply inadequate to encompass all that Wesley understood by the grace of God. Indeed, the conjunctive *style* of his theology is not, after all, fully or aptly expressed in the divine and human roles found in an overarching synergistic paradigm that privileges merely the 'Catholic' or 'Eastern' understanding of grace. On the contrary, more accurate readings suggest that a synergistic paradigm, which contains both divine and human acting, must itself be caught up in an *even larger conjunction* in which the Protestant (and Pauline!) emphasis on the *sole activity* of God (*sola gratia, sola fide*), apart from all human working, is *equally* factored in. Not simply co-operant grace, but the conjunction of co-operant grace and free grace" (*The Theology of John Wesley*, 76; emphasis in original). The concerns for divine sovereignty in salvation that motivate the "*larger conjunction*" that Collins is calling for are achieved in the Thomistic synthesis as exemplified in the distinction between operating and cooperating grace. With some care, we can say that Collins' "free grace" and Maddox' "responsible grace" correspond in turn to Thomas' *gratia operans* and *gratia cooperans*.

125 According to Collins, "since Wesley's doctrine of original sin underscores the notion of total depravity, then it logically follows that "irresistible grace" has to operate at least at some point in the Wesleyan order of salvation. Indeed, this may come as a surprise to those Methodists who have been schooled on the notion that irresistible grace is a topic more suited to Calvinists. Nevertheless, since men and women in the natural state, according to Wesley, do not even have the freedom to accept or reject any offered grace, then this gift itself must be graciously and *irresistibly* restored" (*The Theology of John Wesley*, 80). Collins' assessment of Wesley's understanding of the provenience of grace is accurate

but his utilization of the term "irresistible grace" is, in my opinion, inapt. If, for Wesley, humans lack the freedom to accept or reject the gospel is it accurate to describe the overture of grace as irresistible? Does not the very notion of irresistibility suggest that post-lapsarian humans have the negative freedom to reject the gospel, which is then overridden by grace? Better, and more coherent with the reality that both Wesley and Collins are describing, is the Thomistic concept of *gratia operans*: God acts on the will or infuses operative habits into a person prior to any movement of the human will.

126 Journet, *Meaning of Grace*, 36.

127 Cf. Ephesians 2:13: "it is God who is at work in you, enabling you both to will and to work for his good pleasure."

128 Journet, *Meaning of Grace*, 70.

129 Herbert Boyd McGonigle, *Sufficient Saving Grace: John Wesley's Evangelical Armenianism* (Waynesboro, Ga.: Paternoster Press, 2001), 187–88.

130 McGonigle, *Sufficient Saving Grace*, 201.

131 McGonigle, *Sufficient Saving Grace*, 203.

132 Michał Paluch, *La profondeur de l'amour divin: Évolution de la doctrine de la prédestination dans l'œuvre de saint Thomas d'Aquin* (Paris: Libraire Philosophique J.Vrin, 2004), 206.

133 Paluch, *La Profondeur*, 204; emphasis in original.

134 Paluch, *La Profondeur*, 317; emphasis in original.

135 WJW 7:322, "Hymn 193."

136 In *Responsible Grace*, Maddox suggests that a doctrine of a "self-limiting God" might be a more biblical and Wesleyan solution to the question of divine knowledge and human freedom (53). Perhaps so, but for Thomas such a solution would be problematic because it suggests too much conceptual penetration into the divine mystery. Followers of Thomas who wanted to entertain Maddox' proposal seriously would want to reflect further on how the theologoumenon of the kenotic "self-limitation" of God's knowledge can avoid being flipped on its head into the Feuerbachian divinization of human knowledge that collapses the doctrine of analogical predication into univocal predication.

137 Maritain, *Degrees of Knowledge*, 330.

138 Maritain, *Degrees of Knowledge*, 373; emphasis in original.

139 Maritain, *Degrees of Knowledge*, 373.

140 Maritain, *Degrees of Knowledge*, 373.

141 In this study, I have not been trying to uncover the "catholic Wesley" in the way that some theologians try to retrieve a "catholic Luther." As David Steinmetz argues in "The Catholic Luther: A Critical Reappraisal," *Theology Today* 61 (2004): 187–201, "the debate about Luther as a catholic theologian is really, in the end, a debate about the catholicity of the churches that trace their origin to his reforming work" (199). I am not arguing for the catholicity of Wesley or Methodism, but in a sense, against it.

142 Outler, "Do Methodists Have a Doctrine?" 25.

143 *Unitatis Redintegratio*, 3.

144 ST 1.Pr.

145 WJW 1:103.

Chapter 7

1 Joseph Cardinal Ratzinger, "On the Ecumenical Situation," in *Pilgrim Fellowship of Faith: The Church as Communion* (San Francisco: Ignatius Press, 2005), 253–69.

2 Ratzinger, "On the Ecumenical Situation," 256.

3 John L. Peters, *Christian Perfection and American Methodism* (Nashville: Abingdon, 1956), 193.

4 Cf. the entry *heroïcité des vertus* in De Bonhome's *Dictionnaire de Spiritualité: Ascétique et Mystique, Doctrine et Histoire* (Paris: Beauchesne, 1968), F.XLIV–XLV, 337–43.

5 Cf. *Heilige als Brückenbauer: Heiligenverehrung im ökumenischen Dialog*, ed. Karl Schlemmer (St. Ottilien: EOS Verlag, 1997).

6 WJW 7:465.

7 *Tertio Millenio Adveniente*, 37.

8 Wainwright, *Methodists in Dialogue*, 249.

9 Wainwright highlights the connection between sanctification and unity in Jesus' high priestly prayer of John 17 as a way in which Methodists can come to terms with the Roman Catholic doctrine of infallibility. First of all notice the correlation that Jesus establishes between truth and love, "Since, in God, truth and love, are one, it may be assumed that true teaching is best conducive to love, while love will give insight into the truth of God" (*Methodists in Dialogue*, 64). Truth matters for the sanctification of the believer; hence, the need to reflect on ways in which truth is preserved and delivered by the church. Wainwright's proposal is that "the notions of infallibility and indefectibility could take on more warmth and personal character if the language of assurance were used to make clear the concern for the salvation of individual human beings that underlies the church's claimed need of certitude in its preaching and teaching" (69). In this connection it is important to recall the witness of Blessed Maria Gabriella of Unity. In the words of John Paul II, "Sister Maria Gabriella, called by her vocation to be apart from the world, devoted her life to meditation and prayer centered on chapter seventeen of Saint John's Gospel, and offered her life for Christian unity. . . . The example of Sister Gabriella is instructive; it helps us understand that there are no special times, situations or places of prayer for Christian unity. Christ's prayer to the Father is offered as a model for everyone, always and everywhere" (*Ut unum sint*, 27). Fittingly, Sister Maria Gabriella was beatified at the conclusion of the week of prayer.

10 Chesterton, *Saint Thomas Aquinas: "The Dumb Ox,"* 24.

11 Antonio Rubial García, *La santidad controvertida: Hagiografía y conciencia criolla alrededor de los venerables no canonizados de Nueva España* (México, D.F.: Fondo de Cultura Económica, 1999), 96.

12 Rubial, *La santidad*, 110.

13 WJW 19:294, n. 73; cf. Jean Orcibal, "Les spirituels français et espagnols chez John Wesley et ses contemporains," in *Revue de l'Histoire des Religions* 139 (1951): 50–109.

14 WW 12:294. This statement is a paraphrase from his own abridgment of Losa's account of López' death: "[W]hen, being asked, if he would have the holy candle to go see the secret, he answered with great courage, as is said before, *All is*

clear, there is no secret, it is noon-day with me. Wherein his meaning was not, that his faith was without obscurity, but that, in matters belonging to it, he had no doubt" (Wesley, *The Life of* Mr. *Gregory López*, 95). Compare this statement with Wesley's abridgment, "[W]hen it appeared to me time to give him the parting blessing, I said, 'All is clear; there is no longer anything hid: It is full noon with me.' Plainly declaring, that the light which then shone on his soul, far surpassed that of the noon-day sun" (404).

15 Wesley, *The Life of* Mr. *Gregory López*, 397; cf. Losa, *The Life of* Mr. *Gregory López*, 200.

16 WW 12:44.

17 WJW 21:32, Journal 10, October 15, 1755.

18 WJW 3:627, "On the death of John Fletcher."

19 WJW 3:627, "On the death of John Fletcher."

20 WJW 22:127, Journal 18, April 22, 1779.

21 Wesley, *The Life of* Mr. *Gregory López*, 396.

22 Wesley, *The Life of* Mr. *Gregory López*, 396.

23 Wesley, *The Life of* Mr. *Gregory López*, 396.

24 See, for instance, the exchange that takes place when Losa asks López about any sins that the latter needs absolution for: "Whereto [López] answered, that, *Through the mercy of God, he found nothing that troubled his conscience.* Which is to be understood in the matter of mortal sin: for, he was not ignorant that none ever lived without venial sins, except the Virgin Mary our Blessed Lady; not for that he never committed any; but because having committed none wittingly, and being asked on the sudden, it was very possible that that time he remembered none" (*The Life of* Mr. *Gregory López*, 60).

25 WJW 2:375, "On the Trinity."

26 John Wesley's ecumenical openness in his sermon *On the Catholic Spirit* and his *Letter to a Roman Catholic* is remarkable given the period in which he lived, but they represent only one strand of Wesley's attitude toward the Roman Catholic Church. Regarding this letter, which has been called an olive branch to the Catholics, David Chapman (*In Search of the Catholic Spirit*) rightly cautions us that "it would be misleading to place too much weight on a single letter, written when there was considerable pressure on Wesley to avoid further trouble. Certainly, the letter reveals Wesley at his most irenic and conciliatory, though it is unique in tone and content among his writings on Roman Catholicism. There is little evidence in subsequent works to show that Wesley made any attempt to fulfill its noble resolutions" (33).

27 This recognition would give rise to confusions and condemnations among his contemporaries. As Chapman avers, "Such obvious sympathy for certain Roman Catholic spiritual writers and their interpretation of Christian life distinguished Wesley from the majority of his contemporaries in the Church of England, who were far more Protestant-minded, and inevitably invited the accusation of popery" (*In Search of the Catholic Spirit*, 22).

28 WJW 19:294, Journal 5, August 31, 1742. Indeed, to this day, the hagiographers are often one of the chief obstacles standing in the way of a greater appreciation of the lives of the saints. As Wainwright rightly and wryly suggests, "We are now in need of "lives" of other saints written in styles which avoid those that gave

hagiography a bad name and yet (or rather) encourage us to emulation of their subjects" (*Methodists in Dialogue*, 248).

29 For instance, in comparing the holiness of the recently deceased John Fletcher to that of López and de Renty, Wesley states, "There are two circumstances that deserve consideration. One is, we are not assured that the writers of their lives did not extenuate, if not suppress, what was amiss in them; and some things amiss we are assured there were, viz., many touches of superstition, and some of idolatry, in worshipping saints, the Virgin Mary in particular: But I have not suppressed or extenuated anything in Mr. Fletcher's character; for, indeed, I knew nothing that was amiss, nothing that needed to be extenuated, much less suppressed. A second circumstance is, that the writers of their lives could not have so full a knowledge of them, as both Mrs. Fletcher and I had of Mr. Fletcher; being eye and ear witnesses of his whole conduct. Consequently, we know that his life was not sullied with any mixture of either idolatry or superstition" (WJW 19:294, Journal 5, August 31, 1742). As an aside, I must say that though this attribution of López holiness to the mediation of Mary is in character for Losa, I have not been able to track down the place where Losa actually said this in so many words. However, Losa (in the Woodhead translation) does call Mary the "Star of the Sea" in the spiritual journey (101–2), and López recommends as a valuable aid in the pursuit of perfection (101, 183–84).

30 WJW 3:627, "On the death of John Fletcher."

31 WJW 19:294, Journal 5, August 31, 1742.

32 Wesley, *The Life of Mr. Gregory López*, 342.

33 Wesley, *The Life of Mr. Gregory López*, 343, 345, 367.

34 WW 13:132.

35 WW 12:305.

36 Wesley, *The Life of Mr. Gregory López*, 377.

37 Wesley, *The Life of Mr. Gregory López*, 373.

38 Wesley, *The Life of Mr. Gregory López*, 392.

39 Wesley, *The Life of Mr. Gregory López*, 359.

40 Wesley, *The Life of Mr. Gregory López*, 393. Elsewhere we read, "That presence of God wherein he lived was not barren or unfruitful: seeing it daily produced more and more acts of love to God and his neighbor: that love which is the end of the commandment, and the sum of all perfection" (Wesley, *The Life of Mr. Gregory López*, 366).

41 Losa, *The Life of Mr. Gregory López*, 196.

42 WW 3:122, Journal, November 25, 1762.

43 "A Plain Account of Christian Perfection," 342.

44 WW 12:338.

45 WW 12:299.

46 Jane Cooper, *Letters wrote by Jane Cooper: to which is prefixt some account of her life and death*, 2 (London: 1792). Eighteenth Century Collections Online. Gale Group. http://galenet.galegroup.com/servlet/ECCO. Henceforth referred to as *Letters*.

47 *Letters*, 33.

48 *Letters*, 33.

49 *Letters*, 34.

50 *Letters*, 6.
51 *Letters*, 6.
52 *Letters*, 19: "If I wish any thing, it is for more opportunity for private prayer. Between the sick, the afflicted, and those seeking the Lord, I have very little time to myself. However I feel no desire, but to do and suffer his will."
53 WW 3:122.
54 *Letters*, 10.
55 *Letters*, 12.
56 *Letters*, 12.
57 WW 3:122.
58 ST 2–2.24.8.ad1.
59 Thomas addresses the subject of Papal canonizations in *Quaestiones de quolibet* 9.8: "Utrum omnes sancti qui sunt per Ecclesiam canonizati, sint in gloria, vel aliqui eorum in Inferno." Are the saints listed by the church, really saints? Or could the church have made a mistake and canonized a sinner? For Thomas, the canon of saints though not exhaustive is free from error; the certainty of the church's discernment rests on the conviction that God would not let the church err on a matter of such importance, and the responsibility and focus point for this certainty is the bishop of Rome: "pontifex, cuius est canonizare sanctos, potest certificari de statu alicuius per inquisitionem vitae et attestationem miraculorum; et praecipue per instinctum spiritus sancti, qui omnia scrutatur, etiam profunda Dei" (*Quodlibet* 9.8.ad1). In brief, the church's canonization of saints is a papal act of judgment inspired by the Holy Spirit that the Christian should joyfully and confidently accept: "pie credendum est, quod nec etiam in his iudicium Ecclesiae errare possit" (*Quodlibet* 9.8). The question remains whether, on Thomistic grounds, this Papal charism allows the Pope to judge the holiness of those persons outside the visible boundaries of the Catholic Church. Thomas does not ask this question. Yet his reflections on whether a judge can pass a just judgment on someone not subject to his jurisdiciton might be the place to start (ST 2–2.67.1). Thomas' answer to this question is largely in the negative; one cannot justly judge someone outside one's realm of authority, and yet his mention of Daniel judging certain Babylonian judges of lying suggests that there are exceptional circumstances that warrant such a judgment. As Thomas avers: "In judging those ancients Daniel exercised an authority delegated to him by Divine instinct (*ex instinctu divino*)" (ST 2–2.67.1.ad1).
60 Cf. ST 2–2.178.2.
61 *Letters*, 11.
62 ST 2–2.178.2.ad4.
63 Cf. ST 2–2.178.2.ad4.
64 Cf. ST 1–2.113.9.
65 *Letters*, 10.
66 ST 2–2.185.1.ad2.
67 ST 2–2.21.2.
68 ST 1–2.112.5.ad3: "Sin has for its principal object commutable good, which is known to us. But the object or end of grace is unknown to us on account of the greatness of its light, according to 1 Tim. 6:16: 'Who . . . inhabiteth light inaccessible.'"

69 ST 2–2.18.4.ad2.

70 Cf. ST 1–2.40.5. Does this emphasis on the objective basis of hope mean that experience is of no relevance? No. For Thomas, experience is related to hope in various ways. As Thomas explains, "Experience in matters pertaining to action not only produces knowledge; it also causes a certain habit, which renders action easier" (ST 1–2.40.5.ad1). Experience strengthens hope by showing that one is making progress in overcoming the difficulties that hinder the obtainment of the goal. Of course, negative experiences can turn hope into despair. This is why sometimes old people can become cynical; "experience makes them think something impossible" (ST 1–2.40.5.ad2). Conversely, what passes for hope among the young is often simply inexperience: "Wherefore youths, through inexperience of obstacles and of their own shortcomings, easily count a thing possible; and consequently are of good hope" (ST 1–2.40.6). On the first occasion that Jane Cooper received the assurance of God's pardoning love, she became convinced that she would sin no more. This state did not last long, but Cooper is somewhat at a loss to explain this falling. Was it her lack of sufficient faith? Was the whole experience of assurance a self-delusion? Aquinas might have us question whether her hope and confidence were, at least in part, owing to youthfulness and inexperience. Wesley was well aware of this confusion. In his sermon on "The Repentance of Believers," he explains that: "[W]hen we first find redemption in the blood of Jesus; when the love of God is first shed abroad in our hearts, and his kingdom set up therein; it is natural to suppose that we are no longer sinners, that all our sins are not only covered but destroyed. As we do not then feel any evil in our hearts, we readily imagine none is there" (WJW 1:336, "The Repentance of Believers").

71 Cf. ST 1–2.112.5.

72 ST 2–2.132.1.ad3.

73 *Letters*, 38.

74 *Letters*, 38.

75 As Thomas avers, even among the virtuous, "It is possible, without falsehood, to deem and avow oneself the most despicable of men, as regards the hidden faults which we acknowledge in ourselves, and the hidden gifts of God which others have" (ST 2–2.161.6.ad1).

76 Cf. Hans Urs von Balthasar, *Two Sisters in the Spirit: Thérèse of Lisieux and Elizabeth of the Trinity* (San Francisco: Ignatius Press, 1992), 343–53.

77 Cf. ST 1–2.68.1ad2, ST 1–2.68.2, ST 2–2.159.2

78 As Thomas avers, "A heroic or godlike habit only differs from virtue commonly so called by a more perfect mode (*secundum perfectiorem modum*), inasmuch as one is disposed to good in higher way than is common to all" (ST 3.7.2.ad2).

79 For a brief but detailed account of the use of the category of heroic virtue as a criteria for canonization see Alfred de Bonhome's "Heroïcités des vertus," 337–43. During the canonization proceedings for St. Bonaventure in 1482, Jean François de Pavinis applied the Thomist schema of the virtues albeit in an unsystematic manner and without explicitly employing the term "heroic virtue." It was not until 1602 that this term was first used as a criterion for canonization when the Salamancan theologians promoted the cause of their patronne St. Teresa de Ávila. In 1738 Benedict XIV, as Prospero Lambertini,

published the extremely influential *De servorum Dei beatificatione et beatorum canonizatione*, in which he devotes extensive attention to the role of heroic virtues in the recognition of holiness. According to Lambertini, a heroic virtue is made manifest by the excellence of its acts: "le plus seuvent, le fait qu'il se rencontre plus de difficulté à les accomplir sera un signe de leur 'excellence'" (338–39). However, the excellence of the act needs to be weighed against the concrete circumstances of the act: "les services des malades accompli par le roi saint Louis, par exemple, l'emporte en excellence sur le meme service rendu par un simple particulier" (339). By themselves, these heroic acts are insufficiently perspicuous criteria for sanctity, but when these acts are frequent (*multiplex excellentiae vitae*) the presence of the virtues is made increasingly manifest. However, it is not the difficulty or frequency of the act that is a sign of a heroic habit. "Ces actes multiples d'heroïsme doivent avoir été accomplish 'avec promptitude, facilité et joie' (*prompte, faciliter et cum delectatione*)" (339). The facility of the act is a sign of the presence of the habit; the joy of the act is a sign of the intensity of the habit, and "si en accomplisant un acte mû par le charité surnaturelle, cette joie s'accompagne de *suavitas*, il y a là un signe charactéristique (*nota et signum*) d'heroïcité" (339). Charity is the bond of perfection which animates all moral and theological virtues. When it comes to acts under the rule of charity what matters most is not the outward difficulty of the act or the frequency of the act but the quality of the act: "*non temporis rationalem sed actuum qualitatem perpendendam*" (340).

80 "A Plain Account of Christian Perfection," 342.

81 ST 1–2.68.2.

82 *Letters*, 14.

83 *Letters*, 36.

84 *Letters*, 17.

85 *Letters*, 22.

86 Cf. *Letters*, 12.

87 *Letters*, 30.

88 ST 2–2.139.1.

89 ST 2–2.139.1.

90 Cf. ST 2–2.123.12.ad2: "Virtue essentially regards the good rather than the difficult. Hence the greatness of a virtue is measured according to its goodness rather than its difficulty."

91 Cf. *De caritate* 8.ad17. In this passage, Thomas makes the point that it is more meritorious to love a friend than an enemy. Perfect charity is made more manifest by loving an enemy, but it is not the difficulty that constitutes the basis for merit but the presence of charity that is moved to love the friend with more fervor and God with most. As Josef Pieper argues in *Leisure: The Basis of Culture* (South Bend, Ind.: St. Augustine Press, 1998), the reason that Thomas' argument seems upside down is that we have grown up on Kantian ethics, which claim that the good is the difficult. For Kant, virtue helps us overcome our natural inclinations. "What Thomas says, instead, is that virtue perfects us so that we can *follow* our natural inclinations in the right way" (17).

92 Joseph Ratzinger, as cited in W. H. Woestman, *Canonization: Theology, History, Process* (Ottawa: Saint Paul University Press, 2002), xv.

93 Ratzinger, as cited in Woestman, xvi.
94 Lawrence S. Cunningham, *The Meaning of Saints* (San Francisco: Harper & Row, 1980).
95 Cunningham, *The Meaning of Saints*, 86.
96 Cunningham, *The Meaning of Saints*, 95.
97 Theresa Sanders, "Seeking a Minor Sun: Saints after the Death of God," *Horizons* 22, no. 2 (1995): 184.
98 Sanders, "Seeking a Minor Sun,"184.
99 Edith Wyschogrod, "Exemplary Individuals: Toward a Phenomenological Ethics," *Philosophy and Theology* 1, no. 1 (1986): 9–32. In this connection, Wyschogrod mentions the case of a prostitute whose claim to sanctity is based on the fact that she gave herself freely to men of all castes (19).
100 Wyschogrod, 17.
101 Wyschogrod, "Exemplary Individuals," 21.
102 Cunningham, *The Meaning of Saints,*113.
103 Cunningham, *The Meaning of Saints*, 161.
104 Cf. David M. Matzko, "Postmodernism, Saints and Scoundrels," *Modern Theology* 9, no. 1 (1993): 19–36.
105 Matzko, "Postmodernism," 22. Matzko believes that the postmodern critique of modernity, particularly its opposition to universal notions of rationality and morality, opens the space for the reappropriation of the saints as moral exemplars. Yet, the postmodern allergy to metanarratives seems to me to restrict the significance of the saints to the historical realm and leave little room for the possibility that the ministry of the saints begins in earnest after they die.
106 Chesterton, *Saint Thomas Aquinas: "The Dumb Ox,"* 23.
107 ST 1.73.1; *De veritate* 1.10.ad.s.c.3.
108 This first perfection cannot be lost, for the image of God is present virtually in the habits and even in the powers of the soul, in the same way that the act is present in its principles. So as long as at least the powers of the soul are present, the image of God persists even without actual acts (cf. ST 1.93.8.a3).
109 ST 3.2.10.
110 Cf. Brian S. Hook and R. R. Reno, *Heroism & the Christian Life: Reclaiming Excellence* (Louisville, Ky.: Westminster John Knox, 2000). Reno and Hook consider Albert Camus one of the most eloquent apologists for the antiheroic. "For Camus, the baseline of common decency arises out of the ordinariness of human life, it mediocrity and veniality, as well as its quiet dignity and enduring emotional needs. To transcend this commonality entails cutting oneself off from the taproot of humane existence, and risks making the hero an enemy of humanity" (195).
111 Consider the following exchange between Tarrou and Rieux in Albert Camus, *La Peste* (Saint-Armand: Editions Gallimard, 1947), 230. Tarrou: "En somme, . . . ce qui m'intéresse, c'est de savoir comment on devient un saint." Rieux: "Mais vous ne croyez pas en Dieu." Tarrou: "Justement. Peut-on être un saint sans Dieu, c'est le seul problème concret que je connaisse aujourd'hui." Rieux: "Je n'ai pas de goût, je crois, pour l'héroïsme et la sainteté. Ce qui m'intéresse, c'est d'être un homme." Tarrou: "Oui nous cherchons la même chose, mais je suis moins ambitieux."

112 Cf. Pietro Card. Palazzini, "La Santità coronamento della dignità dell'uomo," in *Miscellanea in occasione del IV centenario della Congregazione per le Cause dei Santi* (Vatican City: Congregation for the Causes of the Saints, 1988), 221–36. According to Cardinal Palazzini, holiness is the manifestation of the *splendor humanitas* (233): "Ora anche il modo con cui la Chiesa procede nella dichiarazione della santità uffiizialata dimostra non è altro che la maturità umana, portata al suo più alto livello per il potenziamento della grazia" (229). The saint is the most powerful apology for the worth of the person. The apologetic significance of the saints is one of the reasons for the record numbers of beatifications and canonizations during John Paul II's papacy. The official declaration of sanctity constitutes the church's strongest defense of human dignity in the face of a culture of death.

113 W. E. Sangster, *The Pure in Heart: A Study in Christian Sanctity* (Nashville: Abingdon, 1954), 90–91.

114 Sangster, *The Pure in Heart*, 61.

115 Sangster, *The Pure in Heart*, 59.

116 Cf. WJW 7:465.

117 Cf. WJW 7:465.

118 Karl Jaspers, *Von der Wahrheit* (München: R. Piper Verlag, 1947), 925.

119 *Scriptum super sententiis*, 2.10.1.1.ad 3.

120 *Ut unum sint*, 84.

121 Sangster, *The Pure in Heart*, 61.

122 Wainwright, *Methodists in Dialogue*, 248. One question that needs to be explored is whether the naming of those saints outside one's ecclesial bounds is an ecumenical step toward unity or one of the fruits of unity. In the 2000 Père Marquette Lecture in Theology, *Is the Reformation Over?* (Milwaukee, Wisc.: Marquette University Press, 2000) Wainwright seems to suggest or at least underscore the former. "My suggestion is that a tremendous fillip would be given to ecclesial reconciliation if the Catholic Church were to adopt a number of Protestant heroes and heroines into its official sanctorale, for that would bestow liturgical recognition upon the communities in whose bosom these saints grew in the Spirit of holiness and bore their conspicuous witness to Christ. Certainly the idea of an "exchange of saints" would merit ecumenical exploration" (56). I strongly agree with Wainwright on the ecumenical potential of such recognition and hence the need for further exploration. One aspect that would need to be explored is the relation between the communion of saints and the Eucharist. How much "reconciliation of memories" must precede the incorporation of each other's saints into the anamnesis?

123 Sangster, *The Pure in Heart*, 91.

Appendix

1 ST 1.93.7.ad2.

2 ST 1.93.4.ad1.

3 ST 1.92.2.

4 Sister Prudence Allen, *The Concept of Woman: The Aristotelian Revolution 750 B.C.–A.D. 1250* (Grand Rapids: Eerdmans, 1985), 386.

5 Allen, *The Concept of Woman*, 389.

6 Allen, *The Concept of Woman*, 407.
7 Allen, *The Concept of Woman*, 407.
8 Pia Francesca de Solenni, *A Hermeneutic of Aquinas' Mens through a Sexually Differentiated Epistemology: Toward an Understanding of Woman as Imago Dei* (Rome: Edizioni Università della Santa Croce, 2000), 15.
9 De Solenni, *A Hermeneutic*, 154.
10 De Solenni, *A Hermeneutic*, 155.
11 De Solenni, *A Hermeneutic*, 156.
12 De Solenni, *A Hermeneutic*, 157.
13 De Solenni, *A Hermeneutic*, 160.
14 De Solenni, *A Hermeneutic*, 163.
15 De Solenni, *A Hermeneutic*, 165.
16 De Solenni, *A Hermeneutic*, 167.
17 De Solenni, *A Hermeneutic*, 169.

Bibliography

Reports from the Methodist Catholic Dialogue

The Apostolic Tradition. Singapore, 1991.

Authority, Moral Decisions, Family. Honolulu, 1981.

Christian Home and Family. Denver, 1971.

The Grace Given You in Christ: Catholics and Methodists Reflect Further on the Church. Seoul, 2006.

Growth in Understanding. Dublin, 1976.

Methodist Statement of the World Methodist Council on the 1999 Joint Declaration on the Doctrine of Justification. Seoul, 2006.

Speaking the Truth in Love: Teaching Authority among Catholics and Methodists. Brighton, 2001. *Toward an Agreed Statement on the Church*. Nairobi, 1986.

The Word of Life: A Statement on Revelation and Faith. Rio de Janeiro, 1996.

Primary Sources for John and Charles Wesley

Wesley, Charles. *Hymns for Ascension Day*. Madison N.J.: Charles Wesley Society, 1994.

Wesley, Charles, and John Wesley. *Hymns on the Lord's Supper*. Madison, N.J.: Charles Wesley Society, 1995.

Wesley, John. A *Christian Library. Consisting of extracts from and abridgments of the choicest pieces of practical divinity, which have been publish'd*. Vol. L. Bristol, 1749–1755: 337–406.

——. *Explanatory Notes upon the New Testament*. London: Epworth Press, 1976.

——. *The Letters of John Wesley*. Edited by John Telford. London: Epworth Press, 1931.

——. *The Works of John Wesley*, eds. Albert Outler et al. Nashville: Abingdon, 1984.

——. *The Works of John Wesley*, ed. Thomas Jackson. Grand Rapids: Baker Book House, 1984.

Wesley, John, and Charles Wesley. *John and Charles Wesley: Selected Prayers, Hymns, Journal Notes, Sermons, Letters and Treatises*. Edited byFrank Whaling. Mahwah, N.J.: Paulist Press, 1981.

Primary Sources for Thomas Aquinas

Aquinas, St. Thomas. *The Aquinas Catechism*. Translated by L. Shapcote. Manchester, N.H.: Sophia Institute, 2000.

——. *Comentario a las Sentencias de Pedro Lombardo*. Translated by Juan Cruz. Pamplona, Spain: Ediciones Universidad de Navarra, 2002.

——. *On Charity*. Translated by L. H. Kendzierski. Milwaukee, Wisc.: The Marquette University Press, 1960.

——. *On Evil*. Translated by John A. Oesterle and Jean T. Oesterle. Notre Dame, Ind.: University of Notre Dame Press, 1995.

——. *The Perfection of the Spiritual Life*. Translated by F. J. Procter. Westminster, Md.: Newman Press, 1950.

——. *Quaestiones disputatae de veritate*. Paris: J. Vrin, 2002.

——. *Sancti Thomas de Aquino opera omnia iussu Leonis XIII O.M. edita*. Rome: Ex Typographia Polyglotta S.C. de Propaganda Fide, 1882.

——. *Summa contra Gentiles*. Translated by A. C. Pegis et al. Notre Dame, Ind.: University of Notre Dame Press, 1975.

——. *The Summa Theologica of St. Thomas Aquinas*. Translated by Fathers of the English Dominican Province. Allen, Tex.: Christian Classics, 1948.

——. *Summa Theologiae*. 5th ed. Madrid: Biblioteca de Autores Cristianos, 1994.

——. *Truth*. Translated by Robert Mulligan. Indianapolis: Hackett Publishing, 1954.

——. *The Ways of God for Meditation and Prayer*. Manchester, N.H.: Sophia Institute, 1995.

Secondary Literature

Abraham, William. "The End of Wesleyan Theology." *Wesleyan Theological Journal* 40, no. 1 (2005): 7–25.

Albin, Thomas. "'Inwardly Persuaded': Religion of the Heart in Early British Methodism." In *"Heart Religion" in the Methodist Tradition and Related Movements*. Edited by Richard Steele. Lanham, Md.: Scarecrow Press, 2001: 33–66.

Allen, Prudence. *The Concept of Woman: The Aristotelian Revolution 750 B.C.–A.D. 1250*. Grand Rapids: Eerdmans, 1985.

Augustine, *The Trinity* in *Augustine: Later Works*. Edited by John Burnaby. Philadelphia: Westminster Press, 1955.

Aumann, Jordan. *The Pastoral and Religious Lives*. Vol. 47: *St. Thomas Aquinas, Summa Theologiae*. Chicago: Blackfriars, 1973.

Baker, Frank. "Practical Divinity: John Wesley's Doctrinal Agenda for Methodism." *Wesleyan Theological Journal* 22, no. 1 (1987): 7–16.

Bartels, Laura. "The Political Image as the Basis for Wesleyan Ecological Ethics." *Quarterly Review* 23 (2003): 294–301.

Benedict XVI. *Deus Caritas Est*. Vatican City: Libreria Editrice Vaticana, 2006.

Berger, Teresa. *Theology in Hymns? A Study of the Relationship of Doxology and Theology According to a Collection of Hymns for the Use of the People Called Methodist*. Translated by Timothy E. Kimbrough. Nashville: Kingswood Books, 1995.

Beuchot, Mauricio. "La noción de la persona en santo Tomás." In *Atti del IX Congresso Tomistico Internazionale*, III. Vatican City: Libreria Editrice Vaticana (1991): 138–48.

Blanchette, Oliva. *The Perfection of the Universe According to Aquinas: A Teleological Cosmology*. University Park: Pennsylvania University Press, 1992.

Bouillard, Henri. *Conversion et Grâce Chez S. Thomas d'Aquin*. Paris: Aubier, 1941.

Bowmer, John. *The Sacrament of the Lord's Supper in Early Methodism*. London: Dacre Press, 1951.

Brantley, Richard E. *Locke, Wesley, and the Method of English Romanticism*. Gainesville: University of Florida Press, 1984.

Brockwell, Charles. "Methodist Discipline: From Rule of Life to Canon Law." *Drew Gateway* 54 (1984): 1–24.

Bruno, Daniel A. "Fundamentos teológicos de la ética wesleyana. Alcanzes y limitaciones." *Cuadernos de Teología* 23 (2004): 89–108.

Büchler, Pierre, ed. *Humain à l'image de Dieu*. Geneve: Labor et Fides, 1989.

Byrne, Brendan. "Ignatius Loyola and John Wesley: Experience and Strategies of Conversion." *Colloquium* 19 (1986): 54–66.

Campbell, Ted. *John Wesley and Christian Antiquity*. Nashville: Kingswood Books, 1991.

Camus, Albert. *La Peste*. Saint-Armand: Editions Gallimard, 1947.

Cannon, William. *The Theology of John Wesley with Special Reference to the Doctrine of Justification*. Nashville: Abingdon-Cokesbury, 1946.

Carver, Frank. "Growth in Sanctification: John Wesley and John of the Cross." *The Tower: The Journal of Nazarene Theological Seminary* 3 (1999): 33–70.

Cell, George Croft. *The Rediscovery of John Wesley*. New York: University Press of America, 1935.

Cessario, Romanus. *Christian Ethics and the Theological Life*. Washington, D.C.: Catholic University of America Press, 1996.

——. *The Moral Virtues and Theological Ethics*. Notre Dame, Ind.: University of Notre Dame Press, 1991.

——. *A Short History of Thomism*. Washington, D.C.: Catholic University of America Press, 2005.

——. *The Virtues, or the Examined Life*. New York: Continuum, 2002.

Chapman, David. *In Search of the Catholic Spirit: Methodists and Roman Catholics in Dialogue*. Peterborough, England: Epworth Press, 2004.

Chesterton, G. K. *Saint Thomas Aquinas: "The Dumb Ox."* New York: Doubleday, 1956.

Christensen, Michael. "Theosis and Sanctification: John Wesley's Reformulation of a Patristic Doctrine." *Wesleyan Theological Journal* 31, no. 2 (1996): 71–94.

Christmann, Heinrich. *Stände und Standespflichten*. Vol. 24: *Summa Theologica: Deutsch-lateinische Ausgabe*. Salzburg: Gemeinschaftsverlag, 1952.

Clapper, Gregory. *John Wesley on Religious Affections*. Metuchen, N.J.: The Scarecrow Press, 1989.

Clarke, Norris. *Explorations in Metaphysics: Being-God-Person*. Notre Dame, Ind.: University of Notre Dame Press, 1994.

Clement of Alexandria. *Stromata* in *The Ante-Nicene Fathers*. Vol. 2: *Fathers of the Second Century*. Edited by Alexander Roberts and James Donaldson. Peabody, Mass.: Hendrickson, 1994.

Cobb, John. *Grace & Responsibility*. Nashville: Abingdon, 1995.

Collins, Kenneth. *John Wesley: A Theological Journey*. Nashville: Abingdon, 2003.

——. "John Wesley and the Fear of Death as a Standard of Conversion." In *Conversion in the Wesleyan Tradition*. Edited by Kenneth Collins and John H. Tyson. Nashville: Abingdon, 2001: 56–68.

——. "John Wesley's Topography of the Heart: Dispositions, Tempers and Affections." *Methodist History* 36, no. 3 (1998): 162–75.

——. *The Scripture Way of Salvation: The Heart of John Wesley's Theology*. Nashville: Abingdon, 1997.

——. *The Theology of John Wesley: Holy Love and the Shape of Grace*. Nashville: Abingdon, 2007.

Cooper, Jane. *Letters Wrote by Jane Cooper: To which is prefixt, some account of her life and death*. London, 1792. Eighteenth-Century Collections Online. Gale Group. http://galenet.galegroup.com/servlet/ECCO.

Cox, Leo. "John Wesley's Conception of Sin." *Bulletin of the Evangelical Theological Society* 5, no. 1 (1962): 18–24.

Cubie, David. "John Wesley's Concept of Perfect Love: A Motif Analysis." Ph.D. diss., Boston University, 1965.

Cunningham, Lawrence S. "Current Theology: A Decade of Research of the Saints." *Theological Studies* 53 (1992): 517–33.

——. *The Meaning of Saints*. San Francisco: Harper & Row, 1980.

——. "The Politics of Canonization." *Christian Century* 100 (1983): 454–55.

Dauphinais, Michael, and Matthew Levering. *Knowing the Love of Christ: An Introduction to the Theology of St. Thomas Aquinas*. Notre Dame, Ind: University of Notre Dame Press, 2002.

Davies, Brian. *The Thought of Aquinas*. Oxford: Clarendon, 1992.

De Bonhome, Alfred. "Heroïcités des vertus." In *Dictionnaire de Spiritualité: Ascétique et Mystique, Doctrine et Histoire*. Paris: Beauchesne, 1968: 337–43.

de Lubac, Henri. *The Mystery of the Supernatural*. New York: Herder & Herder, 1998.

de Oliveira Ribeiro, Claudio et al., ed. *Teologia e prática na tradição wesleyena: Uma lectura a partir da América Latina e Caribe*. São Bernardo do Campo, Brazil: Editeo, 2005.

de Solenni, Pia Francesca. *A Hermeneutic of Aquinas's Mens through a Sexually Differentiated Epistemology: Toward an Understanding of Woman as Imago Dei*. Rome: Edizioni Università della Santa Croce, 2000.

Dorman, Ted. "Forgiveness of Past Sins: John Wesley on Justification, A Case Study Approach." *Pro Ecclesia* 10, no. 3 (2001): 275–94.

Driscoll, Martha. *A Silent Herald of Unity: The Life of Maria Gabriella Saghedu*. Kalamazoo, Mich.: Cistercian Publications, 1990.

Duque, José, ed. *La tradición protestante en la teología latinoamericana. Primer intento: lectura de la tradición metodista*. San José, Costa Rica: DEI, 1983.

Emery, Gilles. *Trinity, Church, and the Human Person*. Naples, Fla.: Sapientia, 2007.

——. *Trinity in Aquinas*. Naples, Fla.: Sapientia, 2003.

Flannery, Austin, ed. *Vatican Council II*. Vol. 1: *The Conciliar and Post-Conciliar Documents*. Northport, N.Y.: Costello Publishing, 1998.

Flew, R. Newton. *The Idea of Perfection in Christian Theology: An Historical Study of the Christian Idea for the Present Life*. London: Oxford University Press, 1934.

Ford, David. "Saint Makarios of Egypt and John Wesley: Variations on the Theme of Sanctification." *Greek Orthodox Theological Review* 33, no. 3 (1988): 285–312.

Frost, Francis. "Méthodisme." In *Catholicisme: hier, aujourd'hui, demain*. Edited by G. Jacquement, IX, 1948: 48–71.

——. "The Power of Spiritual Powerlessness in the Missionary Outreach of John Wesley." *Methodist History* 37, no. JI (1999): 253–65.

——. "The Three Loves: A Theology of the Wesley Brothers." *Epworth Review* 24, no. 3 (1997): 86–116.

Gallup, George H. *The Saints among Us: How the Spiritually Committed Are Changing Our World*. Harrisburg, Pa.: Morehouse Publishing, 1992.

Garrigou-Lagrange, Reginald. *Christian Perfection and Contemplation: According to St. Thomas Aquinas and St. John of the Cross*. Rockford, Ill.: Tan Books & Publishers, 2004.

Gilson, Etienne. *The Christian Philosophy of St. Thomas Aquinas*. Notre Dame, Ind.: University of Notre Dame Press, 1956.

Gondreau, Paul. "The Humanity of Christ, the Incarnate Word." In *The Theology of Thomas Aquinas*. Edited by Rik van Nieuwenhove and Joseph Wawrykow. Notre Dame, Ind.: University of Notre Dame Press, 2005: 252–76.

González, Justo L. *Juan Wesley: Herencia y promesa*. Hato Rey, Puerto Rico: Publicaciones Puertorriqueñas, 1998.

Griffiths, Paul, and Reinhard Hütter, eds. *Reason and the Reasons of Faith*. New York: T&T Clark, 2005.

Gunter, W. Stephen. *The Limits of "Love Divine": John Wesley's Response to Antinomianism and Enthusiasm*. Nashville: Kingswood Books, 1989.

Hauerwas, Stanley. *Character and the Christian Life: A Study in Theological Ethics*. San Antonio, Tex.: Trinity University Press, 1975.

——. *Sanctify Them in the Truth: Holiness Exemplified*. Nashville: Abingdon, 1998.

Heitzenrater, Richard P. "Great Expectations: Aldersgate and the Evidences of True Christianity." In *Aldersgate Reconsidered*. Edited by Randy Maddox. Nashville: Kingswood Books, 1990: 49–91.

——. *The Poor and the People Called Methodists*. Nashville: Kingswood Books, 2002.

——. *Wesley and the People Called Methodists*. Nashville: Abingdon, 1995.

Hipp, Stephen A. *"Person."* In *Christian Tradition and the Conception of Saint Albert the Great: A Systematic Study of Its Concept as Illumined by the Mysteries of the Trinity and the Incarnation*. Münster: Aschendorff Verlag, 2001.

Hook, Brian S., and R. R. Reno. *Heroism and the Christian Life*. Louisville: Westminster John Knox, 2000.

Hütter, Reinhard. "*Desiderium Naturale Visionis Dei–Est autem Duplex Hominis Beatitudo sive Felicitas*: Some Observations about Lawrence Feingold's and John Milbank's Recent Interventions in the Debate over the Natural Desire to See God." *Nova et Vetera* 5, no. 1 (2007): 81–132.

——. "St. Thomas on Grace and Freedom in the *Initium Fidei*: The Surpassing Augustinian Synthesis." *Nova et Vetera* 5, no. 3 (2007): 521–53.

Jaspers, Karl. *Von der Wahrheit*. Munich: R. Piper Verlag, 1947.

John Paul II. *Ut Unum Sint*. Boston: Pauline Books and Media, 1995.

Johnson, Elizabeth. *Friends of God and Prophets: A Feminist Theological Reading of the Communion of Saints*. New York: Continuum, 1998.

Jones, Ivor H., and Kenneth B. Wilson, eds. *Freedom and Grace*. London: Epworth Press, 1988.

Jones, Scott. *John Wesley's Conception and Use of Scripture*. Nashville: Kingswood Books, 1995.

Journet, Charles. *The Meaning of Grace*. Princeton, N.J.: Sceptre Publishers, 1960.

Keating, James, and David McCarthy. "Moral Theology with the Saints." *Modern Theology* 19, no. 3 (2003): 203–18.

Kerr, Fergus. *After Aquinas: Versions of Thomism*. Malden, Mass.: Blackwell Publishing, 2002.

Kimbrough, S. T. "Charles Wesley and the Poor." In *The Portion of the Poor: Good News to the Poor in the Wesleyan Tradition*. Edited by M. Douglas Meek. Nashville: Kingswood Books, 1995: 166.

Klaiber, Walter, and Manfred Marquardt. *Gelebte Gnade: Grundriss einer Theologie der Evangelisch-methodistischen Kirche*. Stuttgart: Christliches Verlagshaus, 1993.

Knight, Henry H., III. "The Relation of Love to Gratitude in the Theologies of Edwards and Wesley." *Evangelical Journal*, no. 6 (1988): 3–12.

Krämer, Klaus. *Imago Trinitatis: Die Gottebenbildlichkeit des Menschen in der Theologie des Thomas von Aquin*. Freiburg: Herder, 2000.

Langford, Thomas A. *Practical Divinity: Theology in the Wesleyan Tradition*. 2 vols. Nashville: Abingdon, 1998.

Law, William. *The Works of William Law*. Vol. 3: *A Practical Treatise upon Christian Perfection*. Eugene, Ore.: Wipf & Stock, 2001.

Leonhardt, Rochus. *Glück als Vollendung des Menschseins: Die beatitudo-Lehre des Thomas von Aquin im Horizont des Eudämonismus-Problems*. Berlin: de Gruyter, 1998.

Lessmann, Thomas. *Rolle und Bedeutung des Heiligen Geistes in der Theologie John Wesleys*. Stuttgart: Christliches Verlagshaus, 1987.

Levering, Matthew. *Christ's Fulfillment of Torah and Temple: Salvation according to Thomas Aquinas*. Notre Dame, Ind.: University of Notre Dame Press, 2002.

———. *Scripture and Metaphysics: Aquinas and the Renewal of Trinitarian Theology*. Malden, Mass.: Blackwell Publishing, 2004.

Lewis, C. S. *The Voyage of the Dawn Treader*. New York: Macmillan, 1952.

Lindström, Harald. *Wesley and Sanctification: A Study in the Doctrine of Salvation*. Nashville: Abingdon, 1946.

Lonergan, Bernard. *Grace and Freedom: Operative Grace in the Thought of St. Thomas Aquinas*. Toronto: University of Toronto, 2000.

Long, D. Stephen. *John Wesley's Moral Theology: The Quest for God and Goodness*. Nashville: Kingswood Books, 2005.

Losa, Francisco de. *The Holy Life of Gregory López, a Spanish hermite in the West-Indies*. Translated by A. Woodhead. London, 1675.

———. *The life of Gregorie Lopes that great servant of God, native of Madrid, written in Spanish by Father Losa curate of the Cathedrall of Mexico. And set out by Father Alonso Remon of the Order of our Lady de la Merced, with some additions of his owne*. Paris, 1638.

Luby, Daniel Joseph. *The Perceptibility of Grace in the Theology of John Wesley: A Roman Catholic Consideration*. Rome: Pontifical University of St. Thomas, 1994.

Lumen Gentium in *Vatican Council II*. Vol. 1: *The Conciliar and Post Conciliar Documents*. Northport, N.Y.: Costello Publishing, 1998: 402.

Maddox, Randy. "Anticipating the New Creation: Wesleyan Foundations for Holistic Mission." *Asbury Journal* 62 (2007): 49–66.

——. "John Wesley: Practical Theologian?" *Wesleyan Theological Journal* 23, no. 1–2 (1988): 122–47.

——. "Karl Rahner's Supernatural Existential: A Wesleyan Parallel?" *Evangelical Journal* 5 (1987): 3–14.

——. *Responsible Grace: John Wesley's Practical Theology*. Nashville: Abingdon, 1994.

——. "Wesley as Theologian in the History of Methodist Theology." *Rethinking Wesley's Theology for Contemporary Methodism*. Edited by Randy Maddox. Nashville: Kingswood Books, 1998: 213–25.

——. ed. *Aldersgate Reconsidered*. Nashville: Kingswood Books, 1990.

Magallanes, Hugo. *Introducción a la vida y teología de Juan Wesley*. Nashville: Abingdon, 2005.

Mann, Mark H. *Perfecting Grace: Holiness, Human Being, and the Sciences*. New York: T&T Clark, 2006.

Maritain, Jacques. *The Degrees of Knowledge*. Translated by Phelan Gerald. Vol. 7: *The Collected Works of Jacques Maritain*. Edited by Ralph McInerny. Notre Dame, Ind.: University of Notre Dame Press, 2002.

——. *De la grâce et de l'humanité de Jésus*. Bruges, Belgium: Desclée de Brouwer, 1967.

——. *A Preface to Metaphysics*. New York: Mentor Omega Book, 1962.

Marshall, Bruce D. "*Quod Scit Una Uetela*: Aquinas on the Nature of Theology." In *The Theology of Thomas Aquinas*. Edited by Rik van Nieuwenhove and Joseph Wawrykow. Notre Dame, Ind.: University of Notre Dame Press, 2005: 1–35.

Marty, François. *La Perfection de l'homme selon Saint Thomas d'Aquin: Ses fondements ontologiques et leur vérification dans l'ordre actuel*. Rome: Gregorian University Press, 1962.

Matzko, David Matthew. "Postmodernism, Saints and Scoundrels." *Modern Theology* 9, no. 1 (1993): 19–36.

McCormick, Steve. "Theosis in Chrysostom and Wesley: An Eastern Paradigm on Faith and Love." *Wesleyan Theological Journal* 26 (1991): 38–103.

McGonigle, Herbert Boyd. *Sufficient Saving Grace: John Wesley's Evangelical Arminianism*. Waynesboro, Ga.: Paternoster Press, 2001.

Meistad, Tore. *Martin Luther and John Wesley on the Sermon on the Mount*. Lanham, Md.: Scarecrow Press, 1999.

Merriell, D. Juvenal. *To the Image of the Trinity: A Study in the Development of Aquinas' Teaching*. Toronto: Pontifical Institute of Medieval Studies, 1990.

Metz, Johann Baptist. "Theologie als Biographie: Eine These und ein Paradigma." *Concilium* (May 1976): 311–15.

Molloy, Noel. "Hierarchy and Holiness: Aquinas on the Holiness of the Episcopal State." *The Thomist* 39, no. 2 (1975): 198–252.

Morency, Robert. *L'Union de Grâce selon saint Thomas*. Montreal: Les Éditions de L'Immaculée Conception, 1950.

O'Meara, Thomas F. *Thomas Aquinas: Theologian*. Notre Dame, Ind.: University of Notre Dame Press, 1997.

O'Neill, C. E. "L'Homme Ouvert à Dieu (Capax Dei)." In *Humain à l'image de Dieu*. Edited by Pierre Büchler. Geneve: Labor et Fides, 1989: 241–60.

Orcibal, Jean. "Les spirituels français et espagnols chez John Wesley et ses contemporains." *Revue de l'Histoire des Religions* 139 (1951): 50–109.

Osborne, Thomas. "Perfect and Imperfect Virtues in Aquinas." *The Thomist* 71, no. 1 (2007): 39–64.

Outler, Albert C. "Do Methodists Have a Doctrine of the Church?" In *The Doctrine of the Church*. Edited by Dow Kirkpatrick. Nashville: Abingdon, 1964.

——. *Evangelism and Theology in the Wesleyan Spirit*. Nashville: Discipleship Resources, 1996.

——, ed. *John Wesley*. New York: Oxford University Press, 1964.

Palazzini, Pietro. "La Santità coronamento della dignità dell'uomo." In *Miscellanea in occasione del IV centenario della Congregazione per le cause dei Santi (1588–1988)*. Vatican City: Congregation for the Causes of the Saints, 1988: 221–36.

Paluch, Michal. *La profondeur de l'amour divin: Evolution de la doctrine de la prédestination dans l'oeuvre de saint Thomas d'Aquin*. Paris: Libraire Philosophique J. Vrin, 2004.

Pesch, Otto H. "Existential and Sapiential Theology—The Theological Confrontation between Luther and Aquinas." In *Catholic Scholars Dialogue with Luther*. Edited by Jared Wicks. Chicago: Loyola University Press, 1970: 61–81.

——. *Theologie der Rechtfertigung bei Martin Luther und Thomas von Aquin. Versuch eines systematisch-theologischen Dialogs*. Vol. 4. Walberberger Studien der Albertus-Magnus-Akademie. Theologische Reihe. Mainz: Matthias-Grünewald-Verlag, 1967.

Peters, John L. *Christian Perfection and American Methodism*. Nashville: Abingdon, 1956.

Pieper, Joseph. *Leisure, the Basis of Culture*. South Bend, Ind.: St. Augustine Press, 1998.

——. *The Silence of St. Thomas: Three Essays*. New York: Pantheon, 1957.

Piette, Maximin. *John Wesley in the Evolution of Protestantism*. New York: Sheed & Ward, 1937.

Pinckaers, Servais. *The Pinckaers Reader: Renewing Thomistic Moral Theology*. Edited by John Berkman and Craig Steven Titus. Washington, D.C.: The Catholic University of America Press, 2005.

——. *The Sources of Christian Ethics*. Washington, D.C.: The Catholic University of America, 1995.

Pope, Stephen J., ed. *The Ethics of Aquinas*. Washington, D.C.: Georgetown University Press, 2002.

Porter, Jean. "Virtue and Sin: The Connection of the Virtues and the Case of the Flawed Saint." *Journal of Religion* 75, no. 4 (1995): 521–39.

Rack, Henry D. *Reasonable Enthusiast: John Wesley and the Rise of Methodism*. Nashville: Abingdon, 1989.

Rahner, Karl. *Theological Investigations*. Vol. 3: *The Theology of the Spiritual Life*. Translated by Karl H. and Boniface Kruger. Baltimore: Helicon Press, 1967.

Ramírez, Santiago. *Los Dones del Espíritu Santo*. Madrid: Biblioteca de Teólogos Españoles, 1978.

Ratzinger, Joseph Cardinal. "On the Ecumenical Situation." In *Pilgrim Fellowship of Faith: The Church as Communion*. San Francisco: Ignatius Press, 2005.

Riestra, José Antonio. *Cristo y la Plenitud del Cuerpo Místico: Estudio sobre la cristología de Santo Tomás de Aquino*. Pamplona, Spain: Ediciones Universidad de Navarra, 1985.

Rigl, Thomas. *Die Gnade wirken lassen: Methodistische Soteriologie im ökumenischen Dialog*. Paderborn, Germany: Bonifatius, 2001.

Rodríguez y Rodríguez, Victorino. "Estructura metafísica de la persona humana." In *Atti del IX Congresso Tomistico Internazionale* III. Vatican City: Libreria Editrice Vaticana, 1991: 113–48.

Roldán, Alberto Fernando. "La santificación como 'perfección cristiana' en Juan Wesley." *Cuadernos de teología* 22 (2003): 175–89.

Rowell, Geoffrey, Kenneth Stevenson, and Rowan Williams, eds. *Love's Redeeming Work: The Anglican Quest for Holiness*. New York: Oxford University Press, 2001.

Royo Marín, Antonio. *Teología de la Perfección Cristiana*. 3rd ed. Madrid: Biblioteca de Autores Cristianos, 1958.

Rubial García, Antonio. *La santidad controvertida: Hagiografía y conciencia criolla alrededor de los venrables no canonizados de Nueva España*. México, D.F.: Fondo de Cultura Económica, 1999.

Runyon, Theodore. *The New Creation: John Wesley's Theology Today*. Nashville: Abingdon, 1998.

Ryan, Thomas. "Revisiting Affective Knowledge and Connaturality in Aquinas." *Theological Studies* 66 (2005): 49–68.

Saarinen, Risto. "Theosis." In *Theologische Realenzyklopädie* 33. Berlin: de Gruyter, 2002: 389–93.

Saavedra, Alejandro. "Fundamentación metafísica de la dignidad de la persona humana." In *Atti del IX Congresso Tomistico Internazionale* III. Vatican City: Libreria Editrice Vaticana, 1991: 162–71.

Sanders, Theresa. "Seeking a Minor Sun: Saints after the Death of God." *Horizons* 22, no. 2 (1995): 183–97.

Sangster, W. E. *The Path to Perfection: An Examination and Restatement of John Wesley's Doctrine of Christian Perfection*. Nashville: Abingdon, 1943.

——. *The Pure in Heart: A Study in Christian Sanctity*. Nashville: Abingdon, 1954.

Schlemmer, Karl, ed. *Heilige als Brückenbauer: Heiligenverehrung im ökumenischen Dialog*. Vol. 1. Andechser Reihe. St. Ottilien: EOS Verlag, 1997.

Seckler, Max. *Instinkt und Glaubenswille nach Thomas von Aquin*. Mainz: Matthias-Grünewald-Verlag, 1961.

——. *Das Heil in der Geschichte*. Munich: Kösel Verlag, 1964.

Shanley, Brian J. *The Thomist Tradition*. Boston: Kluwer Academic, 2002.

Sherwin, Michael. *By Knowledge & by Love: Charity and Knowledge in the Moral Theology of St. Thomas Aquinas*. Washington, D.C.: Catholic University of America Press, 2005.

Smith, Timothy L. *Thomas Aquinas' Trinitarian Theology: A Study in Theological Method*. Washington, D.C.: Catholic University of America Press, 2003.

Somme, Luc-Thomas. *Fils adoptifs de Dieu par Jésus Christ: La filiation divine par adoption dans la théologie de Saint Thomas d'Aquin*. Paris: Librairie Philosophique J. Vrin, 1997.

——. *Thomas d'Aquin, la divinisation dans le Christ*. Genève: Editions Ad Solem, 1998.

Steele, Richard, ed. *"Heart Religion" in the Methodist Tradition and Related Movements*. Lanham, Md.: Scarecrow Press, 2001.

Steinmetz, David C. "The Catholic Luther: A Critical Reappraisal." *Theology Today* 61 (2004): 187–201.

Stump, Eleonore. *Aquinas: Arguments of the Philosophers*. New York: Routledge, 2005.

Te Velde, Rudi. *Aquinas on God: The "Divine Science" of the Summa Theologiae*. Burlington, Vt.: Ashgate, 2006.

——. *Participation and Substantiality in Thomas Aquinas*. New York: E. J. Brill, 1995.

Thompson, William M. *Fire and Light: The Saints and Theology*. New York: Paulist Press, 1987.

Todd, John M. *John Wesley and the Catholic Church*. London: Hodder & Stoughton, 1958.

Torrell, Jean-Pierre. *Aquinas' Summa: Background, Structure, & Reception*. Washington, D.C.: The Catholic University of America Press, 2005.

——. *Saint Thomas Aquinas*. Vol. 1: *The Person and His Work*. Washington, D.C.: Catholic University of America Press, 1996.

——. *Saint Thomas Aquinas*. Vol. 2: *Spiritual Master*. Washington, D.C.: Catholic University of America Press, 2003.

Tschipke, Theophil. *L'humanité du Christ comme instrument de salut et de la divinité*. Fribourg: Academic Press Fribourg, 2003.

Tuttle, Robert G. *Mysticism in the Wesleyan Tradition*. Grand Rapids: Zondervan, 1989.

Tyson, John R. *Charles Wesley on Sanctification: A Biographical and Theological Study*. Grand Rapids: Francis Asbury Press, 1986.

United Methodist Hymnal. Nashville: United Methodist Publishing House, 1989.

Valsecchi, Alfonso. *Il fine dell'uomo nella teologia di Tommaso d'Aquino*. Rome: Gregorian University Press, 2002.

van Nieuwenhove, Rik. "Bearing Marks of Christ's Passion." In *The Theology of Thomas Aquinas*. Edited by Rik van Nieuwenhove and Joseph Wawrykow. Notre Dame, Ind.: University of Notre Dame Press, 2005: 277–302.

van Nieuwenhove, Rik, and Joseph Wawrykow, eds. *The Theology of Thomas Aquinas*. Notre Dame, Ind.: University of Notre Dame Press, 2005.

Vickers, John. "'Begotten from everlasting of the Father': Inadvertent Omission or Sabellian Trajectory in Early Methodism?" *Methodist History* 44 (2006): 251–66.

von Balthasar, Hans Urs. *The Christian State of Life*. San Francisco: Ignatius Press, 1983.

——. *Explorations in Theology*. 4 vols. San Francisco: Ignatius Press, 1989.

——. *The Theology of Karl Barth*. San Francisco: Ignatius Press, 1951.

——. *Thomas und die Charismatik: Kommentar zu Thomas von Aquin Summa Theologica Quaestiones II–II*. Vol. 23: *171–182*. Deutsche Thomas-Ausgabe. Einsiedeln, Freiburg: Johannes Verlag, 1996.

——. *Two Sisters in the Spirit: Thérèse of Lisieux and Elizabeth of the Trinity*. San Francisco: Ignatius Press, 1992.

Wainwright, Geoffrey. *The Ecumenical Moment: Crisis and Opportunity for the Church*. Grand Rapids: Eerdmans, 1983.

——. *Is the Reformation Over? Catholics and Protestants at the Turn of the Millennia*. Milwaukee: Marquette University Press, 2000.

——. *Methodists in Dialogue*. Nashville: Kingswood Books, 1995.

——. "The Saints and the Departed: Confessional Controversy and Ecumenical Convergence." *Studia Liturgica* 34 (2004): 65–91.

——."Trinitarian Theology and Wesleyan Holiness." In *Orthodox and Wesleyan Spirituality*. Edited by S. T. Kimbrough Jr. Chestwood, N.Y.: St. Vladimir's Seminary Press, 2002: 59–80.

——. "Vollkommenheit." In *Theologische Realenzyklopädie* 35. Berlin: de Gruyter, 2003: 273–85.

——. "Wesley's Trinitarian Hermeneutic." *Wesleyan Theological Journal* 36, no. 1 (2001): 7–30.

——. *Worship with One Accord: Where Liturgy and Ecumenism Embrace*. Oxford: Oxford University Press, 1997.

Watson, David Lowes. *The Early Methodist Class Meetings*. Nashville: Discipleship Resources, 1985.

Wawrykow, Joseph P. *God's Grace and Human Action. 'Merit' in the Theology of Thomas Aquinas*. Notre Dame, Ind.: University of Notre Dame Press, 1995.

——. "Hypostatic Union." In *The Theology of Thomas Aquinas*. Edited by R. van Nieuwehove and J. Wawrykow. Notre Dame, Ind.: University of Notre Dame Press, 2005: 222–51.

Weber, Theodore R. *Politics in the Order of Salvation: Transforming Wesleyan Political Ethics*. Nashville: Kingswood Books, 2001.

Weinandy, Thomas. "The Beatific Vision and the Incarnate Son: Furthering the Discussion." *The Thomist* 70 (2006): 605–15.

——. "'Jesus' Filial Vision of the Father." *Pro Ecclesia* 13, no. 2 (2004): 189–201.

White, Thomas Joseph. "Jesus' Cry on the Cross and His Beatific Vision." *Nova et Vetera* 5, no. 3 (2007): 555–81.

——. "The Voluntary Action of the Earthly Christ and the Necessity of the Beatific Vision." *The Thomist* 69 (2005): 497–534.

Williams, A. N. *The Ground of Union: Deification in Aquinas and Palamas*. New York: Oxford University Press, 1999.

Williams, Colin. W. *John Wesley's Theology Today*. Nashville: Abingdon, 1960.

Wilson, David Dunn. *Many Waters Cannot Quench: A Study of the Sufferings of Eighteenth-century Methodism and Their Significance for John Wesley and the First Methodists*. London: Epworth Press, 1969.

Wippel, John F. *The Metaphysical Thought of Thomas Aquinas: From Finite Being to Uncreated Being*. Washington, D.C.: Catholic University of America Press, 2000.

Woestman, William H. *Canonization: Theology, History, Process*. Ottawa: Saint Paul University, 2002.

Wood, A. Skevington. *Love Excluding Sin: Wesley's Doctrine of Sanctification*. Ilkeston, England: Moorley's Bible & Bookshop, 1980.

Woodward, Kenneth L. *Making Saints: How the Catholic Church Determines Who Becomes a Saint, Who Doesn't, and Why*. 2nd ed. New York: Simon & Schuster, 1996.

Wynkoop, Mildred Bangs. *Foundations of Wesleyan-Arminian Theology*. Kansas City, Mo.: Beacon Hill Press, 1967.

——. *A Theology of Love: The Dynamic of Wesleyanism*. Kansas City, Mo.: Beacon Hill Press, 1972.

Wyschogrod, Edith. "Exemplary Individuals: Toward a Phenomenological Ethics." *Philosophy & Theology* 1, no. 1 (1986): 9–31.

Index of Selected Names

Index of Subjects